Documenting Socialism

Documenting Socialism
East German Documentary Cinema

Edited by
Seán Allan and Sebastian Heiduschke

berghahn
NEW YORK · OXFORD
www.berghahnbooks.com

First published in 2024 by
Berghahn Books
www.berghahnbooks.com

© 2024 Seán Allan and Sebastian Heiduschke

All rights reserved. Except for the quotation of short passages for the purposes of criticism and review, no part of this book may be reproduced in any form or by any means, electronic or mechanical, including photocopying, recording, or any information storage and retrieval system now known or to be invented, without written permission of the publisher.

Library of Congress Cataloging-in-Publication Data

Names: Allan, Seán, editor. | Heiduschke, Sebastian, 1974– editor.
Title: Documenting socialism : East German documentary cinema / edited by Seán Allan and Sebastian Heiduschke.
Description: New York : Berghahn, 2024. | Includes bibliographical references and index.
Identifiers: LCCN 2024014192 (print) | LCCN 2024014193 (ebook) | ISBN 9781805396574 (hardback) | ISBN 9781805396581 (epub)
Subjects: LCSH: Documentary films—Germany (East)—History and critcism. | Socialism and motion pictures—Germany (East) | Germany (East)—In motion pictures. | DEFA. Studio für Dokumentarfilme—History. | LCGFT: Essays.
Classification: LCC PN1995.9.D6 D5784 2024 (print) | LCC PN1995.9.D6 (ebook) | DDC 070.1/809431—dc23/eng/20240409
LC record available at https://lccn.loc.gov/2024014192
LC ebook record available at https://lccn.loc.gov/2024014193

British Library Cataloguing in Publication Data

A catalogue record for this book is available from the British Library

ISBN 978-1-80539-657-4 hardback
ISBN 978-1-80539-658-1 epub
ISBN 978-1-80539-659-8 web PDF

https://doi.org/10.3167/9781805396574

Contents

List of Illustrations   viii
Acknowledgements   xi

Introduction. Documenting Socialism   1
   Seán Allan and Sebastian Heiduschke

Part I: Studios, Systems and Networks

1. 'Mountains of Material': Gerhard Scheumann and the
   Cinéma Vérité Debate in the GDR   35
   Matthew Bauman

2. The DEFA 'Foreign Ministry Films': Presenting the GDR to the
   World, 1962–90   53
   Thomas Maulucci

3. Diary of the Ordinary: Reinventing the Newsreel. DEFA
   Kinobox, 1981–90   74
   Reinhild Steingröver

Part II: Documentary Auteurs

4. The Archives Testify: The Compilation Films of Annelie and
   Andrew Thorndike   97
   Helen Hughes

5. 'How Far Can You Go?': Everyday Lives in the Films of Kurt
   Tetzlaff   116
   Nick Hodgin

6. Peter Voigt: Socialist Documentary and the Legacy of Brecht   137
   Seán Allan

7. Critical Truths: Documenting Disillusionment in the Films of
   Helke Misselwitz, Petra Tschörtner and Angelika Andrees   156
   Jennifer L. Creech

Part III: Transnational Documentary

8. East German Documentary Films by and about Sorbs   179
   Andy Räder

9. 'Are These Pictures a Deception?' Socialist Self-Reflexivity in
   the Cambodia Trilogy of Studio H&S   201
   Martin Brady

10. Polycentric Images of Africa in East German Documentary
    Film   222
    Sebastian Heiduschke

11. East Germany's Anti-racist Politics and Black Abjection in
    Documentary Film   241
    Priscilla Layne

Part IV: Documenting Alterity

12. *Ein Tagebuch für Anne Frank* (*A Diary for Anne Frank*, 1958):
    The GDR's Answer to Alain Resnais' *Nuit et Brouillard* (*Night
    and Fog*, 1956)?   265
    Elizabeth Ward

13. A Woman's Work? Women Soldiers, Masculinities and Binary
    Panic in Documentaries of the East German Army   287
    Tom Smith

14. The Queer Cipher in East German Documentary: *In Sachen
    H. und acht anderer* (*In the Matter of H. and Eight Others*,
    1972) and Queer Activist Super 8 Films   307
    Kyle Frackman

Part V: The Presence of the Past: Reconstructing the Socialist Imaginary

15. The Socialist City and Utopian Temporality in Halle-Neustadt
    Documentaries   329
    Stephan Ehrig

16. The Rubble of History: Searching for the German Past in a European Present in Andreas Voigt's *Ostpreußenland* (*Tales of East Prussia*, 1995) and Volker Koepp's *Kalte Heimat* (*Cold Homeland*, 1995)   350
   Jason Doerre

Filmography   370

Index   377

Illustrations

Figures

0.1. Poster for *Lied der Ströme* (1954)   9

0.2. Jürgen Böttcher, *Stars* (1963)   15

2.1. In Heinz Hafke's *Sie, wie viele andere* (1969) our heroine can do it all, including (maybe!) finally repairing her son's bike, which had resisted her husband's best efforts   63

2.2. SED Chairman Erich Honecker, Congress President Freda Brown and GDR head of state Willi Stoph on the grandstand amidst international delegates and Free German Youth members at the October 1975 World Congress of Women in East Berlin in *DDR-Magazin 13/1975—Weltkongreß im Internationalen Jahr der Frau*   67

3.1. Dieter Schumann's straightforward portrait of the cook Inge Thieme in *Gulaschkanone* [*Kinobox*, 9/1982]   87

3.2. The locomotive in Jochen Kraußer's *Lok im Garten - ein ungewöhnliches Hobby* [*Kinobox* 27/1983]   89

4.1. A portrait of Bertha Krupp, together with a figure denoting the wealth of the estate, and an entry in the book *Jahrbuch der Millionäre 1912*. Annelie and Andrew Thorndike *Du und mancher Kamerad* (1956)   102

4.2. A young woman queues in Red Square to walk by the body of Lenin. Annelie and Andrew Thorndike, *Das russische Wunder* (Part 2) (1963)   106

5.1 Workers like silhouettes in the snow in Kurt Tetzlaff's *Im Januar 1963* (1963)   123

5.2. Industrial sublime in Kurt Tetzlaff's *Alltag eines Abenteuers* (1976)   132

6.1. *Theaterarbeit* (Peter Voigt, 1975)   147

6.2. *Dämmerung* (Peter Voigt, 1993)   151

7.1. Gundula Schulze holds one of her photographs. *Aktfotographie, z.B. Gundula Schulze* (Helke Misselwitz, 1983)   160

7.2. Collective loneliness in *Unsere alten Tage* (Petra Tschörtner, 1989)   166

8.1. Camera set up in the classroom to capture the school children's performances in Toni Bruk's *Briefe – In Gedenken an Dr. Maria Grollmuß; Listy* (1985)   189

8.2. Shooting of the hand puppet scene in *Sokol – P.S. zu einem Kapitel unserer Geschichte* (1990)   195

9.1. Studio H&S, *Kampuchea – Sterben und Auferstehn* (1980)   206

9.2. Studio H&S, *Die Angkar* (1981)   212

10.1. Orderly traffic, controlled by a Black police officer in a white uniform in in Joachim Hellwig's *Der schwarze Stern* (1965)   227

10.2. Ballet performance featuring polyrhythmic dancing in Moussa Kémoko Diakité and Gerhard Jentsch's *Hirde Dyama* (1970)   233

10.3. Visualized ideals of Kuxa Kanema in Lisa and Joachim Hadaschik's *Grüße aus Maputo* (1979)   235

11.1. In this shot from Ella Ensink's *Abschied von Afrika* (1961), Black South African women collect water from an outdoor tap. The sign above them reads the 'fountains are designated for the Indigenous', an example of the apartheid system   247

11.2. In this shot from Walter Heynowski's *Kommando 52* (1965), through editing, Tshombe slowly fades out, leaving the focus on the West German mercenaries who are fighting on his behalf   250

12.1. The former commandant of Westerbork concentration camp, Albert Konrad Gemmeker, walks alongside CDU election posters in Joachim Hellwig's *Ein Tagebuch für Anne Frank* (1958)   278

12.2. In Joachim Hellwig's *Ein Tagebuch für Anne Frank*, viewing the truth is positioned as the successor to 'reading the truth'   280

13.1. Interview with Gabi Arzt surrounded by soft toys. Still from Uwe Belz's *Gabi – Vermittlung Platz 12* (1984)   297

13.2. Mixed-gender training exercise at the Unteroffiziersschule Perleberg, from Dietmar Schürtz's *Neugier und Bewährung* (1988)   299

14.1. The judge extensively questions the accused, mediating information for both the legal case and the viewer in Richard Cohn-Vossen's *In Sachen H. und acht anderer* (1972)   315

14.2. HIB members gather conspiratorially before their participation in the 1 May celebrations in Michael Unger's *Auf der Suche nach dem Glück* (*In Search of Happiness*, 1977)   321

15.1. Aerial shots highlighting the masterplan model view. *Der Mensch muss auch wohnen – Bilder über das Leben in Halle-Neustadt* (Wolfgang Bartsch, 1974)   339

15.2. Mural mosaic *Gaben der Völker* (*Gifts of the People*), designed by Martin Hadelich (1968) from *Der Mensch muss auch wohnen – Bilder über das Leben in Halle-Neustadt* (Wolfgang Bartsch, 1974)   343

16.1. Cinematographer Thomas Plenert capturing a cold winter landscape in Volker Koepp's *Kalte Heimat* (1995)   358

16.2. Single mother, farmer, and cinéaste in Andreas Voigt's *Ostpreußenland* (1995)   364

Acknowledgements

Many people contributed in all sorts of ways to the making of this volume. We would particularly like to thank the DAAD and the German Screen Studies Network (GSSN), who provided the financial assistance without which it would not have been possible to stage a three-day workshop to bring the contributors together in St Andrews. Sabine Söhner at the DEFA-Stiftung, Kerstin Lommatzsch at Progress Film, Hiltrud Schulz at the DEFA Film Library of the University of Massachusetts Amherst, and Manja Meister at the Deutsches Rundfunkarchiv all played vital roles in providing advice, film material and still photographs. Julia Hussels and Anett Schubotz (Bertolt-Brecht-Archiv at the Akademie der Künste, Berlin) Tim Storch (Bundesarchiv Berlin), Vickie Cormie (University of St Andrews Library) and Renate Göthe (Filmuniversität Konrad Wolf, Babelsberg) were all instrumental in providing and curating additional archival material.

In addition, we would particularly like to thank: Sam Herring for his work on subtitling the film *A Diary for Anne Frank*; the two anonymous reviewers for their invaluable comments on the manuscript; and the production team at Berghahn Books – and especially Amanda Horn, Sulaiman Ahmad, Lizzie Martinez, Julia Powers, Keara Hagerty, Melissa Gannon, and Jon Lloyd. Carla Steinbrecher at the University of St Andrews also provided expert editorial assistance on the volume. We are are particularly indebted to Elizabeth Ward for her work on indexing the volume. Last but not least, we are grateful for the help and support of Dora Osborne, Paul Flaig, Birgit Röder, Jutta Voigt, Mariana Ivanova and the late Ralf Schenk, all of whom contributed in many different capacities to our project.

Introduction
Documenting Socialism

Seán Allan and Sebastian Heiduschke

Looking back at the *Wende* and the events leading up to German unification in 1990, few would have predicted the rapid expansion of scholarship focusing on East German cinema that has taken place over the past thirty years. Thanks to the efforts of the DEFA-Stiftung, PROGRESS Film, ICESTORM, Kanopy and the DEFA Film Library, a large number of feature films produced at the DEFA studio in Potsdam-Babelsberg are readily available in streamed or DVD format (many of them in subtitled versions). In the past, many scholars were all too inclined to dismiss these films as crude works of propaganda designed to shore up the position of the Socialist Unity Party (SED) in the German Democratic Republic (GDR). However, the increased availability of DEFA's feature films has brought about a much more differentiated approach to the analysis and appreciation of this rich film culture. No longer seen simply as a window onto life in East Germany, these films have become embedded into debates about memory studies, representations of gender, sexuality, race, and film aesthetics. Moreover, as the very concept of national cinema has increasingly been called into question, recent research into DEFA's transnational entanglements has opened up new avenues of research that no longer see the studio's output in terms of the cinema of a small nation.

However, in the case of nonfictional film, the picture is much less clear. While some of the better-known East German documentaries have been released on DVD, very few are available in subtitled versions, and many are only accessible in archives and/or in unrestored versions. In part this is understandable for, as this volume demonstrates, although the DEFA-Studio für Wochenschau und Dokumentarfilme (DEFA Studio for Newsreel and Documentary Films) had the main responsibility for documentary production, some of the most interesting films were produced by specialist subunits of the DEFA Studio such as defa futurum, by independent units such as the East German army's Armeefilmstudio (Army Film Studio [AFS]) or by radical collectives and activist filmmakers. Some of these collectives – the Homosexuelle Interessengemeinschaft Berlin is an obvious example – operated on the margins of mainstream film production in the GDR, while others – such as Studio H&S – grew out of, and were subsequently reintegrated into, the DEFA Studio itself. Although the works of such celebrated filmmakers as Annelie and Andrew Thorndike, Karl Gass, Jürgen Böttcher, Winfried and Barbara Junge, Kurt Tetzlaff, Volker Koepp, Gitta Nickel, Helke Misselwitz and Petra Tschörtner might be approached in terms of quasi-auteurist models of filmmaking, one of the aims of this volume is to serve as a reminder of the limitations of such an approach when dealing with the broader output of filmmakers in the GDR. If our volume succeeds in contributing to a deeper understanding of art and filmmaking under state socialism in all its diversity and contradictions, then it will have realized one of its key aims.

While scholarly interest in DEFA in the English-speaking world initially focused on feature films, it has become increasingly clear just how incomplete our picture of East German film production is if we ignore the huge number of nonfiction films (including newsreels and related productions such as *Kinobox*) that were released in the GDR. As this volume shows, many of these nonfictional films reflect the transnational aspirations of some East German filmmakers insofar as they were often conceived of as a means of exercising soft power and targeted at developing nations during the Global Cold War. The discovery of such entanglements has been encouraged by a paradigm shift in film studies in recent years as contemporary scholars seek to decolonize the discipline and explore ways in which it might move beyond conventional European and US agendas and engage more fully with the Global South. As several of the chapters in our volume demonstrate, East German documentary filmmakers were heavily engaged in reporting the liberation movements that had arisen in the wake of postwar decolonization, even if they sometimes struggled to escape the limitations of their own European perspective.

In an age in which mainstream national television networks have become ever more timid in criticizing political orthodoxy, it is not hard to understand why there has been such an upsurge of interest in radical documentary filmmaking in recent years. At the same time, developments in digital technology have made it possible for many more individuals to have access to the equipment needed for the production of nonfictional film and – albeit indirectly – to reflect on the ethics and aesthetics of documentary representation. As both scholars and viewers have become increasingly sensitive to concepts of positionality and issues of bias (whether conscious or unconscious), the limitations of often unquestioned notions of (pseudo-)objectivity are now an integral aspect of cultural analysis. The ability to draw a distinction between crude propaganda and something that might be termed partisan filmmaking goes some way towards explaining the recent rediscovery of East German documentary. Nowhere is this revival of interest more clearly the case than with the films of Studio H&S, which have now become the focus of intense scholarly debate in a way that would have been almost unthinkable a decade ago.[1]

As the editors of the first full-length English-language publication on East German documentary, we cannot aspire to complete coverage. Inevitably there are some notable gaps; for example, the fact that there are no chapters devoted exclusively to the work of such key figures as Jürgen Böttcher and Winfried and Barbara Junge is not a judgement on our part on their significance for East German cinema, but rather an acknowledgement of the fact that there is already a considerable body of scholarship (in English) on these filmmakers.[2] Rather, our aim is to provide a sociohistorical context for a broader understanding of the production of nonfictional film in the GDR, to highlight some of the major players, to remind readers of the vital contributions made by those working on the margins of DEFA and to offer a range of different theoretical approaches in the hope that this volume will inspire others to explore this rich – but largely undiscovered – body of work.

Anno Zero?

For many cultural historians, 17 May 1946, the date on which DEFA was granted its licence by the Soviet Military Administration in Germany (SMAD), marks the beginning of East German film history. Nonetheless, as early as January 1946, work on the first newsreels and non-fictional films was being undertaken by members of the Filmaktiv, a precursor of DEFA set up under the auspices of the SMAD to oversee film production in the Soviet Zone of Occupation (SBZ). Like their Soviet counterparts, the Western Allies also recognized that a thoroughgoing overhaul of the German educational system and the close monitoring of all forms of mass media would be necessary to combat the legacy of fascism. However, with the founding on 27 July 1945 of the Deutsche Zentralverwaltung für Volksbildung (German Administration of Culture and Education [DVV]) under the leadership of Paul Wandel, it was the Soviets who seized the initiative in ensuring that, in the SBZ at least, pro-communist Germans would be at the forefront of a revival of German culture. While many writers and artists in the immediate postwar period were driven by a desire to rekindle the spirit of German classical humanism, one of the most pressing problems for the new generation of filmmakers was the legacy of the Nazi film industry. Writing in the first issue of the periodical *Theater der Zeit* in July 1946, the director Kurt Maetzig noted that 'for many years we were shown thousands of authentic images which were used to construct a completely false image of reality'.[3] In the case of feature films, the founding generation of directors at DEFA attempted (not always successfully) to avoid the sentimental clichés of melodrama, a genre that Goebbels had mobilized so successfully in the service of ideological indoctrination during the Third Reich. But those involved in newsreel and documentary production in the SBZ were confronted with the problem that the propagandistic character of the Nazi newsreel *Die deutsche Wochenschau* (1940–45), together with such notorious documentaries such as Fritz Hippler's *Der ewige Jude* (*The Eternal Jew*, 1940), had undermined public confidence in the capacity of nonfictional film to distinguish between truth and ideology.

The date of 19 February 1946 saw the launch in the SBZ of the first episode of the newsreel *Der Augenzeuge*, an event that prompted its founding editor, Kurt Maetzig, to note that 'this new newsreel is designed not to have anything in common with the fascist war newsreel droning with bombastic pathos . . . It should prompt viewers to think for themselves'.[4] The efforts of Maetzig and his colleagues at DEFA to address the viewing public's lingering scepticism regarding film as a news medium are perhaps most clearly reflected in the slogan 'Sie sehen selbst, Sie hören selbst, urteilen Sie selbst!' (See for yourself, listen for yourself, judge for yourself!), which, from the thirteenth episode onwards, prefaced the then weekly editions of *Der Augenzeuge*. The newsreel – which ran continuously from 19 February 1946 until 19 December 1980 – was also instrumental in paving the way for the production of longer documentaries such as Maetzig's *Einheit SPD-KPD* (*Unity SPD-KPD*), a 19-minute film about the merger of the Communist and Social Democratic Parties and the rise of the Socialist Unity Party (SED) released in May 1946. When viewed from today's perspective, *Einheit*

SPD-KPD comes across as a curious blend of 're-staged' events, political reportage and propaganda; however, as Günter Jordan notes, in 1946 many contemporary reviewers praised the documentary precisely because of its 'modern composition and lack of pathos'.[5]

Another way of combating the unwelcome legacy of Nazi propaganda was through the production of hard-hitting films focusing on German culpability such as Richard Brandt's *Todeslager Sachsenhausen* (*Sachsenhausen Death Camp*, 1946), a film that to some extent draws on the approach adopted by Hanuš Burger and Billy Wilder in *Die Todesmühlen* (*Death Mills*, 1945) and that presented German viewers with uncompromising images of the suffering endured by concentration camp victims. Technological constraints in both filming and sound recording meant that certain sequences – notably those in which an SS officer describes the executions at the camp – had to be shot several times with overdubbed sound. However, while that was not in itself seen as detracting from the film's authenticity, it soon became apparent that the dramaturgical underpinning of this type of documentary left spectators cold and unable to engage with the ethical issues being presented. In the light of this and the low morale of the German population generally, the Filmaktiv proposed a series of short documentaries about postwar reconstruction – Kurt Maetzig's *Berlin im Aufbau* (*Rebuilding Berlin*, 1946) is just one example – which rather than condemning Germans for wartime atrocities highlighted the contributions of forward-looking citizens to the construction of a modern, antifascist society. Just how enduring a trope reconstruction (*Aufbau*) would become in the history of East German film and literature is evident in Stephan Ehrig's discussion of films about the construction of new towns such as Halle-Neustadt in the GDR of the 1970s (see Chapter 15).

In their search for progressive models of documentary filmmaking, there were essentially two traditions on which the new generation of filmmakers at DEFA could draw: on the one hand, there were those films that deployed the avant-garde cinematic techniques of the late 1920s such as Walter Ruttmann's *Berlin – Die Sinfonie der Großstadt* (*Berlin – Symphony of a City*, 1927) or Dziga Vertov's *Man with a Movie Camera* (1929); on the other hand, there was the proletarian cinema of the Weimar years associated with Prometheus-Film GmbH set up by the German Communist Party (KPD) in 1926, and Weltfilm, which was established a year later in 1927.[6] Examples of such films included short factual documentaries such as Phil Jutzi's short *Blutmai* (*Bloody May Day*, 1929) and Slatan Dudow's *Zeitprobleme. Wie der Berliner Arbeiter wohnt* (*Problems of Our Time: How the Berlin Worker Lives*, 1929). Given the hostility in the GDR from the early 1950s onwards towards so-called formalist aesthetics, it is hardly surprising that, over time, the model provided by the proletarian film culture of the 1920s and 1930s would prove more acceptable to the SED's cultural theorists than Ruttmann and Vertov's more formally innovative work. However, as Günter Jordan has noted, the dominance of Nazi film culture in the previous decade meant that names like Ruttmann, Vertov, Jutzi and Dudow were but distant memories, and the political vacuum of the immediate postwar period required a more affirmative aesthetic that promoted the activities of the SED and the reconstruction of society along socialist principles. Accordingly, as the vicissitudes of the Cold War came to be felt ever more keenly during the Berlin Blockade and the run-up to the founding of the GDR on 7 October 1949, the DEFA studio found itself under pressure to produce a series of partisan documentaries in support of the SED and its Two-Year Plan. Increasingly from 1948 onwards, documentary films such as Eva Fritzsche's *Die Brücke von Caputh* (*The Bridge of Caputh*, 1949) – the first DEFA documentary produced by a female director – were explicitly politicized in accordance with the SED's needs and, like Maetzig's *Einheit SPD-KPD*, had to resort to the re-staging of historical events to make their political point. Made by DEFA's department for short films, the Abteilung Kurzfilm, Fritzsche's film used actors to re-stage the construction of a bridge that that had already been rebuilt and, in the process, anticipated the forms of agitprop filmmaking that stood in the sharpest possible contrast to the more aesthetically complex documentary forms of the later years and indeed the appeal to spectator autonomy encapsulated in the opening slogan of *Der Augenzeuge*.

Structure and Organization in the Early Years

During the period from 1946 to 1949, the SED was responsible for supplying much of the needed film stock and equipment, while the SMAD initially censored and approved both newsreels and documentaries up until the founding of the GDR. Due to the financial constraints of these early years, many documentaries filmed under DEFA's licence had to be commissioned and/or externally funded, and some films made in this period were even subcontracted to the privately owned company Produktion Brandt (named after its owner, Richard Brandt, the producer and director of *Todeslager Sachsenhausen*).[7] After the founding of the GDR in 1949, the SED gradually nationalized such private companies and turned them into publicly owned enterprises known as Volkseigene Betriebe (VEB).[8]

The year 1952 saw a complete restructuring of film production in the GDR, including its centralization under the supervision of a newly created central film administration, the Hauptverwaltung (HV) Film. As part of the Ministry of Culture, the HV Film was in overall charge of censoring, producing, distributing and exhibiting films in the GDR. Two studios, the DEFA-Studio für Populärwissenschaftliche Filme (DEFA Studio for Popular Science Films) and the DEFA-Studio für Wochenschau und Dokumentarfilme (DEFA Studio for Newsreel and Documentary Films), now oversaw the production of documentaries, newsreels and the satirical cabaret film series *Das Stacheltier* (*The Porcupine*, 1953–64) that provided a space for critical and dissenting voices. Over the course of the 1950s, the DEFA-Studio für Wochenschau und Dokumentarfilme experimented with a variety of internal structures, including allocating production staff to specific genres in the early 1950s and setting up dedicated production teams under the leadership of a group of (exclusively male) heads in 1959.

History and Ideology

During the early 1950s, the efforts of the DEFA-Studio für Wochenschau und Dokumentarfilme were largely focused on films designed to convince postwar Germans that, in backing socialism, they were standing on the right side of history, both politically and materially. Nowhere is this more clearly the case than in the struggle for the cultural legacy of prewar Germany where a succession of anniversaries provided the perfect opportunity for the GDR to portray itself as the natural heir to the humanist legacy of the past. Films such as Ernst Dahle's *Johann Sebastian Bach* (1950), Max Jaap's *Beethoven* (1954) and Wernfried Hübel's *Händel* (1960) are just some of the key documentaries produced by DEFA during this period. These films, which sought to situate contemporary developments in German politics in the context of historical events such as the Reformation, the Thirty Years' War and the French Revolution, and that presented their revolutionary protagonists as embracing a proto-socialist outlook,[9] were conceived at a point in history where in both East and West, the division of Germany was seen as simply a provisional state of affairs.[10] Underpinning these and other documentaries of this kind was the view that, as the GDR's then Prime Minister Otto Grotewohl put it in a speech of 1950, 'what is at stake is German culture itself, something that cannot simply be divided. Our goal is to nurture and preserve the notion of a genuinely national German culture'.[11]

What Grotewohl envisaged – and what remained enshrined in the GDR's constitution up until the early 1970s – was a unified Germany under socialism, and to that end it was vital to demonstrate the technological and historical progress being achieved in the East. Alongside DEFA's contribution to the culture wars of the 1950s, there was a wave of films about technology and improvements in production, typified by documentaries such as Joop Huisken's *Stahl* (*Steel*, 1950) and *Turbine 1* (1953), which highlighted the achievements of socialist labour in the GDR. These were complemented by a range of films contextualizing the rise of the GDR including Andrew Thorndike and Karl Gass' *Der Weg nach Oben: Chronik eines Aufstiegs* (*The Way up: Chronicle of an Ascent*, 1950), which focused on economic progress in the GDR, and Annelie and Andrew Thorndike's *Du und mancher Kamerad* (*The German Story*, 1956) which traced the roots of fascism back to German Imperialism and sought to position the GDR as a progressive state that had arisen in response to the catastrophe of the Third Reich.

Opportunities for documentary filmmaking at DEFA also attracted left-wing filmmakers from outside Germany, and in March 1953 the Dutch cinematographer Joop Huisken was joined at DEFA by his former mentor and fellow countryman, Joris Ivens.[12] Ivens is perhaps best known in the GDR for his groundbreaking documentary *Lied der Ströme* (*The Song of the Rivers*, 1954), a transnational production that not only showcased the benefits of technology and socialism in a global context, but also drew in a network of collaborators from all over the world, including Bertolt Brecht, Ernst Busch, Pablo Picasso, Paul Robeson and Dmitri Shostakovich (Figure 0.1).

In Ivens' film, the viewer is invited to draw a metaphorical comparison between the six great rivers of the world – the Volga, the Mississippi, the Nile, the Yangtze, the Amazon and the Ganges – all heading towards their common destination, the sea, and the common goal of the Weltgewerkschaftsbund (World Federation of Trades Unions) to implement socialism on a global scale. Given the film's reliance on political affect, it is perhaps hardly surprising that the result is a highly poeticized, but essentially uncritical, picture of the communist bloc generally and of the Soviet Union under Stalin in particular.

Although the East German filmmakers Annelie and Andrew Thorndike also produced a series of highly partisan documentaries, the compositional techniques underpinning their work – especially their use of documented archival sources – were quite different from Ivens' more

Introduction • 9

Figure 0.1. Poster for *Lied der Ströme* (1954). © DEFA-Stiftung/Kurt Geffers

self-consciously poeticized style. However, as Helen Hughes notes in her discussion of the Thorndikes (see Chapter 4), to focus exclusively on the propagandistic aspect of their films is not only to ignore their personal histories and the political context in which they worked, but also to downplay the genuinely innovative character of their approach. Alongside films such as *Du und mancher Kamerad* and *Das russische Wunder* (*The Russian Miracle*, 1959–63), which presented idealized histories of the GDR and the Soviet Union respectively, the Thorndikes were perhaps best known for their contributions to the series *Die Archive sagen aus* (*The Archives Testify*), including *Urlaub auf Sylt* (*Holiday on Sylt*, 1957) and *Unternehmen Teutonenschwert* (*Operation Teutonic Sword*, 1958). These films, which presented documentary evidence showing how former high-ranking Nazis had been entrusted with prominent positions of power and influence in the Federal Republic of Germany (FRG) and the North Atlantic Treaty Organization (NATO), reflected a new strategy in film production at DEFA that was designed to bolster the SED's mythologization of the postwar division of Germany whereby the GDR was presented a state made up exclusively of antifascists, while in the FRG the legacy of German fascism lived on. Moreover, as Elizabeth Ward's analysis of Joachim Hellwig's *Ein Tagebuch für Anne Frank* (*A Diary for Anne Frank*, 1958) demonstrates (Chapter 12), even a documentary ostensibly about Holocaust memory could be mobilized to expose the rehabilitation of former National Socialist perpetrators in the Federal Republic.

The global resonance of such films as Iven's *Lied der Ströme* and the Thorndikes' *Das russische Wunder* (which Andrew Thorndike claimed had been viewed by 140 million viewers in 86 countries) served as a reminder of the power of cinema to reach viewers well beyond the GDR. Just how important documentary film would be in promoting the GDR was to become even more apparent following the introduction in 1955 of the so-called Hallstein Doctrine as a key strategy in the Federal Republic's foreign policy. Named after the West German Foreign Minister Walter Hallstein, the policy was an attempt to isolate the GDR politically by declaring that, with the exception of the Soviet Union, any state that formally recognized the GDR would be regarded as having committed a hostile act towards the FRG. The policy, which followed hard on the heels of the Western Allies' decision in 1955 to recognize the FRG (but not the GDR), was driven by the determination of the West German Chancellor Konrad Adenauer and his Christian Democratic Union (CDU) government to present the FRG as having an exclusive mandate to speak for the whole of Germany. Although the Hallstein Doctrine remained in place until the end of the 1960s, the foundation of the Warsaw Pact in 1955 and the resulting system of alliances made it impossible to apply it consistently. Nevertheless, it was not until the 'Basic Treaty' (Grundlagenvertrag) initiated by Chancellor Willy Brandt's Social Democratic government came into effect in June 1973 that the GDR was formally recognized by the Federal Republic.

Faced with the impossibility of establishing embassies abroad, the GDR had little choice but to resort to alternative measures if it was to cultivate relations with foreign powers. Such measures included establishing trade missions and associated cultural/information centres, which, it was hoped, would be upgraded over time into consular missions. Not surprisingly, the screening of documentary features about the GDR played an increasingly important role in the exercise of such soft power. As Thomas Maulucci notes (see Chapter 2), the East German Ministerium für Auswärtige Angelegenheiten (Ministry for Foreign Affairs) regularly approached the DEFA with commissions for documentary shorts that were designed to be screened to audiences outside the GDR. These films, many of which were produced by the Camera DDR production group that was established in 1968, presented reports not only on East German science, technology, health, sport and culture, but also included footage of East German politicians in international settings. In addition, they portrayed the GDR as a technologically advanced country in which socialist society had brought about the emancipation of women in the workplace (a claim that would be subjected to intense critical scrutiny by female documentary filmmakers such as Gitta Nickel, Helke Misselwitz, Róża Berger-Fiedler and Petra Tschörtner in the 1970s and 1980s). Finally, these films engaged in a form of public diplomacy that supported the postwar programme of decolonization and independence in the Global South, and wooed potential political allies, notably in the emerging Arab world, and in other global hotspots of anti-Americanism, such as Chile and Vietnam.

Cinéma Vérité and the Challenges of Modernism

In 1962, the DEFA-Studio für Wochenschau und Dokumentarfilme implemented a model that the DEFA-Studio für Spielfilme (feature films) had launched three years earlier in 1959, and created five artistic collectives (Künstlerische Arbeitsgruppen [KAGs]) and added two more in 1965. In a similar undertaking, five KAGs covering educational films, television commercials and animation films were established in the DEFA-Studio für Populärwissenschaftliche Filme. The KAGs were an important innovation in East German film production, providing semi-autonomous spaces for permanent collectives of industry professionals, including screenwriters, cinematographers and production designers under the leadership of a director. The KAGs all had their own budgets and were responsible for the successful planning and production of their films within the overall guidelines of the DEFA studio under which they operated. The KAGs were very male-dominated; Ingeborg Bissert was the only woman to head up a KAG – Sach- und Zeichentrick (animation) – in the DEFA-Studio für populärwissenschaftliche Filme, which at the time was under the overall leadership of Gerhard Haufe. Inge Kleinert directed the DEFA-Studio für Wochenschau und Dokumentarfilme between 1962 and 1966, and appointed another female employee at DEFA, Renate Wekwerth, to be head of the KAG Wochenschau.

While the building of the Berlin Wall on 13 August 1961 created significant and, for many, insurmountable boundaries to travelling to the

West, the relative stability that ensued made it possible for East German politicians and filmmakers alike to focus increasingly on the social and material conditions of life and work in the GDR itself. Now that the German-German question seemed, at least temporarily, to have been 'resolved', many filmmakers felt confident in adopting a more critical stance concerning contemporary East German society.[13]

In part this change of direction was also facilitated by developments in technology, and the use of concealed cameras together with the possibility of recording sound on location made it possible for filmmakers like Karl Gass in his documentary *Feierabend* (*Leisure*, 1963) to observe at close quarters the after-work activities of a brigade of workers at an oil refinery in Schwedt an der Oder.[14] Gass' largely unflattering portrait of workers in one of the more remote industrial outposts of the GDR – the workers clearly prefer the temptations of the local bar over the opportunities for self-development provided by the plant's lending library – unleashed a vigorous debate about the concept of realism underpinning the film. While the East German weekly *Sonntag* condemned the film, the *Nationalzeitung* praised it as a precursor of the new direction for documentary production at DEFA.[15] However, it was the foreign press – the French journal *Cinéma* described the film as a revival of what is usually referred to as 'cinéma vérité' – that sought to situate *Feierabend* within broader developments in contemporary European cinema.[16]

Industrial documentaries such Karl Gass' *Feierabend* and Jürgen Böttcher's *Ofenbauer* (*Furnace Builders*, 1962) also need to be seen in the context of the so-called 'Bitterfelder Weg' that was adopted as a cultural policy in the GDR in the late 1950s and early 1960s. In November 1958 a conference had been staged at the VEB Leuna petrochemical works located in the town of Bitterfeld entitled 'Chemie bringt Brot, Wohlstand und Schönheit' (Chemistry – A Source of Bread, Prosperity and Beauty). The conference was designed to promote the role of the polymer industry in boosting material standards of living in the GDR, but it also provided the launchpad for a new conceptualization of East German cultural life in which the SED seconded creative practitioners to industrial plants where, through their engagement with the working classes and the process of production, they would contribute through their creative work to the development of what was termed the 'allseitig sozialistische Persönlichkeit' (the all-round-socialist personality), while encouraging members of the working classes to become writers and artists themselves. At the same time, the mediation of such collectivist activity in art, literature and film would be deployed to combat accusations that the alienation of the working classes was no less prevalent in socialist command economies that it was in Western capitalism.

While many socialist realist projects created in the spirit of the 'Bitterfelder Weg' are immediately forgettable, a number of documentarists such as Karl Gass and Jürgen Böttcher were able to bring their keen understanding of developments in European cinema – above all the emergence of cinéma vérité – to bear on documentaries filmed in industrial settings. Likewise, as Nick Hodgin (Chapter 5) notes, a similar quest for authenticity and engagement with individual members of the collective is evident in the early films of Kurt Tetzlaff, including *Im Januar 1963* (*In January 1963*). That East German documentary filmmakers were very familiar with developments in international filmmaking was largely due to the annual Leipzig Film Festival, which, over time, became one of the most important festivals of its kind. Established in 1955 as the *All-German* Leipzig Festival of Cultural and Documentary Films (*Gesamtdeutsche* Leipziger Woche für Kultur- und Dokumentarfilm – our emphasis), the festival was seen as the East German counterpart to the Mannheim Culture and Documentary Film Week in the FRG. Although it was suspended from 1957 to 1959, it resumed in 1960, and a year later was renamed the *Internationale* Leipziger Dokumentar- und Kurzfilmwoche (*International* Leipzig Documentary and Short Film Week). While the building of the Berlin Wall made it much more difficult for East German filmmakers to travel to the West after 1961, filmmakers from both East and West were able to travel to the annual festival in Leipzig and, as Caroline Moine has noted, in both 1961 and 1962, the festival was attended not only by filmmakers from the USSR, Czechoslovakia and Poland, but also by a number of delegates from the Federal Republic who defied the embargo placed on the festival by the (West) German Filmmakers Union.[17] Despite the political tensions of the 1960s, the festival provided an opportunity for DEFA's directors to gain firsthand experience of the new wave cinemas that were emerging across Europe and, above all, in France, Poland and Czechoslovakia. In particular, the presence of the French director Chris Marker and the screening of his film *Le Joli Mai* (*The Lovely Month of May*, 1963) – a documentary shot using lightweight Éclair cameras with synchronized sound – was to make a profound impression on East German filmmakers at the time. Other filmmakers associated with the stylistic approaches of cinéma vérité and/or Direct Cinema who attended the Leipzig festival included the Americans Richard Leacock, Albert Maysles and the Scot John Grierson. Given the retrospective of Dziga Vertov's work at the 1960 festival and the award of the Golden Dove to *Le Joli Mai* in 1963, it is hardly surprising that, as Matthew Bauman points out (Chapter 1), the politics of cinéma vérité were vigorously debated not only at the festival, but also in the pages of the GDR's leading film periodical *Filmwissenschaftliche Mitteilungen* during the early 1960s.

What was at stake in such discussions was the very nature of cinematic realism. While some saw the methods of cinéma vérité as a form of modernism that captured the external world in all its complexity and invited the viewer to become not a passive recipient, but rather a spectator actively involved in the interpretation of that reality, others condemned it for its failure to provide an analysis couched within the supposed objectivity of a Marxist-Leninist framework. Accordingly, at the 1963 festival, Chris Marker observed that:

> [T]he essence of film is that the spectator himself participates, either with admiration or with scepticism, in what is happening on the screen. I believe that viewers ... are becoming increasingly well-informed and conscious of the complex character of the problems of life. As a result, they no longer believe in straightforward solutions to problems, and they see the need to recognise how these problems are bound up with each other, to embrace the contradictions they give rise to, and to resist arriving at simplistic solutions.[18]

Such a view stood in marked contrast to the more orthodox Marxist approach espoused by the Soviet filmmaker Sergei Yutkevich:

> Is it sufficient just to take a camera out onto the street and film life? Is that really a form of cinematic truth? ... Film seeks to capture the dialectical character of life as a process, because truth lies in our hands. There is one and only one truth, and it can only be revealed by means of a scientific Marxist ideology.[19]

While at one level this type of exchange can be seen as a reprise of the ongoing debate between socialist realism and a more pluralist and multivalent concept of modernism, at another it also reflects the transition during the 1960s from the more dogmatic approach of the Thorndikes, and the rise of a quite different type of realism that, in time, came to be associated first with the likes of Karl Gass and the more *nouvelle vague* style films of the rising star, Jürgen Böttcher, whose most recent film *Stars* (Figure 0.2) was singled out for special praise by Chris Marker at the 1963 festival.

At the same time, these debates were a foretaste of the aesthetic conflicts that would come to a head during the infamous Eleventh Plenum of December 1965 where several feature films were banned because of their critical view of contemporary life in the GDR.

Introduction • 15

Figure 0.2. Jürgen Böttcher, *Stars* (1963). © DEFA-Stiftung

Films like Marker's *Le Joli Mai* and Gass' *Feierabend*, which exploited new developments in camera and sound technologies, played a pivotal role in bringing about a paradigmatic shift during what many would regard as, potentially at least, one of the richest periods of East German filmmaking: the first half of the 1960s. The Eleventh Plenum of 1965/1966 was instrumental in preventing the emergence of a distinctively East German nouvelle vague of feature film production in the second half of the decade. The banning of so many films together with the replacement of the more liberally minded studio manager Jochen Mückenberger by Franz Bruk contributed to a marked reluctance on the part of filmmakers to engage in formal experimentation and had a negative impact in terms of both the quantity and quality of DEFA's output during the final years of the Ulbricht era.

However, while DEFA's documentary production was not hit as hard as its feature films, the banning of Tetzlaff's *Es genügt nicht 18 zu sein* (*Being 18 Is Not Enough*, 1965/1989) – an uncompromisingly realistic portrait of a brigade of workers at a drilling rig in Mecklenburg – shows that even documentary cinema, with its more restricted target audiences, was not immune to the sanctions that followed in the wake of the Eleventh Plenum. Even before the fateful events of 1965, the difficulties Böttcher had experienced with both *Drei von vielen* (*Three of Many*, 1961/1989) – a film that suggested that the working classes might be more interested in modernist art than the proponents of the Bitterfelder Weg had imagined – underline how sensitive the GDR's Ministry of Culture still was to narratives that deviated from more conventional socialist realist aesthetics.[20] Likewise, the controversy surrounding *Barfuß und ohne Hut* (*Barefoot and without a Hat*, 1964), another film seen as presenting a distorted image of young East Germans, merely prefigured the banning of Böttcher's nouvelle vague masterpiece, *Jahrgang '45* (*Born in '45*, 1966/1990).

While Böttcher emerged as a highly influential figure during the 1960s, the decade also saw two important, and interlinked, developments: the rise of television in the GDR and the setting up of what would be the state's only truly independent documentary production unit, the Studio H&S. Although many DEFA documentaries were screened on East German television, the relationship between DEFA and the Deutscher Fernsehfunk (DFF) in the GDR was quite different from that in the West. Whereas in the FRG television exercised a profound influence on documentary production, in the GDR, as Peter Zimmermann has noted, television and film production at the DFF and DEFA respectively were to a large extent independent of one another.[21] One of the most important figures linking East German television and DEFA was Gerhard Scheumann, who founded and moderated the television show *Prisma*, which was broadcast between 1963 and 1965 and presented a critical account of current affairs in the GDR.[22] In 1965, together with his colleague, Walter Heynowski, Scheumann turned his attention to the legacy of colonialism and the impact of US foreign policy in the Global South. Their place in the East German media landscape was ensured, following the success of *Der lachende Mann* (*The Laughing Man*, 1966), a documentary about the West German mercenary and former Wehrmacht soldier Friedrich Müller fighting in the Republic of the Congo against the leftist supporters of the former President Patrice Lumumba, who had been murdered in 1961. Now enjoying the backing of the rising political star, Erich Honecker, the DEFA-Gruppe Heynowski und Scheumann was established on 28 February 1967. Although the group still operated officially under the auspices of DEFA, it had its own budget (including access to some 300,000 West German marks), had permission to recruit the West German cameraman Peter Hellmich and was exempted from the usual requirement to have its films formally signed off by the DEFA studio management.

Following the success of the group's next project, *Piloten im Pyjama* (*Pilots in Pyjamas*, 1967) in which a series of American POWs shot down over Vietnam are subjected to intense questioning about their attitudes to the conflict, the unit was allowed, quite exceptionally in the GDR, to operate as a completely autonomous production unit under the name Studio H&S from 1969 to 1982. Not only could most of the team travel freely outside of the GDR, but they were also allowed to retain the foreign currency generated by sales to capitalist countries and, as a result, could purchase sophisticated editing equipment from the United States and Western Europe with which they could generate further income.[23] However, as Priscilla Layne also notes (Chapter 11) in her study of Black abjection in *Kommando 52* (1965), the films of Studio H&S are never quite what they seem. Despite their exotic settings, both *Kommando 52* and *Piloten im Pyjama* are as much about the German-German problem and the covert role of the FRG in the Global Cold War as they are about the situation in Africa and Vietnam specifically. Even so, to dismiss these films as simply propaganda is to fail to do justice to their complex aesthetics. In revealing the constructed artificiality of the onscreen image, there is an obvious relationship between their work and that of Peter Voigt, who, although employed by Studio H&S, was effectively allowed to work independently at the headquarters of Studio H&S in Berlin's Kronenstraße. Voigt was a multitalented documentarist who had worked at the Berliner Ensemble with Bertolt Brecht in the early 1950s and whose particular expertise lay in the integration of still photographs into documentary films. Like the films of Studio H&S, Voigt's documentary work in both film and other media privileges form over content and is as much about how to decode the images on display as it is about the images themselves. As Seán Allan notes (Chapter 6), it is the mobilization of the Brechtian concept of the *gestus* that makes not only Voigt's work but also the work of the Studio H&S generally so much more complex than just conventional works of propaganda. These elements of self-reflexivity are also evident in the cycles of films about the Pinochet coup in Chile and the Vietnam War that were released by Studio H&S during the 1970s. As Martin Brady (Chapter 9) demonstrates in his chapter on Studio H&S's so-called Cambodia Trilogy of the 1980s, a close reading of the films reveals the ways in which Heynowski and Scheumann foreground the cinematic apparatus as an integral part of political analysis and thereby contribute to a cinematic tradition of self-reflexivity.

Winds of Change in the Wake of the Eleventh Plenum

Discussions at DEFA following the Eleventh Plenum prompted further changes to the organizational structure of DEFA documentary production, including the establishment in 1967 of an independent studio, the DEFA-Gruppe 67, under the leadership of Andrew Thorndike who reported directly to the Ministry of Culture. At the same time, an additional collective, KAG Gass, was established as a quasi-autonomous production unit with its own studio, editing and duplication facilities under the leadership of Karl Gass. In response to a palpable climate of societal and political disquiet in the GDR following the Prague Spring in 1968, a greater centralization of documentary filmmaking took place in 1969 with a view to ensuring a greater consistency between the DEFA studio's output and the political messaging of the SED. As a result, the Studio für populärwissenschaftliche Filme and the Studio für Wochenschau und Dokumentarfilme were combined into a new structure, the DEFA-Studio für Kurzfilme (short films), which comprised nine KAGs, including the former KAG Auslandsinformation (foreign information) – now renamed Camera DDR – together with the addition in 1971 of the production of a hybrid unit, defa futurum, covering both documentary and fictional film.

The replacement of Walter Ulbricht by Erich Honecker as First Secretary of the SED's Central Committee on 19 June 1971 is often regarded as ushering in a new phase of liberalization in East German cultural policy, a development that was consolidated by the formal recognition of the GDR by the Federal Republic in June 1973. However, the expatriation of the singer/songwriter Wolf Biermann in November 1976 following his criticism of the GDR at a concert in Cologne showed how short-lived such cultural thaws could be. Although several important writers, artists and performers left the GDR in the wake of the Biermann affair, as Eduard Schreiber notes, the impact on the (restructured) DEFA-Studio für Dokumentarfilme was minimal, because to abandon the GDR was also to abandon the infrastructure, technical support and security of employment that made for such favourable conditions for documentary filmmakers at DEFA.[24]

Alongside the more hard-hitting productions emerging from Studio H&S that engaged with the Cold War in its transnational context, many filmmakers at DEFA – especially Gitta Nickel, Volker Koepp and Jürgen Böttcher – exploited improvements in camera and sound technology that enabled them to observe everyday life in the GDR and to do so relatively unobtrusively. Increasingly, these investigations of everyday life were approached from the perspective of the GDR's female workforce who often had to combine the demands of the workplace with the demands of childcare and family life. Some of the most interesting examples of this tendency include Böttcher's *Wäscherinnen* (*Laundresses*, 1972), Nickel's *Wir von ESDA* (*Working for ESDA*, 1976), and Koepp's series of films about female workers in Wittstock, *Mädchen in Wittstock* (*Girls in Wittstock*, 1975) and *Wieder in Wittstock* (*Wittstock Once Again*, 1976). A more extensive – and historically grounded – panorama of East German life is to be found in the so-called 'Langzeit-Dokumentarfilme' (long-term documentaries) produced by Barbara and Winfried Junge about a group of children born in 1954/1955 and living in the village of Golzow in the Oderbruch region.[25] The origins of the project can be traced back to 1961 – some three years earlier than Michael Apted's television series *Seven Up!* (1964) in the United Kingdom – and Junge's film *Wenn ich erst zur Schule geh'* (*When I Go to School*). Remarkably, the series survived the reunification of Germany in 1990 and it was not until 2007 that it was finally brought to a close. As Nora Alter has observed, the Golzow films are much more than just an account of life in a provincial East German village; they also reflect the developments in documentary filmmaking in the GDR from the 1960s through its demise and beyond.[26]

Many of the films produced in the final decade of the GDR's existence are, as Nick Hodgin has observed, infused with a sense of Romantic melancholy that manifests itself in particular in films such as Peter Rocha's *Hochwaldmärchen* (*High Forest Fairy Tale*, 1987) and *Schmerzen der Lausitz* (*The Pain of Lusatia*, 1990) that focus on the destruction of the natural world by the brown coal mining industry in the GDR. 'Where images of machinery in DEFA's documentary films once connoted progress, the GDR's self-sufficiency or proud industrial character, in Rocha's film they are indiscriminate, ominous, dwarfing the people who operate them'.[27] As Seán Allan notes (Chapter 6), a similar sense of melancholy regarding the future of the East German cultural sphere is also evident in a film such as Peter Voigt's *Dämmerung –Ostberliner Bohème der 50er Jahre* (*Dusk*, 1993). Seen from this perspective, it is perhaps unsurprising that the new generation of filmmakers – especially the emerging female talents Helke Misselwitz, Petra Tschörtner and Gabriele Denecke – should turn their attention to the experiences of those who, by virtue of their gender, age or disability, had been consigned to the margins of socialist society. Misselwitz's *Winter Adé* (1989) and Tschörtner's *Unsere alten Tage* (*In Our Old Age*, 1989) present the viewer with a range of vignettes covering the lives of individuals who would otherwise remain hidden from view. Yet, as Jennifer Creech argues (Chapter 7), it is precisely through the mobilization of such marginalized figures that the work of these two female directors is imbued with a profound sense of authenticity. Following the collapse of the GDR in 1989, further marginalized groups – notably those Germans from East Prussia had had been displaced following the end of the Second World

War – started to emerge in the wake of discussions about where exactly the boundaries of a new unified Germany should be drawn. As Jason Doerre demonstrates in his discussions of the work of Volker Koepp and Andreas Voigt (Chapter 16), the complex relationship of the presence of the past in post-unification German culture became a prominent – and enduring – theme for many documentary filmmakers working in the post-Wende period.

Studio Structures: The Final Phase

By 1973, all the KAGs had been stripped of their autonomy and converted into so-called Production Groups (Produktionsgruppen [PG]), which, in 1975, had fallen under the remit of the recently renamed DEFA-Studio für Dokumentarfilme (a name that would be retained even after unification and privatization). For the first time, a newly formed PG Kinderfilm (children's film) oversaw films aimed at children and teenagers, and over the next decade and a half, the number of PGs grew to a total of eighteen distributed across three studio locations in Potsdam-Babelsberg, Kleinmachnow and Berlin (Kronenstraße), along with the group defa futurum that was located in the Berlin studios alongside the production facilities for the puppet animation show *Unser Sandmännchen* (*The Sandman*), which had been screened on East German television since 1959 and was hugely popular with audiences in both the GDR and the FRG.

On 18 December 1980, DEFA ended production of *Der Augenzeuge* – at that time the world's longest-running newsreel – and, in order to maintain the relationship with the International News Reel Association INA, replaced it the following year with a new current affairs programme *Kinobox* produced by a dedicated unit, the PG defa kinobox. As Reinhild Steingröver (Chapter 3) notes, this production unit attracted some of the outstanding talents in the GDR's final generation of filmmakers. In 1983, further changes took place in DEFA's organizational when Studio H&S was stripped of its autonomous status, reintegrated into the DEFA-Studio für Dokumentarfilme, and renamed PG Kronenstraße (after the street in which it was located). Nonetheless, even after 1983, many still referred to as Gruppe H&S or Werkstatt H&S in recognition of its historical origins. Four years later in 1987, a new group PG Video was added to the DEFA-Studio für Dokumentarfilme after video technology was adopted with a view to facilitating the production of advertising films.

Despite the constant restructuring and renaming of production units, most remained under the leadership of the same (male) individuals who often remained in their positions for more than a decade. This left few opportunities for younger generations of directors and producers or female employees to take on responsibilities and/or initiate change. In 1988, a group of young DEFA filmmakers drafted a manifesto to be read and discussed at the Fifth Congress of the Verband der Film- und Fernsehschaffenden der DDR (Association of Film and Television Workers of the GDR).[28] Although the rapidly changing political landscape in the GDR meant that this discussion never took place, the Studio für Dokumentarfilme decided to form the short-lived PG 117 Nachwuchs (Young Generation). When the political changes eventually led to German unification in 1990, the studio briefly changed into a limited liability corporation. DEFA folded for good in 1998, after the Kirch media group had purchased portions of it in 1992 and liquidated it over the course of the next six years, while other parts became the companies DOKFILM, Park Studios, Ö Film, Cintec and Thomas Wilkening Film Production. A key factor in hastening the demise of the DEFA-Studio für Dokumentarfilme was the fact that, for a number of reasons, it lacked the latest technology that was available at comparable studios in Central and Western Europe, and as a result was unable to transform itself into a profitable corporation as judged by the prevailing standards. As a result, West German and other international investors often showed little interest in maintaining film production or modernizing outdated equipment and facilities, and focused on the acquisition of the valuable real estate instead.

Technology and Exhibition

Changes in approach and documentary style have always been closely linked to developments in technology, and limited supplies of convertible currency meant that the cost – and restricted availability – of high-quality film stock and advanced camera technology was a constant issue for the DEFA-Studio für Dokumentarfilme. When DEFA created the various KAGs in 1952, those shooting newsreel and documentary footage received larger ARRIFLEX 35 cameras and the smaller, more portable Debrie cameras left over from the (prewar) inventory of UFA. They also had access to state-of-the-art Swiss-manufactured NAGRA audio recorders, West German Sennheiser microphones, Osram lights and various high-spec lenses. However, limited access to hard currency and Western markets following the building of the Berlin Wall in 1961 made it increasingly challenging to obtain replacement parts. It is striking that when discussing the obstacles he faced in making the documentary *Stars* (1963), Jürgen Böttcher cited both the noisiness of the Arriflex cameras at his disposal and the lack of high-quality recording equipment.[29] Moreover as his cameraman Christian Lehmann noted in an interview with the film historian Caroline Moine, filmmakers working for East German television had greater access to better equipment than those whose work was targeted at cinema audiences.[30] Despite obligations to trade technology with other Comecon nations, the difficulties in accessing advanced technologies led to the establishment of repair facilities at each of the DEFA studios. There, technicians became experts in adapting, modifying and compounding whatever technologies they had at their disposal. This expertise expanded into sound technology as well, and the DEFA Studio für Dokumentarfilme piloted magnetic sound recording technology for all DEFA studios and eventually introduced 4-channel recording as early as 1956.

However, by far the most impressive development was Georg Maidorn's invention of an East German 70 mm camera in 1964, the so-called DEFA-Reflex or 70 Reflex, which made the GDR only the third nation after the Soviet Union and the United States to have access to such technology.[31] However, the DEFA-Studio für Dokumentarfilme was only able to produce three 70 mm documentaries – Werner Bergmann's experimental *DEFA 70* (1967) and Annelie and Andrew Thorndike's films *Du bist min – Ein deutsches Tagebuch* (*You Are Mine – A German Diary*, 1969) and *Wladimir Iljitsch Uljanow Lenin* (1970) – before 70 mm film production became too expensive and was abandoned. Studio standards for film material were the 35 mm format for documentaries and newsreels and 16 mm film for educational and training films, both of which were manufactured in the state-owned Filmfabrik Wolfen under the historic Agfa brand. It was renamed in 1964 as ORWO (Original Wolfen) to settle a legal dispute with the West German Agfa company. The first DEFA documentaries were still shot on combustible nitrate film stock. For 16 mm films, the studio imported expensive raw material for acetate film to avoid dangerous fires in schools and factories that were still a possibility with nitrate film. While colour film stock was rare and not on a par with the international standard set by Kodak's Eastman Colour stock, Kurt Maetzig and Feodor Pappe had permission to film *Immer Bereit* (*Always Prepared*) about the first Free German Youth's Deutschlandtreffen in colour as early as 1950. The limitations of the colour film stock at their disposal coupled with the much greater availability of the East German ORWO NP 55 black-and-white film stock (universally regarded as a top-quality product) goes some way towards explaining why many DEFA documentary filmmakers still filmed in black and white right up until the 1980s.

Over the forty years or so of DEFA's existence, ingenuity and innovation prevailed and made it possible for the DEFA-Studio für Dokumentarfilme in its various iterations to produce well over 4,000 films that were viewed by domestic and international audiences in both East and West. During the late 1940s and throughout the 1950s, documentaries would often be screened in film clubs, in regular cinemas and in so-called Zeitkinos (cinemas in close proximity to railway stations) that specialized in the screening of 60-minute shows consisting of 'zeitnahe' (recent) documentaries and newsreels.[32] Starting in 1952, the East German railway company Deutsche Reichsbahn operated multiple carriages (Kinowagen) with facilities for screening films[33] and, in addition, dozens of trucks were equipped with mobile projector units to take documentaries to spectators who lived too far from the nearest movie theatre.[34] Although the modes of screening changed – especially with the availability of television from 1952 – over the decades of the GDR's existence, the SED ensured that access to DEFA newsreels and documentaries was both easy and affordable for all its citizens.

Documenting Socialism

Given the DEFA studio's prolific output and the large number of filmmakers who worked outside the auspices of the mainstream studio, it is scarcely possible to do justice to the phenomenon of East German documentary in a volume of this size. Many of the individual filmmakers and production studios such as Studio H&S referenced in the volume could easily be the subject of a monograph in their own right. Likewise, the production of Super 8 film – a crossover phenomenon that embraces not only activist documentary but also home movies with their more intimate forms of personal memory – merely underlines what a complex and diverse field the production of nonfictional film in the GDR was. Accordingly, our volume seeks to reflect that complexity by offering a range of different approaches to the analysis of East German documentary cinema. However, no study of this kind exists in a vacuum, and in constructing this volume we have sought to build on the comprehensive overview presented in Günter Jordan and Ralph Schenk's landmark volume of 1996 *Schwarzweiß und Farbe. DEFA-Dokumentarfilme 1946–92*, and on the detailed analysis of the sociopolitical context of the early years provided in 1994 by Christiane Mückenberger and Günter Jordan, *'Sie sehen selbst, Sie hören selbst. . . .' Eine Geschichte der DEFA von ihren Anfängen bis 1949*. It is also striking that, perhaps mindful of the need to preserve the memories of an ageing generation, these well-established studies have been supplemented either by compilations of interviews with key figures – such as the volume *Das Prinzip Neugier. DEFA-Dokumentarfilme erzählen* (2012), edited by Ingrid Poss, Christiane Mückenberger and Anne Richter – or by volumes containing multiple contributions by former practitioners at DEFA, such as Peter Zimmermann's landmark volumes *Deutschlandbilder Ost. Dokumentarfilme der DEFA von der Nachkriegszeit bis zur Wiedervereinigung* (1995) and the more recent *Dokumentarfilm in Deutschland. Von den Anfängen bis zur Gegenwart* (2022).

In German-language scholarship, recent in-depth studies of the filmmakers Joris Ivens[35] and Volker Koepp[36] have underlined the importance of both for an understanding of both the early phase of DEFA documentary and its afterlife. Likewise, Rüdiger Steinmetz and Tilo Prase's monograph of 2002 on *Dokumentarfilm zwischen Beweis und Pamphlet. Heynowski & Scheumann und Gruppe Katins* on Studio H&S might be seen as the first step towards a more nuanced understanding of Heynowski and Scheumann's films that have too often been dismissed as nothing more than simplistic propaganda. While English-language scholarship has been reliant on a series of disparate articles and chapters covering a rage of filmmakers and topics,[37] the recent translation and publication in 2018 of Caroline Moine's monograph *Screened Encounters: The Leipzig Documentary Film Festival, 1955–1990* provides a wealth of detail on what was perhaps the most important event in the calendar of the DEFA-Studio für Dokumentarfilme. Last but not least, Nora M. Alter's *Projecting History: German Nonfiction Cinema 1967–2000* (2002) represents a rare attempt to situate East German documentary filmmaking alongside its West German counterpart.[38]

As a number of the contributions volume reveal, East German documentary was a transnational undertaking that, even in its earliest phase, drew on the talents of foreign filmmakers such as Joop Huisken and Joris Ivens. Even in the darkest periods of the Cold War, the networking opportunities provided by the Leipzig Documentary Film Festival ensured that it remained in constant dialogue with filmmakers from both East and West (including the United States). Indeed, as the very title of Hermann Herlinghaus' anthology *Dokumentaristen der Welt in den Kämpfen unserer Zeit* (*Global Documentary Film and the Struggles of Our Time*, 1982) underlines, East German filmmakers clearly saw themselves and their work in the context of a progressive global movement that embraced figures such as Paul Rotha, Mikhail Romm, Patricio Guzmán, Lionel Ngakane, Chris Marker and Richard Leacock. We have discussed elsewhere the dangers of approaching East German film history in terms of a narrow conception of national cinemas,[39] and while it is impossible to disassociate the individuals and topics from the immediate political context in which they operated, almost all of the chapters in the volume – Sebastian Heiduschke's reading of DEFA documentaries through the lens of African Cinema (Chapter 10) is but one example – remind us that to see DEFA as the cinema of a small nation is to ignore its richness and complexity. Moreover, as Andy Räder points out in his discussion of Sorbian documentary (see Chapter 8), the GDR was anything but a homogenous political entity.

However we choose to define DEFA, one thing is certain, namely that the studio consistently sought to position itself as Other in respect to mainstream commercial filmmaking and the type of fare served up by Hollywood. In the sphere of documentary filmmaking, this created a relationship of affinity with those filmmakers from other parts of the world who, by virtue of focusing on documentary (rather than feature filmmaking), found themselves consigned to the margins of their own film industries. This sense of alterity is particularly evident in the ways in which DEFA documentaries sought to position the GDR as Other in respect to its near neighbour, the Federal Republic. While this sense of political alterity comes across clearly in the statements and testimonies of those former employees recorded in the collections from the 1990s, our attempt to reimagine DEFA documentary some thirty to forty years later reveals the presence of several blind spots in respect of race, gender and sexuality. In many ways these blind spots, which are hardly confined to East German cinema, suggest that DEFA had rather more in common with other national cinemas than would appear to be the case at first sight. Kyle Frackman's queer re-reading (Chapter 14) of the film *In Sachen H. und acht anderer* (*In the Matter of H. and Eight Others*, 1972) exposes contradictions in the East German government's handling of sexualities that did not conform to conventional heterosexual models. By the same token, Tom Smith's analysis (Chapter 13) of the representation of female soldiers in short documentaries produced by – and for – the Nationale Volksarmee (National People's Army [NVA]) shows how these films oscillate between constantly problematizing and reinforcing binary gender norms in ways that challenge conventional concepts of masculinity and reveal the gender binary to be under increasing pressure in the GDR. At the same time, both Frackman and Smith's chapter point to alternative forms of film production that could not always be easily aligned with state socialism in the GDR.

The fascination – and challenge – of DEFA documentaries is that often the ostensible subject of a given film was simply a pretext to discuss the Cold War and the situation of the GDR in respect of the FRG within that framework. As Priscilla Layne (Chapter 11) notes, at one level discussions of Black abjection appear to present a progressive view of postcolonial politics, but at another this trope is instrumentalized in ways that are clearly designed to highlight the progressive political credentials of the GDR itself. Nonetheless, it is important not to fall into the trap of dismissing East German documentary as simply crude propaganda. Even the Studio H&S, often condemned by scholars as nothing more than an anti-FRG agitprop unit, has started to attract greater scholarly attention as critics have become more attuned to the elements of self-reflexivity that are evident in their films. Likewise, many will object that filmmakers like Annelie and Andrew Thorndike, Karl Gass, Peter Voigt, Gerhard Scheumann and Walter Heynowski presented partisan ideology in the guise of supposedly objective historical narratives. However, such a view downplays not only the aesthetic complexity (and self-reflexivity) of a number of these films, but also the highly politicised context of the Cold War in which the filmmakers operated, as well as their personal biographies and first-hand experiences of the legacy of German fascism. By contrast, those willing to engage with East German documentary – both mainstream and marginal – on its own terms will discover a rich and provocative collection of films that, if anything, underlines just how interconnected filmmakers in the GDR were with postwar developments in global cinema.

Seán Allan is Professor of German at the University of St Andrews and holds a Joint Research Professorship for Neuere Deutsche Literaturwissenschaft at the University of Bonn. His main research areas are Heinrich von Kleist, the culture of the European Enlightenment and the cinema in the GDR. His publications include *DEFA: East German Cinema, 1946–1992* (co-edited with John Sandford, Berghahn Books, 1996), *Unverhoffte Wirkungen. Erziehung und Gewalt im Werk Heinrich von Kleists* (co-authored with Ricarda Schmidt and Steven Howe, K&N, 2014), *Re-imagining DEFA: East German Cinema in Its National and Transnational Contexts* (co-edited with Sebastian Heiduschke, Berghahn Books, 2016), *Screening Art: Modernism and the Socialist Imaginary in East German Cinema* (Berghahn Books, 2019) and *Inspiration Bonaparte: German Culture under Napoleonic Occupation* (Camden House, 2021).

Sebastian Heiduschke is Professor of World Languages and Cultures at Oregon State University. His film publications include the books *East

German Cinema: DEFA and Film History (2013 in English, 2019 in a Japanese edition), *Re-imagining DEFA: East German Cinema in its National and Transnational Contexts* (co-edited with Seán Allan, 2016), as well as essays in *Camera Obscura, Feminist German Studies, German Studies Review, Monatshefte* and various edited collections.

Notes

1. A notable exception in this respect is Rüdiger Steinmetz and Tilo Prase's study: *Dokumentarfilm zwischen Beweis und Pamphlet. Heynowski & Scheumann und Gruppe Katins* (Leipzig: Leipziger Universitätsverlag, 2002).
2. On Jürgen Böttcher, see, for example, Richard Kilborn, 'The Documentary Work of Jürgen Böttcher. A Retrospective', in Seán Allan and John Sandford (eds), *DEFA: East German Cinema 1946–1992* (New York: Berghahn Books, 1999), pp. 267–82. On Barbara and Winfried Junge and their *Kinder von Golzow* project, see, for example, Barton Byg, 'GDR-Up: The Ideology of Universality in Long Term Documentary', *New German Critique* 80(1) (2001), 126–44.
3. Kurt Maetzig, 'Vom Wesen des Dokumentarfilms', *Theater der Zeit* 1 (1946), 24. All translations of original German sources are the authors' own unless otherwise stated.
4. Kurt Maetzig, 'Wir sind alle Augenzeugen', *Vorwärts*, 14 August 1946.
5. Christiane Mückenberger and Günter Jordan, *'Sie sehen selbst, Sie hören selbst'. Eine Geschichte der DEFA von ihren Anfängen bis 1949* (Marburg: Hitzeroth, 1994), pp. 243–45 (at p. 244).
6. For a more detailed account of the role and history of Prometheus and Weltfilm, see Bruce Murray, *Film and the German Left in the Weimar Republic. From* Caligari *to* Kuhle Wampe (Austin: University of Texas Press, 1990), pp. 186–224.
7. Produktion Brandt/Sonderfilm, Bericht 8.8.1947 (= BArch, DR IV 2/906/202).
8. For an encyclopaedic overview of DEFA's structures and organization, see Günter Jordan, *Film in der DDR. Daten – Fakten – Strukturen* (Potsdam: Filmmuseum Potsdam, 2009). See also the corresponding website: https://www.defa-stiftung.de/defa/geschichte/daten-und-fakten/filmwesen-der-ddr/ (retrieved 3 August 2023).
9. As Stephan Ehrig has noted, these protagonists were often referred to as 'teleological precursors'. See Stephan Ehrig, 'Deconstructing Revolutionary Traditions: Stefan Schütz's *Kohlhaas*', in Stephan Ehrig, Marcel Thomas and David Zell (eds), *The GDR Today: New Interdisciplinary Approaches to East German History, Memory and Culture* (Oxford: Lang, 2018), pp. 83–98.
10. See Seán Allan, *Screening Art: Modernism and the Socialist Imaginary in East German Cinema* (Oxford: Berghahn Books, 2019), pp. 60–78.

11. Otto Grotewohl, 'Die deutsche Kultur ist unteilbar', *Neues Deutschland*, 23 March 1950.
12. Following his first visit to the DEFA studio in August 1951, Ivens had been involved in a number of short-term collaborations. See Günter Jordan, *Unbekannter Ivens. Triumph, Verdammnis, Auferstehung. Joris Ivens bei der DEFA und in der DDR 1948–1949* (Berlin: Bertz + Fischer, 2018), p. 23.
13. Karl Gass notes that 'at that time I was very much in favour of the Wall, indeed I felt it should have been built much earlier as the open border was causing us huge damage'. See Karl Gass, 'Ich habe nicht umsonst gelebt', in Ingrid Poss, Christiane Mückenberger and Anne Richter (eds), *Das Prinzip Neugier. DEFA-Dokumentarfilmer erzählen* (Berlin: Neues Leben, 2012), pp. 34–57 (at p. 48). This goes some way towards explaining the political thrust behind what is probably Gass' best-known (but perhaps least representative) documentary outside the GDR, namely *Schaut auf diese Stadt* (*Look at This City*, 1962).
14. See Gass' remarks on sound recording technology: Karl Gass, 'Von der filmischen Hymne zur realistischen Dokumentation. Auf den Spuren des Bitterfelder Weges', in Peter Zimmermann (ed), *Deutschlandbilder Ost. Dokumentarfilme der DEFA von der Nachkriegszeit bis zur Wiedervereinigung* (Konstanz: UVK Medien/Ölschläger, 1995), pp. 77–108 (especially p. 92). See also Michael Biegholdt, Werner Wüste and Karl Gass, 'Unsere Arbeit an dem Dokumentarfilm *Feierabend*', *Filmwissenschaftliche Mitteilungen* 2 (1964), 264–75.
15. *Sonntag* 9/1964 and *Nationalzeitung*, 17 October 1964.
16. *Cinéma 64*, No. 85/April 1964.
17. On the early history of the festival, see Caroline Moine, *Screened Encounters: The Leipzig Documentary Film Festival, 1955–1990* (New York: Berghahn Books, 2018), pp. 43–70.
18. Protokoll der VI. Leipziger Dokumentar und Kurzfilmwoche 1963, pp. 42–43 (cited in Günter Jordan and Ralf Schenk (eds), *Schwarzweiß und Farbe. DEFA Dokumentarfilme, 1946–92* (Berlin: Jovis, 1996), p. 380)
19. Ibid.
20. For a discussion of Böttcher's *Drei von vielen*, see Allan, *Screening Art*, pp. 95–104.
21. Peter Zimmermann, 'Der Dokumentarfilm der DEFA zwischen Propaganda, Alltagsbeobachtung und subversiver Rezeption', in Zimmermann (ed.), *Deutschlandbilder Ost*, pp. 77–108 (at p. 92).
22. For a more detailed discussion of *Prisma*, see Heather L. Gumbert, *Envisioning Socialism: Television and the Cold War in the German Democratic Republic* (Ann Arbor: University of Michigan Press, 2014), pp. 144–49.
23. A more detailed account of the founding and economic basis of the studio is presented in Rüdiger Steinmetz and Tilo Prase, pp. 45–67.
24. Eduard Schreiber, 'Zeit der verpassten Möglichkeiten, 1970 bis 1980' in Jordan and Schenk, *Schwarzweiß und Farbe*, pp. 129–79 (at p. 159).

25. For a detailed study of the Golzow film project, see Byg, 'GDR-Up', as well as Britta Hartmann and Marian Petraitis, '". . . sich später mal als DDR-Bürger wiedersehen zu können": Vom ethnografischen zum historiografischen Modus in der dokumentarischen Langzeitstudie *Die Kinder von Golzow*', in Dominik Orth and Heinz-Peter Preusser (eds), *Mauerschau – Die DDR als Film. Beiträge zur Historisierung eines verschwundenen Staates* (Berlin: De Gruyter, 2020), pp. 273–96.
26. Nora M. Alter, *Projecting History: German Nonfiction Cinema 1967–2000* (Ann Arbor: University of Michigan Press, 2002), pp. 195–210 (at p. 199).
27. Nick Hodgin, 'DEFA's Last Gasp: Ruins, Melancholy and the End of East German Filmmaking', in Seán Allan and Sebastian Heiduschke (eds), *Re-imagining DEFA. East German Cinema in its National and Transnational Contexts* (New York: Berghahn Books, 2016), pp. 271–91 (at p. 272).
28. For a translation and discussion of the manifesto, see Laura G. McGee, 'Revolution in the Studio? The DEFA's Fourth Generation of Film Directors and Their Reform Efforts in the Last Decade of the GDR', *Film History* 15(4) (2003), 444–64.
29. Jürgen Böttcher, 'Bemerkungen zu meinem Film *Stars*', *Filmwissenschaftliche Beiträge* 1 (1964), 1–12.
30. Cited in Moine, *Screened Encounters*, p. 94. For a discussion of the relationship between the film studio DEFA and the East German broadcaster Deutscher Fernsehfunk, see Thomas Beutelschmidt, *Kooperation oder Konkurrenz? Das Verhältnis zwischen Film und Fernsehen in der DDR* (Berlin: DEFA-Stiftung, 2009).
31. Ralf Schenk. 'Ein Hauch von Welt. Vor 30 Jahren kamen die ersten 70mm-Filme der DEFA auf die Leinwand', film-dienst 19/1997, https://www.defa-stiftung.de/defa/publikationen/artikel/191997-ein-hauch-von-welt/ (retrieved 24 July 2023).
32. Jeanpaul Goergen, 'Vorwiegend aus politischen Gründen', *Leuchtkraft. Journal der DEFA-Stiftung* 3 (2020), 131–34.
33. Jeanpaul Goergen, 'DEFA auf Schienen. Die Kinowagen der Deutschen Reichsbahn', *Leuchtkraft. Journal der DEFA-Stiftung* 2 (2019), 100–4.
34. Günter Jordan, 'Die frühen Jahre', in Jordan and Schenk, *Schwarzweiß und Farbe*, pp. 40–41.
35. Günter Jordan, *Unbekannter Ivens. Triumph, Verdamnis, Auferstehung. Joris Ivens bei der DEFA und in der DDR 1948–1989* (Berlin: Bertz + Fischer, 2018).
36. Grit Lemke (ed.), *Unter hohen Himmeln. Das Universum Volker Koepp: Gespräche und Reflexionen* (Berlin: Bertz + Fischer, 2019).
37. Key examples include, but are not limited to, Sarah Blaylock, 'Bringing the War Home to the United States and East Germany: *In the Year of the Pig* and *Pilots in Pajamas*', *Cinema Journal* 56(4) (2017), 26–50; Patricia A. Simpson, 'Allegories of Resistance. The Legacy of 1968 in GDR Visual Cultures', in Christina Gerhardt and Marco Abel (eds), *Celluloid Revolt. German Screen*

Cultures and the Long 1968, (Rochester, NY: Camden House, 2019), pp. 201–18; Nick Hodgin, 'Alternative Realities and Authenticity in DEFA's Documentary Films', in Marc Silberman and Henning Wrage (eds), *DEFA at the Crossroads of East German and International Film Culture: A Companion* (Berlin and Boston: Walter de Gruyter, 2014), pp. 281–304; Richard Kilborn, 'The Documentary Work of Jürgen Böttcher: A Retrospective' in Seán Allan and John Sandford (eds), *DEFA: East German Cinema, 1946–1992* (New York: Berghahn Books, 1996), pp. 267–82; Franziska Noessig, 'Artists and Artworks in the Films of Jürgen Böttcher' (unpublished PhD Thesis, Kings College London, 2019); and Lauren Cuthbert, '"Ich hatte Befehle": Multidirectional Memory and the Vietnam War in Heynowski and Scheumann's Piloten im Pyjama (1968)', *German Life and Letters* 75(4) (2022), 521–39.
38. See also Matthias Steinle, 'Visualizing the Enemy: Representations of the "Other Germany" in Documentaries Produced by the FRG and GDR in the 1950s', in John E. Davidson and Sabine Hake (eds), *Framing the Fifties: Cinema in a Divided Germany* (New York: Berghahn Books, 2007), pp. 120–36.
39. Seán Allan and Sebastian Heiduschke, 'Introduction: Re-imagining East German Cinema', in *Re-imagining DEFA*, pp. 1–18.

Select Bibliography

Allan, Seán, and Sebastian Heiduschke (eds). *Re-imagining DEFA: East German Cinema in its National and Transnational Contexts*. New York: Berghahn Books, 2016.
Alter, Nora M. *Projecting History. German Nonfiction Cinema, 1967–2000*. Ann Arbor: University of Michigan Press, 2002.
Beutelschmidt, Thomas. *Kooperation oder Konkurrenz? Das Verhältnis zwischen Film und Fernsehen in der DDR*. Berlin: DEFA-Stiftung, 2009.
Böttcher, Jürgen. 'Bemerkungen zu meinem Film *Stars*', *Filmwissenschaftliche Beiträge* 1 (1964), 1–12.
Byg, Barton. 'GDR-Up: The Ideology of Universality in Long Term Documentary', *New German Critique* 80(1) (2001), 126–44.
Davidson. John E., and Sabine Hake (eds). *Framing the Fifties: Cinema in a Divided Germany*. New York: Berghahn Books, 2007.
Ehrig, Stephan, Marcel Thomas and David Zell (eds). *The GDR Today: New Interdisciplinary Approaches to East German History, Memory and Culture*. Oxford: Lang, 2018, pp. 83–98.
Hermlinghaus, Hermann (ed.). *Dokumentaristen der Welt in den Kämpfen unserer Zeit. Selbstzeugnisse aus zwei Jahrzehnten (1960–1981)*. Berlin: Henschel, 1982.
Heynowski, Walter, 'Walter Heynowski: Einen Film macht man 1:1', in Ingrid Poss, Christiane Mückenberger and Anne Richter (eds), *Das Prinzip Neugier. DEFA-Dokumentarfilmer erzählen*. Berlin: Neues Leben, 2012, pp. 59–97.

Hodgin, Nick. 'Alternative Realities and Authenticity in DEFA's Documentary Films', in Marc Silberman and Henning Wrage (eds), *DEFA at the Crossroads of East German and International Film Culture: A Companion*. Berlin: Walter de Gruyter, 2014, pp. 281–304.
Jordan, Günter. *Unbekannter Ivens. Triumph, Verdamnis, Auferstehung. Joris Ivens bei der DEFA und in der DDR 1948–1989*. Berlin: Bertz + Fischer, 2018.
Jordan, Günter, and Ralf Schenk (eds). *Schwarzweiß und Farbe. DEFA-Dokumentarfilme, 1946–92*. Berlin: Jovis, 1996.
Lemke, Grit (ed.). *Unter hohen Himmeln. Das Universum Volker Koepp: Gespräche und Reflexionen*. Berlin: Bertz + Fischer, 2019.
McGee, Laura G. 'Revolution in the Studio? The DEFA's Fourth Generation of Film Directors and Their Reform Efforts in the Last Decade of the GDR', *Film History* 15(4) (2003), 444–64.
Moine, Caroline. *Screened Encounters: The Leipzig Documentary Film Festival, 1955–1990*. New York: Berghahn Books, 2018.
Mückenberger, Christiane, and Günter Jordan. *'Sie sehen selbst, Sie hören selbst.' Eine Geschichte der DEFA von ihren Anfängen bis 1949*. Marburg: Hitzeroth, 1994.
Poss, Ingrid, Christiane Mückenberger and Anne Richter (eds). *Das Prinzip Neugier. DEFA-Dokumentarfilmer erzählen*. Berlin: Neues Leben, 2012.
Silberman, Marc, and Henning Wrage (eds). *DEFA at the Crossroads of East German and International Film Culture: A Companion*. Berlin: Walter de Gruyter, 2014.
Steinle, Matthias. 'Visualizing the Enemy: Representations of the "Other Germany" in Documentaries Produced by the FRG and GDR in the 1950s', in John E. Davidson and Sabine Hake (eds), *Framing the Fifties: Cinema in a Divided Germany*. New York: Berghahn Books, 2007, pp. 120–36.
Steinmetz, Rüdiger. 'Heynowski & Scheumann: The GDR's Leading Documentary Film Team', *Historical Journal of Film, Radio and Television* 24(3) (2004), 365–79.
Steinmetz, Rüdiger, and Tilo Prase. *Dokumentarfilm zwischen Beweis und Pamphlet. Heynowski & Scheumann und Gruppe Katins*. Leipzig: Leipziger Universitätsverlag, 2002.
Zimmermann, Peter (ed.). *Deutschlandbilder Ost. Dokumentarfilme der DEFA von der Nachkriegszeit bis zur Wiedervereinigung*. Konstanz: UVK Medien/Konstanz, 1995.
Zimmermann, Peter. *Dokumentarfilm in Deutschland. Von den Anfängen bis zur Gegenwart*. Bonn: bpb, 2022.

PART I
Studios, Systems and Networks

CHAPTER 1

'Mountains of Material'
Gerhard Scheumann and the Cinéma Vérité Debate in the GDR

Matthew Bauman

At the beginning of the 1960s, the documentary film industry in East Germany found itself in a state of crisis. The increasing popularity of cinéma vérité and Direct Cinema documentaries in the West led those involved in East German documentary filmmaking to engage in a debate about how (and indeed whether) to modernize production by bringing their output in line with film festival submissions by filmmakers from countries such as France, the United States, the United Kingdom and Canada, who were at the forefront of these new styles. This chapter investigates the response of Gerhard Scheumann, one of East Germany's most prominent documentary filmmakers, to this debate during the early 1960s. Scheumann's contributions in this period to *Filmwissenschaftliche Mitteilungen*,[1] the journal associated with East Germany's Hochschule für Film und Fernsehen,[2] reveal his assessment of the merits of the movement; even into the mid-1970s, he and co-director Walter Heynowski tacitly engaged with the phenomenon of cinéma vérité in their own films. Scheumann's approach also invites a comparison with that adopted by Joris Ivens, another important figure not only in the history of DEFA but also in the overall history of global documentary filmmaking. However, Ivens' origins in (and subsequent return to) the film industry in the West underline how he was able to reconcile his creative work with such innovatory approaches to documentary and did so in a way that was quite different from Scheumann.

One of the primary arenas in which this debate played out was the journal *Filmwissenschaftliche Mitteilungen*, which began publication in 1960. Edited by Heinz Baumert, the journal published three issues a year, and these were often supplemented by special numbers dedicated to specific themes. From 1962 to 1965, there were fifteen contributions by filmmakers, critics and scholars from both East and West that dealt with matters concerning developments in documentary film related to cinéma vérité. Some of these articles were transcripts or expansions of papers delivered at the annual Leipzig Documentary Film Festival, some were direct rebuttals of (or commentaries on) articles from previous issues, and there were also transcripts of interviews with filmmakers from the West such as Chris Marker and Richard Leacock. Together, these documents provide evidence of East Germany's attempts to define the role of documentary cinema within both its media industry and its political system as it sought the best way to compete with the sudden global popularity and technical sophistication of Western documentaries.

The cinéma vérité debate as it played out in the journal is a fascinating example of East Germany's efforts to deal with a major aspect of Western culture that, in the early 1960s, had penetrated the recently erected Berlin Wall.[3] These developments became impossible to ignore in East German documentary circles when the French director Chris Marker was awarded the Golden Dove at the 1963 Leipzig Documentary Film Festival for *Le joli mai* (*The Lovely Month of May*). The jury's unexpected decision further raised the stakes of the debate on the merits of the cinéma vérité style and exerted a profound influence on East German documentary as DEFA's directors continued to evaluate their own filmmaking against the global documentary scene where techniques associated with the cinéma vérité style were becoming increasingly mainstream.

One of the most important approaches to the phenomenon is that adopted by Gerhard Scheumann, a frequent contributor to *Filmwissenschaftliche Mitteilungen* and an active participant in the cinéma vérité debate. In what follows I will introduce Scheumann and his writings on cinéma vérité in the early 1960s before turning to discuss his cinematic engagement with the style ten years later in the short Studio H&S documentary *Meiers Nachlaß* (*Meier's Legacy*, 1975). Scheumann's contributions to the cinéma vérité debate in *Filmwissenschaftliche Mitteilungen* are early examples – pre-dating his famous 1965 '*Prisma*-Testament' – of his willingness to prod the East German media industry into exploring themes that were more overtly critical of the German Democratic Republic (GDR) and using more technically innovative forms (an impulse that ultimately cost Studio H&S its independence in 1982).

Gerhard Scheumann was born in 1930 and, despite having attended one of the infamous Nazi Nationalpolitische Erziehungsanstalten (National Political Institutes of Education), emerged from the war a committed communist. Scheumann came to East German television in 1962 after working as a reporter and editor for radio and as an instructor at the Weimar Fachschule für Rundfunkwesen (College of Radio). Later that year, he founded and moderated the television programme *Prisma*, which investigated social and political issues inside the GDR. He left the programme in 1965 and began his partnership with Walter Heynowski, with whom he founded the independent Studio H&S two years later. After being ordered to shut down Studio H&S in 1982, he and Heynowski returned to the DEFA Studio for Documentary, where they remained until its dissolution in 1991. It was subsequently revealed that Scheumann, who died in Berlin in 1998, had served as an informant (Inoffizieller Mitarbeiter) for the Ministerium für Staatssicherheit (Stasi) from 1957 onwards.

Scheumann recognized the potential of television well before most of his fellow GDR citizens,[4] and his writings for *Filmwissenschaftliche Mitteilungen* also boosted his reputation as a media studies scholar with practical experience. Rüdiger Steinmetz has remarked on Scheumann's talent for combining his filmmaking talent and Marxist-Leninist theory into an intellectual approach to film and television documentary.[5] As someone working primarily in television at a time when the medium was only beginning to have an impact on the GDR – and despite his position on the editorial committee – Scheumann did not fit the profile of the other contributors to *Filmwissenschaftliche Mitteilungen*, who came almost exclusively from the film industry. However, Scheumann recognized that television-style reportage and live broadcasting had much in common with cinéma vérité, a position he outlined at length in his 1962 article 'Das Fernsehen – die Chance des Dokumentarfilms' (Television – An Opportunity for Documentary). This perspective presented him with a unique vantage point – one less encumbered by the conventions of the film industry – from which to analyse both cinéma vérité and documentary production.

Many discussions of the concept of cinéma vérité have suffered from a tendency on the part of scholars and practitioners to deploy the term very loosely; accordingly, anyone using the term must first set out their own understanding of its meaning.[6] There are several competing claims regarding who first invented the term and what its exact definition should be.[7] In addition, cinéma vérité is often conflated with its most prominent competing style, the so-called Direct Cinema prominent in the United Kingdom and North America, even though for some the two styles are regarded as significantly different. Generally speaking, however, cinéma vérité is primarily associated with French filmmakers such as Jean Rouch who regularly appeared on camera in their own films and engaged with their subjects through interviews and discussion. Direct Cinema, on the other hand, is more often used to refer to British, Canadian and US filmmakers, such as Richard Leacock and D.A. Pennebaker, who minimized their appearances on film and adopted a 'fly-on-the-wall' approach to their subjects.[8] In the context of the GDR during the first half of the 1960s, the term 'cinéma vérité' was generally deployed as a catch-all expression for contemporary trends in documentary production, i.e. films employing lightweight, 16 mm cameras, synchronized sound recording, everyday themes and 'person-on-the-street'-style cinematography. Even so, some contributors to *Filmwissenschaftliche Mitteilungen* (notably the Polish director Wanda Wertenstein) still argued for the need for greater precision in the use of the term.[9]

Scheumann presents his own assessment of the theoretical aspects of this understanding of cinéma vérité in his 1964 article 'Noch einmal: Cinéma-vérité' (Cinéma Verité Once Again),[10] which was written in response to several earlier contributions on the topic.[11] This is his most direct and prolonged engagement with the concept of cinéma vérité and it sets out clearly the terms of the debate during the early 1960s as well as what he sees as its most pressing issues: the quality of film equipment in the GDR compared to other countries; the reliance of East German filmmakers on narration to rescue substandard recorded material; and the often unrealistic ambitions regarding what a GDR documentary can be expected to tackle. He begins with an (implicit) reminder that in East German culture, the philosophical is intimately bound up with the political. This is then followed by a backhanded compliment for those cinéma vérité filmmakers trying to arrive at the truth without the benefit of socialism:

> It is most welcome when filmmakers in capitalist countries (like France, Canada and the USA) attempt to reveal the truth through an unmediated observation of their immediate reality even if they only deal with small slices of life... Even this supposed 'criticism of symptoms' that result from the prevailing conditions in the capitalist world can be a step towards uncovering the truth. Ultimately, the recognition of surface appearances (Erscheinungen) precedes the recognition of underlying reality (Wesen).[12]

Having conceded that even capitalist approaches to documentary filmmaking might provide a means (albeit one that is less direct) of capturing the truth of a given situation, Scheumann nevertheless identifies what he perceives as the central problem of the cinéma vérité method. He points out that appearance and underlying reality are rarely identical, and that if they were, the documentary truth that is revealed would be self-evident, would not require explanation and would obviate the need to make a film about a given topic in the first place. Moreover, the article suggests that, regardless of a filmmaker's intention, carrying on filming until the 'moment of truth' (*Sternstunde*) dawns would merely result in the production of mountains of material. Even if the resulting footage had any value, it would remain hidden from view due to the sheer quantity of film material that would have to be processed.[13] Scheumann argues that cinéma vérité cannot see the wood for the trees, and its adherents cannot capture documentary truth on film because they are so focused on the surface-level facts presented to a supposedly objective camera. In saying as much, Scheumann makes the (implicit) claim that, by contrast, he and his documentary films do have the capacity to capture that which remains hidden in the work of filmmakers embracing cinéma vérité.

Scheumann's article goes on to propose a solution to the shortcomings of cinéma vérité when he contends that any documentary truth that is revealed ultimately stems from the vision of the filmmaker and that the film itself plays only an intermediary role. By drawing attention to the ways in which the resulting footage is always subject to the manipulation of those making the film, Scheumann reminds his readers that films do not emerge *ex nihilo*.[14] In addition, he seeks to reinforce his argument by rebutting the celebrated cinéma vérité director Jean Rouch's claim that the use of montage usually resulted in low-quality films. For Scheumann, by contrast, montage is a vital tool in political documentary.[15] By the same token, he also rejects another of Rouch's implicit claims, arguing that it is not possible to make an objective film that is untainted (*verfälscht*) by the filmmaker's subjectivity:

> In my experience there is no emotionally detached, impartial camera. In each individual shot the filmmaker's perspective on reality is already discernible; life 'as it really is', is in every case life as the film's creators see it according to the particular development of their thinking.[16]

It is but a short leap from Scheumann's claim that to make a film is to engage in a process of manipulation to the related claim that other manipulative acts on the part of the director are necessary to show life as it really is. The necessity of such interventions to reveal the reality behind the surface images captured on film is a fundamental tenet of Scheumann's ideological approach to filmmaking and one that is clearly recognizable to anyone familiar with Studio H&S's output.

The specific truth that Scheumann wishes to reveal to viewers is that of a Marxist-Leninist concept of society; in his view, a documentary should aspire to guide the viewer to a practical confirmation of the theoretical truth derived from this underlying ideology. Nevertheless, he admits that socialist documentary has not yet quite mastered the art of proving abstract theses by selecting, recording, editing and commenting on events that will demonstrate the validity of this ideological stance.[17] Ultimately, for Scheumann, it is the director's task to set up the cinematic experiment in such a way as to yield the desired result. This is Scheumann's fundamental disagreement with the cinéma vérité school: his ideological conviction means that he is already wholly confident in the concept of a 'truth' that exists prior to the making of the film (and so has only to be demonstrated), whereas the more empirically oriented cinéma vérité directors believe that it is precisely the process of filmmaking itself that leads to the discovery of truths of which they (and the viewer) were originally unaware.

What Scheumann the television professional recognized well before many of his colleagues at DEFA[18] was that the theories of the cinéma vérité school were not inextricably linked to technologies such as handheld cameras and synchronized sound that made them possible. Indeed, he believed these technologies might be put to good use producing documentaries that capitalized on the popularity of the cinéma vérité form, while still maintaining a commitment to revealing a Marxist-Leninist analysis of reality. Accordingly, in the first of three action points listed at the conclusion of 'Noch einmal: Cinéma-vérité', Scheumann exhorts the East German documentary industry to modernize its equipment by investing in 16 mm cameras, synchronized recording equipment and the equipment for transferring 16 mm to 35 mm, thereby allowing filmmakers to deploy these technological advances for their own benefit.[19] In addition, he makes it clear that, in the right hands, the tools used to develop cinéma vérité can also be used to create films that serve as valuable instructional material for audiences in socialist countries. The key is to embrace the technology of cinéma vérité while rejecting the more passive shooting methods of its directors: 'The most important component of a documentary film is its exposed material. Raising its quality through the precise and patient observation of life remains the crucial task.'[20] Scheumann held firm in this belief throughout his professional career, which extended well beyond the cinéma vérité debate of the early 1960s in *Filmwissenschaftliche Mitteilungen* and into his own work as a documentary filmmaker in the 1970s.

Less than two years after the publication of Scheumann's essay, the Eleventh Plenum of the ruling Socialist Unity Party (SED) in December 1965 ushered in a return to the aesthetics of Socialist Realism in virtually all spheres of East German cultural production and put an abrupt end to public discussion of formal innovations such as cinéma vérité.[21] The pre-Plenum debate around cinéma vérité during the early 1960s in *Filmwissenschaftliche Mitteilungen* was something of a last hurrah of open discourse for the journal in a period of cultural thaw that saw a greater than usual tolerance on the part of the SED for debates that departed from the party line. After 1965, the abrupt return to classic Soviet-style Socialist Realism led to the removal of Heinz Baumert as the managing editor of the journal and a temporary ban on publication.[22] When the journal resumed in 1966 under a new managing editor, Hermann Herlinghaus, its content reflected an unmistakeable turn toward partisanship (*Parteilichkeit*) regarding film aesthetics and criticism.[23]

Despite the rather artificial resolution to the East German cinéma vérité debate in the mid-1960s, Heynowski and Scheumann continued to use the style as a foil against which to frame their own approach to documentary film well into the 1970s. This is particularly the case with their 1975 documentary short *Meiers Nachlaß*. In 1974 the duo received permission to leave the GDR – a privilege afforded them due to the special status of their independent Studio H&S – and travelled to Munich to film the auction of the estate of Adolf Hitler's second-in-command, Hermann Göring. The film crew recorded the auction, held by and for the benefit of the Free State of Bavaria, on 25 October 1974. The resulting twenty-one-minute documentary uses that footage juxtaposed with archival footage of Göring and other Nazi leaders and their atrocities to excoriate not only the Bavarian government for profiting from the sale of these tainted belongings, but also those bidding at auction who are willing to pay prices well exceeding the material value of the goods, presumably because of the identity of their former owner.

A text and montage book, published to accompany the film, begins with a quasi-rhetorical question on the part of the directors: 'What should a documentary filmmaker do upon receiving the news that the estate of the Hitler regime's second-in-command is going under the hammer...?'[24] Though the piece is attributed jointly to both Heynowski and Scheumann, like most texts credited to the creative duo, it bears the hallmarks of Scheumann's distinctive polemical style[25] and takes up many of the same themes dealt with in his contributions to *Filmwissenschaftliche Mitteilungen*. The provocative question at the start of the text reflects the directors' understanding that their job is to reveal hidden truths that cannot be imparted simply by presenting authentic footage of the event. The text's answer to its own question is, unsurprisingly, to create a film that uses montage and narration to unpack the underlying significance of the auction by documenting the event in three interrelated layers. The first is the basic documentation of the event itself: the auction of Göring's estate. The second layer is the explanation of the objects and their provenance: the lavish lifestyle that the 'pseudo-baroque figure'[26] Göring enjoyed. The third sets out Göring's legacy of suffering and war crimes. Taken together, Heynowksi and Scheumann explain that their film reveals Göring's true legacy and why the auction alongside the Bavarian government's intention to profit from it elicit such a strongly negative response from the filmmakers.

In the final paragraph of the text, Heynowski and Scheumann explain that they understand their role as documentary filmmakers to be more than 'just presenting authentic images'. Instead, and in a way that is consistent with Scheumann's negative assessment of cinéma vérité a decade earlier, they posit that it is precisely the use of montage that makes it possible to 'expose the internal context that exists between images' and 'to render the invisible visible'.[27] Indeed, adopting a cinéma vérité-style approach to this film project would only present the first layer of documentation that Heynowski and Scheumann discuss: the filming of the auction itself. Simply rolling the cameras, recording the auction and presenting that footage as the finished product would provide viewers with a surface-level documentation of the event, but in the absence of any additional contextualising information, the reasons for filming this particular auction would remain opaque.

These images of items being auctioned are not enough to give viewers the information they need to understand the significance of what they are seeing: 'Marcus Aurelius said in his *Meditations* that objects are without consciousness and without the ability to express themselves . . . The objects needed to be explained in the context of the milieu in which they originated.'[28] As if to demonstrate this point, such objects are exactly what the viewer sees for nearly the first third of the film. Only after six minutes does the twenty-one-minute film betray the owner of the ostentatious items being auctioned off.[29] This surprise reveal is intended to shock the audience while, in effect, refuting the methodology of cinéma vérité by demonstrating the limitations of simply offering unmediated footage of the auction itself. Heynowski and Scheumann do not intend to simply allow Göring's reputation with the film's viewers to precede him. Instead, they add the second and third layers referred to above to establish what they consider to be the relevant contextual information about Göring's life and career. The auction scenes are now liberally intercut with photographs and documentary footage contrasting the opulence of Göring's life as Hitler's second-in-command with the gruesomeness of the suffering he inflicted on Spanish Republicans, concentration camp inmates, inhabitants of Nazi-occupied territories and, ultimately, his fellow citizens (the latter being represented in this film by Richard Peter's photographs of charred corpses in a Dresden air raid shelter). Only when all three layers are combined does the true historical significance that Heynowski and Scheumann want to impart to this event become clear.

The use of montage is explicitly deployed to communicate the filmmakers' point of view – in this case, their perception of the moral bankruptcy of the capitalist West as exemplified by the Bavarian government's attempt to profit from a war criminal's collection of luxury items. Proponents of cinéma vérité see documentary truth as an emergent phenomenon and, to varying degrees, attempt to remove themselves from the filmmaking process to allow that truth to manifest itself both to the filmmaker and to the viewer. Due to their desire to communicate what they regard as very specific truths about the world and particular events – complex, systemic truths that cannot be explained or made self-evident by simply running a camera – Heynowski and Scheumann exploit the power of montage and juxtaposition to convey their ideological message effectively to their audience.

Cinéma vérité emerged at the very beginning of Scheumann's career, and his practical experience of the movement was necessarily limited when he began thinking about its potential impact on documentary film and television. The arrival of cinéma vérité was the first major paradigm shift in documentary that he had directly experienced, and he had only been working for one year in television when he wrote his first contribution to *Filmwissenschaftliche Mitteilungen*. A helpful comparison to Scheumann's experience of cinéma vérité is provided by that of Dutch director Joris Ivens, who made his first film in 1912. Ivens' career paralleled the rise of documentary as an international genre, and he witnessed (and influenced) its development right up until the advent of cinéma vérité. In many ways, his seventy-five-year career can be seen as a microcosm of the history of documentary cinema in the twentieth century. Like Scheumann, he was a committed communist, but his longer career and greater experience of shooting films across the globe made it possible for him to adopt a more differentiated approach in his evaluation of cinéma vérité.

By the time Ivens came to work for DEFA in 1951, he was already a giant on the international documentary stage with a worldwide network of contacts, and he looms large in the cinéma vérité debate documented in the pages of *Filmwissenschaftliche Mitteilungen* even though he never actually published in the journal himself.[30] During his time at DEFA, Ivens was involved with seven documentaries to varying degrees. Most prominent among these are *Lied der Ströme* (*Song of the Rivers*, 1954) extolling workers on the Volga, Mississippi, Ganges, Nile, Amazon and Yangtze Rivers, and *Die Windrose* (*The Compass Rose*, 1957) about women workers fighting for equal rights in the Soviet Union, Brazil, France, China and Italy.[31] Despite receiving official directing credits, much of Ivens' work at DEFA centred on organising and commissioning footage that was shot by others,[32] tasks that he found offputtingly bureaucratic and that prompted him to leave the studio in 1962.[33] Nonetheless, Ivens remained a key figure on the East German documentary scene by virtue of his continued involvement in the Leipzig Documentary Film Festival up until 1968.[34]

Given his stature in the field, his thoughts on cinéma vérité were often solicited, and he expressed his opinion on the emerging style in several publications.[35] In the early part of the 1960s, Ivens regarded cinéma vérité as essentially a technological advance rather than a theoretical or methodological approach, and one that filmmakers – himself included – had yet to fully grasp and exploit to the full. In a discussion with Hermann Herlinghaus in 1963, Ivens asserted:

> I believe we are in a transitional period. The smaller sound equipment and the influence of television have directed our attention more to the details of our surroundings, and that is a good thing. The traditional documentary film had distanced itself too much from direct, current, everyday reality. Through cinéma vérité we have once again been faced with, so to speak, the actuality that is the source of our life and our entire creative work. In so doing, however, we have clung too much to a reportage style focused on quantity, and there exists the danger of aesthetic detriments.[36]

Fundamentally, Ivens sees the objectives of documentary film as more or less unchanged from the beginning of his career, and claims that he and his peers were just as interested in truth as the new generation of documentary filmmakers using the techniques of cinéma vérité. Two years after his discussion with Herlinghaus, in an interview with the magazine *Image et Son* reprinted in his autobiography *The Camera and I*, Ivens remarks:

My generation used light, easily manageable cameras, but now technique, thanks to synchronization of sound and photography and highly sensitive film material making lighting superfluous allows even greater authenticity – although no greater truthfulness of the filmed material.[37]

Again, echoing Scheumann's assertion in *Filmwissenschaftliche Mitteilungen* that cinéma vérité techniques are essentially a tool, the effectiveness of which lies in the hands of the filmmaker, he concludes:

I'm convinced that 'Cinema Direct' [Ivens' term for cinéma verité] is both indispensable and insufficient – indispensable because it gives material authenticity to certain parts of a film; but insufficient because only commentary can express the complete, responsible, personal action – the involvement of the author, director or commentator.[38]

Thus, Ivens saw cinéma vérité as an idea whose potential was as yet unfulfilled, but even in expressing his reservations, he retained a characteristic optimism that the new generation of filmmakers would exploit the possibilities of the new technologies to the full.[39]

As the decade progressed, the novelty of ultra-mobile cameras and synchronized sound waned as equipment became increasingly available and the technology and related practices became more widely adopted. As Waugh puts it, 'the technical and stylistic innovations were gradually absorbed into the mainstream documentary lexicon and thus increasingly defused of any radical import'.[40] By 1966, Ivens himself was employing the methodology of cinéma vérité in his films about the Vietnam War[41] – evidently without any of Scheumann's ideological compunctions. Working once again for Western film companies, Ivens was able to access the equipment that allowed cinéma vérité practitioners the flexibility and mobility they needed, while remaining free from any overt ideological restrictions on the deployment of the technology or its associated techniques.[42] Like most Western filmmakers, Ivens was able to disentangle the equipment from the 'quantitative' or 'slice-of-life' approaches developed by the filmmakers who originally employed the technology and adapt it to his own filmmaking ethos.[43] While Ivens' return to the West allowed him greater freedom to engage with the technologies and aesthetics of cinéma vérité than the majority of East German documentary filmmakers, the fact that Scheumann was still using the concept as a strawman a decade after the debate had ended underlines its impact in that country as well.

This chapter has considered two key contributions to the East German debate around the cinéma vérité movement in the early 1960s, but it is important to remember that both Scheumann and Ivens were decided exceptions among East German documentarians in terms of their published engagement with the movement. The cinéma vérité debate took place largely on the level of theory, and unless a filmmaker is being interviewed directly, contributors to *Filmwissenschaftliche Mitteilungen* seldom refer to specific films in their discussions. They address cinéma vérité almost exclusively in terms of general production methods or, at most, a handful of specific directors (such as Rouch, to whom Scheumann refers on multiple occasions). Only later does Scheumann use the Studio H&S film *Meiers Nachlaß* as a practical demonstration of his opposition to the form.

Because of its largely generic tenor, the debate that played out among East German film scholars and critics often seems detached from the actual practice of filmmaking and the output of the DEFA studio, even when both are featured in the same journal.[44] DEFA documentary directors such as Jürgen Böttcher and Karl Gass were also highly attuned to international trends, including cinéma vérité, as is evident in films such as Böttcher's *Stars* (1963) and Gass' *Feierabend* (*Leisure*, 1964).[45] Though both films were featured in the 'Workshop Report' (*Werkstattbericht*) section of an issue of *Filmwissenschaftliche Mitteilungen* published at the height of the cinéma vérité debate,[46] curiously neither report references the term directly.

More research is needed to fully understand the disconnect between Ivens, Scheumann and the other participants in the cinéma vérité debate on the one hand, and Böttcher, Gass and the DEFA documentarians who actively responded to the documentary *Zeitgeist* in their filmmaking on the other. One possible explanation for these disparate approaches could be the relationship between cinéma vérité and the use of lightweight 16 mm cameras with synchronized sound. Because DEFA worked exclusively in 35 mm until at least the end of the 1960s (and afterward with only sparing exceptions),[47] it is possible that DEFA filmmakers saw what they were doing in 35 mm as, from a technical point of view, not sufficiently similar to cinéma vérité to warrant a comparison. In 1995 Karl Gass rejected the suggestion that he had sought to imitate cinéma verité in his work,[48] and Eduard Schreiber remarked on filmmakers needing specific technology that was rarely available if they were to participate in the documentary paradigm shift of the 1960s.[49] More research into the history of DEFA's acquisition of 16 mm cameras capable of synchronized sound recording and their deployment on particular projects could begin to provide clarity in this area.

No matter how closely intertwined the theoretical and practical responses to cinéma vérité were in the run-up to the Eleventh Plenum of 1965/1966, when the movement's once-groundbreaking innovations had become standard items in filmmakers' toolkits, creative responses in the form of documentary films dominated at the expense of more abstract academic discussions. An analysis of post-1965 documentaries in the context of earlier arguments made about the merits of cinéma vérité would allow us to gain a clearer idea of the kind of impact these earlier debates had on the development of East German documentary. Comparing DEFA's in-house productions to films made by the independent Studio H&S could also throw more light on the extent to which Scheumann's opinions on cinéma vérité were aligned with those of other East German filmmakers who did not contribute theoretical texts to the debate. Additionally, comparing Ivens' output from the late 1960s onwards (when he began adopting cinéma vérité techniques) with East German documentaries from the same time would provide us with further insights into the kinds of cinéma vérité styles East German documentary was subsequently able to incorporate.

Assessing his editorship of the pre-Plenum *Filmwissenschaftliche Mitteilungen* at the turn of this century, Heinz Baumert quotes from an essay he published in *Neues Deutschland* in 1957 about the purpose of film scholarship: 'we call for and wish for the development of film scholarship and journalism in their roles in service to praxis and the further development of our filmmaking'.[50] Though it was thwarted in its goal, the East German cinéma vérité debate of the early 1960s was a key step in the realization of that vision as its participants attempted to sift through the aesthetic and ideological implications of a Western documentary paradigm shift in order to advance documentary in their own country.

Matthew Bauman is a Ph.D. candidate at the University of Cincinnati where he is completing his dissertation on DEFA and New German Cinema documentaries between 1961 and 1989. He led the German Studies Program at Transylvania University for six years, and he has previously published on director Jürgen Böttcher's experimental *Transformations* trilogy. His further research interests include Weimar period film and literature as well as adaptation theory.

Notes

1. Subsequently renamed *Filmwissenschaftliche Beiträge* (1968–81) and later *Beiträge zur Film- und Fernsehwissenschaft* (1982–2009).
2. Now known as the Filmuniversität Babelsberg KONRAD WOLF.
3. The scope of the debate is captured by Hermann Herlinghaus' remarks at the opening of the Free Forum at Leipzig in 1961 along with the chain of responses they engendered: Hermann Herlinghaus, 'Die Perspektiven des Dokumentarfilms', *Filmwissenschaftliche Mitteilungen* 3(1) (1962), 36–61; Tadeusz Makarczynski, 'Probleme des künstlerischen Dokumentarfilms', *Filmwissenschaftliche Mitteilungen* 3(2) (1962), 177–201; Gerhard Scheumann, 'Das Fernsehen – die Chance des Dokumentarfilms', *Filmwissenschaftliche Mitteilungen* 3(3) (1962), 444–66; and Péter Bokor, 'Dokumentarfilm und Fernsehdokumentation: Gedanken zur Diskussion Herlinghaus-Makarczynski-Scheumann', *Filmwissenschaftliche Mitteilungen* 4(3) (1963): 639–50.
4. Rüdiger Steinmetz and Tilo Prase, *Dokumentarfilm zwischen Beweis und Pamphlet. Heynowski & Scheumann und Gruppe Katins* (Leipzig: Leipziger Universitätsverlag, 2002), p. 370.
5. Ibid, p. 33.
6. See Thomas Waugh, *The Conscience of Cinema: The Works of Joris Ivens, 1912–1989* (Amsterdam: Amsterdam University Press, 2016), pp. 681–83. For the sake of simplicity, I am deploying the term as it was understood in the GDR at the time.
7. See Richard M. Barsam, *Non-fiction Film: A Critical History Revised and Expanded* (Bloomington, IN: Indiana University Press, 1992), p. 412, n. 7.
8. Betsy A. McLane, *A New History of Documentary Film* (New York: Continuum, 2012), pp. 232–33.
9. Wanda Wertenstein, 'Das Wahre und das Falsche der "Cinéma-vérité"', *Filmwissenschaftliche Mitteilungen* 5(1) (1964), 100–6.
10. Gerhard Scheumann, 'Noch einmal: Cinéma-vérité', *Filmwissenschaftliche Mitteilungen* 5(3) (1964), 610–21.
11. Primarily to Herlinghaus, 'Perspektiven' and Makarczynski, 'Probleme' (see note 3).
12. 'Es ist aus vollem Herzen zu begrüßen, wenn Filmschaffende in kapitalistischen Ländern (wie Frankreich, Kanada, USA) durch unmittelbare Beobachtung der sie umgebenden Wirklichkeit, sei es auch nur "scheibchenweise", zur Enthüllung der Wahrheit zu gelangen versuchen . . . Auch die sogenannte "Symptomkritik" kann unter den in der kapitalistischen Welt herrschenden Bedingungen ein Schritt zur Wahrheit sein. Schließlich geht der Erkenntnis des Wesens der Dinge die Erkenntnis ihrer Erscheinung voraus' (Scheumann, 'Noch einmal', 611–12).
13. Ibid., 611–12. Indeed, the idea of shooting endless rolls of film in case something interesting might happen must have seemed especially frivolous to Scheumann, who was working within the constraints of the limited supply of film available in the GDR.

14. Ibid., 613.
15. Ibid., 618.
16. 'Erfahrungsgemäß gibt es keine leidenschaftslose, unparteiische Kamera. In jeder einzelnen Kameraeinstellung realisiert sich bereits das Urteil der Filmschöpfer über die Wirklichkeit; das Leben, "wie es wirklich ist", ist in jedem Fall das Leben, wie es die Gestalter eines Films kraft ihrer ideellen Reife zu sehen vermochten' (ibid., 613).
17. Ibid., 614.
18. Scheumann's article explicitly calls out filmmakers for their dismissive attitude towards his medium, arguing that the aesthetics of live television now inform much of the current documentary film ethos (ibid., 610).
19. Ibid., 620.
20. Ibid.
21. Nevertheless, formal innovation did resume in some areas. For example, Stefanie Mathilde Frank and Ralf Schenk assert that after 1965, DEFA genre cinema still looked to Hollywood as its model and was able to forge a 'dialectical unity' out of US films and SED mandates. See Stefanie Mathilde Frank and Ralf Schenk, 'DEFA-Genrekino – das gibt's doch nicht . . .', in Stefanie Mathilde Frank and Ralf Schenk (eds), *Publikumspiraten. Das Genrekino der DEFA und seine Regisseure (1946–90)* (Berlin: Bertz + Fischer, 2022), p. 16.
22. The abruptness of the change is evidenced by the first issue of volume 6, the penultimate before the Eleventh Plenum, which highlighted the work of English-born Direct Cinema pioneer Richard Leacock and contained contributions advocating for more collaboration between the film and television industries and for investing heavily in modern recording equipment. East German television's innovations in both form and content – detailed in Heather L. Gumbert, *Envisioning Socialism: Television and the Cold War in the German Democratic Republic* (Ann Arbor: University of Michigan Press, 2014) – as well as its access to portable filming equipment made it an attractive partner for the documentary film studio.
23. The publication ban resulted in the cancellation of the third issue of volume 6 at the end of 1965, with Herlinghaus taking over for the first issue of volume 7 in 1966. Examples from this issue of the journal's shift towards party orthodoxy include articles such as 'Partei und Kunst' (Party and Art) and 'Filmkunst und ihre Wissenschaft in den ideologischen Kämpfen unserer Zeit' (The Filmic Arts and Criticism in the Ideological Struggles of Our Time), *Filmwissenschaftliche Mitteilungen* 7(1) (1966), 6–25 and 46–77. For more on the journal during and after the Eleventh Plenum, see Stephen Brockmann, 'The Eleventh Plenum and Film Criticism in East Germany', *German Life and Letters* 66(4) (2013), 432–48.
24. Walter Heynowski and Gerhard Scheumann, 'Zu diesem Film', in *Meiers Nachlaß. Text und Montagebuch* (Berlin: Progress Film-Verleih, 1975), p. 2.
25. Steinmetz and Prase, *Dokumentarfilm*, p. 33.
26. Heynowski and Scheumann, 'Zu diesem Film', p. 3.

27. Ibid.
28. Ibid.
29. The use of 'Meier' in the title – an ironic reference to a likely apocryphal Göring quote – further obscures the owner's identity.
30. However, four pieces about him appear during this time, further attesting to his prominence: an abridged translation of an article by an unknown author from the journal *Cine Cubano*: 'Joris Ivens in Kuba', *Filmwissenschaftliche Mitteilungen* 3(3) (1962), 467–77; a two-chapter preview of Sergei Drobashenko's *The Filmmaker Joris Ivens* (Moscow, 1964); 'Joris Ivens – Das Geheimnis seines Talents', trans. Ruth Herlinghaus and 'Was sah die Seine in Paris', trans. Ruth Herlinghaus, *Filmwissenschaftliche Mitteilungen* 4(2) (1963), 442–62 and 463–76; as well as an essay by Drobashenko on the eponymous film: 'Lied der Ströme', trans. Hermann-Ernst Schauer, *Filmwissenschaftliche Mitteilungen* 4(3) (1963), 715–28.
31. Ivens' time at DEFA and his relationship with the GDR in general is extensively documented in Günter Jordan, *Unbekannter Ivens. Triumph, Verdammnis, Auferstehung. Joris Ivens bei der DEFA und in der DDR 1948–1989* (Berlin: DEFA-Stiftung, 2018).
32. For example, the DEFA-Stiftung credits cinematographers from more than thirty countries as contributors to *Song of the Rivers. Lied der Ströme*, DEFA-Stiftung. See https://www.defa-stiftung.de/filme/filme-suchen/lied-der-stroeme (retrieved 11 December 2023).
33. Waugh, *Conscience*, p. 403.
34. Ibid., p. 560.
35. Waugh cites four 'major pronouncements on cinéma vérité', all in French. Ibid., p. 684. To this I would add 'Joris Ivens, Niederlande, 1963: Zur Dialektik von Poesie und Soziologie', interview by Hermann Herlinghaus in Hermann Herlinghaus (ed.), *Dokumentaristen der Welt in den Kämpfen unserer Zeit: Selbstzeugnisse aus zwei Jahrzehnten, 1960–1981* (Berlin: Henschelverlag, 1982), pp. 33–45.
36. Ibid, pp. 40–41.
37. Joris Ivens, *The Camera and I* (New York: International Publishers, 1969), p. 260.
38. Ibid., p. 261.
39. For example, Ivens often cited Chris Marker's *Le joli mai* as a film that put the new equipment to impressive use: ibid.; Ivens, 'Niederlande', p. 40.
40. Waugh, *Conscience*, p. 505.
41. *Le ciel, la terre* (*The Threatening Sky*, 1966), *Loin du Vietnam* (*Far from Vietnam*, 1967), *Le 17e parallèle* (*The 17th Parallel*, 1968), *Le peuple et ses fusils* (*The People and Their Guns*, 1970) and the short *Rencontre avec le président Hô Chi Minh* (*Meeting with President Hô Chi Minh*, 1970).
42. This is unevenly distributed across the films – for example, Ivens talks about the dearth of professional recording and editing equipment, especially tape recorders, in Vietnam during the filming of *Le ciel, la terre*. See Ivens, *Camera*, p. 259.

43. For the specifics of Ivens' incorporation of cinéma vérité techniques into partisan activist films, see Chapter 7 of Waugh, *Conscience*, pp. 503–62.
44. Scheumann was still working in television throughout the debate, and Ivens returned to the West in 1962.
45. For more on the overall relationship between cinéma vérité and East German documentary, see Günter Jordan, 'Zu den Anfängen zurück, um weiterzukommen. Die Geburt des neuen DEFA-Dokumentarfilms', in Klaus Stanjek (ed.), *Die Babelsberger Schule des Dokumentarfilms* (Berlin: Bertz + Fischer, 2012), pp. 49–116; and Hans-Jörg Rother, 'Auftrag: Propaganda. 1960 bis 1970', in Günter Jordan and Ralf Schenk (eds), *Schwarzweiß und Farbe. DEFA-Dokumentarfilme 1946–92* (Berlin: Jovis, 2000), pp. 92–127.
46. Respectively, Jürgen Böttcher, 'Bemerkungen zu meinem Film "Stars"', *Filmwissenschaftliche Mitteilungen* 5(1) (1964), 1–12; and Michael Biegholt, Werner Wüste and Karl Gass, 'Unsere Arbeit an dem Dokumentarfilm "Feierabend"', *Filmwissenschaftliche Mitteilungen* 5(2) (1964), 264–76.
47. See Eduard Schreiber's comments in Peter Zimmermann, Hans-Jürgen Brandt, Karl Gass, Lutz Haucke, Winfried Junge, Eduard Schreiber and Heinz Kersten, 'Zur Entwicklung des Dokumentarfilms in der DDR. Podiums- und Plenumsdiskussion (gekürzte Fassung)' in Peter Zimmermann (ed.), *Deutschlandbilder Ost. Dokumentarfilme der DEFA von der Nachkriegszeit bis zur Wiedervereinigung* (Konstanz: UVK Medien/Ölschläger, 1995), p. 115; and Jordan, 'Zu den Anfängen zurück', p. 86.
48. Karl Gass, 'Von der filmischen Hymne zur realistischen Dokumentation. Auf den Spuren des Bitterfelder Weges?', in Zimmermann, *Deutschlandbilder Ost*, p. 106.
49. Zimmermann et al., 'Zur Entwicklung', p. 115.
50. Quoted in Heinz Baumert, 'Das verbotene Heft. film-wissenschaftliche mitteilungen 2/1965', in Günter Agde (ed.), *Kahlschlag. Das 11. Plenum des ZK der SED. 1965* (Berlin: Aufbau, 2000), p. 381.

Select Bibliography

Bokor, Péter. 'Dokumentarfilm und Fernsehdokumentation: Gedanken zur Diskussion Herlinghaus-Makarczynski-Scheumann'. *Filmwissenschaftliche Mitteilungen* 3 (1963), 639–50.
Herlinghaus, Hermann. 'Die Perspektiven des Dokumentarfilms', *Filmwissenschaftliche Mitteilungen* 1 (1962), 36–61.
Heynowski, Walter, and Gerhard Scheumann. 'Zu diesem Film', in *Meiers Nachlaß. Text und Montagebuch*. Berlin: Progress Film-Verleih, 1975, pp. 2–3.
Scheumann, Gerhard. 'Das Fernsehen – die Chance des Dokumentarfilms', *Filmwissenschaftliche Mitteilungen* 3 (1962), 444–66.
———. 'Noch einmal: Cinéma-vérité', *Filmwissenschaftliche Mitteilungen* 3 (1964), 610–21.

Steinmetz, Rüdiger, and Tilo Prase. *Dokumentarfilm zwischen Beweis und Pamphlet. Heynowski & Scheumann und Gruppe Katins*. Leipzig: Leipziger Universitätsverlag, 2002.

Wertenstein, Wanda. 'Das Wahre und das Falsche der "Cinéma-vérité", *Filmwissenschaftliche Mitteilungen* 1 (1964), 100–6.

CHAPTER 2

The DEFA 'Foreign Ministry Films'
Presenting the GDR to the World, 1962–90

Thomas Maulucci

Between 1962 and 1990, the East German Ministry of Foreign Affairs commissioned over 500 short documentaries and newsreels from DEFA to support the German Democratic Republic's (GDR) public diplomacy (Auslandsinformation). These films sought to depict conditions in the GDR truthfully and objectively to win support for its policies, both in the socialist and the nonsocialist worlds.[1] Created for foreign audiences, these 'Foreign Ministry films' were made available to every East German institution that worked abroad, including GDR friendship societies. They represented a major portion – some 10 per cent – of the output of the DEFA-Studio für Wochenschau und Dokumentarfilme (DEFA Studio for Newsreel and Documentary Films) in the various iterations of its existence.[2]

East German public diplomacy served the purpose of 'nation branding', which can be defined as efforts over a broad range of areas by both governmental and nongovernmental actors to create a positive image of their state and thereby increase its influence. As the editors of a recent volume on the topic note, 'successful branding enables people at home and abroad to view a state as legitimate and credible, thereby meriting their allegiance and support'.[3] By most measures, East German nation branding between the 1960s and 1980s was highly successful. The GDR gained recognition as a legitimate representative of part of the German people and established a global reputation as the economic powerhouse of the communist world and as a dominant force in international athletic competitions.[4] Other aspects of the brand included its continuation of Germany's humanist cultural traditions and the joint Soviet bloc emphases on peaceful international policies and a generous social-welfare state.

After a short production history, this chapter will focus on the films' portrayal of East German women, a recurrent theme not only in the Foreign Ministry Films, but also in DEFA's feature films generally. Strong female protagonists committed to building a new socialist Germany figure prominently in several from the 1950s, including Hans Müller's *Bürgermeister Anna* (*Mayor Anna*, 1950), Slatan Dudow's *Frauenschicksale* (*Destinies of Women*, 1952) and Kurt Maetzig's *Schlösser und Katen* (*Castles and Cottages*, 1956). However, despite such exceptions, male leads dominated even as the ideological certainties of the early films were replaced with portrayals of a society in transition in the 1960s. It was only in the 1970s, as Henning Wrage has argued, that heroines start to predominate in DEFA feature films, which now portrayed a 'developed socialist society' that had largely lost its ideological purpose and in which these women seemed to have little ability to change things.[5] In contrast, women in the Foreign Ministry documentaries possess a good deal of agency, play an active role in society and, with rare exceptions, are true believers in the socialist cause.

As Jennifer Creech has also observed, during the GDR's final decades, its documentary filmmakers repeatedly used films about women to portray 'social contradictions and rupture' between the state's official narratives about life under socialism and the realities of everyday existence. This occurred as part of a broader trend to focus on aspects of everyday life instead of overtly political themes.[6] Foreign Ministry films, which were supposed to present conditions in the GDR objectively, were also subject to a similar development. For example, they frequently and perhaps intentionally lead us to question how much equality women had achieved and whether equality vis-à-vis the means of production promoted satisfying private lives. They also openly discuss other East German problems like the poor housing situation, which, as they remind us, the GDR planned to solve by 1990. By the 1980s, we even find some Foreign Ministry documentaries on women that focused so much on the everyday that an overall sense of ideological purpose is largely missing.

A Brief Organizational History

In the late 1950s, the GDR began a major effort to secure diplomatic recognition from noncommunist states in which foreign cultural policy played a significant role.[7] On 15 December 1959, the SED (Socialist Unity

Party) Politburo approved general guidelines for public diplomacy that would remain in place until the early 1970s. Public diplomacy was to strengthen the GDR's position internationally and to win international recognition by informing 'the broadest masses abroad' about the East German state, its economic and social successes and its peace-loving foreign policy. Moreover, this type of material – so-called 'Auslandspropaganda' (propaganda for use outside the country) – should 'expose the aggressive, imperialistic and revanchist policies of the Bonn government'.[8]

Documentary film played a crucial role in these efforts. Just before the creation of the Berlin Wall on 13 August 1961, the Politburo commissioned DEFA to develop films on West Berlin, on 'Berlin – The GDR's Capital' and on the need for a German peace treaty.[9] In January 1962, the Ministry of Foreign Affairs asked the Politburo's Secretariat for permission to create a special DEFA production group for documentaries depicting the GDR in a positive light that would be dubbed into major world languages and shown to foreign audiences. It argued that film was one of the most effective means of public diplomacy because it could reach broad circles of the population, even in countries with high illiteracy rates. While capitalist countries already devoted considerable resources to film work in foreign countries, the GDR needed to catch up, and the ratio of its film to print propaganda needed to be increased. Public diplomacy required films that directly addressed themes of interest to foreign audiences. The Ministry believed that short documentaries were best suited for this purpose and were most likely to be shown on foreign television, an increasingly important medium.[10] By November 1962, the DEFA-Studio für Wochenschau und Dokumentarfilme had begun work on twenty short public diplomacy documentaries. The Ministry provided the basic ideas for each, and the studio then worked out a sketch of the plot and later a full scenario or script that had to be approved by the Ministry. These films included the *DDR-Magazin* newsreel, a project the Foreign Ministry took over from the Gesellschaft für kulturelle Verbindungen mit dem Ausland (Society for Cultural Relations with Foreign Countries) that DEFA would produce until 1981.[11]

The first years of collaboration between DEFA and the Foreign Ministry were extremely rocky. Initially both the studio and the Ministry thought that just one official from each partner would be sufficient to oversee the work, and that it was unnecessary to create a special Künstlerische Arbeitsgruppe (Artistic Working Group, KAG) within the DEFA-Studio für Wochenschau und Dokumentarfilme. Projects were simply allocated to as many as seven existing KAGs, which often gave them low priority. There was insufficient thematic planning and an underestimation of the time and resources necessary to produce the films, as well as repeated problems with insufficient capacity at the film copying works and with poor dubbing into foreign languages. Although by 1964 these films were already being sent to thirty-four different countries, East German institutions provided very little feedback on how effective they were with foreign audiences. The underlying problem was that many of these documentaries were of poor quality and directors needed additional guidance on how to make successful public diplomacy films.[12]

Early Foreign Ministry films that focused on the GDR's position on the German and Berlin questions proved especially ineffective with foreign audiences and were removed from circulation. Dagobert Loewenberg's *Revanchismus in West-Berlin – Was wird aus West-Berlin?* (*Revanchism in West Berlin – What Will Become of West Berlin?*, 1963) was highly didactic and at times stylistically clumsy. Another, Winfried Junge's *Der Kinder wegen – Flucht ins Vaterland* (*For the Sake of the Children – Escape to the Fatherland*, 1963), suffered not from poor execution, but rather from the fact that it depicted the flight of West Germans to the GDR, a topic that was not invented, but one that foreign audiences apparently did not find credible in 1963.

By contrast, other documentaries that focused on aspects of life in the GDR fared far better. These included Heinz Müller's *Dorfkinder* (*Village Children*, 1962), about a village school in the Thuringian Forest, and Junge's *Ferientage* (*Holidays*, 1963), about a group of enthusiastic young readers from Altenburg in Saxony who visit one of their favourite authors, Alex Wedding, in Berlin and receive a return visit from her.[13] Both films make the point that one can get a quality education anywhere in the GDR. Dutch director Max Jaap contributed *Drei Briefe* (*Three Letters*, 1962), which depicted the vocational training of young people from Cuba, Togo and Iraq in East Germany through their letters home, which they read aloud in Spanish, French and Arabic. This internationalist theme was echoed in Heinz Fischer's *Institut der Freundschaft* (*Academy of Friendship*, 1964), about foreign students at the Herder Institute in Leipzig. Jürgen Böttcher contributed two excellent films: *Im Pergamonmuseum* (*In the Pergamon Museum*, 1962) and *Charlie und Co* (*Charlie & Co*, 1963). The latter is about an amateur circus group consisting of workers from a VEB machine factory in Leipzig. Böttcher's films emphasized the GDR's cultural offerings for the masses and were especially effective for public diplomacy because they relied on hardly any dialogue.

The Foreign Ministry also commissioned a feature-length documentary from the renowned Belgian director Frans Buyens called *Deutsch-*

land – Endstation Ost (*Talking with Germans*, 1964). It hoped that a film made by a sympathetic foreigner would have high credibility with audiences (a strategy for public diplomacy called 'others about us'). Besides its length, this film also stands out alongside Böttcher's contributions as the most auteurist work produced for the Foreign Ministry. The director himself is the protagonist, personally interviewing East Germans both on the street and in places of work and study, and then pausing to make observations as an outsider on the communist system, assisted by photomontages and cartoon graphics. The Foreign Ministry, some SED leaders and foreign critics thought highly of the film, which indeed presented the GDR in a favourable light, even though some of the interview subjects were critical of official policies. However, its production complicated work on other Foreign Ministry films, other established DEFA documentary filmmakers disapproved of it, and finally the SED decided that its overall message was too controversial. *Deutschland – Endstation Ost* became a victim of the clampdown ('Kahlschlag') on DEFA films following the Eleventh Plenum in 1965.[14]

By this time, the collaboration between the Foreign Ministry and DEFA was clearly in crisis. In October 1964, Paul Ickler, who led DEFA's production of Foreign Ministry films, wrote a long memo that proposed solutions. These included an ideologically unified nation branding in the films based around five main themes. The GDR was committed to peace and international understanding both morally and politically. East Germany proved that the working class could successfully build and lead a highly developed society. Its economic development, not that of West Germany, was the true 'German economic miracle'. East Germany had experienced 'outstanding successes' in building 'socialist democracy' on all levels of society, including the creation of 'a new national culture'. Finally, the GDR was a legitimate representative of the German people, and its policies pointed to the sole way of overcoming the division of Germany. Ickler also proposed creating a new KAG within the DEFA-Studio für Wochenschau und Dokumentarfilme to better coordinate production.[15]

The next year, DEFA created the KAG Auslandsinformation (Public Diplomacy) under Ickler's leadership, and through 1968 it would produce increasingly sophisticated documentaries that reflected his suggested themes. Joop Huisken's *Die Alliierten* (*The Allies*, 1966) interviewed representatives of the four victor powers from the Second World War in their home countries to argue that only East Germany had been democratized, de-Nazified, demilitarized and decartelized according to the stipulations of the Potsdam Accords. Joachim Hadaschik's *Berlin heute* (*Berlin Today*, 1966) presented East Berlin as the GDR's capital and culminated with some very effective shots of the 1 May 1966 parade intended to highlight the city's internationalism (the camera focuses on people of colour), as well as the easy interaction between the political leadership and the population. The film emphasized the social and economic progress made since 1945, including the 'true German economic miracle'. Buyens' *Für das Selbstbestimmungsrecht der Völker* (*For the Sake of National Self-Determination*, 1966) is a traditional documentary largely based on archival footage that documented the GDR's solidarity with peoples around the world who suffered under the yoke of imperialism. Other films documented the creation of a new culture in the GDR based on Germany's humanist traditions. These included two films by Heinz Müller. *Häuser unterm Kreuz* (*Churches in the GDR*, 1966) portrayed Christian traditions in the GDR, focusing on the Halberstadt Cathedral, while *Revolution einer Kultur* (*Revolution of a Culture*, 1968) presented an overall history of the GDR's cultural life. Lotte Thiel's beautifully shot *Die Spur von meinen Erdentagen* (*The Trace of My Earthly Days*, 1968) depicted the Weimar of Goethe and Schiller. Still other documentaries that stood out included Junge's portrait of Rostock, *Jubiläum einer Stadt – 750 Jahre Rostock* (*A City's Anniversary – Rostock at 750 Years*, 1968) and Böttcher's *Tierparkfilm* (*Tierpark Berlin*, 1967–68) on the East Berlin Zoo.

Despite this progress, by early 1968 East German diplomatic missions and cultural centres abroad were complaining about the lack of both feature and documentary films for use in public diplomacy.[16] The reference to feature films reflects just what a state of disarray the entire DEFA Film Studio was in after the Eleventh Plenum of 1965/1966. A further consequence of the Plenum was that ideological pressures increasingly came to bear. Rolf Schnabel, a director who had completed his studies at the SED's academy for Party members, took over the DEFA Documentary Film Studios in 1967 and began devoting considerable attention to the problems facing the KAG Auslandsinformation. A major priority was developing a cadre of filmmakers properly trained not just as documentarists but also in international politics, in foreign languages and most importantly in Marxism-Leninism.[17] On 22 October 1968, the Ministry of Foreign Affairs and DEFA agreed to create a new production group called Camera DDR to develop the Foreign Ministry films. For the first time, it would have the personnel and resources necessary to produce its own films and be responsible for dubbing and copying the finished product.[18] Joachim Hadaschik, another graduate of the SED's academy, took over as Camera DDR's leader in 1969.[19] This reorganization proved workable until the collapse of the GDR in 1989–90.

The Foreign Ministry documentaries display a wide variety of cinematic styles, as might be expected for a body of work that stretched over nearly thirty years. Technology itself dictated the style to some extent. During the 1960s, static camera angles and nondiegetic sound (standard narration, musical soundtracks, etc.) predominate, and some early documentaries were obviously staged. Lotte Thiel's *Das Gesetz heißt Glück* (*Care for Mothers and Infants in the GDR*, 1965) even used actors to portray a couple expecting a child. By the early 1970s, portable cameras and audio were being widely utilized and created more possibilities for filmmakers. In some Camera DDR films of the 1980s, the camera itself begins to move. In Alfons Machalz's *Eine Lehrerin* (*A Teacher*, 1987), we see Erich Honecker and other GDR personalities waving from the grandstand from the perspective of marchers during the 1 May parade, and in Dieter Raue's *Wenn die Erde weiß vom Schnee* (*Winter Sports in Oberhof*, 1986), the world-class double lugers Jörg Hoffmann and Jochen Pietzsch carry the camera with them on a practice run.

Camera DDR itself promoted standardization. It branded its films with intertitles in six world languages (German, English, French, Spanish, Arabic and Russian) followed by its own logo (films were dubbed into additional languages as necessary). It also promoted a sharper ideological message. Indeed, the pressure to publicize the regime's leaders and their current policies found its critics even among Camera DDR's co-workers. As director Alfons Machalz mockingly put it, 'public diplomacy meant expounding on the history of the GDR and the resolutions of all the SED Party Conferences as much as possible in each film! The film's subject didn't matter'.[20] Somewhat unfairly, Camera DDR also gained a reputation for using its cutting-edge filmmaking equipment – one of the perks of doing public diplomacy – to produce formulaic and boring films about state visits and industrial exhibitions.[21] However, these were exactly the themes that the SED prioritized because they illustrated the international importance of the state, its leading representatives and its economy. It is important to note that nation branding also aims to win legitimacy with domestic audiences and therefore to serve nation building.[22] As a result, East German television broadcast Hadaschik's Camera DDR films about Honecker's visits to foreign countries to strengthen the government's legitimacy at home, since they emphasized the GDR's growing international importance.[23]

The wide range of topics covered in the Foreign Ministry films also serves as an argument against seeing them as formulaic. Hadaschik recognized that producing films for public diplomacy placed special demands on their creators. Above all, these documentaries had to be suitable for foreign audiences with the overriding goal of getting them on television to reach the largest circles possible. However, this meant that they could neither go too far in attacking capitalism (a sure way to get them banned by authorities in nonsocialist states) nor focus on contemporary events lest they become quickly outdated. For this last reason, Hadaschik in 1971 advocated transforming the *DDR-Magazin* from a standard-style newsreel into a topical news magazine.[24] Three years later, he also emphasized in an interview that foreign audiences in nonsocialist states were most interested in everyday life under 'real existing socialism'.[25] Camera DDR therefore focused increasingly on portraying the GDR and its system, including its interactions with the outside world, instead of documenting larger Cold War issues like the German question or the Vietnam War, which had sometimes featured in Foreign Ministry films through the early 1970s. The only major exception to this trend was a series of documentaries in the late 1970s and early 1980s on the new nuclear arms race purportedly started by the North Atlantic Treaty Organization (NATO). This strategy fit well with the new guidelines for public diplomacy approved by the SED's Politburo in 1973 and 1974. Due to the inter-German détente of the early 1970s and East Germany's admission to the United Nations (UN) in 1973, the German problem and diplomatic recognition were now issues of the past. Public diplomacy in Western and developing countries now had to promote the socialist bloc's peace policy, encourage progressive forces, and counter imperialist attacks and disinformation. In the socialist world, it had to demonstrate the prospects for further progress towards communism. These goals could be achieved most effectively by promoting the GDR and its accomplishments.[26]

Branding the GDR: Films about Women

The East German state viewed its efforts to emancipate women as an important accomplishment that demonstrated the superiority of socialism over capitalism. Under socialism, women's emancipation meant 'freedom from social dependence on men and equality in relation to the means of production'. In theory, men and women had equal career and educational opportunities regardless of their marital or parental status. Official policies towards women also aimed at ensuring the availability of trained female labour for the workforce while promoting a higher birth rate. By the 1980s, over 90 per cent of East German women worked.[27] Starting in the late 1970s, a modest baby boom occurred in response to new SED initiatives, including a 'baby year' of paid leave for a second child. Thereafter, East German fertility rates exceeded those in the Federal Republic until German reunification in 1990. State policies, including guaranteed employment, help explain why East German women also married younger than their West German counterparts and were much less likely to be childless.[28] This was the official picture and, by the standards noted above, was a success story. However, as scholars of GDR women's history have noted, the communist authorities viewed gender relations exclusively through the lens of class conflict. If women were expected to have more responsibility in the workplace, they also received little relief in terms of their domestic responsibilities, and there was scant evidence of a significant change in society's attitudes towards them. The persistence of a 'glass ceiling' throughout the GDR's history suggests that mere lip service was paid even to the narrow objective of workplace equality.[29]

Throughout their history the Foreign Ministry films featured women. As early as 1964, a segment of Buyens' *Deutschland – Endstation Ost* discussed the GDR's system of kindergartens and creches, which was expanding but not yet sufficient to meet the needs of working women. We see shots of various women in an urban setting, some taking care of children, and Buyens speculates about what had brought them out and whether they worked: 'Women and work. Here in the GDR, I can't think about one word without the other.' As still photos of women in different occupations appear on the screen, Buyens lists reasons why they might want employment and concludes that 'they have the wish to affirm themselves as human beings and because they believe that work can help them in this regard'.

An important theme of nation branding was that all East Germans enjoyed the same opportunities for their personal development due to progressive state policies. *Das Gesetz heißt Glück* follows a young couple from Dresden, who are having their first child, through the year of the pregnancy, with every doctor's visit, day off for the mother and state subvention included. An animated map of the GDR illustrates that no pregnant woman had to travel more than 20 kilometres to receive care. Heinz Hafke's *Sie, wie viele andere* (*Portrait of a Woman*, 1969) goes still further by emphasizing how women's lives have changed for the better in general, allowing them to combine family life with interesting careers. The heroine, an unnamed married mother, has considerable responsibility as a mechanical engineer at a locomotive factory near Berlin. The plot revolves around her successful attempt to repair the automated oxyacetylene torch that is vital for production at the plant. She must work through the night, but she has a supportive husband (who is shown caring for their son and household) and colleagues. Hafke repeatedly uses montages of black-and-white still photos to illustrate her life, which includes growing up in a working-class family, belonging to the Free German Youth (FDJ), and taking advantage of the career and educational opportunities offered through the factory. Our heroine also narrates the film by reading aloud a letter she has written to a foreign woman who is curious about the state of sexual equality in the GDR:

> Perhaps you think I am an exceptional case (as a female engineer with male subordinates). But that too has something to do with the planned development here [*die planmäßige Entwicklung bei uns*]. What was indeed an exceptional case yesterday is part of almost all cooperatives [*Betriebe*] today as a matter of course and will be normal and ordinary tomorrow. Automation. Electronics. Data processing.

And, she might have added, women. *Sie, wie viele andere* has very high production values, and the Foreign Ministry recommended it as one of the selections for a planned GDR documentary festival in 1969 in Colombo, Sri Lanka.[30] Both *Das Gesetz heißt Glück* and *Sie, wie viele andere* challenge our understanding of documentary film, since they are based on fictional persons and situations. They are scripted and filmed (at least in part) on sound sets.

Camera DDR continued to make documentaries on the possibilities the GDR offered to its women to become 'well-rounded developed socialist personalities', in part through what was known as the 'scientific-technological revolution', but it abandoned the use of sound sets and fictionalized scenarios. The first segment of *DDR-Magazin* 1971/04 is devoted to Edelgard Rißland, who ran a ready-made clothing cooperative in Thuringia. Now in her mid-thirties, she had begun work fifteen years earlier as a seamstress in the same plant. The narrator stresses that modern technology will be increasingly employed in the clothing industry, so that it was necessary for the workers to learn: 'And every enhancement of knowledge means an enrichment of character.' The segment's conclusion shows women at the plant learning to further qualify themselves, which subsidized care and education for their children helps them to do. Rißland herself had completed studies while on the job to become one of the 200,000 East German women with a higher degree and one of 1,500 who managed plants.

Several Foreign Ministry documentaries feature single mothers. At first glance, this topic seems an uneasy fit with the GDR's nation-branding attempts. During the state's first decades, the SED emphasized the

Figure 2.1. In Heinz Hafke's *Sie, wie viele andere* (1969) our heroine can do it all, including (maybe!) finally repairing her son's bike, which had resisted her husband's best efforts. ©DEFA-Stiftung/Heinz Borrmann.

nuclear family as a model, although with a working mother (in contrast to capitalist countries). Divorce, adultery and sex out of wedlock all qualified as signs of 'social disorganization'. However, Donna Harsch writes that in the communist worldview, 'childbearing defined womanhood more than did marriage', even if this view was seldom openly expressed.[31] Single mothers therefore fell into an ambiguous zone. As the state expanded its benefits, especially during Honecker's 'welfare dictatorship' of the 1970s and 1980s, it became easier to raise a child out of wedlock.[32]

Camera DDR filmmakers depicted single mothers to demonstrate how socialism had emancipated women and allowed them to live fulfilled lives within the collective. Helga Weist, the subject of Joachim Hadaschik's *Eine Delegierte* (*A Female Delegate*, 1971), operates a massive conveyor bridge that dug, moved and processed brown coal at an open pit mine in the Lausitz region. Now in her mid-thirties, she began there as an apprentice and acquired further qualifications. Weist is a dedicated member of SED, which the narrator says was 'like a mother', and is portrayed as a politically forward-thinking and confident women who her colleagues look to for advice and leadership. As the name of the film indicates, she was chosen to speak about the coal industry at the SED's Eighth Party Congress in 1971. In one scene she stands atop the conveyor bridge and says that what they have accomplished at the mine was 'wonderful', but it was only possible because 'we feel ourselves fully responsible [*mitverantwortlich*]. We know what it means to help govern [*mitregieren*], to pitch in [*mitarbeiten*]', a play on the GDR's slogan '*Arbeite mit, plane mit, regiere mit!*' (Work with us, plan with us, govern with us!). In the final segment of *DDR-Magazin* 1973/09, an even younger single mother, twenty-four-year-old Regina Wichmann, is introduced as the mayor of the rural community of Jaebetz, part of a collective farm in Brandenburg. Besides her responsibilities as mayor and mother of the four-year-old Simone, Wickmann is completing a degree in agricultural science and becoming an SED member. She is depicted as competent and popular, especially among younger villagers, and is described by her former teacher as 'a true child of our republic' and by the narrator as 'a young woman of our times'.

Other Camera DDR films feature single women who were celebrities, including athletes, such as in two of the three segments in *DDR-Magazin* 1974/02. The first is middle-distance runner Gunhild Hoffmeister, who had won a medal at the 1972 Olympics (and would again in 1976). She also served as a delegate from Cottbus to the GDR's national parliament, the Volkskammer, and was studying to become a sports instructor, all while raising a young daughter as a single parent. The other is singer and actress Vera Oelschlegel, who is depicted as an engaged socialist. The film culminates with her spirited rendering of the German version of a song associated with Salvador Allende's socialist government in Chile, '*Venceremos*' ('We Shall Prevail'), at a major FDJ event with prominent SED politicians like Honecker in attendance. Support for the Chilean left represented a major part of the GDR's internationalism even before the 1973 coup in that country and was featured in several Foreign Ministry films. *DDR-Magazin* 1979/07, directed by Heinz Sobiczewski, is a sympathetic portrait of yet another famous athlete, Roswitha Krause, who still holds the distinction of being the only women to medal in two different Olympics in two different sports (silver in the 4x100 metre freestyle swim relay in Mexico City in 1968 and in team handball in Montreal in 1976). Krause narrates the film herself and is shown training and playing with her club handball team (TSC Berlin), studying to become a licensed sports teacher, and socializing with friends and family. She also serves as a representative to the Berlin city parliament. The film takes us on visits to Potsdam, Rostock and the Baltic Sea (one of the purposes of these documentaries was to show the country and its tourist attractions). Krause states that the construction of socialism in East Germany was instrumental to the sport movement that she had so benefited from and that being successful in sports required being part of a well-functioning collective.

A key function of the Foreign Ministry films was to commemorate important events and anniversaries in the GDR. During the United Nations 'International Year of the Woman' in 1975, East Berlin hosted a World Congress of Women in East Berlin in October organized by communist governments and international nongovernmental organizations (NGOs). The Congress, according to historian Celia Donert, 'represented the culmination of post-war efforts by state socialist regimes to use women's rights for the purpose of gaining international legitimacy', although they would continue with some success to champion a socialist perspective on women's rights throughout the Cold War.[33] Hosting the Congress also allowed the GDR to profile itself as an important international actor just one year after officially joining the UN (which sanctioned the event) and just as it was able to establish diplomatic relations with states around the world as a result of inter-German détente. Heinz Müller and Erwin Nippert's *Für das Glück der Frauen und Familien* (*For the Happiness of Women and Families*, 1975), an overview of the status of East German women during the 'International Year', concludes with footage from the Congress. The narrator describes the choice of East Berlin as host as 'a great acknowledgement of women and of the entire country'.[34]

However, the main document of the Congress was *DDR-Magazin 1975/13 – Weltkongreß im Internationalen Jahr der Frau* (*World Congress in the International Year of the Woman*), directed by Barbara-Christa Enseleit, Joachim Hadaschik, Rolf Hempel, Alfons Machalz, Kurt Plickat and Heinz Sobiczewski. The voice of an unnamed East German woman, supposedly a delegate, narrates the film. We see the work of the Congress and its committees, which emphasized the communist position that women's emancipation depended on assuring their legal and workplace equality, preserving world peace and ending colonization. The magazine also introduced the East German state. Congress delegates visit sites that highlight the GDR's traditions of anti-fascism (the Buchenwald and Ravensbrück concentration camps and the Seelow Heights USSR War Memorial, where the camera catches several older women, presumably Soviet citizens, weeping) and humanism (the Berlin State Opera and Dresden's art museums). Additional visits to a factory in Berlin, a rural co-op, a retirement home, a kindergarten and the *Pionierrepublik Wilhelm Pieck* (a *Free German Youth* (FDJ) summer camp in Brandenburg named after the GDR's first president) provide an opportunity to discuss the GDR's social state. 'To be sure they also have their concerns and still unfulfilled desires', concludes the narrator, 'but the GDR's citizens know the word "crisis" only from hearsay.'

DDR-Magazin 1975/13 also emphasizes East Germany's internationalism, starting with Honecker's message at the Congress's opening session that the GDR pursued an 'open-minded policy of promoting peace and friendship among nations' by working with people of diverse backgrounds and views from around the world. Prominent foreign visitors like the Congress's chairwoman, Freda Brown of Australia, Soviet Cosmonaut Valentina Tereshkova (the first woman in space) and Salvador Allende's widow Hortensia are either shown making speeches or featured in interviews.

Throughout the film, the camera focuses on women of colour, including multiple shots of Congress guest Angela Davis. East German leaders, including Honecker and his wife Margot, the Minister of Education, also figure prominently. The SED leadership and the Foreign Ministry wanted films that documented such moments faithfully as proof of the GDR's growing importance in the world. And the magazine delivered by making the Congress look like a harmonious and even joyful occasion, culminating in a visit from 2,200 East German Young Pioneers, who congratulated the delegates with flowers and hugs, and led them in chanting 'long live international solidarity!' We do not learn of the behind-the-scenes tensions involving certain Western NGOs who found the Congress' focus on the exploitation of women under capitalism and imperialism too limited a perspective on the obstacles to gender equality.[35]

Camera DDR films that strayed too far from the official themes for nation branding ran into trouble with the authorities, even if they were well done. An example is *Eine Lehrerin* (*A Teacher*), which portrays Monika Iben. She teaches in the *Oberstufe* (grades 7–10) of a Berlin polytechnic secondary school, the standard ten-class GDR institution. *Eine Lehrerin* begins and ends with scenes from a reunion held in Iben's apartment with recent graduates. She offers them the familiar form of address, 'Du', as a sign of their close relationship. *Eine Lehrerin* only makes occasional and subtle references to the communist system. Iben, who is not a member of the SED, is shown participating in a meeting of her class's 'Thälmann Pioneers' (a FDJ group) and a May Day parade, but no context is provided. If a viewer somehow missed those two brief scenes and was also unfamiliar with the inside of a typical GDR apartment in the late 1980s, they might be forgiven for asking if the docu-

Figure 2.2. SED Chairman Erich Honecker, Congress President Freda Brown and GDR head of state Willi Stoph on the grandstand amidst international delegates and Free German Youth members at the October 1975 World Congress of Women in East Berlin in *DDR-Magazin* 13/1975 – *Weltkongreß im Internationalen Jahr der Frau.* © DEFA-Stiftung/K. Schulze, G. Becher, G. Münch et al.

mentary was shot in East or West Germany. After her former students have gone home, Iben says that 'the sweetest reward [*der schönste Lohn*]' for a teacher is sensing that students trust you 'and see you as a true partner'. The focus is on individuals and not society. Alfons Machalz had to defend his film to representatives of the state certification board [*staatliche Abnahme*]. Although they found it realistic and likeable, they thought that it did not depict the socialist goals of the GDR's education system or the social role of its teachers.[36]

Perhaps the most interesting aspect of the Foreign Ministry documentaries is the fact that although their task was nation branding, many of them implicitly and sometimes explicitly point out problems with the official narrative. This is true of the films about women that suggest, for example, the persistence of traditional societal norms. In *Deutschland – Endstation Ost*, blue-collar female workers interviewed by Buyens tell him that they felt equal to their male colleagues. In contrast, white-collar women hint that they face a 'glass ceiling'. One relates that it took a long time for gender equality to become an established principle at their workplace, and another states that she had not been considered for an assignment simply because she was a woman. Subsequent Camera DDR films also touched on the difficulties women faced combining careers with family life and on the persistence of the 'glass ceiling'. These problems are discussed most dramatically in one of the final films it produced, Willi Urbanek's *Edeltraud D./Protokoll einer Erkundung* (*Edeltraud D./Protocol of an Investigation*, 1988), which documented the success and challenges of a woman who managed a large collective farm near Weimar. *DDR-Magazin* 1972/04 (directed by Johanna Kleberg), dedicated to the twenty-fifth anniversary of the foundation of the GDR's Demokratischer Frauenbund Deutschlands (Democratic Women's League of Germany), ends with a segment that takes us to a beauty parlour and a fashion show. The female narrator explains that 'personal hygiene (Körperpflege)', cosmetics and fashion were no longer limited to just privileged women.

One wonders what the early German communist and feminist Clara Zetkin, featured in the magazine's first segment, would have made of this aspect of the 'well-developed socialist personality'. The female protagonists of *Das Gesetz heißt Glück* and *Sie, wie viele andere* are immaculately dressed and coiffured, as is Helga Weist in several scenes from her private life. *Eine Delegierte* also emphasizes Weist's 'feminine side' by showing her window shopping for the latest fashions. And at a wedding reception in *DDR-Magazin* 1979/07, the single Roswitha Krause, who is nearly thirty years old, must discuss when and whom she plans to marry.

Conclusion

One of the most difficult questions to answer in respect to the Foreign Ministry films is their reception. East German diplomatic missions showed them to key foreign partners and to commemorate GDR or bilateral anniversaries. The cultural ministries of socialist countries and GDR friendship groups elsewhere around the world were important partners for organizing screenings, including in theatres or film festivals. The films were also available in East German cultural centres, through the mobile film wagons of the Liga für Völkerfreundschaft (League for People's Friendship, since late 1961 the umbrella organization for the GDR's friendship groups) in the developing world, and in some Western countries through film distributors. As a 1978 public diplomacy manual emphasized, opportunities to reach the masses through television were greatest in countries that were socialist 'or whose TV stations still stood in the build-up phase', i.e. in the developing world.[37] However, film was only one of many methods used by the GDR for nation branding. We know that Foreign Ministry productions like Buyens' *Deutschland – Endstation Ost* and Rudi Hein's *Made in GDR* (1981), which depicted the GDR's modern export economy, were well received by foreign audiences.[38] But it is hard to estimate their individual contribution to establishing the brand. Moreover, reception depended on multiple factors ranging from the quality of the individual films to the interest level of foreign partners (the French Communist Party was especially engaged)[39] to the availability of the necessary projection technology (East Germany was slow to react to the global transition from film to videotape in the 1980s).[40] However, there was no question that the East German authorities believed that documentary film played an important role in their nation-branding attempts. In the weeks after the fall of the Berlin Wall on 9 November 1989, the Ministry of Foreign Affairs desired to continue its public diplomacy efforts using most of the old techniques but under a new name, '*Öffentlichkeitsarbeit*' (Public Relations). Like Auslandsinformation, 'public relations' would provide an objective look at developments in the GDR, but with a new emphasis on presenting the diversity of views in the country.[41] Only at the end of June 1990, little more than three months before the reunification of Germany, did the Ministry inform DEFA it was cancelling further production of Foreign Ministry films due to lack of funding.[42]

Thomas Maulucci teaches history and serves as HIST 1400 faculty coordinator for the Early College Experience Program at the University of Connecticut. Among other publications, he has written *Adenauer's Foreign Office. West German Diplomats and Diplomacy in the Shadow of the Third Reich, 1945–1955* (Northern Illinois University Press, 2012) and with Detlef Junker co-edited the volume *G.I.s in Germany: The Social, Economic, Cultural and Political History of the American Military Presence* (Cambridge University Press, 2013). He is currently preparing a monograph on DEFA's Foreign Ministry Films.

Notes

1. On *Auslandsinformation*, see Nils Abraham, *Die politische Auslandsarbeit der DDR in Schweden. Zur Public Diplomacy der DDR gegenüber Schweden nach der diplomatischen Anerkennung (1972–1989)* (Berlin: Lit Verlag, 2007), pp. 43–61.
2. DEFA produced around 5,200 documentary films and newsreels between 1946 and 1994. See Rosemary Stott, 'The State-Owned Cinema Industry and Its Audience', in Seán Allan and Sebastian Heiduschke (eds), *Re-imagining DEFA: East German Cinema in Its National and Transnational Contexts* (New York: Berghahn Books, 2016), pp. 19–40 (at p. 20).
3. Carolin Viktorin, Jessica C.E. Gienow-Hecht, Annika Estner and Marcel K. Will, 'Introduction: Beyond Marketing and Diplomacy: Exploring the Historical Origins of National Branding', in Carolin Viktorin, Jessica C.E. Gienow-Hecht, Annika Estner and Marcel K. Will (eds), *Nation Branding in Modern History* (New York: Berghahn Books, 2018), pp. 1–26 (at p. 2).
4. Ernest D. Plock, *East German-West German Relations and the Fall of the GDR* (Boulder: Westview Press, 1993), pp. 41–43.
5. Henning Wrage, 'Powerless Heroines: Gender and Agency in DEFA Films of the 1960s and 1970s', in Kyle Frackman and Faye Stewart (eds), *Gender and Sexuality in East German Film: Intimacy and Alienation* (Rochester, NY: Camden House, 2018), pp. 42–61 (at pp. 42–43).
6. Jennifer L. Creech, *Mothers, Comrades, and Outcasts in East German Women's Film* (Bloomington: Indiana University Press, 2016), pp. 197–98.
7. Frank Trommler, *Kulturmacht ohne Kompass. Deutsche auswärtige Kulturbeziehungen im 20. Jahrhundert* (Cologne: Böhlau Verlag, 2014), pp. 666–70.
8. Protocol No. 56/59 of the Politburo meeting on 15 December 1959, 'Richtlinien zur Erweiterung und Verbesserung unserer Auslandspropaganda' (= BArch DY 30/42657).
9. Protocol No. 37/61 of the Politburo meeting on 25 July 1961, 'Verstärkung unserer Auslandspropaganda im Zusammenhang mit dem Abschluß eines Friedensvertrages und der Lösung der Westberlinfrage' (= BArch DY 30/42757).
10. 'Vorlage für das Kollegium des Ministeriums für Auswärtige Angelegenheiten zur Verstärkung der Filmpropaganda im Ausland', with four attachments, 27 January 1961, Politisches Archiv des Auswärtigen Amts, Berlin (hereinafter cited as PA AA), Papers of the East German Ministry of Foreign Affairs (hereinafter cited as MfAA) M 1-LS-A/443/folios 30–38. The MfAA's Kollegium, its highest advisory body under the foreign minister, discussed the proposal on 29 January 1962. 'Protokoll über die 3. Sitzung des Kollegiums am Montag, den 29. Januar 1962', signed Lothar Bolz (Foreign Minister) and Horst Grunert (Head of the Cultural Division), 31 January 1962, ibid./folios 3–6.

11. 'Produktion Ministerium für Auswärtige Angelegenheiten', 28 November 1962. (= BArch DR 118/4465); copy of the contract between the MfAA (signed Horst Grunert, Head of the Kulturabteilung) and the VEB DEFA Studio für Wochenschau und Dokumentarfilme (signed Inge Kleinert, Director), 8 Febuary 1963, ibid.
12. Paul Ickler (DEFA Studio für Wochenschau and Dokumentarfilme), 'Vorlage zur Verbesserung der filmischen Auslandspropaganda', 15 October 1964 (= BArch DR 117/194; Ministerium für Kultur (signed Erich Wendt, State Secretary and First Deputy of the Minister) and MfAA (signed Georg Stibi, Deputy of the Minister), 'Gegenwärtiger Stand und weitere Entwicklung der Arbeit mit dem Film und Filmexport. Vorlage für den Beirat für Auslandsinformation beim Zentralkomitee der SED', 27 August 1964 (= BArch DR 1/4538/78–103).
13. Alex Wedding, a pseudonym for Grete Weiskopf (1905–66), was an author of children's and young adult socialist books that became part of the GDR's required school curriculum.
14. Thomas Heimann, 'Wie ein Ausländer die DDR mit eigenen Augen sehen wollte. Frans Buyens bei der DEFA', in Ralf Schenk and Erika Richter (eds), *Apropos: Film 2001. Das Jahrbuch der DEFA-Stiftung* (Berlin: Verlag Das Neue Berlin, 2001), pp. 105–32.
15. Ickler, 'Vorlage zur Verbesserung der filmischen Auslandspropaganda'.
16. No author, 'Gespräche mit Presse-Attachés und Leitern unserer Kulturzentren', 4 May 1968. (= BArch DR 118/4486).
17. See the memo by Erika Wiens, editor in the KAG-Auslandsinformation, 'Gedanken zur Arbeitsweise und zur Struktur der Gruppe Auslandsinformation', 14 September 1968 (= BArch DR 118/4486).
18. 'Aktennotiz', signed Schnabel, 25 October 1968 (= BArch DR 118/4465).
19. On Hadaschik, see Günther Jordan and Ralf Schenk (eds), *Schwarzweiß und Farbe: DEFA-Dokumentarfilme 1946–92* (Berlin: Jovis, 2000), pp. 399–400.
20. See Machalz's handwritten note, probably from the 2010s (= Filmmuseum Potsdam/Sammlungen/NL Alfons Machalz/vol. 1/staple 1).
21. For example, see Ralf Schenk, 'Die Klügsten gehen in den Osten', *Berliner Zeitung*, 3 May 2007.
22. Viktorin et al., 'Introduction', pp. 17–20.
23. One example is *Begegnungen der Freundschaft*, a.k.a. *Afrika 1979* (*Meeting Friends*, 1979), about Honecker's official visits to four states on that continent, which was well received in screenings to the SED leadership and played on East Germany's First Programme on 2 May 1979. Commissioned by the SED Central Committee, it was a compilation of materials also used for four 1979 Camera GDR films on each separate visit directed by Hadaschik and Rolf Hempel (= BArch DR 118/4622).
24. Joachim Hadaschik, 'Politische Journalistik im Dokumentarfilm für die Auslandsinformation', in Abteilung Auslandsinformation, Institut für Internationale Beziehungen der Deutschen Akademie für Staats- und Rechtswis-

senschaften 'Walter Ulbricht', *Aus Theorie und Praxis der Auslandsinformation* (Potsdam-Babelsberg, Sonderheft, February 1971), pp. 70–76.
25. Interview with Hadaschik in Wolfgang Noa, *Werkstatt – Dokumentaristen und Publizisten im 25. Jahr der DDR über sich* (Potsdam-Babelsberg: DEFA-Studio für Kurzfilme, 1974), pp. 35–41 (at p. 41).
26. Protocol No. 12/73 of the Politburo meeting on 27 March 1973, attachment 5, 'Konzeption für die Gestaltung der Auslandsinformation der DDR gegenüber jungen Nationalstaaten und kapitalistischen Länder nach der Herstellung diplomatischer Beziehungen' (= BArch DY 30/43419); Protocol No. 22/74 of the Politburo meeting on 21 May 1974; 'Konzeption für die Gestaltung der Auslandsinformation der DDR in den sozialistischen Ländern' (= BArch DY 30/43486).
27. Corey Ross, *The East German Dictatorship: Problems and Perspectives in the Interpretation of the GDR* (London: Arnold, 2002), p. 56.
28. Josie McLellan, *Love in the Time of Communism: Intimacy and Sexuality in the GDR* (Cambridge: Cambridge University Press, 2011), pp. 65–66; Donna Harsch, *Revenge of the Domestic: Women, the Family, and Communism in the German Democratic Republic* (Princeton: Princeton University Press, 2006), pp. 304–7.
29. McLellan, pp. 69–76, 82; Lenora Ansorg and Renate Hürtgen, 'The Myth of Female Emancipation: Contradictions in Women's Lives', in Konrad H. Jarausch (ed.), *Dictatorship as Experience: Towards a Socio-Cultural History of the GDR*, trans. Eve Duffy (New York: Berghahn Books, 1999), pp. 163–76; Dagmar Langenhan and Sabine Roß, 'The Socialist Glass Ceiling: Limits to Female Careers', in ibid., pp. 177–91.
30. Köhn (Abt. Auslandsinformation, MfAA) to Rolf Schnabel (director, Camera DDR), 7 July 1969. (= BArch DR 118/4464).
31. Harsch, p. 199.
32. McLellan, pp. 66–68, 82.
33. Celia Donert, 'Whose Utopia? Gender, Ideology, and Human Rights at the 1975 World Congress of Women in East Berlin', in Jan Eckel and Samuel Moyn (eds), *The Breakthrough: Human Rights in the 1970s* (Philadelphia: University of Pennsylvania Press, 2014), pp. 68–87 (at p. 85).
34. *DDR-Magazin* 1974/02 and *DDR-Magazin* 1975/01 were also dedicated to the 'International Year'.
35. Donert, 'Whose Utopia?', pp. 80–85.
36. Camera DDR (signed Seidel), 'Protokoll der staatl. Abnahme "Die Lehrerin", Regie: A. Machalz, am 9.12.87', 9 December 1987 (= Filmmuseum Potsdam/Sammlungen/NL Alfons Machalz/vol. 3/staple 5).
37. W. Lorenscheit (Arbeitsgruppe 'Diplomatische Praxis' Institut für Internationale Beziehungen, Akademie für Staats- und Rechtswissenschaft der DDR), 'Die auslandsinformatorische Arbeit an der Auslandsvertretung', 1978, pp. 35–37 (= PA AA, MfAA Press Division (hereinafter cited as M 62)/11986–93).

38. On *Made in GDR*, see Inge Schönherr (GDR Embassy, London) to the MfAA, 'Bericht über die auslandsinformatorischen Aktivitäten während der Vorbereitung und Durchführung der Informationstage des DDR-Außenhandels in Großbritannien (vom 8.–11. Juni 1982) sowie Schlussfolgerungen für künftige Aktivitäten', 17 June 1982 (= PA AA M 62/488).
39. Perrine Val, *Les relations cinématographiques entre la France et la RDA: entre camaraderie, bureaucratie et exotisme, 1946–1992* (Villeneuve-d'Ascq: Presses universitaires du Septentrion, 2021).
40. Press Department, MfAA, 'Statement on Agenda Item 2 at the 10th Multilateral Consultations of Directors of Departments and Divisions for Press and External Information of the Foreign Ministries of Socialist Countries' (Warsaw, 10–11 September 1987) (= PA AA M 62/12246–93).
41. Abteilung Auslandsinformation (MfAA), 'Staatliche Öffentlichkeitsarbeit gegenüber dem Ausland', with three attachments, 28 December 1989 (= PA AA M 62/12243–93).
42. Otto Pfeiffer (Referat Presse/Öffentlichkeitsarbeit, Bereich Oeffentlichkeitsarbeit, MfAA) to F. Seidel (Director, DEFA Studio for Documentary Film), 29 June 1990 (= PA AA M 62/3245–94).

Select Bibliography

Abraham, Nils. *Die politische Auslandsarbeit der DDR in Schweden. Zur Public Diplomacy der DDR gegenüber Schweden nach der diplomatischen Anerkennung (1972–1989)*. Berlin: Lit Verlag, 2007.

Creech, Jennifer L. *Mothers, Comrades, and Outcasts in East German Women's Film*. Bloomington: Indiana University Press, 2016.

Heimann, Thomas. 'Wie ein Ausländer die DDR mit eigenen Augen sehen wollte. Frans Buyens bei der DEFA', in Ralf Schenk and Erika Richter (eds), *Apropos: Film 2001. Das Jahrbuch der DEFA-Stiftung*. Berlin: Verlag Das Neue Berlin, 2001, pp. 105–32.

Jarausch, Konrad H. (ed.). *Dictatorship as Experience: Towards a Socio-cultural History of the GDR*, trans. Eve Duffy. New York: Berghahn Books, 1999.

McLellan, Josie. *Love in the Time of Communism: Intimacy and Sexuality in the GDR*. Cambridge: Cambridge University Press, 2011.

Stott, Rosemary. 'The State-Owned Cinema Industry and Its Audience', in Seán Allan and Sebastian Heiduschke (eds), *Re-imagining DEFA: East German Cinema in Its National and Transnational Contexts*. New York: Berghahn Books, 2016, pp. 19–40.

Val, Perrine. *Les relations cinématographiques entre la France et la RDA: entre camaraderie, bureaucratie et exotisme, 1946–1992*. Villeneuve-d'Ascq: Presses universitaires du Septentrion, 2021.

CHAPTER 3

Diary of the Ordinary: Reinventing the Newsreel
DEFA *Kinobox*, 1981–90

Reinhild Steingröver

'See for yourself, hear for yourself, judge for yourself.' The slogan of DEFA's newsreel *Der Augenzeuge* (*The Eyewitness*) reflects its origins as an information service for the postwar German population. Launched in 1946 at the same time as the founding of the studio in first monthly, then weekly and (from 1957 onwards) twice-weekly formats, *Der Augenzeuge* was intended to be 'primarily a political-journalistic voice, but also an agitator and reminder, an educator, informant, and mediator of all things new and beautiful'.[1] Outlasting its rival in the Federal Republic, *Die neue deutsche Wochenschau* (1949–78), it would become the longest running cinematic newsreel in Germany. But with the widespread availability of television in the German Democratic Republic (GDR) from the 1970s onwards, DEFA took the decision to cease production of the newsreel on 18 December 1980. The newly founded artistic production group *Kinobox* was established with the task of producing a magazine of up to five short films (with a total running time of 15 minutes) that would be shown in cinemas before the main feature film presentation. Initially ten such magazines per year were expected, a target that was later reduced to just six. While *Kinobox* as *Der Augenzeuge*'s direct successor was liberated from the burden of being a straightforward news bulletin, it was immediately confronted with the task of first defining its artistic and formal identity. In 1980 the DEFA dramaturg Ulrich Burkhardt described *Kinobox*'s remit in the broadest of terms:

Journalistic formats such as newspaper feuilleton, satirical reports, short portraits, popular science stories, animation, jokes, collages, treasures from the early days of cinema, performances and caricatures should all be included.[2]

With such a loose definition of its form, the new magazine sought to distance itself from coverage of daily news and politics that had been the hallmark of its predecessor. But while its main focus lay on reaching and entertaining younger audiences, the legacy of *Der Augenzeuge* is still evident in its self-understanding as an 'educator, informant, and mediator'.

The *Kinobox* artistic group was relatively young by DEFA standards and the average age of its directors was just thirty-five. Its members had ambitious artistic goals:

> To reflect our reality with the artistic-aesthetic means of cinema, to present convincing positions about current problems and events, to provide intellectual and emotional stimulation, and to be entertaining – that is the DEFA-*Kinobox*'s credo.[3]

However, as becomes evident from the surviving archival production documents, with its small number of core staff and many freelance contributors, the group struggled throughout its decade-long existence to fulfil this mission. In its annual reports, the group's first leader Joachim Hellwig (from 1980 to 1981) and his successor Bernd Burkhardt stressed the need to define the magazine's goals. Even so, after three years of production, one report assesses that 'the cultural-political function of the magazine' remained unclear.[4]

As I will argue, on the one hand, the structural context of the DEFA-Studio für Dokumentarfilme's new production group in 1981 contributed to its failure to realize its own self-imposed goals, but on the other hand, it also offered unexpected opportunities for the production of a significant number of remarkable short films. While many of the roughly 300 films it produced are aesthetically conventional and politically affirmative reports about socialist progress, some 15 per cent of the group's output consisted of aesthetically innovative films, moving portraits of ordinary people, pointed satire and carefully documented time capsules of forgotten places and landscapes. The films in this latter category are GDR-specific and rooted in the time and place of their production. Nonetheless, they also transcend their origins insofar as they deliberately probe universal humanist questions about art, life, work and history. As such, these films underline the potential for innovation that *Kinobox* had, despite its relatively marginalized status within the organization of DEFA as a whole. Films by Jochen Kraußer, Helke Misselwitz, Jörg Foth, Andreas Voigt and Thomas Heise that I will discuss in this chapter belong to this category.

If, as Günter Jordan has suggested, the *Kinobox* production group offered filmmakers an 'ideal environment for formal and stylistic experiments',[5] then how are we to explain the failure of the first cooperation between *Kinobox* and the Babelsberg Hochschule für Film und Fernsehen (HFF) in 1982? The film *Erfinder '82* (*Inventors '82*) remained unfinished and its director, Thomas Heise, abandoned his studies at the film school as a result. What was it that enabled some highly innovative films to pass through the cumbersome process of approval, while others languished in storage for years or were never screened? What were the particular interests of the filmmakers in this group? And what were the opportunities and limitations of the short film format? As we shall see, institutional practices and loopholes, individual agency and sometimes just serendipity all played a key role in these production histories.

Right from the start the attempt to make films lasting between 30 seconds and five minutes that were entertaining, aesthetically compelling, up to date and politically committed on such a tight production schedule proved to be a challenge. In order to reach the broadest possible audience, an edition of *Kinobox* might contain a rare archival film from the silent era, followed by an enthusiastic report about modern conditions of production in one of the GDR's copper-wire factories, and all of this followed by a music video on the annual Festival des politischen Liedes (Festival of Political Song). Rounding out an edition, audiences might be treated to a brief satirical spoof or animation of just a few seconds' length. Such a random juxtaposition of shorts on topics as diverse as the genetics of the soya bean, the history of the Zeppelin and rice farmers in China, frequently resulted in magazines that, far from appealing to everyone, satisfied almost no one. Concerns about curatorial and aesthetic arbitrariness led to attempts on the part of the group to compile thematically coherent magazines on a number of occasions, but even then, as the collection of films on love (*Kinobox* 20/1983) underlined, these themes tended to be very broad.

Additionally, the question of what subjects might lend themselves to a short film format that was compatible with the group's artistic goal 'to reflect reality with artistic-aesthetic means' remained unclear. In many cases, the shorts resemble superficial journalism. Many contributing directors had experience of working for the newsreel or other types of journalistic filmmaking, such as acting as a foreign correspondent, working for the studio for documentaries on popular science produced by both the DEFA-Studio für populärwissenschaftliche Filme (DEFA Studio for Popular Science Films) and the DEFA-Studio für Dokumentarfilme. Finally, Progress Film, the GDR's sole film distribution company, paired *Kinobox* magazines with feature films, which often led to clashes between audience expectations and the shorts that were screened.[6]

As Rosemary Stott notes, even in the late 1980s, cinema remained the most popular form of entertainment in the GDR and was generously supported by the state as an important way of promoting its goals and achievements:

> In 1988 there were 50.2 million visits to the cinema as opposed to 9.6 million visits to the theatre; and 7,045 people were employed by cinemas, representing a total of 7.76% of employees in the cultural industries. The importance of cinema in the state's eyes is also confirmed by the fact that spending on the film industry increased steadily despite a slight fall in the number of cinemas; in 1980, government spending was 209.5 million (East German) Marks and by 1988, it was 281.5 million Marks.[7]

This robust infrastructure reflects the East German government's focus on cinema in general, and on documentary film in particular. Throughout its existence, DEFA produced short features that ran prior to the main attraction, regardless of whether that was a fictional film or a documentary. The cinema visit was designed to be a cultural event, with the entertaining and educational appeal of a collective experience. DEFA thus concerned itself not just with the production of films, but also with the production of cinema culture itself.

The creation of the *Kinobox* magazine has to be understood in this cultural context. Instead of simply abolishing the newsreel when the rise of television had rendered it superfluous, the programme of films before the main attraction consisting of the *Kinobox* magazine, as well as additional 20-minute short documentaries (Beiprogrammfilme), was designed to create a receptive and engaged audience for the main feature, as had been customary since the earliest days of cinema. The early advertising pioneer Julius Pinschewer, for example, produced not only commercials for Maggi seasoning and aspirin, but also ads for major exhibits, government health programmes and war bond purchasing campaigns during the First World War. The challenge was that audiences had many other attractions competing for their attention and, by the 1980s, had become disillusioned with the ever-growing discrepancy between official proclamations of socialist progress and their own experience of reality.

With the impending release of the first *Kinobox* in September 1981, the new artistic group had to determine what kinds of films to make and how to make them. Archival documents reveal that differences of opinion soon emerged prompting a change of leadership after less than one year. The group's founding leader was Joachim Hellwig, who had led *defa-futurum* from 1971 to 1981. In one of the earliest documented minutes about the planned *Kinobox* group, the question of what to do with the 'well established name futurum'[8] arose. Hellwig had directed and promoted intergenre films that crossed the boundaries between popular science, science fiction, animation and documentary. As Doreen Mende explains, defa futurum was initiated 'to present a vision of a socialist future by reflecting on the present' through films that were developed in a workshop system based on Marxist dialectics.[9] In his 1975 dissertation on the artistic design of socialist cine-futures in film, Hellwig offers a diagram to describe how politicians, dramaturgs, writers and directors create such films in a collective workshop process that originates in the material existence (*Sein*) and shapes social consciousness towards socialist ideals (*Bewusstsein*).[10] In Hellwig's words:

> The experiences we were able to gather in non-fiction filmmaking mostly arose from the documentary approach this genre requires. It was partially enhanced by the new methods and modes of representation we developed under the rubric of the inter-genre film.[11]

In his dissertation – co-authored with Claus Ritter – Hellwig outlined a utopian vision of a workshop for film production that would merge the different methods of artists and scientists:

> Scientific representations of the future, i.e., prognoses, are the work of sometimes hundreds of people who rely on the work of hundreds more; they employ the most modern means, scientific methods and technologies. The creator of artistic portrayals, by contrast, works in isolation in the process of artistic creation. Must things always be that way? Are today's social conditions, which manifest themselves in manifold ways in the union of the processes of life and creation, adequate to the composition of a future? If an artist chooses to grapple with this subject – the future – does it even make sense for them to work in isolation, or will new forms need to be found? Are consultations sufficient, or should we seek to devise new methods?[12]

These aspirations for collective creative processes – originally articulated for the defa futurum group in the documentary film studio – seem to have guided Hellwig's concept of *Kinobox*'s hybrid style as a kind of intergenre magazine that at the same time had to contend with the realities of tight production schedules, cumbersome bureaucratic structures and generational differences. Even in its utopian form, such a workshop was never intended to be democratically structured, but rather one controlled by its leader. The hierarchical nature of this conceptual planning reflected the propagandistic goals for filmmaking. According to the youngest generation of filmmakers like Jörg Foth or Andreas Voigt, by pairing young directors with established teams of production workers, Hellwig replicated one of the key structural obstacles to aesthetic innovation and prevented the directors from using the new production group as a way of finding their own artistic style. Studio officials aimed to reach young viewers by creating formats such as the 'Disco film' (for example, Hellwig's 1972 film *Liebe 2002* [*Love in the Year 2002*]) and several of the *Kinobox* directors had made films in that genre in the previous decade. When the studio wished to gauge the effectiveness of their first few releases for young viewers in March 1982, they attempted to commission a survey from the Leipzig-based Zentralinstitut für Jugendforschung (Central Institute for Research on Youth). When the researchers in Leipzig were too busy, *Kinobox* hired a consultant, Gisela Harkenthal, for the task.

The studio's expressed interest in the feedback from young audiences did not translate into their willingness to grant young filmmakers easy permission to produce films that actually dealt with the sensibilities and worldviews of teenagers, as Dieter Schumann wrote in his proposal for a *Kinobox* short on *Rock-Report in der DDR* (*Rock Report in the GDR*). Schumann's film was first proposed in 1982 and again in 1983, and was further elaborated in 1985. The director had argued that rock music was the perfect medium to embark on a nuanced exploration of the contradictory and difficult process of teenage identity formation: 'In this way, music becomes the mirror of the existential needs and emotions of the younger generation.'[13] The film was not realized until 1988 when it became an instant hit under the title *flüstern & SCHREIEN* (*whisper & SHOUT*). Schumann's initial proposal from 1982 suggested demonstrating his effectiveness to work with teenage amateur musicians for a feature film project through several short contributions for *Kinobox*. Schumann's desire to give voice to the teenagers' views in a 'loose and informal' format also clashed with Hellwig's practice of sticking to highly scripted and staged intergenre films.

Records of planning meetings in 1981, highlighting improved processes for resolving complaints within the group, suggest that working relationships between group members were not always harmonious.

Joachim Hellwig was replaced less than one year after the group was founded by, first, an interim leader, Irina (Gregor) Lepke, and then, in 1982, by the dramaturg Bernd Burkhardt. Burkhardt remained in this position for the duration of the group's existence and oversaw the production of what were for the most part conventional shorts, but he also wrote letters in support of projects that ran into difficulties. He acted as dramaturg on several films by Helke Misselwitz, for example, her *TangoTraum* (*TangoDream*, 1985), *Winter Adé* (*After Winter Comes Spring*, 1988) and *Wer fürchtet sich vorm schwarzen Mann* (*Who's Afraid of the Bogeyman*, 1989) as well as Sybille Schönemann's *Verriegelte Zeit* (*Locked up Time*, 1990). Here, as elsewhere in the history of the DEFA studio, it is remarkable to observe the impact that a particular individual, such as a group leader, could have on the production outcomes despite the complex structures of the system.

Kinobox files contain many laments about the lack of a unified style and shared goals (einheitliche Führungslinie) throughout its decade-long existence.[14] However, suggested solutions remained at the level of theoretical ideas about operational restructuring. Should the number of permanent directors in the group be reduced from seven to just four? Or should the auteur principle (the so-called 'writer-director principle') be reconsidered? Instead of delving into discussions about aesthetics and politics, the dominant focus was on logistics: 'In general, it should be assumed that each employee cannot realize their individual socialist programme.'[15] While on one level, this observation seems to point to the concern for a unified political message, on another, it hints at far less lofty goals: 'Specifically, this means maintaining fixed working hours. The accumulation of weekend overtime for the purpose of earning a second vacation is to be avoided.'[16] The minutes of the meeting advise the group leader to keep track of unavoidable overtime and instruct the group members that those hours are 'to be claimed between shoots'.[17] Even after the change of leadership, logistical and economic concerns continued to dominate internal discussions about cinematic quality or content. In one of the discussions about the poor image quality of interpolated film sections from foreign films, we read 'content trumps image quality' (*Inhalt über Bildqualität*).[18]

The ambitious target of producing six to ten editions of *Kinobox* per year meant that a significant number of freelance authors and directors had to be employed, despite the group leaders' concern for further loss of cohesiveness. The thematic plan for the production year 1982/1983 dated 15 May 1982 summarizes this challenge in terms of concrete numbers: the production of *Kinobox* magazines for 1981 had exhausted all the scripts that had been developed since the autumn of 1980, and because production was simultaneously ongoing, there had been no time for new script development. Since the annual number of short films required was between forty and fifty – and the ratio of script ideas and film production lay between 1:2 and 1:3 – some 80–150 film topics were needed annually.

This discrepancy between supply and demand offered freelance artists, underemployed writers and directors, and even students a rare – but welcome – opportunity to make a short film for the DEFA documentary studio. As we shall see, a significant number of the most interesting *Kinobox* films were made by young directors, such as Andreas Voigt, Helke Misselwitz, Herwig Kipping and Jörg Foth, all of whom experienced difficulties obtaining permanent contracts as directors in the DEFA studio after graduating from film school.[19] Other guest directors hailed from the group for DEFA short documentaries aimed at children (Jochen Kraußer), children's films (Konrad Weiss) or the HFF at Babelsberg (Thomas Heise and Peter Badel). *Kinobox* also sought to fulfil its production plan by reaching out to other artistic groups in the DEFA Studio für Dokumentarfilme, as well as to groups outside DEFA by contacting the Akademie der Künste (Academy of Arts), the FDJ (Free German Youth), various trade unions and even amateur film clubs.[20] This offered tremendous opportunities for external filmmakers to gain professional experience and to learn how to realize a larger project by practising on a short film. For Helke Misselwitz, the short films about working women led to the contract for her breakthrough film *Winter Adé*:

> Then a door opened after all and I made small contributions for the *Kinobox*. I narrated thirty-five years of an East German life in three and a half minutes and presented a completely ordinary biography in thirty-five photos. That film was not approved for screening, but I had lengthy discussions with the studio director who then asked me whether I would like to make a film about women. That became *Winter Adé*.[21]

Jörg Foth credits his *Kinobox* short *Tuba Wa Duo* (1989) as an excellent practice for adapting a script by cabaret duo Wenzel & Mensching for cinema, as he did in *Letztes aus der Da Da eR* (*Latest from the Da-Da-R*, 1990).[22]

The basic need for a sufficient number of subject proposals as well as films overshadowed more abstract considerations like Hellwig's model of the ideal creative workshop or Lepke's questioning of the writer-director principle. For *Kinobox*'s freelancers, an additional attraction was money and above-average rates of pay. The average *Kinobox* short cost 15,000 marks, of which several thousand went to the writer and director, respectively. Upon release, further premiums were possible if the film earned a favourable rating in the approval process.[23] This applied to film students as well. Production costs for Thomas Heise's planned 15-minute short *Inventors '82* were budgeted at 13,000 marks. According to an agreement between the DEFA Studio für Dokumentarfilme and the HFF dated 13 January 1983, students in directing and cinematography were permitted to direct independent shorts for *Kinobox* to gain practical experiences. Thomas Heise and Peter Badel, a student of cinematography, were contracted as early as the spring of 1982 for *Erfinder '82*. The *Kinobox* leadership was hoping that Heise and his film could answer the question of how a group of workers might turn into an inventors' collective (*Neuererkollektiv*). The GDR had an organized a system – the so-called *Neuererbewegung*, which encouraged and rewarded innovation among workers of any trade. It resembled in many ways corporate strategies designed to encourage entrepreneurial thinking in Western capitalist economies. Ironically, the film project was terminated when Heise, the rebellious cinematic 'innovator' exmatriculated from the film school. Heise made a film for the medium-length (20-minute) *Kinobox* series of *Beiprogrammfilme* in 1989, *Imbiss Spezial* (*Snack Bar Special*, 1990). Gerd Kroske described that film in his assessment for the studio approval process as follows: 'A film that allows us to both see and hear once again. Bravo!'[24]

The voluminous paper trail on the unfinished *Erfinder '82*, for which Günter Jordan was the assigned mentor, reflects just how much ink was spilled to connect the many different institutions that had to be notified and granted their cooperation for a 15-minute portrait of a group of young workers in an electronics factory: numerous offices within the documentary studio, the HFF, the FDJ, the relevant factory and more. The film's exposé opens with the seemingly optimistic view in the inventor collective: 'I believe every person has a chance to become an inventor. There is nothing that is impossible.' A stern pledge to continuous innovation was offered at the end: 'There is no room for complacency when something has been achieved.'[25]

The exposé appears to describe a film in full alignment with the goals of the Socialist Unity Party (SED) and its hopes for entrepreneurial workers in large and small companies throughout the GDR. The above observations clearly articulate the desired spirit of optimism and striving for continual improvement at a time when many citizens in the GDR were increasingly disillusioned regarding the socialist project. Heise's film was shelved after the rough-cut screening. Archival files describe (in neutral terms) the 'voluntary exmatriculation of the former student Thomas Heise', offer thanks for the mutual support between documentary studio and film school, and express concern about the gap in the production plan due to the almost completed but now unsalvageable film. In a video interview of 2005 with the DEFA scholar Ralf Schenk, Heise explains that in January 1982 he could hardly turn down the commission for this project, but had no intention of complying with the request for a conformist film. Instead, he and Peter Badel had wanted to create a cinematic version of the company brochure about the inventors' collective and then contrast this with candid shots of the workers' everyday experiences in the factory. As indicated in the script, Heise accompanied the workers to the May Day demonstration, but filmed them waiting around for long periods and playing with their flags, while at the same time panning across endless rows of police and catching Erich Honecker looking at his watch. He then juxtaposed these candid shots with footage of the same workers' group in the parade as shown on TV. These contrasting edits exposed the staged nature of the official coverage, including the artificial soundtrack of enthusiastic applause. The film was not approved and Heise refused to make the requested changes. In the 2005 interview, Heise describes a meeting between himself and Bernd Burkhardt, who laid out the options: make the changes or accept the end of his studies at the HFF. Heise comments: 'I found that fair and that is how it was documented in the files.'[26] He opted to 'voluntarily' apply for his exmatriculation in order to minimize the damage and avoid being banned from all subsequent filmmaking activities in the GDR. In the end, he was able to work for the GDR's radio broadcasting network (Rundfunk der DDR), the state film documentation office (Staatliches Filmarchiv der DDR) and later again for the DEFA-Studio für Dokumentarfilme. As described by Heise, the *Kinobox* leader Burkhardt was both straightforward and supportive, and was invited by Heise to an unofficial screening of his next film.

This failed film project illustrates the limits of the new production group's political and aesthetic possibilities. The *Kinobox* mission 'to reflect our reality with the artistic-aesthetic means of cinema, [and] to present convincing positions about current problems and events',[27] as articulated barely a year prior to Heise's unfinished film project, was not approved by the studio leadership, which reverted to the newsreel mission to educate and agitate. As we will see, some bitingly satirical short films, such as Jochen Kraußer's *Lok im Garten* (*Locomotive in the Garden*, *Kinobox* 27/1983) and Konrad Weiss' *Zeltplatzgeschichten*

(*Camping Stories*, *Kinobox* 15/1982), slipped past the multiple levels of control, sometimes aided by inconspicuous descriptions in the production material by Bernd Burkhardt. This became easier in the late 1980s and in the case of short films dealing with everyday events rather than subjects such as political rallies or socialist prestige projects like the inventors' collectives. In addition to the political scandal around a failed film, it also created practical pressures for the production plan and budget, since not enough films could be delivered to fill their contracts to the distributor Progress Film.

Operational challenges also hampered long-term planning for the small number of staff employed at *Kinobox*:

> The fact that the centenary of Karl Marx's birth will take place next year has been known to us for at least ninety-nine years. The only question is whether and how we at *Kinobox* intend to plan for this.[28]

While this sarcastic comment mocked the group's lack of long-term planning, the *Kinobox* staff were also expected to respond flexibly to current events: 'But there are also topics where one could say: *Kinobox* came, saw and reported. The question of victory can be posed later.'[29]

Such criticism, along with demands for greater access to Western media (especially visual material) and the desire for more internal discussion of how to speed up production processes, reflect the ongoing frustrations of the middle years.[30] Bernd Burkhardt's increasingly explicit comments concerning both the magazine's mediocre quality and lack of discussion about aesthetics and goals appear to mirror the concerns of the youngest generation of filmmakers in the fiction film studio of that time. Yet the reams of memos, minutes and reports never quite amounted to the kind of urgent manifesto and strong sense of group identity that inspired the authors of the paper delivered by the director Jörg Foth at the Verband der Film- und Fernsehschaffenden (Association of Film and Television Workers) on 5 February 1988.[31] Instead, the passive and rigidly technocratic viewpoint we find in the *Kinobox* production materials suggests that, ultimately, the real goal of such criticism was not structural reform, but rather plan fulfilment.

Burkhardt's dissatisfaction with *Kinobox*, his support for films that ran into difficulty,[32] and the overall lack of a coherent vision for the films' content and style may all have contributed to filmmakers from diverse backgrounds (writers, directors, dramaturgs and cinematographers) finding an opening to make short films that have stood the test of time. In some cases, it took years for these short films to be approved for release by the central film board of the GDR's Ministry of Culture, the Hauptverwaltung Film. Dieter Schumann's above-mentioned *Rock-Report in der DDR* is but one example. Even Bernd Burkhardt's interventions on behalf of films that ran into difficulty, including Jochen Kraußer's satirical *Der Auftrag* (*The Mission*, 1983) had limited effect. Burkhardt described the film, inauspiciously, as a 'film about the manufacturing of Marx busts' in the report on topics suggested for inclusion in the special edition of *Kinobox* (*Kinobox* 61/1988) devoted to Marx's centenary (an edition which also contained Misselwitz's *Familie Marx* (*The Marx Family*) that had been originally shot in 1983). Kraußer's film does indeed depict the serial production of Marx plaster heads, their uniform glazing with black paint and the dry voiceover: 'the heads must become hard and firm' and 'these are the pliers, that hold the heads together' as rows and rows of identical little Marx heads roll past. It is unclear whether the film referenced Heiner Müller's eponymous play about a cancelled revolution, which was first performed in the GDR in 1981, but the pointed satire about the stifling uniformity of technocratic rule in place of revolutionary energies in the GDR was unmistakable regardless.

As is the case for all DEFA films, it is sometimes difficult today to understand why some films were not immediately approved for release, such as Dieter Schumann's straightforward portrait of the cook Inge Thieme in *Gulaschkanone* (*Field Kitchen*, *Kinobox* 9/1982), while Konrad Weiss' openly ironic *Zeltplatzgeschichten* was screened without any problems from January 1983 until early 1984 in East German cinemas. Despite having earned the category 'especially valuable' (*besonders wertvoll*), its licence was abruptly revoked by the then film minister Horst Pehnert himself after the film had been screened in an event featuring particularly successful satirical films.[33]

Weiss' satire took an original song by Thomas Natschinski about the pleasures of escaping the stresses of urban life and unspoiled nature, and set it against sequences showing petit-bourgeois behaviour on overcrowded campgrounds where ubiquitous signage lists dozens of petty rules for the vacationers. One poignant shot of a young GDR family breakfasting directly next to a chain link fence – a blatant reminder to viewers of the limits on travel in the GDR – may have been too much for Pehnert and the film was withdrawn from all cinemas. While all shorts had to undergo the customary group approval screenings and discussions, the short film format was certainly subject to less high-level scrutiny than more costly and prestigious projects.

Schumann's *Die Gulaschkanone* belongs to the category of miniature portraits of individuals in forgotten places and situations. In four minutes, Schumann provides a glimpse into the daily routine of fifty-year-old cook Inge Thieme, who prepares gallons of hearty soup in her mobile cooker, which she wheels every day to its concession stand near the city wall of Ascheberg (Figure 3.1).

Pensioners, workers and schoolchildren gather in the chilly outdoors around standing tables, and spoon their warm lunch for just one mark and a friendly word to the cook. The images picture the unspectacular routine in a small community. They may not have conformed with the goals for cine-futuristic depictions of modern socialism, but they reflect a simple and literally fulfilling way of everyday life. *Gulaschkanone* as the story of an early food truck, operated by the energetic cook and enjoyed by her satisfied regulars, both celebrates and remembers long-forgotten forms of labour and community.

These time capsules tell the story of life in a now non-existent GDR, but do so in a way that is not limited by being purely GDR-specific. Short portraits about individual humans as opposed to typecast GDR figures, such as 'the antifascist resistance fighter', 'the emancipated GDR woman' or 'the innovative GDR researcher', offer glimpses of individual experiences of life in the GDR that do not have to signify socialist biographies. Siegfried Gebser's short about the ninety-four-year-old Urbans, butterfly entomologists in the Müritz region (20/1982), Nina Freudenberg's story about Helga Zippel, a roofer in Frankfurt/Oder (6/1981), and Andreas Voigt's portrait of a senior citizen recalling acts of civil disobedience during the 1930s Berlin (36/1984) appear as small ethnographic documents in the sense of novelist and anthropologist Amitav Gosh's idea of 'ethnography as conversation between individuals'.[34]

While these shorts cannot simply be reduced to presenting GDR-typical biographies, they do, nonetheless, illuminate GDR-specific content. Helga Zippel in Frankfurt/Oder appears as a passionate roofer whose satisfaction derives from her self-determined work and its value for her customers: 'people are happy when it doesn't rain into their homes' (6/1981). Director Nina Freudenberg articulated what may have attracted many directors to the *Kinobox*, namely the opportunity to portray interesting individuals in their own environment: 'What really motivated me was my interest in humans and their life stories'.[35] While Helga is not presented as a female worker in a typically male profession who has been liberated by socialism, her story is a reminder that, in the Federal Republic of Germany (FRG), women were employed in far smaller numbers than in the GDR and were even less likely to be found in traditionally male trades. Even in 2021, the publication of the German Roofers' Association, *Das Dachhandwerk*, found it appropriate to feature a story about a female roofer under the title 'Dachdeckermeisterin kann

Figure 3.1. Dieter Schumann's straightforward portrait of the cook Inge Thieme in *Gulaschkanone* [*Kinobox* 9/1982]. © DEFA-Stiftung/Rainer Schulz.

auch exzellente Torten backen' (Female Roofer Can Also Bake Terrific Cakes).[36] However, Helga Zippel's matter-of-fact narration of her pleasure in working on the roofs of Frankfurt/Oder presents a self-confident and self-determined professional who – unlike the female roofer featured in *Das Dachhandwerk* – is not to be patronized through the use of adjectives, such as 'modest' or 'cleanly'.

In addition to the many predictable films that celebrate the superiority of socialist production innovation in GDR factories and use workers simply as extras, the *Kinobox* vault contains films about ordinary individuals and their relationship to their work. While all documentary film might be regarded as a 'creative treatment of actuality', to cite Grierson's well-worn phrase, many of the shorts discussed here aim to unearth a tiny slice of lived experience and present individual voices as directly as possible.[37] This might occur by consciously omitting an explicatory voice-over or by allowing subjects to narrate their own stories, as, for example, in Helke Misselwitz's *35 Fotos-Blick ins Familienalbum* (*35 Fotos – A Family Album*, *Kinobox* 39/1985). In this short, Karin selects photos from her family album that reflect important moments in her life, such as birth, school, graduation, marriage, children, divorce and new career, and holds them up to the camera. As she explains their significance, she reconsiders her own interpretation of them, suggesting that while one photo seems to display a couple's happiness, their impending divorce was already in preparation. The film not only quite literally gives voice to Karin's own version of her biography, but it also demonstrates the unreliability of historical images in general. As Misselwitz's film suggests, they can serve many different narratives and it is up to the agent of the story to tell her version.

The memorable shorts often derived from local encounters with charismatic individuals, for example, Trutz Meinl's 1981 miniature about Lothar Berfelde (aka Charlotte von Mahlsdorf), whom Rosa von Praunheim would portray over a decade later in their feature film *Ich bin meine eigene Frau* (*I Am My Own Woman*, 1992). Meinl's treatment of the subject, unlike that of von Praunheim, does not explicitly discuss the challenges of Lothar/Charlotte's transgender identity under the Nazis or in the GDR. The film was included in one of the earliest *Kinobox* editions (6/1981) and would almost certainly not have been approved for release had it been more political. Instead, Meinl focuses on his protagonist's work of preserving the nineteenth-century villa in Mahlsdorf with its old instruments and period furnishings. Meinl clearly shows Charlotte in both male and female attire without comment, and instead the voice-over stresses values like hard work, resourcefulness and generosity: 'He restores and repairs, lays bricks and paints, he dusts, scrubs floors, and cleans thirty-two large double windows. All by himself.' It is remarkable that this frank portrait of a transgender protagonist and community of friends was aired widely in East German cinemas some eight years before Heiner Carow's groundbreaking portrayal of gay culture, *Coming Out* (1989).

Other shorts are rooted in the tradition of 1920s cinema's fascination with machines and the serial production of goods, such as the uncommented visual meditations we find in *Kleiderbügel* (*Clothes Hangers*, 35/1984), *Flaschenballett* (*Bottle Ballet*, 34/1984) or cinematographer Thomas Plenert's *Schiffshebewerk Niederfinow* (*Shipyard Niederfinow*, 32/1984). Andreas Voigt's short *Bilder aus der Giesserei* (*Images from the Foundry*, 37/1984) depicts the young Leipzig painter Albrecht Gehse at work in a loud and hot foundry in Meuselwitz, painting steel workers on location. Gehse explains: 'You feel close and yet quite separate. Understanding and non-understanding of the other reaches its peak in the process of painting.' Voigt's film zooms in on the process of image making as steel workers and painter eye each other up with obvious curiosity. Gehse's pictures and Voigt's film share the same interest in the individuality of the depicted subjects as well as the process of representation.

Voigt also contributed one of the most bizarre shorts with his *Mann mit Krokodil* (*Man with Crocodile*, 34/1984), which opens with the highly provocative sentence 'Once a year, Jonas is tied up' and proceeds to tell the story of Jonas, the alligator, and his annual taxi ride from Berlin Prenzlauer Berg to a dacha in Rosenthal. After Jonas has been transferred to a garden pond, his owner explains the fascination with exotic animals: 'one cannot really get away here', and quickly adds 'because of the large family and so on'. As in Weiss' camping stories, the ironic commentary about the limitations on travel and adventure in the GDR were obvious to any viewer.

Without a doubt, the most pointed critique of such limitations can be found in a number of Jochen Kraußer's shorts. In addition to *Der Auftrag*, Kraußer also directed *Kreuzschnabellegende* (*The Legend of the Crossbill*, 8/1981) and *Lok im Garten*.[38] The latter depicts in four minutes the laborious preparations for the ride of a steam locomotive (Figure 3.2).

Figure 3.2. The locomotive in Jochen Kraußer's *Lok im Garten - ein ungewöhnliches Hobby* [*Kinobox* 27/1983]. © DEFA-Stiftung/Manfred Schreyer

In a tightly framed image, the viewer observes much hammering and banging on engine parts, boarding of passengers in period costumes, including a cameo by the director himself, and finally the conductor's all-clear signal. The camera then zooms out to a bird's-eye view of the train to reveal a track length of just 20 metres till the garden fence (Figure 3.2): 'Twenty meters of track remained. Twenty meters till the fence. In between she stands, stands and waits for her next ride in Mr. Reckzeh's garden.'

On a more sombre note, Kraußer tells the legend of the crossbill bird in the Thuringian forests. The birds were believed to absorb illnesses from children when placed in a little cage into the sick child's bedroom. The bird died while the child was cured. Kraußer uses the storyteller Bruno Greiner Petters, whom he deployed in a longer television film to tell this tale and demonstrate the practice of capturing the birds. While the camera lingers on a close-up of the tiny bird in the cage, the voiceover states: 'Bruno made a remarkable discovery about life in a cage.' Bruno then explains that crossbills lose their red colour in captivity and can only regain it upon release, concluding: 'Nobody knows the explanation for this riddle.'

The history of the DEFA *Kinobox* artistic group offers an insight into the interaction between filmmakers and studio structures and the changing valency of East German cultural policies in the 1980s. The studio made attempts to innovate (by adopting the format of a cinematic magazine rather than that of a newsreel), but it was also dependent on trusted leadership (Hellwig's 'intergenre cine-futurism') and experienced administrators (Burkhardt's skilful manoeuvring) to fulfil ambitious production plans. Talents and projects that pushed the envelope especially in the early 1980s were rejected, delayed or remained incomplete, as a number of examples discussed above illustrate. Despite repeated calls for a more far-reaching discussion of aesthetics and content, and a sense that the *Kinobox* magazines were of limited relevance for contemporary viewers, the group's operational structures remained largely unchanged throughout its existence. But these very structures also facilitated a steady output of short films by external writers and directors from a wide range of backgrounds that were essential if the studio's targets were to be met. Whether brilliant satire, moving miniature portraits, aesthetic experiments or historical time capsules of events and landscapes, these films represent an important and lasting legacy of documentary filmmaking in the GDR. Günter Jordan's assessment of *Kinobox* as an 'ideal environment for formal and stylistic experiments' might be dismissed as wishful thinking, as considering what could have been had the leadership had a greater desire to unshackle the ideological hold, but it does contain a degree of truth. Many young filmmakers seized the opportunities given to them by *Kinobox* to test new ideas. For some, the experiment also showed them just how far they could and could not go politically. However, for others, the experiment led to further opportunities. *Kinobox* films serve as a reminder of the value of short documentary films, not despite but precisely because of their marginalized status.

Reinhild Steingröver is Associate Dean of Faculty Affairs and Professor of German at the Eastman School of Music. She is also an Affiliate Professor of Film Studies in the Program of Film and Media Studies at the University of Rochester. Her publications include essays on East German Cinema, documentary and experimental film, autobiographical writing and contemporary feminist writing. She is the author of *Last Features: East German Cinema's Lost Generation* (Camden House, 2014), which appeared in German translation as *Spätvorstellung – Die chancenlose Generation der DEFA* (Bertz+Fischer, 2014). The book was named Outstanding Academic Title by *Choice* magazine in 2014. She also authored a monograph on Thomas Bernhard (Peter Lang, 2000) and co-edited with Randall Halle the volume *After the Avant-Garde: Engagements with Contemporary German and Austrian Experimental Film* (Camden House, 2008), as well as the anthology *Not So Plain as Black and White; Afro-German History and Culture 1890–2000* (with Patricia Mazón, University of Rochester Press, 2005).

Notes

1. Harald Budde, 'Der Augenzeuge hat ausgedient', *Rheinischer Merkur*, 16 January 1981.
2. Ulrich Burkhardt, 'Die Boxer', *DEFA Blende* 10 (1980).
3. Ibid.
4. This lament can be found in almost every annual report, for example, 'Rechenschaftsbericht der Parteigruppe defa-kinobox', 16 September 1983, p. 4 (= DR 118/3040).
5. Günter Jordan, 'Der Augenzeuge', in Günter Jordan and Ralf Schenk (eds), *Schwarzweiss und Farbe. DEFA-Dokumentarfilme, 1946–92* (Berlin: Jovis, 1996), pp. 270–93 (at p. 289).
6. Gisela Harkenthal, 'KinoBox', *Sonntag*, 11 July 1982.
7. Rosemary Stott, 'The State-Owned Cinema and Its Audience', in Séan Allan and Sebastian Heiduschke (eds), *Re-imagining DEFA: East German Cinema*

in Its National and Transnational Contexts (Oxford: Berghahn Books, 2016), pp. 19–40 (at pp. 19–20).
 8. 'Gesprächsdiposition zur Gründung der künstlerischen Arbeitsgruppe Kinobox', not dated, but likely 1980 (= BArch DR 118/3036).
 9. Doreen Mende, 'The Time Lag of DEFA-Futurum: A Socialist Cine-futurism from East Germany', in Aga Skrodzka, Xiaoning Lu and Katarzyna Marciniak (eds), *The Oxford Handbook of Communist Visual Culture* (Oxford: Oxford University Press, 2020), pp. 293–313 (at p. 310).
 10. Joachim Hellwig and Claus Ritter, 'Erkenntnisse und Probleme, Methoden und Ergebnisse bei der künstlerischen Gestaltung sozialistischer Zukunftsvorstellungen im Film unter der besonderen Berücksichtigung der Erfahrungen der AG defa-futurum'. PhD dissertation (Leipzig Karl-Marx-University, 1975).
 11. Mende, 'The Time Lag of DEFA-Futurum', p. 301.
 12. Ibid.
 13. Dieter Schumann, 'Rock-Report in der DDR', annotation 17 April 1985 (= BArch DR 118/3067).
 14. 'Rechenschaftsbericht der Parteigruppe defa-kinobox' (= DR 118/3040).
 15. 'Protokoll der Jahresanfangsberatung der defa *Kinobox*', 30 January 1981, led by Joachim Hellwig. (= BArch DR118/3037).
 16. Ibid.
 17. Ibid.
 18. Ibid.
 19. See Reinhild Steingröver, *Last Features: East German Cinema's Lost Generation* (Rochester, NY: Boydell & Brewer, 2014), pp. 141–42.
 20. 'Themenplan *Kinobox*', 15 May 1982 (= BArch DR 118/3591).
 21. Helke Misselwitz, Interview with Wolfram Pilz, *Filmgespräche Schwerin*, October 2015. https://www.youtube.com/watch?v=Bljf5iGkBcc (retrieved 22 March 2024) (at 36:12–38:55). See also Jennifer L. Creech's chapter in this volume as well as my 'Reimagining Woman: The Early Shorts of Helke Misselwitz', in Kyle Frackman and Faye Stewart (eds), *Sex and Gender in East German Film: Intimacy and Alienation* (Rochester, NY: Camden House: 2018), pp. 204–25.
 22. Jörg Foth in Ingrid Poss and Lothar Warneke (eds), *Spur der Filme: Zeitzeugen über die DEFA* (Berlin: Ch. Links Verlag, 2006), p. 465. For more on Foth's short Kinobox films, see Steingröver, *Last Features*, pp. 46–48.
 23. Bill for honoraria, *kinobox* 23, March 1982 (= BArch DR 118/3039).
 24. Gerd Kroske, 'Einschätzung des Filmes *Imbiss Spezial*', 23 March 1990 (= BArch DR 118/5329).
 25. Thomas Heise, *Erfinder '82*, Exposé, 15 March 1982 (= BArch DR 118/3038).
 26. 'Zeitzeugengespräch: Thomas Heise', led by Ralf Schenk (PROGRESS Film GmbH, 2005).
 27. Burkhardt, 'Die Boxer'.
 28. 'Rechenschaftsbericht der Parteigruppe defa-kinobox', 10 March 1982 (= BArch DR 118/3039).

29. Ibid.
30. Ibid.
31. Members of the last generation of film artists in the studio had worked for years to demand reforms for less burdensome production processes and prepared a manifesto for the convention of film and television workers. Under pressure from the party, the young artists voted at the last minute to withdraw the manifesto and director Jörg Foth delivered a speech entitled 'Unsere Welle war keine'. See Steingröver, *Last Features*, pp. 5–7, n. 9.
32. See memo to studio director Rüsch on 2 August 1982 in support of films by Weiss, Kraußer, and Voigt for distribution to the CSSR (= BArch in DR 118/3040). All three films were either withdrawn from circulation or not distributed on the orders of Burkhardt's superiors.
33. Letter from Konrad Weiss to studio director Rüsch, 14 June 1984 (= BArch DR 118/3040).
34. Amitav Gosh in conversation with the author on 8 April 2022 at the University of Rochester.
35. Barbara Felsmann, 'Nina Freudenberg. Ich wollte die Wirklichkeit und nicht irgendwelche Fantasiegebilde', in Cornelia Klauss and Ralf Schenk (eds), *SIE. Regisseurinnen in der DEFA und ihre Filme* (Berlin: Bertz & Fischer, 2019), pp. 95–101 (at p. 96).
36. Michael Podschadel, 'Dachdeckermeisterin kann auch exzellente Torten backen', *dach.live*, 10 August 2021, https://dach.live/dachdecker-lifestyle/dachdecker-werden/dachdeckermeisterin-kann-torten-backen (retrieved 19 April 2022).
37. John Grierson's famous definition from 1933, cited in Lorenzo Ferrarini, 'Documentary Hybrids', in Philip Vannini (ed.), *Routledge International Handbook of Ethnographic Film and Video* (Abingdon: Routledge, 2020), pp. 164–72 (at p. 165).
38. The film was originally titled *Auf freier Strecke* (*Full Speed Ahead*).

Select Bibliography

Frackman, Kyle, and Faye Stewart (eds). *Sex and Gender in East German Film: Intimacy and Alienation*. Rochester, NY: Camden House, 2018.

Hellwig, Joachim, and Claus Ritter. 'Erkenntnisse und Probleme, Methoden und Ergebnisse bei der künstlerischen Gestaltung sozialistischer Zukunftsvorstellungen im Film unter der besonderen Berücksichtigung der Erfahrungen der AG defa-futurum', PhD dissertation. Leipzig: Karl-Marx-University, 1975.

Jordan, Günter. 'Der Augenzeuge', in Günter Jordan and Ralf Schenk (eds), *Schwarzweiss und Farbe. DEFA-Dokumentarfilme, 1946–92*. Berlin: Jovis, 1996, pp. 270–93.

Klauss, Cornelia, and Ralf Schenk (eds). *SIE. Regisseurinnen in der DEFA und ihre Filme*. Berlin: Bertz & Fischer, 2019.

Mende, Doreen. 'The Time Lag of DEFA-Futurum: A Socialist Cine-Futurism from East Germany', in Aga Skrodzka, Xiaoning Lu and Katarzyna Marciniak (eds), *The Oxford Handbook of Communist Visual Culture*. Oxford: Oxford University Press, 2020, pp. 293–313.

Poss, Ingrid, and Lothar Warneke (eds). *Spur der Filme: Zeitzeugen über die DEFA*. Berlin: Links Verlag, 2006.

Steingröver, Reinhild. 'Reimagining Woman: The Early Shorts of Helke Misselwitz', in Kyle Frackman and Faye Stewart (eds), *Sex and Gender in East German Film: Intimacy and Alienation*. Rochester, NY: Camden House: 2018, pp. 204–25.

Stott, Rosemary. 'The State-Owned Cinema and Its Audience', in Séan Allan and Sebastian Heiduschke (eds), *Re-imagining DEFA: East German Cinema in Its National and Transnational Contexts*. Oxford: Berghahn Books, 2016, pp. 19–40.

PART II
Documentary Auteurs

CHAPTER 4

The Archives Testify
The Compilation Films of Annelie and Andrew Thorndike

Helen Hughes

Annelie and Andrew Thorndike were creative partners who made a series of documentaries that in the 1950s and 1960s reached millions of viewers. Produced by the DEFA-Studio für Wochenschau und Dokumentarfilme (DEFA Studio for Newsreels and Documentary), and the DEFA-Gruppe 67, their films were shown not only on East German television, but were also distributed worldwide, and their oeuvre spanned the period from the foundation of the German Democratic Republic (GDR) in 1949 up to the late 1980s. Travelling with their films all over the world, speaking and writing about them, and explaining their working methods and the political motivation for their filmmaking, they also became personalities representing the socialist GDR and established their place in film history as converts to communism who believed in the power of cinema to influence the 'dictatorship of the proletariat' by evidencing both its and their own history.

This chapter focuses on four key films from the period 1954–69 when their global reputation reached its highest point. *Du und mancher Kamerad* (*The German Story*, 1956) was advertised in the East German film magazine *Progress Filmillustrierte* as the product of processing some 1.5 million metres of footage and led to the DEFA Studio collectively being awarded the Nationalpreis der DDR, second class. *Urlaub auf Sylt* (*Holiday on Sylt*, 1957), made as part of a series named *Archive sagen aus* (*The Archives Testify*), exposed the fact that former National

Socialists were still in high office in the West and weaponized the archive documentary as a form.[1] According to the directors, *Das russische Wunder* (*The Russian Miracle*, 1959–63) – which was seen by 140 million spectators in 86 countries[2] – had involved travelling all over the Soviet Union visiting regional museums in search of their 'treasures'.[3] In recognition of these efforts, they were flown to Moscow to show the film to a select group of Soviet heroes and to receive the Order of Lenin (the highest honour in the Soviet Union) from Leonid Brezhnev personally. Their determination to embrace innovative techniques of filmmaking is reflected in *Du bist min* (*You Are Mine*, 1968/1969), which was not only the first 70 mm colour film to be made in the GDR but also a bold experiment with a first-person narrative reflecting on the life of one of the directors.

Always understood by journalists and commentators as carrying the communist message, their work had an impact on the image of the GDR and influenced the development of archival-based documentary internationally. One important reason for revisiting the Thorndikes' films today is to acknowledge the significance of their work both for GDR cultural historians and for documentary film studies today. They developed a pioneering artistry in merging together not only moving images, but also newspapers, bureaucratic documents, diagrams, photographs, diaries, recorded sounds, eyewitness accounts, animations, re-enactment, period fiction film and visualizations of statistics and absolute numbers. Their creative use of old newsreel footage was particularly pronounced because, as Eric Barnouw put it, 'archival material had become their passion'.[4]

The concept of documentation was a major part of the Thorndikes' approach to filmmaking, but they did not restrict the concept to direct footage of events. Another key reason for revisiting their legacy is to examine what their documentary film aesthetic was and how it related to their primary aim, namely the promotion of socialism. As DEFA films, their works were, as Günter Jordan and Ralf Schenk put it, always in the service of the state.[5] Owing to their success, and as the first generation of GDR filmmakers, they and their films are fully implicated in all that the GDR stood for, including the building of the Berlin Wall. During the Cold War, scholars in the West felt it important to draw attention to the propagandistic nature of their work, highlighting how their manipulation of documentary resources was always in support of their politics and how they used both documentary film and period fiction film (including re-enactment) to promote their complete faith in the message of Marxism-Leninism.

The Thorndikes' films were made in a political environment in which the films had clear goals relevant to the GDR's developing cultural policy. The filmmakers were active party members and participants in constructing not only the voice of DEFA, but also that of the Socialist Unity Party (SED). Taken as a prisoner of war to the Soviet Union in the immediate aftermath of the Second World War, Andrew Thorndike also returned to Moscow in 1952 to observe and work on the film festival there. The techniques he was developing in *Der Weg nach oben: Chronik eines Aufstiegs* (*The Way up: Chronicle of an Ascent*, 1950) should also be situated, as the film historian Jay Leyda notes, within the tradition established by the Soviet filmmaker Esfir Shub and the film *The Fall of the Romanov Dynasty* (1927). As I will argue, focusing exclusively on the propagandistic aspect of the Thorndikes' work has obscured their pioneering contribution to a form of 'archive-based' cinema that, in today's digital age, has been deployed in the service of all kinds of political and nonpolitical projects.

In the years 1946–49, newsreel and documentary production under Kurt Maetzig's leadership at DEFA adopted a sober tone that was designed to distinguish it from the National Socialist *Kulturfilm*. By contrast, the Thorndikes' compilation films of the 1950s promoted the construction of personal feelings of hate towards the fascist past and combined these with demonstrations of love for socialism in the past, the present and future. The reasons for this rejection of sobriety in favour of a more emotional narration of history are rooted in the Thorndikes' biographies. The pair first met during the production of *Der Weg nach oben*, a film made to celebrate the first anniversary of the GDR's foundation. Despite being from very different backgrounds – Annelie Kunigk was a twenty-four-year-old head teacher and political activist from a working-class family, while Andrew Thorndike was sixteen years older and from a prominent bourgeois family background – their partnership evolved from disagreements over how best to make the film. Both were converts to communism, having experienced the end of the Second World War in Eastern Europe.

As party members and experienced political filmmakers, the Thorndikes were trusted to lead the production of a film about the history of Germany. The extensive brochure produced to accompany *Du und mancher Kamerad* – at the time the most expensive film made by DEFA – documents the immense collective effort in consulting archival collections (a process to which Joris Ivens, Bertolt Brecht, Paul Dessau and Karl-Eduard von Schnitzler were all said to have contributed).[6] The work of compilation filmmaking is explained as an extensive process of sorting, identification and consultation that involved multiple institutions engaged in historical research. The great fortune of the filmmakers was to have been given access to the Babelsberg film bunker, which had fallen into the hands of the Soviet army. The sheer number of archives involved also explains why so many co-workers were engaged on the project, which was not only an exercise in historical documentary filmmaking, but also one of identifying, archiving and preserving film material.

The driving force behind this great effort was primarily pedagogical: the film was intended to educate on a national scale. It was not enough, Karl-Eduard von Schnitzler noted in the accompanying brochure, to say that we are all part of history. Just because we have all experienced war and peace does not mean we have understood these experiences or know how to prevent or promote them. Resorting to the film archives was an intensive quest to gather more visible evidence of history: 'Looking at the scenes, the spotlight picked out individuals and groups hidden in the dark who have influenced our lives, and shone a light onto events and omissions that were meant to remain hidden from our gaze.'[7] Accordingly, the film – a 'factual report' – opens with a statement that transforms the archive into a body of evidence waiting for exposure, while the closing (and most controversial) remark claims that 'every shot is a historically verifiable document'.

In her monograph *Archiveology* (2018) on contemporary practices in archive filmmaking, Catherine Russell discusses some important distinctions between found-footage film, compilation film, and films that deal critically with the archive. She acknowledges that all such work 'is always, already about film history, the history of filmmakers filming people, places, and things',[8] and goes on to question whether only critical archive films such as those of Bruce Connor 'interrogate the media sources of the images'.[9] It is difficult to generalize about what archive film is because the term is deployed in a variety of ways in different historical contexts and over a long period of time. However, the statement at the beginning of *Du und mancher Kamerad* provides clear evidence of the assumptions made in the making (and screening) of that film. The Thorndikes' method is to emphasize the historically verifiable character of the film by highlighting their insistence on extensive archival research to identify the provenance of the documented sources. Steered by the ideologue and co-author Karl-Eduard von Schnitzler, they embed their montage techniques – the verified images – within a Marxist-Leninist historiography and regard this as a political act in the service of peace. The film *Du und mancher Kamerad* constitutes perhaps the clearest statement of the GDR's self-understanding as a state from its foundation in 1949 up until the end of the 1960s.

Today the film is worth studying for the pioneering way in which it involved both developing and then deploying an archive to tell the story of the two World Wars. It begins with charming old-world images of traffic in Berlin the late 1890s and a speech of 1893 delivered by an actor playing Friedrich Engels. Schnitzler explains that the authors were particularly proud to present footage of the history of the German workers' movement, including some rare shots of Karl Liebknecht. However, no images of Engels in Germany existed. The decision to create an historical re-enactment of the visit – 'accurate in all its detail right down to the correct buckles and the exact way of clearing the throat' – is justified by Schnitzler in the accompanying publicity materials on the grounds that 'the truthful depiction of history in a documentary film should not be held back by the arbitrary choices of court photographers who only shot what was convenient for the ruling class', as well as the fact that just 7 per cent of the film is presented in the form of re-enactment (all of it relating to scenes taking place before 1920).

Instead of a single dominant voice, three voices – two male, one female – guide the viewer through the story of the German Reich in a register that ranges from calm and intimate to angry and forceful. A portrait is created of a powerful industrial state that generates fabulous wealth for a list of aristocrats and bourgeois speculators while keeping exploited working people in abject poverty. It is important that the workers and agricultural labourers are (somewhat condescendingly) disassociated from the evils of the state by being shown as creating wealth while living in extreme poverty themselves. In this way the film situates its target audience outside the narrative that is to come. Then, in accordance with Brecht's idea that enemies 'have a name, an address and a face',[10] *Du und mancher Kamerad* draws the names of specific individuals out of their supposed darkness by opening up a book – Rudolf Martin's *Jahrbuch der Millionäre 1912* (*Yearbook of Millionaires 1912*) – profiling wealthy industrialists such as Bertha Krupp and her family home the Villa Hügel near Essen (Figure 4.1).[11]

The work of some eleven socialist historical and economic institutes in Berlin went into the voiceover explaining how wealth is generated. The montage skills developed in the DEFA-Studio für Wochenschau und Dokumentarfilme are deployed to bring the theory to life within the audiovisual event. An echoing, strident voice lists the Krupps' ownership of mines, steelworks, docklands and factories, while footage of them appears onscreen. The figure representing Krupp's fortune – estimated

Figure 4.1. A portrait of Bertha Krupp, together with a figure denoting the wealth of the estate and an entry in the book *Jahrbuch der Millionäre 1912*. Annelie and Andrew Thorndike, *Du und mancher Kamerad* (1956). © DEFA-Stiftung/Archivmaterial, K. Stahnke, W. Ruge, W. Fuchs et al.

in 1956 at 187 million Deutschmarks – appears over their images, while dynamic images of complex machinery designed for weapons manufacture connect this wealth to war. In this way the film highlights the enduring personal connections between the aristocracy, entrepreneurs, politicians and government spanning the nineteenth century, the First World War, the Weimar Republic and the Second World War, and posits these as the root cause of Germany's two expansionist wars. This is essentially the SED's explanation for why the German people were prepared to go to war again, but the sequence reveals a personal spin as particular hatred is directed at an image of Privy Councillor Hugenberg (for whom Thorndike's father, Andrew Thorndike III, had worked), a figure described as 'master of the cinema and the press, a spider in a web of ignorance and provocation'.

Both Annelie and Andrew Thorndike commented at different times on the emotional and physical labour that went into the making of *Du und mancher Kamerad*, which in 1956 was rewarded with a collective national prize presented in person by Wilhelm Pieck to co-scriptwriter Günther Rücker, composer, Paul Dessau, and Annelie and Andrew Thorndike.[12] The film's extraordinary success – it was screened not only in cinemas and public educational spaces in the GDR but also abroad – meant that DEFA documentary film gained enormously in prestige. Recognized and celebrated by critics such as Leyda and Barnouw, the filmmakers Annelie and Andrew Thorndike were feted as the pioneers of a new worldwide trend in utilizing similar audiovisual assets.[13]

Writing in *Neues Deutschland*, Andrew Thorndike described the two years they had spent working on the project as a 'journey of discovery' and celebrated the discovery of the footage with Karl Liebknecht while noting that some 'infamous contemporary personalities essential to the story were missing'.[14] However, it was not only re-enactment that was used to address the issue of 'missing' material, but also passages from fiction films, most recognizably Lewis Milestone's *All Quiet on the Western Front* (1930). The issue of the images' authenticity was quickly picked up on by the film's critics. In 1986 Annelie Thorndike commented in detail on their animation of still photographs as well.[15] Looking at these images today, in the light of more recent controversies unleashed by Errol Morris's *Thin Blue Line* (1988) and the use of emotionally laden iconography, the use of such material appears more acceptable as a pragmatic solution to a practical problem of representation.

Some years later, Annelie Thorndike described the process of carrying out archival research in terms that suggest it was a traumatic experience and is reported to have said that one sequence in the completed film had to be cut from two-and-a-half minutes to a minute as 'it was so tragic ... that, in its original version, not only members of the audience but even projectionists fainted'.[16] The sequence referred to comes 74 minutes into the film and is announced as classified material from the Third Reich. 'Now, for a minute, images kept secret from the German people. Footage from a secret film of the Reich's Propaganda Ministry'. The footage is visibly damaged and wavering, but images of the Warsaw Ghetto are clearly visible, and the commentary is momentarily paused. A Jewish prayer, sung without accompaniment, is played over the images of children forced to give up some vegetables they have hidden in their clothes.

This experience of finding and using classified film became the basis for a series set up by DEFA with the title *Archive sagen aus*. The Thorndikes provided two contributions, *Unternehmen Teutonenschwert* and *Urlaub auf Sylt*, both of which were controversial international interventions accusing living persons in the Federal Republic of crimes committed during the Third Reich. In these films the relationship between voiceover and image is even more tightly knit, leading to an effect Leyda describes as the nerve tingling sensation of a good crime film.[17] A three-minute sequence from *Urlaub auf Sylt* exemplifies how the Thorndikes' methodical approach was deployed to deliver a specific accusation regarding Germany's National Socialist past. In this early example of investigative documentary, a single voiceover is used to accuse Heinz Reinefarth, the West German Mayor of Westerland, on the island of Sylt, of the crime of the Warsaw massacre. The voiceover addresses Reinefarth directly, as the images first establish the identity of the accused by blending a contemporary portrait of him in civilian clothing with photographs of him as an SS Officer. Having established his identity, footage of fighting in Warsaw during the war is integrated into a narrative in which Reinefarth gives the order for the massacre. An eyewitness account found in the Warsaw archives and voiced by the well-known DEFA actor Raimund Schelcher presents detailed information. On its own, it would already be interesting but possibly difficult to follow. The film supports the account with images of the printed protocol itself, animated with underlining following the words as they are read out. As a factory space is described, the images are replaced by an animated diagram. As the executions that took place there are described, still photographs are inserted. The heightening of signification through superimposition, division of the screen, animation and highlighting serves to improve the comprehensibility of the points made in the film and to contain emotions such as dread or anger as the crimes are described. At the end of the sequence, an alternative portrait of Reinefarth is shown, this time as a serving SS-Gruppenführer, now – as far as the film is concerned – responsible for mass killings in Warsaw during the Third Reich. Like *Unternehmen Teutonenschwert*, *Urlaub auf Sylt* contributed to the ongoing dispute between East and West about the process of de-Nazification and the perceived failure of the FRG in particular to pursue and prosecute known war criminals. However, it was not until 1961 that the evidence against Reinefarth became so clear that he was forced to step back from his campaign to continue as mayor.[18]

The next major Thorndike project in compilation filmmaking was a celebration of the Soviet Union with the two-part film *Das russische Wunder*. The opening of the film with its reference to the flight of the Soviet cosmonaut Yuri Gagarin into space on 12 April 1961 provided an obvious rallying point for transnational communist pride. The congratulatory telegram from Walter Ulbricht to Nikita Khrushchev was published in *Neues Deutschland*: 'Under the sign of socialism, the building of communism, a dream of mankind has become reality.'[19] However, the specific political context for the Thorndikes' new compilation documentary was the construction of the Berlin Wall on 13 August 1961. Looking back on the events from the perspective of the 1990s, Kurt Hager, the politburo member responsible for cultural affairs at that time, wrote: 'National sentiment was deeply affected as further developments would show.'[20] *Das russische Wunder* had the task of distracting attention away from the Wall and the now inaccessible Federal Republic of Germany (FRG) by celebrating the GDR's ties with the Soviet Union, a place some 'sixty-three times the size of Germany', as we are reminded during the film's opening.

Das russische Wunder has a complex structure that makes it both an inward-looking and an epic work of cinema. The outer frame about making the film gives way to the contemporary achievement of the Soviet Union's first manned flight into space, which in turn gives way to the history of the Russian Revolution, beginning with the erection of a statue to Marx and Engels on Revolution Square in Moscow and ending with images of the streams of visitors to the Lenin Mausoleum on Red Square. The 'Russian miracle', to which the film's title alludes, is, the voiceover declares, merely a synonym for communism and it is the story not only of the Soviet Union but of the film's audience too. This complex structure is deployed to narrate an account about the collective achievement of Soviet communism across a shrinking world and turning Moscow's Red Square into the centre of an expanding communist world (Figure 4.2).

Just as *Du und mancher Kamerad* had been celebrated as the collective achievement of those working for DEFA, so too, through a series of animated maps, *Das russische Wunder* is introduced as a film shot by many different camera operators in multiple locations, representing the work of the studio's researchers, technicians and creative departments. It is a compilation of material from many different archives scattered all over the Soviet Union and beyond, and it demonstrates both in its ambition and quality the pinnacle of DEFA's achievements. And just as *Du und mancher Kamerad* brought together many strands of European film history to make a definitive statement on the foundation of the GDR, so too *Das russische Wunder* went global to declare Soviet-style socialism the future of humanity.

The year 1963 was the *annus mirabilis* for the Thorndikes, who became celebrities in the GDR. Their rise to prominence was reflected not only in the award of the Order of Lenin in Moscow, but also in an appearance in *Der Augenzeuge* as guests at the birthday celebrations for

Figure 4.2. A young woman queues in Red Square to walk by the body of Lenin. Annelie and Andrew Thorndike, *Das russische Wunder* (Part 2) (1963). ©DEFA-Stiftung/P. Sürling, W. Kopalin, A. Kotschetkow et al.

Walter Ulbricht's seventieth birthday and the election, in 1963, of Annelie Thorndike to the Volkskammer of the East German Parliament. Accompanying *Das russische Wunder* to Berkeley in the United Staxtes in 1978, Annelie Thorndike was asked about the lack of any explicit comments in the first part of the film about Krushchev's denunciation of Stalin in 1956. Reflecting on their experience and drawing out the emotional situation, she responded hesitantly in English with a description of the filmmakers' sense of embarrassment and nervousness:

> The film was an unusual success in the Soviet Union. It had more than 80 million viewers. It was their story and at that time the new generation hadn't seen the beginning of their country, they hadn't seen the footage, the materials... At this time when we made the film there were some things it was not possible to mention. Events were too fresh... Andrew and I were unsure about going too deep into feelings, into the fate of a country which is not our country and where we were not living with our families.

Continuing with an account of how they received the Order of Lenin from Brezhnev, as head of the Supreme Soviet, she refers in particular to the issue of such a film being made by German rather than Soviet filmmakers:

> Khrushchev was also there. It was in the Kremlin, unusually, and he said 'I don't understand why' – this was not at all easy for us – 'don't understand why our Soviet documentarists haven't made such a film about how it began' . . . He was very temperamental, and it was not at all easy for us or our Soviet colleagues because they and we were embarrassed.[21]

Annelie Thorndike's reflections go some way towards explaining the film's enormous success. Although it is true that some audiences were bussed in, it is indisputably the case that local unofficial screenings all over the Soviet Union were overwhelmed with visitors. Like *Du und mancher Kamerad*, *Das russische Wunder* presents the citizens of a state with their own story, as Thorndike pointed out, by showing unseen footage documenting the historical actions of their forbears. The film gives a special meaning to a period of growing prosperity. The central message overriding every historical document in the film is a quotation from Marx's *Critique of the Golgotha Programme* (1875): 'from each according to his ability, to each according to his needs!' Inserted between the list of countries and archives and the launch of the rocket carrying Gagarin into space, Marx's words describe the 'higher phase of communist society'.[22] The handwritten quotation, white on black, turns the narrative of struggle into pure belief in the stages of development from capitalism to communism.

The Thorndikes had to work hard to get agreement from the Soviet Union to make the film. Their methods as always required enormous investment, and a huge workforce spread far and wide was involved in helping them collect the evidence for the contrasts between the fabulous wealth of the aristocracy and the more modest wealth of the bourgeois classes. Here they were following directly in the footsteps of Esfir Shub and, like their precursor, they turned all the documents relating to the Romanov dynasty – diaries and letters showing how they lived alongside the abject poverty of the peasants and factory workers – into evidence of pitiless exploitation. In the process, an exaggerated account of Russia's economic backwardness is presented. Like Sergei Eisenstein's *October: Ten Days That Shook the World* (1928), the film presents the Bolshevik myth of the October Revolution, an account that downplays the role of the Menshevik party in instigating unrest and recasts the civil war between the two parties as an internationally distorted struggle between imperialist interests and communism. As in *Du und mancher Kamerad*, here too the interests of the White Army are portrayed as orchestrated by the interests of monopoly capitalists in France, Great Britain, Japan and the United States, and as motivated by a desire for the mineral wealth of Siberia and Ukraine in particular. The war is won, according to this mythologization of history, by soldiers acting as both ideological and physical warriors: 'every unit of the Red Army which entered a village became an agitator in the cause of soviet power'.

However, the film's real achievement is its creation of narrative coherence despite the enormous quantity of material. The first part mesmerizes with its epic account of unity and determination in the face of impossible odds. One sequence, comparing the state of Russian industry with that of the United States in the 1920s, introduces slick visualizations of percentages and absolute quantity. The industrial might of the United States is underlined with footage of Ford car manufacture compared with sequences showing the slow and painstaking production of a single automobile, the first and only one of its kind, in Russia. The first part ends just shy of two hours with Lenin's insistence that in order to survive, communism must match and then overtake its rivals – a seemingly impossible task given the evidence presented.

The second part of the film opens by returning to Gagarin – a living embodiment of Soviet superiority – and what the victory of communism has meant more widely for the populations of the Republics. Now the new generation – implicitly the audience watching the film – can see how their modern Soviet Union of the early 1960s has been formed out of all the regional cultures formerly existing under the Tsar. Part 2 begins with a reminder that, for a brief period of the 'Russian miracle', Stalin was leader of the Soviet Union. But in highlighting what it terms 'an unshakable belief in the power of idealism, selflessness and progress even in the bitter years when Stalin abused his power and the party bled from a thousand wounds', the film's primary concern is not to launch a critique of Stalin, but rather to show how ideology overcomes every obstacle in its path. The film's optimism is crucial in countering its failure to confront the costs of party dictatorship and the struggle for power. *Das russische Wunder* is not a film that presents a critical history, but one designed to bolster the resolve to carry on. No expense is spared in the creation of spectacular aerial images of Kazakhstan, demonstrating change by contrasting footage of a medieval culture of exchange (of animals, children and women) still dominant in the late nineteenth and early twentieth centuries with images of contemporary life in modern cities.

Watching the film today, it is difficult not to be swept along by its upbeat tone. As an historical documentary including both archive film and interviews, it preserves a brief moment in the history of communist propaganda when it seemed as though the struggle was over, and the benefits of technological and social progress were freely available in a communist planned economy. However, in the 1960s, the question of how the new generation was to be motivated to protect the communist heritage was becoming a real problem for the GDR. Not having endured the same hardships, the postwar generation was to be presented with typified, heroic stories like these in Part 2 of *Das russische Wunder*.

The personalized stories presented in *Das russische Wunder* provided a template for *Du bist min*, the Thorndikes' next attempt to make a film supporting socialism in the GDR. As in *Das russische Wunder*, here too, the Communist Party's aim of building an everyday socialist society was conceptualized in terms of cultural development. Alfred Kurella, head of the Culture Commission of the Politburo of the SED from 1957 to 1963, understood this process as one requiring the appropriation of Germany's humanist cultural heritage, and in particular the classical texts of Goethe and Schiller.

However, as Jan Palmowski has argued, the SED's failure to succeed in motivating the population to engage with German classical humanism can be explained in terms of the party's capitulation to a deeper and more widespread interest in folk traditions relating to *Heimat* (homeland) in an attempt to develop a sense of a national culture, despite the obvious associations of *Heimat* with National Socialism.[23] Part of the evidence for Palmowski's thesis includes a magazine article entitled 'the beauty of my *Heimat*' put together in 1969 for the twentieth anniversary edition of the *Neue Berliner Illustrierte* and based on still images from *Du bist min*.[24] In a newsreel of 1969, both Andrew and Annelie Thorndike, whose diary provides the structure for *Du bist min*, explained the reasoning behind their combination of autobiographical elements and critical appropriation of the German cultural heritage: 'We just thought it would be good to express a very personal perspective in the film. We also believe that personal opinions are only of public interest if they engage with more general questions.' Annelie also noted that 'I hope that I have – this was my aim – achieved a balance between personal statement and world representation'.[25]

Du bist min represents the Thorndikes' last innovative attempt to use the power of cinema to persuade East German citizens to root for socialism and, given that the film took enormous risks with the ideological orthodoxy, it is hardly surprising that it met with a critical reception. While Andrew Thorndike's bourgeois biography had underpinned their engagement with the history of Germany leading up to National Socialism, Annelie Thorndike's aspirational working-class background provides the new structuring principle for a treatment of postwar German history that featured widescreen aerial shots of the GDR in colour.

The film was also the first 70 mm documentary in colour to be produced in the GDR, making it, along with the United States and the Soviet Union, one of just three countries that had produced a documentary in this format. 'The public has the right to the best', declared Andrew Thorndike. 'We wanted to articulate a big 'yes' for our 20-year-old state', Annelie Thorndike observed.[26] A review of its first screening at a film festival in Moscow to an audience of 7,000 mentions that the opening images of a flock of birds flying over Usedom prompted spontaneous applause and the film received a special jury prize. A completely new aesthetic for documentary cinema was proclaimed – one that showed a beautiful world in rich colours and majestic aerial shots.

However, in both the Federal Republic and the GDR, the film met with mixed reviews. The West German broadsheet *Die Zeit* labelled it kitsch, while East German reviewers oscillated between condemning the whole film and liking it in parts. While the Russian voiceover was presented in a relatively sober style, Cristine van Santen's German-language voiceover highlighted the subjective femininity of the film and its rejection of facts and figures in favour of a more poetic commentary. In their efforts to trigger a discussion of the concept of *Heimat* and the problem of expelling people, including Germans, from their homelands, the Thorndikes organized a series of public debates involving viewers from the Federal Republic, the GDR and Poland (including a Polish couple who get married in the film). The ensuing discussions were published as the last record of the impact of the Thorndikes' filmmaking partnership.[27]

Du bist min is a film that confronts an ongoing issue for the citizens of Central Europe. Rejecting the possibility of presenting merely pretty pictures, Annelie Thorndike insisted on representing the regular meetings of refugees (*Heimatvertriebene*), as well as the election campaign of the far-right party, the Nationaldemokratische Partei Deutschlands (NPD) in Hamburg. Speaking in the film as an expellee herself, she offers a justification for the GDR's acceptance of the Oder-Neisse border. However, it is not this to which GDR critics objected, of course, but instead her attempt to deploy a highly personalized story rather than objective facts and statistics. Although in 1966 she had published her diary, *Jeder Tag war schön* (*Every Day Was Wonderful*), which had become a bestseller and, as she pointed out, prompted many women to write to her personally, for some viewers the use of the diary form in the film crossed a line. However, from today's perspective, we should see *Du bist min* as an attempt to innovate and establish a new form for the representation of national aspiration. Annelie Thorndike's biography must indeed go down as testimony to the success of the East German state in 1969, but what it represents is not quantifiable in terms of numbers of lives saved or increased longevity; rather, it is a story of self-realization, an elusive concept that lies at the heart of much of Marxist thought and that became more pronounced as a new generation challenged the ideas of the founding fathers.

At the very end of the film, there is a dense sequence of montaged images that is intended to represent the author as a key element in the film. In an interview in September 1969 Annelie Thorndike explained the vision underpinning her film:

> It is the cinema-goer's right to know what the author's position is regarding the major questions of our time. What do they think about the state, about our socialist community? Such statements, poetic confessions, help art to fulfil its mission to contribute to the raising of consciousness, to cite Becher, and to show viewers how to adapt themselves to the world that we live in and that we form according to our will.[28]

The image of Annelie Thorndike's handwritten diary appears at the end of the film with footage of German history projected onto it. A sequence of images taken from DEFA's *Der Augenzeuge* traces her own career, beginning with the Two-Year Economic Plan when she was awarded her own prize along with the famous hero of labour Adolf Hennecke. Her walk along the coast of Usedom, the peninsula separating Poland and the GDR, becomes a rich and significant cultural gesture, echoing the heritage of German Romantic painting and projecting it into the future through a stream of DEFA documentary images towards the new German state with its newly defined borders. These images are not only redolent of the life of the generation that, like Annelie Thorndike, reached maturity at the end of the Second World War, but their framing is also readable as an expression of the coming-to-consciousness she cites. First, the images projected onto the diary have sharp edges so that they function as a factual record of history. Then, as the edges become increasingly blurred, diary and the images merge into one and the same identity. In this montage a new subjectivity is apparent: history becomes the memory of living a life, and becomes the present.

In *Du bist min*, the Thorndikes are represented as a couple who temporarily lived together in and through archive film. Andrew Thorndike's view of what a filmmaker in a socialist state should be remained grounded in a concept of political engagement. When he first met Annelie, he met not only a new life partner but also a creative partner in documentary film production too: 'Documentary film has to enlighten, from the socially objective, elevated position of the committed author, who represents the progressive forces in society, the working classes and their leading party.'[29] Out of their lived experience of film as an everyday newsreel medium spanning the Third Reich and the early decades of the GDR, the Thorndikes' personal and political techniques for presenting history through compilation developed into the grand narrative of the mid-1950s *Du und mancher Kamerad*. By the time they started appearing in newsreels, they understood they were placing themselves into a historical narrative and supporting the antifascist cause with films like *Urlaub auf Sylt* and *Unternehmen Teutonenschwert*. The third phase of socialism as represented in *Das russische Wunder* marked a turning point, as it was there that they foregrounded the creative potential of women in fashioning the new society. As their relationship developed, Annelie Thorndike's voice grew ever stronger, stressing the need for documentary to remain connected to contemporary affairs, to the 'controversial topic'.[30]

The films discussed form the core of the Thorndikes' development as socialist filmmakers, but they did much more that has yet to be fully explored and explained for new generations. Always working at the heart of the party and seeking to promote its aims, they accumulated a copious archive of contemporary newsreel and documentary forms, and deployed a unique combination of reality, fantasy and ideology to create a series of definitive socialist narratives for the GDR. They even worked with the State Film Archive production team to create hidden archives for the future, just as Dziga Vertov had developed sound and image archives for the future in the 1920s. Up until the end of the 1960s, they continued to commandeer great international forces for documentary archive research and compilation, and pioneered new techniques, forms and concepts.

Helen Hughes is Senior Lecturer in German and Film Studies at the University of Surrey. Her research has engaged with documentary studies, German-language cinema and environmental humanities. She is the author of *Radioactive Documentary* (Intellect, 2021), *Green Documentary* (Intellect, 2014), co-editor of *The Cinema of Danièle Huillet and Jean-Marie Straub* (Legenda, 2023) and *Documentary and Disability* (Palgrave Macmillan, 2017), and has also published chapters and articles on European cinema.

Notes

1. Jay Leyda, *Filme aus Filmen: Eine Studie über den Kompilationsfilm* (Berlin: Henschelverlag, 1967), pp. 108–13.
2. Andrew Thorndike, *Nur was der Arbeiterklasse nützt*. Berlin: Verband der Film- und Fernsehschaffenden der DDR, 1984. Reproduced as a supplement by *RotFuchs* 220 (May 2016). Available at: https://rotfuchs.net/files/rotfuchs-beilagen-pdf/RF-220-05-16-Beilage-Thorndike.pdf (Accessed 14/03/2023).
3. Tom Luddy, Ronald Holloway and Annelie Thorndike, 'A Tribute to Andrew and Annelie Thorndike' (audio recording 17 October 1978), https://archive.org/details/bampfa-audio_03405 (retrieved 14 July 2022); Annelie Thorndike and Andrew Thorndike. *Das russische Wunder: Bilder, Geschichten, Dokumente*. Berlin: Verlag Kultur und Fortschritt, 1963, p. 3.
4. Eric Barnouw, *Documentary: A History of the Non-fiction Film* (Oxford: Oxford University Press, 1993), p. 178.
5. Günter Jordan and Ralf Schenk (eds), *Schwarzweiß und Farbe: DEFA-Dokumentarfilme 1946–1992* (Berlin: Jovis, 1996), p. 11.
6. Karl-Eduard von Schnitzler, *'Du und mancher Kamerad*: Der große dokumentarische Film über zwei Weltkriege', *Progress Filmillustrierte* 49 (1956), n.p.
7. Ibid.
8. Catherine Russell, *Archiveology: Walter Benjamin and Archival Film Practices* (Durham, NC: Duke University Press), p. 18.
9. Ibid., p. 19
10. Bertolt Brecht, *Kriegsfibel* (Berlin: Eulenspiegelverlag, 1955), n.p.
11. Rudolf Martin, *Jahrbuch des Vermögens und Einkommens der Millionäre in Preußen* (Berlin: Herlet, 1912).
12. *Der Augenzeuge*, 1956, No. 41.
13. Barnouw, *Documentary*, pp. 198–212.
14. Andrew Thorndike, 'Entdeckungsreise durch 50 Jahre Deutsche Geschichte', *Neues Deutschland*, 24 August 1956, p. 4.
15. See Annelie Thorndike, 'Ich mag die ausgetretenen Wege nicht', *Beiträge zur Film- und Fernsehwissenschaft* 32 (1988), 45–64 (at 53–54).
16. Klaus Huhn and Annelie Thorndike, *Der Massenmörder blieb ohne Strafe* (Berlin: Spotless, 2008), pp. 11–12. The Stroller, *Kinematograph Weekly*, 1 August 1957, 4–5 (at 5).

17. Leyda, *Filme aus Filmen*, p. 112.
18. Klaus Huhn and Annelie Thorndike, *Der Massenmörder blieb ohne Strafe*, pp. 77–79.
19. Walter Ulbricht, 'Walter Ulbricht an Chruschtschow, *Neues Deutschland*, 13 April 1961, p. 1.
20. Kurt Hager, *Erinnerungen*. Leipzig: Faber & Faber, 1996, p. 244.
21. Luddy et al, 'A Tribute to Andrew and Annelie Thorndike'.
22. Karl Marx, 'Critique of the Gotha Programme', in David McLellan (ed.), *Karl Marx: Selected Writings*, 2nd edn. (Oxford: Oxford University Press, 2000), pp. 610–616 (at p. 615).
23. Jan Palmowski, *Inventing a Socialist Nation: Heimat and the Politics of Everyday Life in the GDR, 1945–90* (Cambridge: Cambridge University Press, 2009).
24. Ibid, p. 96.
25. *Der Augenzeuge*, 1969, No. 37.
26. BArch FILMSG/1/3134: newspaper cutting: Karl-Heinz Mertins, 'Erregende Schönheit unserer Gegenwart' (interview with Andrew and Annelie Thorndike), *Schweriner Volkszeitung*, 10 September 1969.
27. BArch FILMSG/1/3134: newspaper cutting, Linda Born, 'und wir haben sagen können: "Das ist min"', *Nationalzeitung Berlin*, 18 September 1969. The article reports on a forum held with the Thorndikes as well as guests from Poland and West Germany at the Kulturhaus Neubrandenburg.
28. Ibid.
29. Jordan and Schenk, *Schwarzweiß und Farbe*, p. 31.
30. Annelie Thorndike, 'Ich mag die ausgetretenen Wege nicht', p. 63.

Select Bibliography

Barnert, Anne. *Filme für die Zukunft: Die Staatliche Filmdokumentation am Filmarchiv der DDR*. Berlin: Neofelis Verlag, 2015.

Fritzsche, Sonja. 'The Continuities of an East German Heimat: Gender and Technological Progress in *Du bist min: Ein deutsches Tagebuch*', *German Quarterly* 83(2) (2010), 172–88.

Heimann, Thomas. 'Von Stahl und Menschen 1953 bis 1960', in Günter Jordan and Ralf Schenk (eds), *Schwarzweiß und Farbe: DEFA-Dokumentarfilme 1946–1992*. Berlin: Jovis, 1996, pp. 49–91.

———. '"Lehren aus der Geschichte": Wahrheitstreue und Propaganda im DEFA-Dokumentarfilm', in Martin Sabrow (ed.), *Verwaltete Vergangenheit: Geschichtskultur und Herrschaftslegitimation in der DDR*. Leipzig: Akademische Verlagsanstalt, 1997, pp. 185–215.

Jordan, Günter. 'Die Frühen Jahre 1946–1952', in Günter Jordan and Ralf Schenk (eds), *Schwarzweiß und Farbe: DEFA-Dokumentarfilme 1946–1992*. Berlin: Jovis, 1996, pp. 15–48.

Palmowski, Jan. *Inventing a Socialist Nation: Heimat and the Politics of Everyday Life in the GDR, 1945–90*. Cambridge: Cambridge University Press, 2009.
Thorndike, Annelie and Andrew Thorndike. *Das russische Wunder: Bilder, Geschichten, Dokumente*. Verlag Kultur und Fortschritt: Berlin, 1963.
Von Schnitzler, Karl-Eduard. '… *Du und mancher Kamerad*: Der große dokumentarische Film über zwei Weltkriege', *Progress Filmillustrierte* 49 (1956), n.p.

CHAPTER 5

'How Far Can You Go?'
Everyday Lives in the Films of Kurt Tetzlaff

Nick Hodgin

The film director Kurt Tetzlaff was born on 22 February 1933 in Tempelburg in Pomerania (today Czaplinek in Poland) in the week in which Hitler authorized the first concentration camps, Göring established a new police force and a fire broke out inside the Reichstag. Tetzlaff would die eighty-nine years later, having outlived both the National Socialist and then the East German state, the first of which resulted in the dislocation of his family when they were forced to flee ever-westwards, while the latter served as both crucible for his talents and sometime foil to his political and artistic sensibilities. He was there at the beginning making films for the state and was there as it ended, observing its subjects as they grappled with the changes taking place and the uncertainties of the time. His death in 2022 barely registered in anglophone obituaries; few German directors are honoured with such notices, let alone East German directors and still less East German documentary filmmakers. Despite a career that had spanned some five decades from the 1950s into the 1990s resulting in over seventy films, including his magnum opus *Erinnerung an eine Landschaft – für Manuela* (*Memory of a Landscape – For Manuela*, 1983), *I'm a Negro. I'm an American – Paul Robeson* (1989), children's films, television programmes and a feature (*Looping*, 1975), his passing also largely went unnoticed in Germany. With the exception of the *Tagesspiegel*, eulogies acknowledging his life and work were mostly confined to film organization websites and a few regional East German newspapers, whose commitment to reporting such events is arguably as much about reconnecting an ageing readership with its German Democratic Republic (GDR) past as it is reporting the individual's death.

Reading through the few obituaries, several qualities are consistently highlighted, in particular Tetzlaff's empathy with his subjects and their situations, and the trust established between those in front of and behind the camera. That trust has long been vital to the modern documentarian: establishing some rapport with subjects mitigates suspicion towards a top-down practice, of a distant speaking down to those filmed (though tension and hostility may be an outcome or even intention). However, in East German documentary culture, achieving such proximity posed altogether different kinds of challenges. For Tetzlaff to be remembered for his closeness to those he filmed is to acknowledge a quality that was especially significant in a society in which public expression might be characterized by guardedness, a necessary circumspection born of the awareness that candour, critical comments or stated positions might have serious consequences. East Germany was famously described by Günter Gaus, the Permanent Representative of the Federal Republic to the GDR, as a 'niche society' in which individuals sought to establish private spheres safe from scrutiny and observation. 'In this private burrow', Gaus observed, 'you'll find the average man and his group, canny enough to show only as much as is necessary of the social engagement Party and State demand.'[1] Away from these niches, East German public society was one in which surveillance was more widespread, the 'higher density of informers negatively affect civic capital by undermining individuals' interpersonal trust, co-operative behaviour and political engagement'.[2]

This chapter does not – indeed, could not – provide an overview of the many films Tetzlaff made during his long career. There is a long-held – in my view erroneous – assumption that the political-organizational backdrop to filmmaking in the GDR meant that documentary films were 'too superficially political and too tediously agitational'.[3] Such an opinion is not unique to those who are simply unfamiliar with the genre, nor is it necessarily representative of a Western view of filmmaking in a socialist state, even if it does chime with the kind of reductive and lasting narratives and stereotypes about cultural production in socialist states. Some commentators readily concede that 'there was a lot of rubbish but there were better things too'.[4] That *aperçu* is true of most national film production of course, but not all national film production was created by and intended, whether directly or indirectly, to serve the interests of a single party.

Tetzlaff learned to tread a fine line between studio expectation and a personal commitment to his own values and artistry, to find a means of producing films that might better explore and more realistically represent life in the GDR. He was not always successful in pursuing that course. His reputation oscillated: like other directors, he was a filmmaker who at times experienced censure and at other times was rewarded (already well travelled in some Soviet republics, he was also permitted to visit the United States in order to film his portrait of Robeson, for example). This may suggest inconsistency or a readiness to accommodate, but is more revealing of the sometimes erratic nature of cultural production in the GDR, subject as it was to the ambivalences of the Party.

To focus only on those of Tetzlaff's films that provoked official criticism and political censure would be to present an inaccurate assessment of him as a filmmaker always oriented against the studios and against the state. Instead, I examine how Tetzlaff was driven by a desire to tell 'the quiet authentic stories of everyday life' and how he applied this in particular to the environment of industrial labour.[5] This milieu might seem an obvious choice for filmmakers operating in a socialist society with a centralized industry and, indeed, there are many film documents charting heavy industry, manufacturing, engineering and large-scale building projects, but Tetzlaff routinely sees past the work itself and chooses to examine the workers instead, a commitment to individuals that sometimes caused him problems with the Film Studios and the Ministry of Culture. Inspired by a range of filmmakers and documentary traditions, from early Soviet filmmakers to Italian neo-realists and cinéma vérité filmmakers, Tetzlaff has also explained his modus operandi as the 'subtle ways and means of getting involved'.[6]

Apprenticeship

Tetzlaff's career was busy from the start. He would continue to make documentary films every year for the next twenty-five years, often directing two or three a year. Not unusually for a graduate of the Hochschule für Film und Fernsehen der DDR (Film and Television Academy of the GDR), his early career followed a period of on-the-job training on several short documentaries, during which time his role was primarily that of dramaturge responsible for the overall thematic coherence and ensuring adherence to the script, an important role given that the screenplay and concept were often the deciding factors when authorizing a film. Like many of his peers, Tetzlaff originally hoped to work in feature films, an ambition that was not unrealistic, given his collaboration with admired mentors at the film school. These included Heiner Carow and Kurt Maetzig, whose invitation to join him as an assistant he declined out of fear that the experienced director might either prove too demanding or might stifle his independence.[7] These early documentaries, most of them *Auftragsfilme* (commissioned films), served as an apprenticeship for Tetzlaff, who was then in his early twenties. Directed by reliable, well-established, albeit minor documentary filmmakers, they represent the loyal and didactic filmmaking typical of the early 1950s. In these films we see a nascent society determined to demonstrate its vitality and achievements, reflected in positive portraits of the young state's industry and its agriculture or profiles variously of young people, leisure opportunities, and stars of the communist world.

A more discernible Tetzlaff style – some might argue more an approach than a style – emerged once he took on the role of director. This new position occurred at an important moment in time. The late 1950s and early 1960s was a period that saw important developments in artistic expression and while the new waves elsewhere in Europe were harder to emulate in the GDR, since the political climate was less conducive and filmmaking equipment far more elusive, their influence was not in doubt. New approaches in documentary film culture, too, filtered through into East German filmmaking circles, especially via the Leipzig film festival, and formalist techniques associated with cinéma vérité and then direct cinema generated much interest.[8] It is not hard to understand: the emphasis on spontaneity, on the revelatory potential documentary filmmaking possessed, which had its roots in Vertov's maxim to capture 'life-as-it-is', had an obvious appeal for young DEFA filmmakers who found little to inspire them in the pedestrian celebrations of society that underpinned the bulk of East German documentary.

Personnel, up Close

In 1963 Tetzlaff turned to industrial labour with the film *Im Januar 1963* (*January 1963*), his first documentary proper, using the actor Manfred Krug to narrate a film following the efforts of men laying and repairing tracks at an open cast lignite mine. Where earlier East German documentary films tended towards the verbose, a constant commentary that narrated the images, the voiceover here is notably scant.[9] There is no lyrical account of the hard graft, no socialist verbiage rationalizing and contextualizing the men's labour. Brief sentences, almost staccato in delivery, provide the barest of facts, offer context and reassure the viewer that 'this film is dedicated to our mates in the lignite mining operation'. Readers of German may shudder at the refusal to obey the typographical convention of nouns beginning with an upper-case letter. Is this seemingly minor decision anything more than a question of style? Is it a provocation? An ineffectual gesture of resistance? A clue may be found in the reference to the miners as *Kumpel*, a casual word long used within the industry and suggesting the filmmakers' closeness to those filmed. The profession was glorified in communist lore and especially in the Soviet world, miners had long been a mainstay of propaganda images, the iconography combining representations of strength and masculinity, implying power and virtue, sometimes sacrifice for the greater good, and valorizing above all the worker as social actor of a new society. Coalfields and mines were consistently a backdrop for visiting politicians whose appearance implied a symbiotic relationship between the Party and the Worker. Alexei Stakhanov's legendary 1,400 per cent increase in productivity in 1935 had served to elevate the image of coalminers (the Soviet miner even graced the cover of *TIME* magazine on 16 December that year). This heroic feat had also burdened many working people with unreasonable expectations of their performance, since the honouring of extraordinary accomplishment carried with it the implication that ordinary and average work amounted to underachieving. In contrast to the depiction of Stakhanov and his later German counterpart, Adolf Hennecke, who was likewise celebrated for his quota-breaking shift in 1948 and honoured every year (and likewise loathed by many of his colleagues), Tetzlaff's film demythologizes these workers and their labour.[10] 'Don't expect any dramas', Krug tells us. It sounds like a warning, but it could also be a pledge, a commitment to truth telling and authenticity. Expect no embellishment, none of the exaggeration to which viewers had become accustomed (and suspicious). As the anthropologist Clifford Geertz notes, a challenge facing ethnographers is that of getting 'from a collection of ethnographic miniatures ... to wall-sized culturescapes'.[11] Tetzlaff is conscious of this, I think. We will spend only 15 minutes with them, Krug acknowledges. This, then, is but a snapshot of 'just one of the track construction brigades at one of the lignite mines in one of the opencast mining operations' in the GDR, just one glimpse of a heterogeneous and multifaceted society (the recurring industrial environments that Tetzlaff documents point to similarities that arguably invert a commonplace: they are the same but different). *Im Januar 1963* shows working life, unadorned; the work is hard, the risks high, but the miners' ordinariness is emphasized, as is their comradeship. The font is low key, simple. It is not the upper-case title typically used and boldly announcing, but subtle, not declarative. The choice of 'Kumpel' underscores that, just as it implies, whether accurate or not, a genuine connection between filmmakers and those filmed. These are not anonymized subjects whose work is to be instrumentalized, their efforts used didactically, but individuals.

The film's subversion of more conventional paradigms is better understood by comparison with contemporaneous East German documentaries. Werner Wüste's *Plus und Minus* (*Plus and Minus*, 1963) released the same year, which also reports on industrial labour that cold winter, serves as a useful contrast. Though the director was a contemporary of Tetzlaff, his film is more rooted in the kind of conventional reportage, or the celebratory films (*Jubelfilme*), we associate with the previous decades and which were still being produced by less adventurous filmmakers in the 1960s: rousing music accompanies the dramatic narration by Rolf Schnabel, who wrote the script and would himself later direct (mostly) propaganda films and, trusted employee that he was, enjoy high-ranking positions in the studios. Where Krug's delivery is laconic and unemotional, the register in *Plus und Minus* is that of the avid functionary: Schnabel's description of 'the selfless commitment of many unknown heroes' is markedly different from Tetzlaff's decision in *Im Januar 1963* to introduce members of the brigade, something he had already tried in his first film, the docudrama *Die erste Seite einer Chronik* (*The First Page of a Chronicle*, 1961), a film not yet uncoupled from the precepts of Socialist Realism, but that already hinted at the director's commitment to individuals. The reference by Schnabel to 'Kumpel' sounds distanced, a top-down reference to miners and their new friendships formed as people from different sectors toil together – homogenized into 'the socialist community', a description Walter Ulbricht had used in 1958 and that is heard several times in the film. Other than Paul Scholz, Representative of the Council of Ministers, seen visiting, arriving to inspect efforts, barely anyone is named and then only in passing. Voices remain unheard. In keeping with its narrative of heroic labour, the examples of quotas exceeded and targets surpassed, the script offers an enthusiastic litany of performance vocabulary, a sublexicon of the state bureaucratese, or what Martin Esslin once called the 'fossilized debris of dead language'.[12] The talk here is of 'overcoming', 'achieving' and 'accomplishing'. 'It was about coal', Schnabel proclaims. 'It was about the Plan.'

As with shots seen in *Die erste Seite einer Chronik*, *Im Januar 1963* offers occasional close-ups, images of the individual team members engaged in clearing tracks to allow the train and giant open cast excavators to move and operate in bitterly cold conditions. Approaching photographic portraiture, these lingering shots caught by cameramen Dietrich Schwartz and Franz Thoms present craggy faces and grim expressions, swathed in tattered cloth beneath their hats to protect them from sub-zero temperatures and looking quite unlike the heroic representations of industrial workers. They are more reminiscent of the profiles of workers found in photography publications in the Weimar period, when artists and others were fascinated by physiognomy, than they are, for example, of the graphic art that celebrated workers in poster form in the GDR. The viewer is briefly drawn to focus more on the person and less on the working environment. These brief shots re-individualize the workers, momentarily freeing them from their roles. Medium shot scenes show members of the brigade moving right to left, hunched and bent against the icy winds, tools over shoulders; the chiaroscuro quality, the men in long coats, quilted jackets and hats are near-silhouetted against the bright snowscape, obscuring any period details that might more precisely date the film. These are workers in East Germany in 1963, but in terms of both their framing and their representation, they are reminiscent of van Gogh's images a century earlier – also realized 'without embellishment or idealization' – of Walloon miners in a freezing Belgian winter (Figure 5.1).[13] Notable too is the way in which the film makes use of sound to convey something of the experience out in the snow-swept fields. While the film provides images of place, the sounds seek to provide a sense of that place, the pictorial and the aural combining to offer the viewer a sensorial experience. The sounds, recorded separately and painstakingly matched to the images on film, detail the noise of machinery, the rumble of those massive excavators, whirring engines, the clank of hammers on rails, pickaxes meeting their targets, the firing up of blowtorch as workers lean in to light their cigarettes, and always the sound of gusting winds. These sounds are not incidental but notable, forcing their way into the film, just as the highly charged narration, which had long accompanied East German documentaries, is notable by its absence. Krug's words (scripted by Armin Georgi, Franz Thoms and Tetzlaff) only sporadically lends matter-of-fact detail to the on-screen action between the industrial noise, the sounds of the weather and the sporadic grunts of the men at work. At times, the disparate noises combine to achieve a near-harmony that anticipates modern-day found sound collages and industrial ambient experiments, certain sounds lending a background rhythm, against which the tools striking steel lend a complimentary, percussive counter-rhythm.

Figure 5.1. Workers like silhouettes in the snow in Kurt Tetzlaff's *Im Januar 1963* (1963). ©DEFA-Stiftung/Dietrich Schwartz, Thomas Franz

Tetzlaff later recalled that in an exercise at the film school conducted by Kurt Maetzig, one of his tutors, he and fellow students were asked to re-direct certain scenes from Maetzig's own films. One objective, he recalls, was 'not to recreate the scene, but to find a different approach and different solutions for it'.[14] This, one might argue, was a seminal moment for the young student: to build something new with the same material. *Im Januar 1963* sees him finding a different route through familiar territory, an approach that would come to characterize much of his later work: avoiding prevailing representations, steering clear of epic endeavour as an example of a dynamic and progressive socialism, and focusing instead on emotions seldom seen expressed and voices too rarely heard.

In Search of the Ordinary, Not the Exemplary

The tentative experiments with narration and form in the early films seem to have emboldened Tetzlaff, who in 1965 returned once again to industrial labour, this time the oil fields between Greifswald and Stralsund in the northeast of the GDR in *Es genügt nicht 18 zu sein* (*Being 18 Is Not Enough*, 1964–66). Before any image has appeared, Krug's voice is heard over a jaunty electric guitar instrumental: 'We were advised not to go to Frätow. You won't find the model there we were told.' If the cool tone of the delivery suggests an indifference to advice, the subsequent rhetorical question suggests an attitude that approaches impertinence: 'Were we even looking for a model?' It amounts to a shoulder shrug, a disregard to what was expected. Already then, in less than thirty words, the filmmakers have demonstrated a double refusal: a rejection of guidance given (exactly whose is not revealed) and a refusal to seek out exemplars, to provide stories that should inspire. The film is bookended by a quotation and conclusion spoken by Krug. The quotation (lower case once again) reads:

> jung nenn ich jene unverzagt,
> der zu gelichteten kampfschar der alten
> im namen der nachgeborenen sagt:
> wir wollen das dasein neu gestalten!
> (the young ones / those are they / who, when the fighters' ranks are thinning / in the name of all young folk say / we shall recast the whole of living!)

It is Mayakovsky's poem 'Geheimnis der Jugend' (The Secret of Youth') from which Tetzlaff also borrows his film title. Quoting a poet admired in the GDR and taught in East German schools may have been intended to assuage irritable functionaries, but if the last line did not cause some consternation, the subsequent film would confirm a position that was unambiguous in its representation of young workers.[15] From the final lines Krug speaks, we infer a kind of agreement between filmmakers and those filmed, one that indicates mutual trust: 'They didn't talk about being happy and we certainly didn't provide an example.' It is an acknowledgement that the film has neither searched for nor found the exemplars the studios might have wanted. It ends with a curious observation, one that quietly challenges the assumption that commitment is measured by volume: 'They didn't say they were building socialism either, but are those who always talk out loud the best?' As already attempted in the earlier films, the script is characterized by lack of formality that stands in stark contrast to many more conventional documentaries. Krug was the ideal actor with the perfect voice for the script. Already known for roles that demonstrated wilfulness, confidence and mischief, his enunciation is in equal parts sanguine, amiable and glib (obituary writers would later remember him as 'one who never beat around the bush but was always direct in his opinions. Someone who said what he thought. Krug was always Krug').[16] This diction and the words spoken are more significant when compared to those typically found in other documentaries. These are often characterized by inflated language, bombastic delivery, the detailing of facts and figures that holds fast to superlatives and euphemisms, and drives home an idealized narrative few should question, let alone resist. Few would have misunderstood the reference here to 'those who talk loudest' – the functionaries, the apparatchiks and script readers, whether those who narrate other documentaries or those who echo the stock phrases culled from the discourse of the Party.

Tetzlaff's film is no indictment of either the Party or of socialism. However, in its non-affirmation, it does allow space for doubt, and this doubt creates space for asking questions, even if the answers are not provided, at least not directly. David MacDougall has argued that the value of visual media is that 'they involve the viewer in heuristic processes and meaning-creation quite different from verbal statement, linkage, theory-formation and speculation'.[17] Arguably, this is similar to what Tetzlaff is looking to achieve. The questions Krug asks are not a prelude to supplying answers, but prompts to ask further questions. To borrow from Geertz, we might say the ambiguity and non-affirmation in this film has the viewer 'guessing at meanings, assessing the guesses, and drawing explanatory conclusions from the better guesses'.[18] The Socialist Unity Party (SED) could be extraordinarily sensitive to ambiguity; the sensitivity to criticism, whether actual or perceived, revealed deep anxiety among the authorities, especially in the face of a younger generation whose interests and attitudes appeared to threaten and distend centrally planned values and ideas. Dominic Boyer reminds us that:

> The fundamental objective of media control in the GDR was the harmonization and calibration of the knowledge in circulation in the state-sponsored 'public sphere' . . . in keeping with the vicissitudes of party hermeneutics. The SED felt managing the economy of signs and meanings in its public sphere to be of such vital importance to their *Kulturstaat* that it required an elaborate system of control (Lenkungssystem) to regulate mass media production.[19]

Tetzlaff's aim is not, I think, to highlight the failed ambition of a collective consciousness or to undermine socialism, but to emphasize the polyvocal quality of East German society. That in itself was problematic. Reflecting on the closed circuit thinking that often characterizes a self-declared party of the vanguard, Boyer notes a reductive mode of thinking:

> Intellectual diversity would be thus circumvented and intellectual legitimacy would be clearly defined: one was either 'for' or 'against' the vanguard party's epistemic settlements.[20]

Ironically, such reductionism would also come to shape post-GDR discussions about the state and its citizens.

The film was criticized for being too long. Cuts were made and even then, it found itself caught up in the so-called 'Kahlschlag' ushered in by the Eleventh Plenum of 1965 in which almost an entire year's worth of films were banned.[21] It was finally withdrawn in 1966, not to be seen again until 1990 after the GDR had collapsed along with much of the industry on which the men Tetzlaff had spent time with relied. The director was surprised by the studio's criticism, which stood in contrast to the positive reception the film had enjoyed at an early screening, and the more relaxed conditions and optimism that was felt in the studios in the lead-up to the Plenum. Though criticism focused on the film's length, the reason, Tetzlaff later ruminated, was obviously the film's uncomfortable truths, especially the meagre conditions in which the young workers lived. Accused by colleagues of a portrayal that amounted to a 'denigration of the working class', he tried in vain to rescue the film and was finally required to deliver an unedifying 'self-criticism', the sincerity of which convinced no one.[22] Colleagues gathered to discuss his film remained resistant to his belief that documentary film should 'find life and not invent it', and Tetzlaff would later say of that experience that he finally 'understood how documentary filmmaking worked'.[23]

One Project, Two Attempts

Bruised by his experiences, Tetzlaff spent the next decade pursuing a more cautious course, choosing to work on film portraits of artists, commissioned pieces like *Wer – wenn nicht wir* (*Who – if Not Us*, 1971) and *Auf bald in Berlin* (*See You in Berlin*, 1973), but continuing nonetheless to experience interference from the studio. Finally, in 1975, Tetzlaff and his team embarked on their most ambitious project to date, returning once again to industrial labour, this time to chart the experiences of those working far from home on the massive Druzhba pipe-laying project connecting Eastern Europe to the Urals. The result was two films, *Begegnungen an der Trasse* (*Encounters at the Line*, 1976) and *Alltag eines Abenteuers* (*The Daily Life of an Adventure*, 1977). As in previous films, Tetzlaff concentrates on the effects that such work has on the workers, on the welders and mechanics engaged in long shifts, often working 14 or 15 hours in freezing conditions. And like those earlier films, the director, who spent months with his team living alongside the subjects, privileges the quotidian over the prestige or significance of the project.

'Gruppe Kontakt', the name of the working group of which Tetzlaff was now part, gives a clue to the filmmakers' intention to collapse the traditional distance between filmmakers and subjects, to reach out and seek what fellow filmmaker Jean Rouch calls the 'irreplaceable quality of real contact'.[24] Already evident in his early work, but increasingly important in his films, Tetzlaff moves ever nearer to his subjects, a proximity that enabled the team to gain memorable insights that might otherwise have eluded them, to capture moments that less proximate filmmaking may have missed. Tetzlaff later emphasized the value of being embedded among this community, citing Robert Flaherty's *Man of Aran* (1934) as an example of committed filmmaking: 'You live with the lads in the barracks, in the trailer. You can't eject them, nor can they eject you. It doesn't matter that the camera is there.'[25] In contrast to the earlier films in which he has Krug acknowledge the fleetingness of their time with the crews working on oilwells and emphasize that these are but snapshots of working lives, these films are more ethnographic, more committed, borrowing from Geertz, to 'thick' than to 'thin' description. What was often absent from East German documentaries was a sense of the people at the heart of the enterprise, an insight into their emotional world. Tetzlaff combines techniques: we sometimes hear the director's disembodied voice prompting subjects, asking questions. The early scenes suggest that the rapport is not yet established. There is some hesitancy, some nervousness in the responses. By the end of the film, the cameras are simply there, observing: 'whether we're eating, boozing or chatting: it doesn't matter if the camera is there or not'.[26] Geertz argued that the anthropologist must acknowledge that ethnography is not just documentation but interpretation, that it must provide an account that includes context to enhance knowledge, rounding out what is offered the reader (or viewer) by those whose lives are being documented and whose lifeworld may be incomprehensible to the viewer.[27] Such an approach brings the subjects to the fore, giving them space to articulate emotions and feelings, opinions and attitudes. The commentary occasionally offers context, filling in gaps that might otherwise limit understanding. Geertz's argument might imply that those in front of the camera have more agency than is the case and just as it is true that the anthropologist is ultimately the author, the one who decides what is and what is not recorded, the same is true of the filmmaker. Michael Renov recognizes the value of Geertz's approach, but also a problem that has long occupied documentary filmmakers: 'Geertz's conception creates, but does not acknowledge, representation as trouble for the Other. Who speaks to whom about what? We speak to us about them. This is the trouble. Others are represented (passive tense) without the possibility of self-representation.'[28] However, in the GDR, there were also limits to the manner of representation. Free expression was permissible so long as it was not heterodox; voiceovers could narrate so long as they did not misrepresent or deviate. Many East Germans were sensitive to language and were practised in the art of decoding and deciphering, of reading between the lines. At times, the narration (in *Begegnungen* it is Jaecki Schwarz) offers lines that sound more like obligatory observations, the kind intended to placate functionaries, than sincere opinion. The project, explains Schwarz, whose cadence and delivery is remarkably close to Krug's, will be 'jointly accomplished by the brotherhood of socialist states for the common good', but he follows this with another comment that seems to undermine a transnational socialist consciousness directed towards collective endeavour – 'the young welders don't think about that every hour' – before hurriedly adding what sounds like a parenthetical and not altogether convincing remark, 'but they know it'. Again eschewing hyperbole and the kind of rhetoric that usually accompanied such multinational efforts, the voiceover is primarily explanatory, providing context where necessary and occasionally paraphrasing the subjects. It is not the work but the workers who are front and centre. An early sequence of discussions reveals a range of different experiences and attitudes towards the project. There is little enthusiasm, no fervour or obvious sense of purpose. Opinions are often understated, those speaking often sound underwhelmed. The SED may have understood itself to be 'conscious vanguard of the working class', but on the ground those workers complain – half-joking but not unserious – about work problems, problematic colleagues, the lack of material, difficulties with supplies and the uncertainty that these provoke. The work is no 'Zuckerlecken' as different people are heard to say in both films, no bed of roses. While some are aware that their work represents a contribution to a major undertaking (anticipating future retrospection – to say 'I was there'), most cite more prosaic reasons for toiling out in the harsh Ukrainian winter, acknowledging good pay as motivation for taking on this challenging work with long hours so far from home. Others disclose that they could find no footing in more conventional work and that life has not worked out for them. For them, the temporary contract in a far-off location is a temporary escape, this work apparently offering the kind of comfort sometimes associated with a carceral community, albeit with a well-stocked canteen and free movement in their barracks. What is most notable is that the lives lived in these temporary shelters are defined by absence: no family, no friends from home and a lack of leisure opportunities. Human stories emerge as the story of the industrial project retreats to context. In *Begegnungen an der Trasse*, the emotional register of one scene suddenly changes from a light-hearted exchange between the men and Siggi, the leader of their brigade, whom they admire, to a tearful moment as the latter reads a letter from home. His anguish in front of his colleagues reveals the extent to which the men have become comfortable in each other's company – including the film team. It even prompts another colleague, Werner, mournfully to disclose his failed relationships, to reveal that life along the route (the 'Trasse' of the title) is for him an escape from a life of failure and disappointment. In this provisional location for ever-moving operations, the men find some comfort in each other's company and their sense of community is apparent, as is the mutual support and recognition. Though some scenes reveal their relationship with local Ukrainians (there is a long section showing the wedding celebrations for one of the men and a woman from the village), theirs is a mostly homosocial, largely hermetic existence. For most, it is no replacement for lives at home of course, even if they are well fed and able to enjoy subsidized cigarettes, plentiful food and alcohol. Images of men dancing wildly and drunkenly with each other at one of the social events – a scene reminiscent of *Es genügt nicht 18 zu sein*, in which one of the young men, isolated from social life, is seen dancing alone – looks more like making do than a celebration of men without women, of inseparability and male independence.

The film finishes with the brigade being honoured for their work by an official from the Free German Youth (FDJ) movement. In other, less reflective films, this scene would likely have served to reinforce the rhetoric of performance and reward, to conclude a film with reference to project accomplishments and targets reached. But there is a notable contrast here between the stiff language used in celebrating the men's 'performance within the framework of socialist economic integration' and the unadorned, accented vernacular that has characterized all other dialogue heard in the film. Other films might have focused on the event. Here, the film does not stay with the speaker, but cuts to images of the work sites, reminding the viewers of the hard labour amid bleak landscapes, tractors lumbering through sludge, a lone worker trudging down a path, a broom over his shoulder. Returning to the building site ceremony, Tetzlaff shows the men, standing in puddles and in thick mud, hands in pockets, cigarettes on their lips, looking more bemused than proud at the words being spoken and the little satin pennant awarded to them by the FDJ representative.

Tetzlaff's previous experiences may have given him important insights into how to operate, but experience did not grant him the power of clairvoyance. Knowledge and familiarity could not insulate against inconsistency; what seemed permissible one month might later be impossible. The film was rejected by the Minister and was refused permission to be screened in Leipzig because of its portrayal of the workers. The men on the *Trasse* were assumed to be the state's vanguard, but all the Minister could see were antisocial elements, a misrepresentation he considered 'shameful'.[29] Other aspects must also have caused furrowed brows. If the worker is venerated, it follows that work ought to be edifying. In *Begegnungen an der Trasse*, work is not simply hard and the workers hardy. The account suggests that work is dehumanizing: 'The Plan demands metres', we are told. 'The daily rhythm is: line up, preheat, weld.' When Schwarz later says 'The Plan must be achieved', that more pipes must be laid to honour the anniversary of Wilhelm Pieck's birthday, work begins to sound less like a challenge and more like a punishment.

Making use of the same footage, the director reworked the film into a documentary of similar length to produce *Alltag eines Abenteuers*. Beginning with a brief explanation of the distance the pipelines will cover at the start of the film, Tetzlaff, now narrating, de-emphasizes its relevance to him: 'We knew that we wanted to get to know the men for whom adventure had already become part of everyday life.' By now, we understand this to be what motivates Tetzlaff, a desire to connect. 'Why distance?', he would later say in an interview. 'I want to get close to people, learn something about them, get to know them.'[30] Getting closer to the workers also meant getting closer to issues that nervous studio functionaries preferred to obviate and again Tetzlaff found himself having to justify certain scenes. In a tender moment of quiet sorrow, one man talks about his faraway wife and daughter. It was a scene Tetzlaff would not have captured had he not also been quartered there amongst the men. He happened to visit the canteen late one night and stumbled on Herbert weeping there, and quickly rushed to fetch cameraman Thoms. Embeddedness gained them access to these private moments, allowed room for close observation, for improvisation, chance moments, and the division between preferred reality and lived actuality is never clearer than in the reception to this scene, which was criticized and that the director fought to keep. It was only by including a voiceover that explains this grief as a symptom of 'Trassenmacke' (route sickness), an occasional but fortunately only temporary condition to which everyone is susceptible, he later explained, that meant it made the final cut.[31]

Where the first film was subject to interference and criticism, the second went on to win the Silver Dove at the international documentary film festival in Leipzig and earned the director another award ('Prädikat Besonders Wertvoll') in 1976. The difference in reception is more revealing of the arbitrary nature of decision-making in the GDR's cultural-political sphere than it is of the director's willingness to compromise. Yet there are new features that might also account for the approval. One important difference in this film comes in the form of an experiment: the camera team visits one of the local villages. An elderly villager in a wavering voice speaks of the three sons she lost in the war. Tetzlaff is commenting on the powerful impression this made on the team while an (uncredited) woman translates the words. Suddenly the camera stock switches from monochrome to colour as the camera focuses on the red stars that adorn the buildings, each one in memory of a villager claimed by the conflict, and then finally on the frail old woman staring at the camera. Switching the colour palette is a bold formal decision and might have provoked criticism had it not been employed at a moment in which the film honours those who fell fighting the Nazis, a reference that undoubtedly earned the film kudos, but that feels like an insertion. Other formal experiments are evident in the film's soundscape. Tetzlaff organizes sound quite differently in *Alltag eines Abenteuers*. One sequence of scenes plays out against a constant white noise of a welding torch firing while other work sounds of seen activity come into play: hammering, industrial vehicles, the whirring of a rotary blade as it slices through a pipe (Figure 5.2).

Often Tetzlaff's films present an aestheticized view of actual work, scenes that contribute to the image bank of industrial labour in the twentieth century: close-ups of welders holding steel masks and black visors, sparks flaring about them; stylized shots looking down the length of a pipe at the end of which men amid a shower of fiery particles are silhouetted against the aperture. There is, as so often in films about industry, a tendency in Tetzlaff's films to seek out arresting images of processes and construction, of technology and automation, an approach that aligns him with other image makers. In a review of Maurice Broomfield's work, for example, Greg Thomas describes the British photographer's interest:

> His shots generally focus on the operator, miner or other skilled labourer whose dexterity and attention ensures the smooth functioning of the production line, raising them to the status of agent and protagonist in spite of the difficult conditions in which many of them worked.[32]

Like Broomfield, a near-contemporary working in Britain, Tetzlaff does not shrink the operators into irrelevance or empty the industrial set-

Figure 5.2. Industrial sublime in Kurt Tetzlaff's *Alltag eines Abenteuers* (1976). ©DEFA-Stiftung/Hans Borrmann, Jürgen Greunig

tings of its labourers. One might also apply the title of the Broomfield exhibition, 'The Industrial Sublime', to some of Tetzlaff's films for there is a similar admiration for scale, a similar fascination with the otherworldly environment of factories, mining operations and oil rigs. For all the wonder at the spectacle of work, the workers are always the story and never merely supporting actors.

Conclusion

Studies of East German cultural and social life have increasingly moved away from limited and limiting narratives, seeking, as Sara Jones has suggested in her analysis of East German literature, to widen boundaries and erode binaries.[33] The (West) German film critic Thomas Rotschild once emphasized that knowledge and understanding may be impeded by a too crude reading of facts when he conceded: 'I am not suspicious of every GDR filmmaker who, because their values corresponded, especially in the early years of the GDR, with what the party wanted, allowed themselves to be put under pressure by the party.'[34] More and more, we recognize the need to abandon those binaries that hold to oppositional poles – dutiful versus dissident, loyal versus critical – and be more attentive to nuance. After her death, it was said of the photographer Evelyn Richter, who spent her career documenting life in the GDR, that 'she was not a resistance fighter, was never arrested or deported... had come to terms with the GDR system... But she refused the pathos of propaganda. Unemotionally, she documented, in black and white, life, art and work in the socialist part of Germany'.[35] The same might be said of Tetzlaff, even if the circumstances of the work and the director's personality meant that he was often invested emotionally in the lives and events he was documenting. However, accommodating oneself to the system did not mean accepting and obliging it. Evading some directives while accepting others was a dilemma and required some guile. Sometimes it worked, sometimes it did not, as Richard Ritterbusch, who collaborated with Tetzlaff, admitted when he said: 'We did not always succeed in getting everything through without compromising.'[36] Just as the organizers for the exhibition of Richter's work say 'It's worth opening your eyes to', so the same is true of Tetzlaff's filmography – including those films that are more cautious in their approach and that do not illuminate the halo of the East German artist-as-critic. The value of Tetzlaff's films to our understanding of the GDR lies in his interest in getting closer to the subjects, in moving in and amongst the people he filmed, ordinary people engaged in work that was not extraordinary to them. It was the modus operandi of other East German writers, filmmakers and photographers who also sought a means by which to eschew grand narratives and opt instead for the individual, the incidental, but that, combined, might amount to more than a particular moment in time. Calculating how best to achieve this was something that occupied the director for much of his working life, was a matter that always mattered: 'The question', he asked, is: 'how far can you go? Where do your responsibilities lie?'[37]

Nick Hodgin is Senior Lecturer in German Studies at the University of Cardiff. He has published widely on German film and German cultural studies, including *Screening the East. Heimat, Memory* and Nostalgia in German film since 1989 (Berghahn Books, 2011), and the co-edited volume (with Caroline Pearce) *The GDR Remembered. Representing the East German State since 1989* (Camden House, 2011), the co-edited volume (with Julian Preece) *Andreas Dresen* (Lang, 2016) and the co-edited volume (with Amit Thakkar) *Scars and Wounds: Film and Legacies of Trauma* (Palgrave Macmillan, 2017).

Notes

1. Günter Gaus, *Wo Deutschland liegt* (Hamburg: Hoffman und Campe, 1983), p. 157. All translations are by the author unless otherwise stated.
2. Sebastian Siegloch, Andreas Lichter and Max Löffler, 'The Long-Term Costs of Government. Surveillance: Insights from Stasi. Spying in East Germany', *Journal of the European Economic Association* 19(2) (2021), 741–89 (at 776).
3. Petra S. Hartmann-Laugs and Anthony John Goss, *Unterhaltung und Politik im Abendprogramm des DDR-Fernsehens* (Cologne: Bibliothek Wissenschaft und Politik, 1982), p. 70.
4. 'Zur Entwicklung des Dokumentarfilms in der DDR: Podiums- und Plenumsdiskussion (gekürzte Fassung)', in Peter Zimmermann (ed.), *Deutschlandbilder Ost. Dokumentarfilme der DEFA von der Nachkriegszeit bis zur Wiedervereinigung* (Konstanz: UVK Medien, 1995), pp. 109–19 (at p. 116).
5. Kurt Tetzlaff, 'Wir waren besessen von der Arbeit', in Ingrid Poss, Christine Mückenberger and Anne Richter (eds), *Das Prinzip Neugier: DEFA-Dokumentarfilmer erzählen* (Potsdam: Neues Leben, 2012), pp. 157–93 (at p. 186).
6. Ibid., p. 186.
7. Ibid., p. 165.
8. See Caroline Moine, *Screened Encounters: The History of the Leipzig Film Festival, 1955–1990* (New York: Berghahn Books, 2018), pp. 86–90.
9. Examples are films such as *Kampf um Wasser* (*The Fight for Water*, dir. Richard Groschopp, 1950) and *Nach 900 Tagen* (*After 900 Days*, dir. Joop Huisken and Karl Gass, 1953), which serve to illustrate the point.
10. 'I had very few friends immediately after that', Hennecke would recall some years later in Tetzlaff's film *Wer – wenn nicht wir* (1971).
11. Clifford Geertz, 'Thick Description: Toward an Interpretive Theory of Culture', in *The Interpretation of Cultures* (New York: Basic Books, 1973), pp. 3–30.
12. Martin Esslin, *The Theatre of the Absurd* (Harmondsworth: Penguin, 1968), p. 348.
13. Joan E. Greer, '"To Everything There Is a Season": The Rhythms of the Year in Vincent van Gogh's Socio-religious Worldview', in Sjraar Van Heugten (ed.), *Van Gogh and the Seasons* (Princeton: Princeton University Press, 2018), pp. 60–89 (at p. 82).
14. Tetzlaff, 'Wir waren besessen von der Arbeit', p. 163.
15. On this poem and its reception in the GDR, see John Rodden, *Textbook Reds: Schoolbooks, Ideology, and Eastern German Identity* (University Park: Pennsylvania State Press, 2010), pp. 52–53. The English translation is by Frank Thompson and is referenced in Peter J. Conradi, *A Very English Hero: The Making of Frank Thompson* (London: Bloomsbury, 2013), p. 273.
16. Norbert Wehrstedt, 'Ein Nachruf. Der große Polterkopf – über das Leben Manfred Krugs', *Leipiziger Volkszeitung*, 27 October 2016, https://www.lvz

.de/kultur/der-grosse-polterkopf-ueber-das-leben-manfred-krugs-NVET QLMAMCWSLUZFKKC7FV255A.html (retrieved 12 September 2022).
17. David MacDougall, 'The Visual in Anthropology', in Marcus Banks and Howard Morphy (eds), *Rethinking Visual Anthropology* (New Haven: Yale University Press), pp. 276–95 (at p. 286).
18. Geertz, 'Thick Description', p. 18.
19. Dominic Boyer, 'Censorship as a Vocation: The Institutions, Practices, and Cultural Logic of Media Control in the German Democratic Republic', *Comparative Studies in Society and History* 45(3) (2003), 511–45 (at 522).
20. Ibid., 519.
21. For more on its reception, see Chris Wahl, 'Kurt Tetzlaffs *Es genügt nicht 18 zu sein*', in Andreas Kötzing und Ralf Schenk (eds), *Verbotene Utopie. Die SED, die DEFA und das 11. Plenum* (Berlin: Bertz + Fischer, 2015), pp. 407–26.
22. Tetzlaff, 'Wir waren besessen von der Arbeit', pp. 168–69. It was a bad run, too, for Krug, whose second engagement that year was the lead role in Frank Beyer's *Spur der Steine* (*The Trace of Stones*, 1966), which, having been declared 'unsocialist', was subsequently banned.
23. Ibid., p. 169.
24. Jean Rouch, 'The Camera and Man', in Paul Hockings (ed.), *Principles of Visual Anthropology* (New York: Mouton de Gruyter, 2003), pp. 79–98 (at p. 88).
25. Tetzlaff, 'Wir waren besessen von der Arbeit', p. 173.
26. Ibid.
27. See Geertz, 'Thick Description', pp. 3–30.
28. Bill Nichols, '"Getting to Know You. . .": Knowledge, Power, and the Body', in Michael Renov (ed.), *Theorizing Documentary* (New York: Routledge, 1993), pp. 174–91 (nn. 224–25).
29. Tetzlaff, 'Wir waren besessen von der Arbeit', p. 174.
30. Ibid., p. 175.
31. Ibid., p. 174.
32. Greg Thomas, 'Industrial Sublime', *Aesthetica*, 17 November 2021, https://aestheticamagazine.com/industrial-sublime (retrieved 12 September 2022).
33. Sara Jones, *Complicity, Censorship and Criticism: Negotiating Space in the GDR Literary Sphere* (Berlin: De Gruyter, 2011), p. 207.
34. 'Zur Entwicklung des Dokumentarfilms in der DDR', p. 117.
35. Birgit Koelgen, 'Das Leben der Anderen: Fotografie von Evelyn Richter im Kunstpalast Düsseldorf', *Ddorf-aktuell*, 22 September 2022, https://www.ddorf-aktuell.de/2022/09/22/das-leben-der-anderen-fotografie-von-evelyn-richter-im-kunstpalast-duesseldorf/ (retrieved 25 September 2022).
36. Richard Ritterbusch, 'Seid neugierig!', in Poss et al., *Das Prinzip Neugier*, pp. 99–120 (at p. 109).
37. Tetzlaff, 'Wir waren besessen von der Arbeit', p. 164.

Select Bibliography

Boyer, Dominic. 'Censorship as a Vocation: The Institutions, Practices, and Cultural Logic of Media Control in the German Democratic Republic', *Comparative Studies in Society and History* 45(3) (2003), 511–45.

Hartmann-Laugs, Petra S., and Anthony John Goss. *Unterhaltung und Politik im Abendprogramm des DDR-Fernsehens*. Cologne: Bibliothek Wissenschaft und Politik, 1982.

Jones, Sara. *Complicity, Censorship and Criticism: Negotiating Space in the GDR Literary Sphere*. Berlin: De Gruyter, 2011.

Moine, Caroline. *Screened Encounters: The History of the Leipzig Film Festival, 1955–1990*. New York: Berghahn Books, 2018.

Poss, Ingrid, Christine Mückenberger and Anne Richter (eds). *Das Prinzip Neugier: DEFA-Dokumentarfilmer erzählen*. Potsdam: Neues Leben, 2012.

Wahl, Chris. 'Kurt Tetzlaffs *Es genügt nicht 18 zu sein*', in Andreas Kötzing und Ralf Schenk (eds), *Verbotene Utopie. Die SED, die DEFA und das 11. Plenum*. Berlin: Bertz + Fischer, 2015, pp. 407–26.

Zimmermann, Peter (ed.). *Deutschlandbilder Ost. Dokumentarfilme der DEFA von der Nachkriegszeit bis zur Wiedervereinigung (Close Up 2)*. Konstanz: UVK Medien, 1995.

CHAPTER 6

Peter Voigt
Socialist Documentary and the Legacy of Brecht

Seán Allan

'I'm 20. I'm working for Brecht and Weigel. I couldn't ask for anything more.' Written in 1954, the year in which he was first employed as an assistant director and dramaturg at the Berliner Ensemble, Peter Voigt's words in his 1998 documentary *Der Zögling. Jawohl Brecht!* (*The Apprentice. Yes Indeed, Brecht!*) underline the importance of Bertolt Brecht not only for himself, but also for a whole new generation of artists and filmmakers in East Germany. Together with the likes of Jürgen Böttcher (1931–) and Karlheinz Mund (1937–2016), Peter Voigt (1933–2015) belongs to an elite group of documentary filmmakers whose work, although clearly rooted in the traditions of East German cultural politics, has a transnational dimension that resonates well beyond the parameters of the former German Democratic Republic (GDR). Voigt was a prolific documentarist who was employed by both DEFA and the independent Studio H&S. While his work spans a wide range of themes, much of it is bound up with the enduring legacy of fascism in the contemporary world and the development of a visual aesthetic that would enable the viewer to both recognize that phenomenon and grasp the underlying social and political causes that give rise to it. In this chapter, I will focus on Voigt's lifelong engagement with the artistic and political legacy of his mentor, Bertolt Brecht, and in particular, the importance of Brechtian aesthetics (and the concept of the *gestus*) for an understanding of Voigt's 'histories from below' and the integration of photographic stills into his work as a political filmmaker and artist.

Brecht's relationship to cinema was, by any yardstick, highly ambivalent. On the one hand, film adaptations of his work, such as G.W. Pabst's *Die Dreigroschenoper* (*The Threepenny Opera*, 1930) and Fritz Lang's *Hangmen Also Die* (1943), convinced Brecht that cinema was a flawed medium in which his artistic integrity would inevitably be compromised; but on the other hand, his collaboration with director Slatan Dudow and composer Hanns Eisler on *Kuhle Wampe oder: Wem gehört die Welt?* (*Kuhle Wampe: Or Who Owns the World?*, 1932) resulted in a film that is often cited as a paradigmatic example of radical left-wing cinema. Given Brecht's sceptical view of cinema together with his disdain for the dogmatic forms of socialist realism which the ruling Socialist Unity Party (SED) was trying to promote in the GDR during the early 1950s, it is hardly surprising that his dealings with DEFA were often at best unproductive and at worst acrimonious, and nor were matters helped by a fundamental disagreement between Brecht and the DEFA director Wolfgang Staudte on the right way to adapt his play *Mutter Courage* for the screen. Nevertheless, as Voigt's lifelong engagement with his mentor underlines, the insistence with which Brecht challenged conventional concepts of realism across a wide range of media made him a constant point of reference in East German debates on aesthetics and cultural policy.

Marc Silberman is by no means the only scholar to note that Brecht's engagement with cinema reveals 'a curious mixture of willingness to adapt to the demands of the movie industry and a refusal to compromise on its terms'.[1] Nonetheless, Brecht was a regular cinema-goer, and he remained fascinated by the potential of new and emerging technologies such as cinema and radio to contribute to a process of aesthetic alienation (*Verfremdung*) that, by making the familiar appear strange, would elicit a critical response on the part of the recipient. In an early journalistic article of 1925, Brecht goes out of his way to highlight the relationship between film, epic theatre and the visual arts (including film):

> Film can be of great importance in the epic theatre . . . Film obeys the same laws as graphic art. It is essentially static and must be treated like a series of tableaux. Its effect must arise from the clear interruptions, which would otherwise just be common errors. The tableaux must be so composed that they can be taken in at a single glance like a sheet of paper, but yet they must withstand separation into details so that every detail corresponds in the larger scheme with the centre. This fundamentally static aspect of film gives rise to the following basic rule: film is limited to a vision which itself stands motionless but into which each individual phase leads for greater effect.[2]

Given Brecht's conceptualization of film as a series of static tableaux, and his use of photomontage in his theatrical productions, it is perhaps surprising that he never really developed a systematic theory of photography in the way that his near-contemporaries Siegfried Kracauer and Walter Benjamin did in their writings on the 'New Photography' of the 1920s.[3] Nonetheless, as Tom Kuhn has argued, such references as we do find to photography in Brecht's writings from the 1920s and 1930s – prompted in part by the rapidly expanding genre of photomontage documentary in print media – reflect his increasingly sceptical view that, in the hands of the bourgeoisie, the photographic image had become 'a terrible weapon for the suppression of truth'.[4] Brecht's growing interest in photography is not only reflected in the number of images pasted into the journals he wrote between 1934 and 1955, but also in the albums filled with newspaper cuttings and images such as his *Kriegsfibel* (*War Primer*) that was assembled in the 1940s and published in 1955. In *Kriegsfibel* the emphasis is not on the psychological interiority of individual portraits; rather, we are invited to reflect on the triangular interplay between: (a) the original photographic image (almost always showing the 'subject' in relation to others); (b) the accompanying newspaper caption; and (c) the aesthetic 'interruption' or intervention in the form of Brecht's epigrammatic commentary on the visual and textual ensemble. Such an approach to photography, in which a detached analysis of the underlying sociopolitical attitude – or *gestus* – embodied by the image takes precedence over the psychological interiority of classical photographic portraiture, challenged conventional concepts of photographic realism. Just how important this would become for Voigt and his contemporaries is evident in the documentary *Bertolt Brecht. Bild und Modell* (*Bertolt Brecht. Image and Model*, 2006). As Voigt turns the pages of a copy of *Kriegsfibel*, he reflects that 'Fotografie zeigt wie die wirklichen Dinge sind; aber es geht ihm [Brecht] darum zu zeigen, wie die Dinge wirklich sind' (Photography shows how real things are; but he [Brecht] is concerned with showing how things really are).

Brecht's influence on Voigt's engagement with the visual arts is evident right from the start of his career. Born in Dessau in 1933, Voigt started out as an assistant set designer in 1952 at the Stadttheater Leipzig run by his father. It was there that he witnessed a guest performance of Brecht's 1950 adaptation of J.M.R. Lenz's radical *Sturm und Drang* drama, *Der Hofmeister* (*The Tutor*), a production that is itself archived in the montage of historical footage assembled in Voigt's 1996 film *Episches Theater* (*Epic Theatre*). In this disjointed series of images, which, almost in the manner of time-lapse photography, is assembled into an 18-minute work of cinematic motion, we get a sense of the way in which Brecht's productions were internalized in the memories of Voigt and his near contemporaries as a series of *gestic* tableaux. When Voigt joined the Berliner Ensemble in 1954 working alongside Benno Besson and Peter Palitzsch, he benefited from the patronage of Ruth Berlau whose skills as a photographer were instrumental in maintaining an archival record of Brecht's productions in the form of the *Modellbücher* (model books) she edited. As part of his duties in Berlin, Voigt was entrusted with the task of administering Brecht's library and private archive, and during the five years he spent at the Theater am Schiffbauerdamm (where the Berliner Ensemble had moved to in 1954), he had the opportunity to observe Brecht at work on rehearsals for *Der kaukasische Kreidekreis* (*The Caucasian Chalk Circle*) and *Leben des Galilei* (*Life of Galileo*). In 1961, at the instigation of Peter Palitzsch, Voigt started work at the DEFA-Studio für Trickfilme (DEFA Studio for Animation Film) in Dresden where he worked on a series of animations for the 1957 televised version of Brecht's *Herr Puntila und sein Knecht Matti* (*Mr Puntila and His Man Matti*) and on an (ultimately unrealized) production of an animated version of Karl Marx's *Das Kapital* (*Capital*). For Voigt, who regarded animation as 'the archetypal form of all cinematic art', the experience of making a movie out of an extended sequence of individual drawings was the perfect training in film production.[5] After a brief spell working at the side of Lothar Barke, one of the GDR's leading experts in animation, Voigt was encouraged to develop a hybrid form of animated documentary in which sequences of photographs were integrated into a more conventional full-length documentary format. This marked Voigt's transition away from conventional animation and towards a form of historical photodocumentary grounded in a concept of montage with which he was well familiar from his earlier experiences working at the Berliner Ensemble.

Having returned to Berlin in August 1961, Voigt worked on a series of documentary features for East German television. But it was not until 1965 that his skills as a specialist in documentary photomontage were acknowledged in the form of an invitation to join Walter Heynowski's production group at the DEFA-Studio für Wochenschau und Dokumentarfilme (DEFA Studio for Newsreels and Documentary). It was there that he met Heynowski's collaborator, Gerhard Scheumann, and worked on the photographic images embedded in their film *Der lachende Mann* (*The Laughing Man*, 1965), a documentary about the West German mercenary Siegfried 'Congo' Müller. The film's success was instrumental in establishing Studio H&S as the first and only significant independent film production studio in the GDR on 1 May 1969.[6] Studio H&S employees not only enjoyed greater opportunities for travel to the West than their counterparts at DEFA, but the organization was also allowed to keep a portion of the convertible currency earned from the sales of its films abroad. This was reinvested in the purchase of modern Western technology that they then leased back to other production units including the DEFA studio. Now no longer just a collaborator (*Mitarbeiter*), but a permanent employee at the studio with the freedom to both write and direct his own films, Voigt eagerly exploited the high-tech production facilities available in Berlin's Kronenstraße where Studio H&S was based.

Working as an almost wholly autonomous producer within Studio H&S, Voigt made some seventeen documentaries of his own during his two spells with the company. In his 1974 film *Der goldene Strich. Bilder vom bürgerlichen Kunstbetrieb* (*Gilded Whores. Pictures from the Bourgeois Art Business*), a film about the exhibition of modern art known as the Documenta that was staged every five years in Kassel in the Federal Republic, Voigt returned to the relationship between politics and realist aesthetics. Although, as April Eisman has demonstrated, artists in both East and West were well informed about aesthetic developments in the two German states, in some quarters of the GDR the Documenta was seen as a confrontational event staged in direct opposition to exhibitions of socialist art in the East.[7] In 1972, the Documenta 5, curated by the Swiss Harald Seezmann, bore the highly provocative title 'Befragung der Realität – Bildwelten heute' ('Questioning Reality – Pictorial Worlds Today') and was the subject of a highly critical article by Ullrich Kuhirt in the leading East German art periodical, *Bildende Kunst*.[8]

Like Kuhirt's article, which complained about the huge amounts of capital invested in the exhibition by such institutions as the Deutsche Bank and Daimler Benz, *Der goldene Strich* adopts a highly polemical standpoint, condemning the works on display as little more than 'investments' (*Kapitalanlagen*) attracting tax relief, while at the same time adding:

> all representative exhibitions are simply a demonstration of the power of those galleries which control the marketplace. Here we see assembled those works that will shape the art market for the next five years.

While such critiques of the Western art market's role in capitalist economies are fairly commonplace in East German media, *Der goldene Strich* goes much further and focuses on a series of works by the so-called Photorealists, a group of predominantly American artists who sought by various technical means to produce paintings that were effectively indistinguishable from photographs. Ironically, the 1972 show was the first

Documenta in which photography would be included as a distinct art form in its own right alongside painting and sculpture. Presented in the form of dialogue, the photorealist works singled out for discussion in Voigt's film include Duane Hanson's *Sitting Artist* (1972), Robert Bechtle's *'61 Pontiac*, John de Andrea's *Arden Anderson and Nora Murphy* (1972), Ralph Going's *Airstream* (1970) and Don Eddy's *Wrecking Yard 1* (1971). In each case, 'the photograph is not an aid to producing a painting; rather painting is an aid to producing a photograph realised using paint'.

Voigt's critique homes in on what he sees as a process of dehistoricization in all the photorealist works singled out for analysis: 'You can take a photo of any old scrap yard and, if you like, paint it. What you can't paint is the scrapyard of history. That's not a proper subject for the camera.' One consequence of this process of dehistoricization is the deliberate self-erasure of the artist as a creative moral agent, and a corresponding lack of ethical engagement that he, in common with many East German theorists, sees as typical of *l'art pour l'art*: 'art no longer as anything to say about reality but is itself the only reality'. To put it another way, the images of the Photorealists are, at least for Voigt, images in which the underlying *gestus* remains concealed. The inference to be drawn is that the existence of such dehistoricized and ethically disengaged art is comforting for the bourgeois class because this particular mode of quasi-naturalistic realism brackets out causes and questions of responsibility, and is instrumental in propagating an essentialist vision of the world – Voigt refers to it as a form of *Totenstarre* (*rigor mortis*) – that seeks to render it impervious to critical scrutiny and change.

Voigt's critique of the mimetic realism of photorealist painting calls to mind Brecht's observation about the shortcomings of photography in 'Der Dreigroschenprozeß. Ein soziologisches Experiment' ('The Threepenny Lawsuit. A Sociological Experiment'), where he writes that 'a photograph of the Krupp works or the AEG reveals almost nothing about these institutions'.[9] Nonetheless, while some of the photorealist paintings could be critiqued on the grounds that 'this new mode of realism always holds the object of study at a distance and dispenses with any kind of political engagement', it was much harder to argue such a view in the case of Edward Kienholz's *Five Car Stud* (1969–72), with its nightmarish depiction of racist lynch-mob justice in the United States. Described by the West German magazine *Stern* as 'the most significant political work of art since Picasso's Guernica', Kienholz's shocking work was not put on public display again in the United States until 2011.[10] But in the context of Documenta 5, Voigt argues, the political import of Kienholz's work is simply being exploited to endow the other works on display with a critical political realism they clearly lack: 'The managers of such exhibitions are well-advised to place some works of artistic integrity amidst all this commercial art.'

Der goldene Strich reflects the importance of Brecht's concept of the gestus in launching a critique of bourgeois realist aesthetics not only for Voigt, but also for the documentary output of the Studio H&S generally. As he notes in an essay of 1979, 'Brecht understood the ambivalence of documentary material better than many documentary filmmakers'.[11] Brecht's growing fascination with photographic images especially towards the end of this life is also the subject of the film *Eine Hinterlassenschaft* (*A Legacy*, 2004) in which Voigt reflects on his memories of the early 1950s, when he was driven over to Brecht's home in Buckow and told to collect a picture of Hitler for inclusion in a playbill. As the camera follows the pages of the scrapbook being turned by an invisible hand, we accompany Voigt and his silent interlocutor Brecht, as they contemplate a series of press photographs featuring Hitler, the Second World War, global capitalism and the connections between them. Nonetheless, *Eine Hinterlassenschaft* is much more than just a quasi-autobiographical film about Voigt, the apprentice artist, as he learns from his mentor, Brecht. Increasingly we are presented with a cinematic equivalent of Brecht's *Kriegsfibel*, as Voigt reads out Brecht's analytical commentaries, thereby highlighting the underlying *gestus* that makes it possible to read these images against the grain. Nowhere is this more clearly the case than when we see a newspaper cutting showing Hitler (a man who, Brecht notes, 'understood the importance of photography') sitting alongside Hindenburg at an event to commemorate those who in 1914 lost their lives at the Battle of Tannenberg. Increasingly, this combination of image and text assumes the form of a primer in decoding the *gestus* of the image and what Brecht in *Der Messingkauf* (*The Messingkauf Dialogues*) would refer to as the 'theatricality of fascism'.[12] In a similar way, the integration of still images into Voigt's documentary work becomes an alienating device that draws attention to both the historicity and theatricality of the embedded image.

All the films discussed so far presuppose an aesthetic experience based on a series of moving images being presented to a stationary viewer. However, in Voigt's contribution to Ludwig Engelhardt's Marx-Engels-Memorial (1983), this relationship is reversed: it is the spectator who moves around a series of static images. Together with the photographer Arno Fischer, Voigt was commissioned to develop four 4.75 metre-high stainless-steel pillars onto which a series of photographs were etched depicting the progress of world revolution since the era of Marx and Engels. Although most of the photographs are of unidentifiable individuals (the image of Erich Honecker being an obvious exception), the historical contexts in which they have been photographed – revolutionary junctures in the history of the German and international working classes – are identifiable and include key moments not only in the history of the GDR but also of the Global South. However, despite all appearances to the contrary, the positioning of the images on the four stelae is not arbitrary; to determine where the photographs should be placed on the stelae, Voigt and Fischer encoded a quotation from a letter by Friedrich Engel's – 'Es kommt alles darauf an zu erreichen, dass die Arbeiterklasse als Klasse handelt' (What is really essential is that the working classes acts as a class)[13] – onto a computer punched-hole tape (*Lochstreifen*), shone a light through the resulting holes, and positioned the images in accordance with the resulting pattern of illuminated dots. How we are to evaluate this approach to composition is something of an open question, given that the underlying code was wholly idiosyncratic and would have been completely unintelligible to anyone lacking insider knowledge.[14] When we recall that the monument was conceived of by the SED as a prestige project located in a highly prominent location, it is tempting to speculate whether Voigt and Fischer were perhaps under pressure to develop an underpinning 'rationale' grounded in socialist dogma that would 'explain' the arrangement of the individual components.[15] Whatever one makes of their approach, the resulting installation is one that avoids an overt instrumentalization of art (photography) in the service of a crude didacticism. As Voigt recognizes, 'anyone looking for a documentary statement in this photographic panorama of history will be disappointed'.[16] Part of the reason for this lies in the fact that, in stark contrast to Voigt's documentary films, it is not the images that move, but rather the spectator, who in the manner of a *flâneur* wanders around the photographs assembling them into new and ever-changing combinations that bring into play not only the photographs on the other stelae, but also the surrounding reliefs and sculptures by Werner Stötzer, Margret Middell and Engelhardt.[17] This reversal of the traditional relationship between spectator and image is, at least in part, a reflection of Voigt's conviction that 'even when dealing with documentary material, the only thing you can prove is your subjective view of the world'.[18] At the same time, by showing history to be a dynamic and ongoing process of erasure and rewriting, the installation anticipates the creative response provided by Jürgen Böttcher's avant-garde documentary *Konzert im Freien* (*A Place in Berlin*, 2001) that is played out against the background of Engelhardt's installation.

Just as the irreverent treatment of the socialist icons Marx and Engels is mirrored in the free jazz riffs performed by the East German musicians Günter 'Baby' Sommer and Dietmar Diesner, so too Fischer and Voigt's graffiti-covered stelae bear witness to the rewriting of socialist history from the perspective of a new post-*Wende* generation.

When viewed in the context of Engelhardt's larger-than-life statues of Marx and Engels, the photographs Fischer and Voigt use to narrate their transnational history of the working classes take on the character of a series of miniatures. Nonetheless, the underlying principle of the microimages etched onto the massive stelae serves as a reminder that, in the construction of alternative (nonbourgeois) histories of humanity, it is the *gestus* underpinning a given historical representation that matters more than its size and scale, for, as Voigt notes, 'even a contact print can capture a sense of monumentalism'.[19] Indeed, the power of the miniature (both visual and textual) to disrupt conventional narratives of history is a consequence of the way in which the reduced size and scale of the miniature reveal the attributes of what is being represented with special clarity.

This process of textual and cinematic 'miniaturization' is evident in Voigt's *Martha Lehmann – Eisenbahnerin* (*Martha Lehmann – Railway Worker*, 1972), a short 13-minute film that is often regarded as a cinematic riff on Brecht's short story *Die unwürdige Greisin* (*The Shameless Old Lady*) of 1948/1949. Like the old lady of Brecht's story, the railway worker Martha Lehmann in Voigt's film is a truly unremarkable individual. However, the real impulse behind Voigt's film was the discovery of a vast collection of bank receipts on the back of which the film's protagonist had scribbled brief (miniaturist) observations, which, taken together, offer an incisive commentary on the history of the end of the Second World War and the rise of socialism in the GDR. At the same time, this history filmed 'from below' has an obvious affinity with the discursive strategy adopted by Brecht in his well-known poem of 1935 'Fragen eines lesenden Arbeiters' ('Questions from a Worker Who Reads'), and when we recall Brecht's remark that 'Alle großen Gedichte haben den Wert von Dokumenten' (All great poems have the value of documents), it is easy to understand why Voigt should regard the documentary films that reveal the contradictions of lived experience and situate them within an identifiable historical context as the cinematic counterpart to Brecht's poetry.[20]

In the course of Voigt's brief film, the turning points of postwar German history are played out in the form of trains that pass by Martha Lehmann's remotely situated level-crossing and that, in 1948, carry German prisoners of war (POWs) returning from the Eastern Front (though sadly not her own son, Rudi) and that, in 1951, convey enthusiastic international participants in the III. Weltfestspiele der Jugend und Studenten (3rd World Festival of Youth and Students) to their final destination in East Berlin. In Martha Lehmann's concise formulations that, precisely because of their compressed format – 'Politics and looking after the level crossing'; 'Wishing for peace and working in the garden' – assume an almost epigrammatic quality, the experience of the present is entangled with memories of the past and mediated via the subjective viewpoint of a lowly working woman. In a similar vein, while Martha's donations in support of the victims of the conflicts in Korea and Algeria are given as an act of remembrance for her own son's sacrifice in the Second World War, they offer the viewer an alternative perspective (both in terms of class and gender) from which to reflect on events taking place on the wider political stage. Seen in this light, Voigt's short film *Martha Lehmann* presents us with a miniature of a woman of no importance, but when viewed through the lens of the underpinning *gestus* that the film supplies, her story assumes a significance that exceeds the parameters of her restricted existence.

In *Martha Lehman – Eisenbahnerin*, Voigt's presents a Brechtian critique of conventional (bourgeois) historical discourse by deploying an essentially unknown female protagonist; in his feature-length documentary *Theaterarbeit* (*Theater Work*, 1975), he adopted a similar approach, but here the subject of his analysis was of one of the most celebrated institutions in the GDR, the Berliner Ensemble. Produced by Studio H&S, *Theaterarbeit* was released in 1975 to mark the twenty-fifth anniversary of Brecht's and Weigel's founding of the Berliner Ensemble, and its title contains an obvious allusion to the published volumes in which Brecht documented and commented on the productions of his plays. In stark contrast to films such as Kurt Tetzlaff's short documentary of 1978, *Die Pflaumenbäume sind wohl abgehauen* (*The Plum Trees Have Surely Been Cut Down*), where the focus is predominantly on Brecht's bohemian lifestyle and his rejection of conventional morality, Voigt's film moves away from 'personality'. The film focuses instead on the playwright's rejection of bourgeois norms of art and goes out of its way to present artistic creativity as a process of collective rather than individual labour. But perhaps the most striking aspect of *Theaterarbeit* is the way in which the history of the Berliner Ensemble is narrated primarily from the perspective of the technicians at work behind the scenes at the Theater am Schiffbauerdamm, which, as of 1954, had become home to the Berliner Ensemble.

As the film unfolds, the viewer is offered glimpses of the stars of the ensemble such as Gisela May, Ekkehard Schall, Jutta Hoffmann and the renowned choreographer and opera director Ruth Berghaus. Those familiar with Brecht's oeuvre will also recognize snippets from his plays *Coriolan* (*Coriolanus*), *Im Dickicht der Städte* (*In the Jungle of the Cities*), *Die Mutter* (*The Mother*), *Die Gewehre der Frau Carrar* (*Senora Carrar's Rifles*) and *Die Dreigroschenoper* (*The Threepenny Opera*). However, once again in the spirit of Brecht's poem 'Fragen eines lesenden Arbeiters', the true 'stars' of this history of the Berliner Ensemble from below turn out to be the technicians working backstage, in the lighting booth and in the workshops where the scenery, props and costumes are being fabricated (Figure 6.1).

As the film shows, their work is not preserved for posterity, but is dismantled, packed away and, almost always, discarded. But by making visible what is normally concealed from view, Voigt's film demystifies the process of artistic creativity and emphasises the collectivist character of the work taking place both on and off-stage.

On one level, the film reflects the high esteem in which Voigt held his mentor, Brecht, but on another level, his documentary goes out of its way to emphasize that the work of a creative ensemble cannot be

Figure 6.1. *Theaterarbeit* (Peter Voigt, 1975). © DEFA-Stiftung

equated with the work of just one individual. 'Everyone can be replaced', one of the technicians comments, 'the only question is how?' With that observation in mind, *Theaterarbeit* explores the inevitable threat of stagnation that accompanies artistic reputation. 'When Brecht died', Helene Weigel comments in the voiceover, 'I was worried that the whole thing might become a kind of museum.' Yet just how well the theatre technicians have internalized the basic thrust of Brecht's dialectical materialism aesthetics is evident in their observation that 'elevating Brecht to the status of a god or demigod – so we're afraid to say anything negative about things he wrote a long time ago is a fundamental problem'. And as the enduring popularity of *Der Dreigroschenoper* underlines, no theatrical production – however revolutionary it may have once been – can resist its incorporation over time into the canonical repertoire of bourgeois theatre. Seen from this perspective, the removal of Brecht's production of *Der Dreigroschenoper* after its 600th performance is not only a tribute to Brecht's enduring reputation as a writer and director, but also a reminder of the Berliner Ensemble's efforts to resist the process of musealization through the introduction of new plays and new productions. As the integration of footage from a production of the 1972 drama *Zement* (*Cement*) by Heiner Müller, the dramatist many would see as Brecht's antithetical successor, underlines, Brecht's impact lives on in an ongoing process of dialectical reworking that show few signs of coming to an end.

Brecht and the legacy of his creative activity at the Berliner Ensemble lies at the heart of many of Voigt's films, including *Dämmerung – Ostberliner Bohème der 50er Jahre* (*Dusk – East Berlin Bohemia in the 1950s*, 1993), *Jawohl, Brecht, Der Zögling* and *Bertolt Brecht – Bild und Modell*. However, it is important to remember that the playwright's iconic status in the eyes of Voigt and his contemporaries was, to a large extent, due to his reluctance to toe the line in respect of the ruling SED. Although Brecht's importance for the cultural-political profile of the GDR can hardly be overstated, he was, at least to begin with, reluctant to settle in what was then the Soviet Zone of Occupation. Despite the best efforts of the Soviet Cultural Officer Alexander Dymschitz to entice Brecht to the East in 1947, the playwright felt more inclined to settle in Switzerland, and it was not until October 1948 that he went to the Soviet Zone together with his wife, Helene Weigel.[21] Brecht's production of *Mother Courage* in East Berlin in January 1949 was widely praised in both East and West, and resonated powerfully with postwar German audiences. However, even at this early stage, the tensions in East German cultural politics, which would later be unleashed by the provocative aesthetics of his theory of epic theatre and his distinctive take on realism, are discernible in a review of *Leben des Galilei* published by Fritz Erpenbeck in *Theater der Zeit* on 17 January 1949. Erpenbeck was just one of several cultural theorists in the East who both endorsed the dogmatic version of socialist realism promoted in the 1930s by Andrei Zhdanov in the Soviet Union and who, accordingly, recognized the challenge presented by Brechtian dramaturgy and its renegotiation of the concept of realism. Erpenbeck's criticism of *Mutter Courage* had been just the opening salvo in what would be a series of increasingly acrimonious attacks on Brecht's work, which occurred in the wake of the anti-Formalist campaigns of the early 1950s. In what might be regarded as a rerun of the Expressionist Debate of the late 1930s, critics like Erpenbeck and Wilhelm Girnus (the arts editor of the East German daily *Neues Deutschland*) warned of the threat posed by the fragmentary aesthetics of modernist works of art, which, in their view, emanated from a decadent bourgeois mindset that was ill-suited to re-educating the population of the fledgling Workers and Peasants State. All of this would come to a head in 1951 with the controversy unleashed by the Berliner Staatsoper's production of Brecht and Dessau's modernist opera, *Die Verurteilung des Lukullus* (*The Condemnation of Lukullus*).

Memories of the 1950s are the subject of Voigt's 1993 documentary *Dämmerung – Ostberliner Bohème der 50er Jahre*, a highly ambivalent film released after the collapse of the GDR in which a range of actors, artists and models, many of them connected with the Berliner Ensemble, look back at their bohemian lifestyles during the 1950s. Filmed in the almost derelict restaurant Ganymed formerly frequented by Brecht and his ensemble, the film has an elegiac quality to it without ever lapsing into sentimentalism. Although Brecht does not feature directly in the film, his shadow looms large over many of the sequences, including that shot in Berlin's celebrated Dorotheenstadt Cemetery where he and Weigel are laid to rest and where the funeral of Wolf Kaiser, perhaps best known for his portrayal of Mackie Messer in *Der Dreigroschenoper*, is taking place. Kaiser, who had taken his own life on 22 October 1992, is just one example of those for whom the collapse of the GDR in 1990 was experienced as a personal existential crisis. In the course of Voigt's film, the viewer is presented with a range of conflicting memories of the past, many of which turn out to be either unreliable, contradictory or both. When invited to reflect on the 1950s, an era now often dismissed by cultural historians as a period of dogmatic politics and artistic stagnation, the sculptor Werner Stötzer declares that 'Life was wonderful back then'. Yet the upbeat tone of Stötzer's initial observation is itself relativized through the simultaneous montage of newsreels featuring Stalin and other forms of documentary footage focusing on traumatic events in the East German historical imaginary such as the Workers' Uprising of 17 June 1953 and the Soviet suppression of the Hungarian Revolution of 1956. By portraying Stötzer and his other interviewees against such a background, Voigt's film offers a visual counterpoint to the heady optimism of the bohemians for whom the GDR held out the promise of a radical new departure in the arts. But not all the participants in the film have such positive memories of the East German past as Stötzer, Brecht's daughter Barbara Brecht-Schall and her husband, the well-known actor from the Berliner Ensemble, Ekkehard Schall. The set designer Igael Turmakin, now living and working in Tel Aviv, recounts how he was subjected to antisemitic abuse while working at the Berliner Ensemble; and the masculinist bias of a bohemian world in which women are treated essentially as decorative objectives is painfully revealed when Voigt interviews his wife, the model and journalist, Jutta Voigt, and her friends Barbara Lübbert, a model for the East German fashion magazine *Sibylle*, and the translator Ingrid Lechner (Figure 6.2).

For Rudi Ebeling, the artist and founder of the modernist gallery *Konkret* – shut down in 1961 after less than a year of operation because of the formalist tendencies of the works on display – the memories of his utopian aspirations are inextricably bound up with the disappointments of the past. In the architect Gerd Zeuchner's testimony, the crushing impact of socialist realism is evident in his account of Horst Strempel's 'Trümmer weg – baut auf!' ('Away with the rubble – rebuild!'). Strempel's mural in the manner of Oskar Schlemmer was installed as a work of public art in Friedrichstraße station in 1948 – a transitional moment in history where everything seemed possible – only to be removed in 1951 in the wake of the SED's drive to promote the aesthetics of socialist realism to the exclusion of all else. Finally, the film reminds the viewer of the difficulties experienced by John Heartfield, best known for his photomontages of the 1930s and 1940s ridiculing Hitler, in establishing himself as an artist in the antifascist German state because of the avant-garde character of his works.

However, the film *Dämmerung* is much more than just a nostalgic glimpse of the past and what might have been. As Claus Löser has noted, its very title – connoting simultaneously both dawn and dusk – is shot through with an inherent ambiguity and evokes not only the onset of a new era, the 1950s and the early days of the fledgling state, but also the demise of the last traces of that period in the post-unification world

Figure 6.2. *Dämmerung* (Peter Voigt, 1993). © DEFA-Stiftung

of 1992. At times, the protagonists appear to be almost stranded in a historical no-man's land. Many of those featured identify with a form of socialist modernism in the early phase of the GDR that sought to steer a course between, on the one hand, the monolithic monumentalism of socialist realism in the Eastern Bloc and, on the other hand, the extreme subjectivity of self-referential *l'art pour l'art* aesthetics in the West. Yet, as the film shows, these avant-garde outsiders in the divided Berlin of the 1950s who chose to throw their weight behind the socialist project now find themselves stranded in another waiting room of history, the post-*Wende* Berlin of the 1990s, with only their memories of the past for company.

In *Dämmerung*, Voigt's interviewees are often to be found watching footage of the film on video screens or speaking against a montage of newsreels and documentary features from the past. In this respect, Voigt's film can be seen as a natural extension of his earlier work in which the insertion of photographs into the body of his films serves to both relativize and comment on what we just seen on screen by revealing its underlying *gestus*. Brecht's influence in the development of this aesthetic approach is obvious in an interview with Voigt, conducted by the film scholar Rüdiger Steinmetz, in which he casts his mind back to the situation depicted in *Hinterlassenschaft*: 'That half an hour in which all he did was turn the pages of the photo-album, that was when I knew I could move on from the theatre and do so without turning my back on Brecht.'[22] Whether in the form of his critique of the works of the Photorealists in *Der goldene Strich* or in the arrangement of photographs of proletarian history etched onto the stelae at the Marx-Engels-Forum Voigt's grasp of photomontage and of the importance of the Brechtian *gestus* for the production of politically radical art underpins almost all his work as a political filmmaker. What Voigt succeeds in doing, above all else, is revealing the historical forces that are at work in the construction and reproduction of a contemporary image. Strikingly, the films Voigt completed about his mentor Brecht as well as ultimately unrealized projects such as *Brechts Wände* (*Brecht's Walls*) do not present the viewer with a psychological portrait; rather, they propose a series of images – notably the images hanging on the walls of the playwright's study – as a means of understanding Brecht's significance and modus operandi. However, the real strength of Voigt's work lies in the way in which it deploys Brecht's concept of dialectical materialism as a means of preventing stagnation. Something of this approach is evident in an 1978 essay entitled 'Wozu Brecht für Dokumentaristen?' ('What's the Importance of Brecht for Documentarists?'): 'Anyone wanting to take their cue from Brecht. . . must embrace his way of working in its entirety. . . . They mustn't ask which bits they agree with, rather the key question is what the differences between him and us are.'[23] Written in 1978, these words underpin not only his forward-looking reportage on the Berliner Ensemble at twenty-five that we find in *Theaterarbeit*, but also form the underlying principle of Voigt's lifelong engagement with his mentor Brecht.

Seán Allan is Professor of German at the University of St Andrews and holds a Joint Research Professorship for Neuere Deutsche Literaturwissenschaft at the University of Bonn. His main research areas are Heinrich von Kleist, the culture of the European Enlightenment and the cinema in the GDR. His publications include *DEFA: East German Cinema, 1946–1992* (co-edited with John Sandford, Berghahn Books, 1996), *Unverhoffte Wirkungen. Erziehung und Gewalt im Werk Heinrich von Kleists* (co-authored with Ricarda Schmidt and Steven Howe, K&N, 2014), *Re-imagining DEFA: East German Cinema in Its National and Transnational Contexts* (co-edited with Sebastian Heiduschke, Berghahn Books, 2016), *Screening Art: Modernism and the Socialist Imaginary in East German Cinema* (Berghahn Books, 2019) and *Inspiration Bonaparte: German Culture under Napoleonic Occupation* (Camden House, 2021).

Notes

1. Marc Silberman (ed. and trans.), *Bertolt Brecht on Film and Radio* (London: Methuen, 2000), p. xiv.
2. Ibid., pp. 6–7; 'Aus dem ABC des epischen Theaters', unpublished typescript, 1927. See also Werner Hecht, Jan Knopf, Werner Mittenzwei and Klaus-Detlef Müller (eds), *Bertolt Brecht. Werke. Große kommentierte Berliner und Franfurter Ausgabe*, vol. 21 (Berlin, Weimar and Frankfurt am Main: Aufbau/Suhrkamp, 1992), pp. 210–12 (at pp. 210–11).
3. Siegfried Kracauer, 'Die Photographie', *Frankfurter Zeitung*, 28 October 1927; and Walter Benjamin, 'Kleine Geschichte der Photographie', *Die literarische Welt*, September/October 1931.
4. Tom Kuhn, 'Brecht and Photography', in Stephen Brockman (ed.), *Bertolt Brecht in Context* (Cambridge: Cambridge University Press, 2021), pp. 131–9 (at p. 135). The quotation from Brecht is cited in Kuhn and taken from Bertolt Brecht, 'Zum zehnjährigen Bestehen der "A-I-Z"', *Arbeiter-Illustrierte-Zeitung*, No. 41, October 1931 (cf. *Bertolt Brecht. Werke*, vol. 21, p. 515).
5. '"Der Preis des Elitären": Peter Voigt – Regisseur und Autor', in Ingrid Poss, Christiane Mückenberger and Anne Richter (eds), *Das Prinzip Neugier. DEFA-Dokumentarfilmer erzählen* (Berlin: Neues Leben, 2012), pp. 192–221 (especially at p. 199).
6. See Rüdiger Steinmetz, 'Heynowski & Scheumann: The GDR's Leading Documentary Film Team', *Historical Journal of Film, Radio and Television* 24(3) (2004), 366–78.
7. April Eisman, 'East German Art and the Permeability of the Berlin Wall', *German Studies Review* 38(3) (2015), 597–616 (especially at 601–2).
8. Ullrich Kuhirt, 'Befragung der Realität? Bemerkungen zur "dokumenta" 72 in Kassel', *Bildende Kunst* 11 (1972), 539–42. For a list of artists exhibiting at the exhibition and a reproduction of excerpts from the catalogue, see: https://www.documenta.de/en/retrospective/documenta_5 (retrieved 20 March 2024).
9. Bertolt Brecht, 'The Threepenny Lawsuit', in Silberman, *Bertolt Brecht on Film and Radio*, pp. 147–99 (at p. 164). Cf. *Bertolt Brecht. Werke*, vol. 21, pp. 448–514 (at p. 469): 'Eine Fotografie der Kruppwerke oder der AEG ergibt beinahe nichts über diese Institute.' Although the concept of realism underpinning photorealism is dismissed in *Der goldene Strich* as an essentially bourgeois illusion, it is important to remember that, for scholars from the West at least, the inclusion of photorealist work in the Documenta 5 was seen as a challenge to the then dominant genre of abstract expressionism.
10. 'Das eindrucksvollste politische Kunstwerk seit Picassos *Guernica*', *Stern*, 27 August 1972.
11. Peter Voigt, 'Wozu Brecht für Dokumentaristen? Ein Diskussionsbeitrag', in Günter Agde (ed.), *Peter Voigt: Filmarbeit. Skizzen, Kritiken, Essays, Interviews* (Berlin: Neues Leben, 2018), pp. 9–13 (at p. 12) (originally published

in Werner Hecht and Hahn Karl-Claus (eds), *Brecht 78: Brecht-Dialog Kunst und Politik. 10.–15. Februar 1978* (Berlin: Henschel, 1979), pp. 252–55 [at p. 254]).
12. Bertolt Brecht. *Werke*, vol. 22, pp. 695–869 (at p. 695).
13. Friedrich Engels, 'Letter to Florence Kelley-Wischnewetzky', 28 December 1886.
14. The coding process is outlined in the document 'Verschlüsselung eines Textes. Bericht über die Suche nach einer Methode', dated December 1978 (= Peter-Voigt-Archiv, 241).
15. In a document entitled 'Mitschrift' of 16 June (no year stated, but probably 1979), Kurt Hager complained of a lack of references to the contribution of the GDR to the history of world revolution (which may go some way towards explaining the inclusion of a photographic portrait of Honecker in the final version of the stelae [= Peter-Voigt-Archiv, 241]).
16. Peter Voigt, 'Poesie durch Montage. Die Stelen auf dem Marx-Engels-Forum. Ein Arbeitsbericht', in Agde, *Peter Voigt*, pp. 32–36 (at p. 34) (first published in *Sonntag* 17 [1986]).
17. For a history of the Marx-Engels-Denkmal project, see Bruno Flierl, 'Der zentrale Ort in Berlin. Zur räumlichen Inszenierung sozialistischer Zentralität', in Günter Feist, Eckhart Gillen und Beatrice Vierneisel (eds), *Kunstdokumentation SBZ/DDR. Aufsätze – Berichte – Materialien* (Cologne: Dumont, 1996), pp. 320–57 (especially at pp. 351–57). The photographs deployed in the installation are also the subject of Voigt's film *Fotografien* (*Photographs*, 1983).
18. Voigt, 'Poesie durch Montage', p. 36.
19. Ibid., p. 33.
20. Bertolt Brecht, 'Kurzer Bericht über 400 (vierhundert) junge Lyriker', in *Bertolt Brecht. Werke*, vol. 21, pp. 191–3 (at p. 191).
21. See Stephen Parker, *Bertolt Brecht: A Literary Life* (London: Bloomsbury, 2014), especially pp. 503–96.
22. Judith Kretschmar and Rüdiger Steinmetz, 'Interview mit Peter Voigt (25 March 2004)' (= Peter-Voigt-Archiv, 86).
23. Peter Voigt, 'Wozu Brecht für Dokumentaristen?', in Agde, *Peter Voigt*, pp. 9–13 (at p. 9).

Select Bibliography

Agde, Günter (ed.). *Peter Voigt: Filmarbeit. Skizzen, Kritiken, Essays, Interviews*. Berlin: Neues Leben, 2018.
Eisman, April. 'East German Art and the Permeability of the Berlin Wall', *German Studies Review*, 38(3) (2015), 597–616.
Flierl, Bruno. 'Der zentrale Ort in Berlin. Zur räumlichen Inszenierung sozialistischer Zentralität', in Günter Feist, Eckhart Gillen und Beatrice Vierneisel

(eds), *Kunstdokumentation SBZ/DDR. Aufsätze – Berichte – Materialien*. Cologne: Dumont, 1996, pp. 320–57.

Kuhirt, Ullrich. 'Befragung der Realität? Bemerkungen zur "dokumenta" 72 in Kassel', *Bildende Kunst* 11 (1972), 539–42.

Kuhn, Tom. 'Brecht and Photography', in Stephen Brockman (ed.), *Bertolt Brecht in Context*. Cambridge: Cambridge University Press, 2021, pp. 131–39.

Parker, Stephen. *Bertolt Brecht: A Literary Life*. London: Bloomsbury, 2014.

Silberman, Marc (ed. and trans.). *Bertolt Brecht on Film and Radio*. London: Methuen, 2000.

Steinmetz, Rüdiger. 'Heynowski & Scheumann: The GDR's Leading Documentary Film Team', *Historical Journal of Film, Radio and Television* 24(3) (2004), 366–78.

Voigt, Peter. 'Der Preis des Elitären', in Ingrid Poss, Christiane Mückenberger and Anne Richter (eds), *Das Prinzip Neugier. DEFA-Dokumentarfilmer erzählen*. Berlin: Neues Leben, 2012, pp. 193–221.

CHAPTER 7

Critical Truths
Documenting Disillusionment in the Films of Helke Misselwitz, Petra Tschörtner and Angelika Andrees

Jennifer L. Creech

The documentary form has always presented the problem of hidden or disavowed mediation at the same time that it has been assumed to provide unmediated objectivity, or documentation of the profilmic event. Indeed, the very title of this volume centres this particular anxiety about or reassurance of the genre's supposed claim to objectivity. Yet, as many decades of documentary theory attest, at the most basic level, the primary need to structure film as narrative always already impedes documentary's assertion of 'unstructured actuality'.[1] For DEFA documentarians specifically, the difficulty of establishing truth through form and content was compounded by the political, ideological and formal expectations of and limitations set by the Socialist Unity Party (SED) and, by extension, the documentary studios.[2] Documentarians who interrogated East Germany's historical imaginary attempted to create a public space for what Elke Schieber calls 'critical truth': 'A style (of filmmaking) ... characterized by long, observational takes with few cuts ... (that) didn't interrupt or condense the words spoken by their subjects ... The camera stressed nothing, discredited no one, idealized nothing.'[3] In many of these films, Schieber's notion of critical truth was achieved through a focus on everyday life and the personal or domestic spheres.[4] As I have argued elsewhere, 'woman' served in both feature and documentary films to problematize the public/private distinction under socialism and to represent the truth of everyday life by creating a sense of authenticity for the viewer that subverted official ideologies of gender in the German Democratic Republic (GDR).

In this chapter, I address the issue of documentary truth – both in general as it concerns the genre and in particular as it concerns the DEFA – in relation to the work of three last-generation DEFA documentarians, Helke Misselwitz, Petra Tschörtner and Angelika Andrees, and consider how the different positionalities of the filmmakers' subjects – children, the elderly and married couples – intersect with institutions both physical (nursing homes and orphanages) and ideological (marriage, the nuclear family and the collective) to establish critical truths about the contradictions of lived socialism in East Germany. I argue that these positionalities reveal social incongruity and rupture in relation to lived experiences and official ideologies under socialism, and that these filmmakers rely on certain formal structures – most notably long takes, the talking-heads technique, the use of voiceover monologue or extra-diegetic sound as commentary, and a frequent focus on still images – to imbue their films with an authenticity that made their films and the characters in them truthful documents of disappointment and disillusionment in the GDR.

Helke Misselwitz, *Aktfotographie, z.B. Gundula Schulze* (*Nude Photography: The Case of Gundula Schulze*, 1983)

Helke Misselwitz's documentary *Aktfotographie, z.B. Gundula Schulze* introduces us to a photographer and academic who, at the time of filmmaking in 1983, is writing her dissertation on the topic 'The Female Nude in Photography in the GDR'. Schulze's artistic and academic goal is to problematize the meaning and function of nude photography, specifically photography of the female nude, in the GDR. In Misselwitz's film, Schulze asserts that photography is a 'declaration of love' for a subject's individual characteristics. These characteristics, which often do not reflect ideals of beauty, lead to inhibitions and feelings of shame. Schulze envisions her role as photographer to be that of building trust with her subject so as to help them see their own beauty while overcoming those feelings of shame. In both her artistic and academic work, she is overtly critical of the anachronism – what she calls the 'joke' of nude photography in East German film, magazines and other art forms – that fails to depart from the traditional artistic male gaze and has absolutely nothing to do with the contemporary experiences of women in

East German society. For her, nude photography should be 'a portrait of the whole subject, such that the person is foregrounded, and the body is not repressed, but rather the face and body are unified in such a way that the viewer is able to surmise the richness and multiplicity of the person, what their history is, what life they have led'.

The opening sequence of Misselwitz's short documentary immediately foregrounds the contradictions between official ideologies and gendered experience by overtly questioning the truth of certain images while validating others. The sequence begins with a static close-up of a hand flipping through the print collection, *Aktfotographie*, published by the VEB Foto Kino Verlag in Leipzig, as a woman reads aloud the introduction to the volume by Klaus Fischer in voiceover:

> Inexperienced models often don't know what to do with their legs either. If a model has somewhat too strong thighs, a frontal view should be avoided. In both men and women, the belly and hips are parts of the body where unreasonable eating habits and lack of exercise quickly make themselves noticeable in wretched fat deposits. If, however, the model presses the spine upward and outward, to the point of making their back hollow, immediately the wrinkles disappear, and the belly becomes smooth and taut. Breasts are the most striking sexual feature; generally speaking, they are considered the symbol of femininity. Not every woman, who otherwise has all the advantages of a good model, also has ideally shaped breasts. It is very, very good if the photographer understands how to hide this and that defect.

The camera then cuts to a long shot of Misselwitz's subject, Gundula Schulze, who states: 'An image of female beauty is created in the public sphere that isn't real. It is an illusion. And the woman who co-creates and represents this illusion, the woman being depicted, has nothing to do with this image because her everyday life and her reality look very different.' The camera then cuts to a long shot in black and white of a group of women, cashiers at a grocery store, in their everyday reality, walking to their posts as the store opens. As they walk, the extra-diegetic sound consists of piano notes and a disembodied female voice explaining the importance of poise in what appears to be a dance class. The extra-diegetic sound then abruptly ends as the camera cuts to a medium shot of a young cashier slamming her till drawer closed and audibly yawning.

In this opening sequence, both the subject matter and the formal strategies position us as critical viewers in relation to official ideologies of gender and the institution of art, and to convince us of the truth value inherent in the words of Misselwitz's subject. As the hand flips through pages of perfectly poised female nudes, most of whom either face away from the camera or avert their eyes, we are informed by the volume's male editor – mediated through a disembodied female voice – of how best to handle the imperfections in the model: thighs that are too large, a fatty stomach and imperfectly formed breasts, all of which may or may not be the result of 'unreasonable eating habits and lack of exercise that result in wretched fat deposits'. The words of the volume's editor make it clear that the subject of these images is ultimately an object of desire. Schulze's own assessment of these aesthetic illusions is also made quite clear: women, whose bodies are used to construct these illusions, actually have no relation to them, as women's everyday realities look very different. Misselwitz then underscores Schulze's assertion with a clever juxtaposition between her own black-and-white images of cashiers arriving for their first shift of the day and the extra-diegetic sound of what appears to be a lesson on how best to carry one's (feminine) body. The piano notes and female voice explaining the importance of poise contrast starkly with the documentary footage of the women at work. In cutting off the extra-diegetic sound with the slamming of a till drawer followed by the visible yawn of one young cashier, Misselwitz documents the obvious discrepancies between the ideals of femininity as outlined by Klaus Fischer and the realities of living day to day in a woman's body. Is the inference to be drawn, perhaps, that sitting at the till for too many hours a day might lead to the 'wretched fat deposits' of which Fischer speaks?

The images in the book are starkly contrasted with Schulze's own images, in which women are photographed in their homes and with everyday objects that reveal aspects of their lives. Most important, perhaps, is that they direct their gaze squarely at the viewer rather than averting their eyes, and they stand or sit in ways that are not meant to hide their imperfections or to invite an erotic gaze. The authenticity of Schulze's images is underscored by their placement within the film and by the soundtrack. The sequence begins with Misselwitz's footage of cashiers, but this time we see them in medium shots and long takes as they interact with and check out their customers. An upbeat acoustic guitar has taken the place of the sound of a dance and poise instructor, as we watch these women at work and take in their movements and facial expressions. The camera then cuts to a medium shot of Schulze, sitting in her living room, asserting that she wishes to 'photograph every woman I meet . . . whom I find sympathetic, who lives, who exudes a kind of warmth . . . I want to photograph what is special about her . . . I want to pull that out in the image and also show her body, her face,

Figure 7.1. Gundula Schulze holds one of her photographs. *Aktfotographie, z.B. Gundula Schulze* (Helke Misselwitz, 1983). © DEFA-Stiftung/Jürgen Rudow

how she lives, what she represents, her background, everything that makes her who she is'. The sound of the acoustic guitar then returns, forging a direct connection between Misselwitz's moving images and Schulze's still images (Figure 7.1), underscoring the familiarity and intimacy of the two artists' work.

In this way, Misselwitz's film offers us both the critical truth of the persistent contradictions between official ideologies of gendered emancipation and women's continued role in the East German public sphere as an erotic object of the gaze, as well as a more authentic documentation of East German women by East German women on film.

Petra Tschörtner, *Hinter den Fenstern* (*Behind Closed Doors*, 1983)

As last-generation DEFA documentarians, Helke Misselwitz, Petra Tschörtner and Angelika Andrees were members of a filmmaking cohort that began working at the studios during a period of political stagnation. Beginning in the late 1960s and early 1970s, and intensifying through the last years of the GDR's existence, both documentary and feature films actively resisted utopian narratives of historical progress that overtly reflected SED ideology and instead focused on the halted, stagnant nature of life under real existing socialism.[5] This shift from utopian, progressive narratives of the collective to narratives emphasizing cultural stagnation and the individual's scepticism (or even cynicism) went hand in hand with a shift of narrative focus on the public sphere to one on the private sphere.[6] And despite its attempts to fully collectivize all aspects of life, the East German state never fully resolved the ideological dichotomy of the public/private distinction it inherited from its bourgeois predecessor, thus relegating private issues such as love, marriage and the family to an ideologically grey area.[7]

In her documentary short, *Hinter den Fenstern*, Petra Tschörtner teases out some of the specific contradictions of the public/private divide in the context of three marriages. For the purposes of this chapter, I will focus on Tschörtner's interview of Christel and Rüdiger, whose marriage posits one uncomfortable critical truth, namely that scarcity of housing, particularly for young people, directly influenced this couple's decisions regarding marriage and divorce. Tschörtner's film reveals that personal desires for love and family are intricately bound to the state, particularly through access to housing. The repetitive use of certain formal strategies such as filming on location in the apartments, the talking-heads technique and the camera's fluctuation from medium to close-up shots invites the viewer into an intimate relationship with Tschörtner's subjects, often revealing inconvenient truths about the nature of marriage in East Germany.

The film begins with a mobile camera driving towards a housing development in Potsdam accompanied by Tschörtner's voiceover explaining that the film emerged after speaking with couples of 'our generation' about how they live together. The camera passes rows of mass-produced housing (*Plattenbauten*), eventually turning to stop in front of one building presented in a medium shot. We hear a man's voice answer the door via intercom as the camera shifts to a close-up shot of a section of windows, and then to a montage of smaller sections and groups of windows as he repeats his questioning 'Hello? Do you hear me?' This editing technique from medium to close-up shots will be repeated throughout the film's interviews as the subjects shift from more general speech acts to more vulnerable confessions about their lives together.

Tschörtner's first interview is of Christel and Rüdiger, both thirty-two years old, who have two daughters and share a roomy apartment. Opening shots place the family members in various rooms: one daughter brushes her teeth in the bathroom while the other lies in a bedroom, Christel is seated on one side of the kitchen table smoking a cigarette while Rüdiger is seated on the other side watching TV – both are presented in medium shots. When asked to describe their first years of marriage, Christel answers 'awful': they fought about everything and she threatened to get pregnant as an attempt to stem Rüdiger's excessive drinking. When asked how they sorted things out, Christel answers 'not at all'; she got pregnant and Rüdiger's drinking continued unabated. At one point they separated, and she filed for divorce because he threatened violence, but that only lasted a few months because they were forced to continue living together due to a lack of housing.

As the camera cuts to a close-up, we see Rüdiger smiling about his short-lived return to bachelorhood, going to bars and skipping work, as Christel confesses in a countershot that she spent most of her nonworking hours during the separation caring for their first daughter and had actually hoped to meet someone else. When asked how they decided to stay together, Christel answers that she simply got tired of not being able to watch the television that Rüdiger had kept for himself in the extra room. She then interrupts Tschörtner with a resounding 'yes!' when asked outright if getting this newer, bigger apartment was the reason they stayed together. In one final attempt to tease out some possible declarations of love between the two, Tschörtner asks what their reasons are for remaining together. When Christel answers 'a little bit of love', Rüdiger laughs heartily and says, 'kids . . . and things: we bought a car, new bedroom furniture . . . we put so much work into everything'. Christel's response: 'habit'.

Here, Tschörtner lays bare a rather uncomfortable critical truth of the public/private divide under socialism: it is not love and commitment, but rather scarcity of housing that plays the primary role in Christel and Rüdiger's decision to stay married. The material obstacles to obtaining an apartment of one's own was, in fact, one of the primary reasons why young people in the GDR got married and had children in the first place, often at a much younger age than their Western counterparts, which also led to a much higher divorce rate.[8] The idea that 'a little bit of love' might be the reason they have stuck it out for so long is undermined not only by Rüdiger's laughter, but also by the close-ups of both of their faces. As Christel reacts to Rüdiger's description of his few glorious months of bachelorhood, she maintains a painful smirk and clenches her teeth. While he beams in remembrance of his short-lived bachelorhood, her face is presented in shadow, yet we can see her eyes narrow as she responds: 'I couldn't afford or allow myself to do much; I had a child. I had to be careful that I didn't make any mistakes that would cause them [the state] to take my child away.'[9]

Tschörtner's film relies almost exclusively on the talking-heads technique. A traditionally realist structure, the technique of having subjects speak directly to the camera has been criticized by some documentary theorists for suggesting unmediated veracity when, in fact, it is often the result of pointed questions posed by the director. Yet Tschörtner's use of the technique is similar to the oral tradition of women's history in general and, more specifically, to the protocol form popularized by Maxie Wander in her collection of interviews, *Guten Morgen, du Schöne* (*Good Morning, Beautiful!*), and to Misselwitz's own use of the technique to create a sense of authenticity in *Winter Adé*.[10] As in these examples, Tschörtner's close-up of Christel presents a picture of 'the ordinary details of her life, her thoughts – told directly by the protagonist to the camera – and [her] frustrated . . . attempts to enter and deal with the public world of work and power', what Julia Lesage argues is often an 'urgent public act' that not only makes such experiences accessible and trustworthy, but also demands the viewers' critical engagement with established social narratives.[11]

Petra Tschörtner, *Unsere alten Tage* (*In Our Old Age*, 1989)

In her 1989 film *Unsere alten Tage*, Petra Tschörtner turns her attention from the personal space of the nuclear family to the collective space of the nursing home, where elderly citizens of Berlin live out their final days. The film begins with Tschörtner's own familial story: over a static long shot of the home, we hear Tschörtner in voiceover, reading aloud the last birthday card she received from her grandmother. As she finishes reading, Tschörtner states: 'We never saw each other again. Grandmother died in the hospital alone, amongst strangers.' This final phrase 'alone, amongst strangers' tidily sums up the film's critical truth of growing old in the GDR, a state in which the ideological concept of subjectivity was anchored by a Marxist understanding of collectivity, which is defined as the:

> typical form of life in socialist and communist societies, in which socialist personalities can fully and completely develop themselves through active engagement in the community and for the benefit of society. The collective is, as a form of social union and community of unmediated contact, the foundational form of life and an important link of social organisation in a society free from exploitation ... Upbring-

ing under socialism is therefore essentially the upbringing of the whole person in and through the collective.[12]

The concept of collectivity was so anchored in the East German self-understanding that it formed the second half of a limitless assemblage of compound nouns defining various groupings of socialist subjects – child-, youth- and adult-collective, pupil- and school-collective, educator-, production- and research-collective – revealing the all-encompassing extent to which the concept of the collective characterized East German social structures.[13] Yet, in Tschörtner's film, the nursing home feels less like a collective that enables the so-called 'all-round development of the (ageing) socialist personality' and more like a place where old people are sent to live 'alone, amongst strangers'. The majority of the film's 48 minutes are spent with elderly men and women who require nursing assistance or have been forgotten by their children, and who have left behind the familiar, domestic homes of their adult lives to share institutional space with strangers.

The first encounter is with an ageing couple who move into the nursing home because their children only visit once a year, 'on birthdays'. Upon arrival at the home, or the *Feierabendheim* as it is described during the intake session, one of the first questions the couple is confronted with is that of death, namely: who will be responsible for making decisions about their estate once both have passed away? In the next scene, we see the couple playing cards and hear an East German report on the television in the background about negotiations between East and West Germany regarding the status of East Germans who have fled and are requesting permanent asylum in the West. When asked how their first night in the *Feierabendheim* is going, the husband answers: 'It's just like on vacation!'

Later, the viewer witnesses one woman's uncomfortable acceptance of her new roommate, whose arrival is marked only by repetitive shaking of her head as she remarks 'this place will never be like home'. When Tschörtner asks another woman if she had wanted to move into the home, she answers that she absolutely did not, but none of her six children could (or would?) take her in. She laments the many losses she has endured throughout her life – among them the death of two young children and two adult children – as she rifles through papers and pulls out an Honorary Certificate (Ehrenurkunde) from the Freier Deutscher Gewerkschaftsbund (FDGB) for forty years of trade union membership in the GDR. A third woman, when asked how she ended up in the home, answers: 'I really don't know. I fell down in my apartment and was taken to the hospital. I don't know what happened after that, not how or when I left the hospital, nor how I got here. I also have no idea who arranged this.' When asked who now lives in her three-and-a-half-room Berlin apartment, she answers 'my eldest daughter'. In yet another scene, we see three old women sitting in their room silently watching the *Sandmännchen* on television. As the sound of the *Abendgruß* plays, the camera cuts to still images in the room that reveal each woman's familial history – photos of their husbands in their wartime uniforms, wedding photos and baby photos. In each of these scenes, Tschörtner uses long, observational takes and gives her subjects the opportunity to speak without interruption. The recurring assertions of isolation and abandonment provide a rather stark contradiction to the ideology of collectivity that, even here in the nursing home, is officially proclaimed if not felt.

These contradictions between official notions of collectivity and the real, existing feelings of elderly abandonment (Figure 7.2) are then strategically emphasized in the scenes that follow. Shots and sounds on the television of the national fortieth anniversary celebrations of the GDR, full of cheering crowds and waving SED patriarchs, are viewed by solitary inhabitants in empty rooms. The camera then cuts to the nursing home's communal space, where a small band of the home's tenants and a group of children from a local crèche attempt to make the collective celebration palpable, singing patriotic songs for those tenants who have assembled. Yet, as the camera pans and settles on those who have come to watch, there is little sense of collectivity and belonging reflected in the images.

The patient, observational camera and the lonely confessions caught on tape enable Tschörtner to fashion an authentic documentation of real, existing socialism that starkly contrasts with the pomp and party *Parolen* one sees in the official representation of the fortieth anniversary celebrations on television. In the final interview, Tschörtner asks a nurse working in the home if it is not depressing to spend every day with the old, sick and dying. 'Absolutely', she answers, explaining that she became a nurse because it was her calling (*Berufung*). She then clarifies:

> Those who live here and spend their last years and last portion of life here are giving up a great deal. They have left a home behind them. That's a rather large piece of one's personality, and they are hoping to find that again here. We certainly can't provide them with a substitute for the home they've left behind. For that, of course, we would need

Figure 7.2. Collective loneliness in *Unsere alten Tage* (Petra Tschörtner, 1989). ©DEFA-Stiftung/Michael Lösche

> enormous support from their relatives, perhaps even from the caregivers. Anyone who is willing should take a look around here and see how these old people are living, after they've left home.

With these words, Tschörtner documents the abandonment of the elderly – not just by their family members, but also by the collective. In order for these ageing comrades to find 'a substitute for the home they have lost', both family members and the state must offer support. Yet, the nurse's suggestion to those 'who are willing' to come and witness life in the *Feierabendheim* feels more like a challenge than an invitation. To take up that challenge is to confront and engage with the inconvenient truth of a collectivity that is performative rather than (trans)formative.

Angelika Andrees, *Heim* (*The Home*, 1978/1989)

The problem of collective neglect also lies at the heart of Angelika Andrees' film *Heim*, released the same year as *Unsere alten Tage*, but filmed more than a decade before. The film takes up the problem of abandonment and marginalization of those who live in the care of the state, but from a rather different perspective. Where Tschörtner's film focused on the elderly, Andrees' film documents the lives of children being raised in an orphanage. However, in both films, the collective's ability to successfully tend to the emotional wellbeing and ensure the all-round development of the individual is called into question.

Andrees' documentary short was originally conceived as a supporting film to be shown in theatres prior to the full-length feature *P.S.* (1978) by Roland Gräf.[14] In short, Gräf's *P.S.* is an orphanage success story that tells the story of a young man who encounters hurdles and failures upon his departure from the home, but eventually realizes and commits to his personal responsibilities as a result of lessons learned in the collective. The film went on to win several awards, including the Special Jury Prize at the Author's Film Festival in Bergamo (1980), as well as Best Director and Best Supporting Actor (for Barbara Dittus) at the GDR National Feature Film Festival in Karl-Marx-Stadt (Chemnitz) in 1980. Andrees' film *Heim* traversed a decidedly different narrative (and historical) trajectory from Gräf's *P.S.* Unlike *P.S.*, *Heim* documents aspects of East German daily life otherwise disavowed in official East German ideologies and refuses to provide the viewer with an uplifting narrative resolution. As a result, the film was shelved before completion and not released until 1989. The film is constructed around observational takes of, and interviews with, children and teenagers living at the orphanage in Mentin, a former estate converted into a *Normalheim*[15] for children and youth aged 6–16. While *P.S.* deals overtly with the struggle to build committed relationships after living in the care of the state, *Heim* poignantly reveals the precarious situation of the children living in this *Normalheim* such that the viewer must question the state's ability to provide children living in their care with the tools to live happy, committed lives once they leave. Over the course of 25 minutes, *Heim* reveals cycles of neglect that follow these children from their nuclear families into the state-run home, painting a devastating picture of emotional abandonment, rampant alcoholism and intergenerational violence.

The film's opening sequence immediately suggests feelings of abandonment and disorientation. The sequence begins with the camera following the morning routine of children in the home being woken by their caregivers and helped to dress. We see children half-asleep being put into a sitting position and dressed, though they are neither awake nor aware of their surroundings. At the same time, the disembodied voice of a young child describes how they came to be living in the home:

A woman picked us up with a man and then afterwards we had to get out of the car here. Then we were down in the office. They just said that we were going to the children's home. Afterwards they said, when we were almost here, they said, 'now we are in Mentin'. Then we knew right away that we had been sent to the home in Mentin.

The child's confused description of their transfer from 'at home' to 'the home' is strangely similar to the moment in Tschörtner's later film, *Unsere alten Tage*, when one woman explains that she doesn't know how she came to be living in the elderly home after falling in her apartment. The child's voice suggests that they were unprepared for the transition from the parental home to the state-run orphanage and that they did not know where they were headed once they had been picked up. The voiceover combined with the images of sleepy children being forcibly pulled out of bed and dressed by a caregiver thus immediately allude to the disorienting and often secretive nature of East Germany's institutionalization of children, which was a common, though officially disavowed, problem.[16]

The remainder of the film reveals both widespread alcoholism and intergenerational violence as ubiquitous, both within the nuclear families from which the children emerge and in the alternative families they find in the home. In the first few minutes, Andrees separately films three teenage boys in static medium-long shots. Each describes their parents as 'heavy drinkers', 'always drinking' or 'drunk most days'. In one instance, we see a young man leaning against the window, obsessively rubbing his forehead, never shifting his gaze from the floor as he talks. The third boy, a blonde eighteen year old who has been in the home for approximately seven years, admits that his parents' alcoholism led to his staying out of the house, getting into fights and being too cheeky with his teachers. These interviews are followed by a cut to a medium close-up of two small hands holding pictures of a young woman, smiling at the camera, and of the same woman with what seem to be older family members sitting on a couch. As we look at these family photos, we hear a young voice off-camera saying: 'My mommy is good. My daddy is good, too.'

The discrepancy between the stories told by the teenage boys and the assertions of this young child cherishing photos of their 'good' parents creates a tension that the viewer cannot ignore. While the young voice mentions nothing of alcohol, the positioning of this voice immediately after those of the three teenagers leads the viewer to wonder if this child has also been placed in the care of the state for similar reasons. Given the well-documented, though for decades officially ignored, epidemic of alcoholism in the GDR,[17] the viewer is left to assume that the young child is simply unaware of their mother's neglect or that their love and longing for her has coloured their memory. The primacy of parental alcoholism in many of the children's recollections nearly ensures this assumption on the part of the viewer, and also reminds us of Christel's assertions in Tschörtner's film *Hinter den Fenstern*: 'I couldn't afford or allow myself to do much; I had a child. I had to be careful that I didn't make any mistakes that would cause them [the state] to take my child away.'[18]

However, the film is not wholly bleak, and Andrees captures numerous moments that reflect the carefree and joyful aspects of living in the home. The former estate itself is nothing short of idyllic: we see children playing hide and seek in the rooms of the home, teenagers walking hand in hand along the grounds, and youngsters balancing on the wide, stone banister of a garden staircase. The former estate is surrounded by fields and forest, and Andrees documents children playing on a swing set in the middle of a field and later hiding in a self-built fort in the forest accompanied by the diegetic sound of crickets, birds, frogs and rustling leaves. In a rare moment of intergenerational care, we see the blonde teenager from the first three interviews serving as a jungle gym for one of the younger children. Throwing the child up into the air, holding them steady while they swing down between his legs, both of their faces light up. The desire for a 'happy ending' is certainly present in Andrees' camera work and particularly in her use of sound. The scenes in the forest and on the estate grounds are sometimes accompanied by whimsical piano music that is reminiscent of a Buster Keaton film, and during one evening gathering, we watch teens dancing to The Beatles and the Beach Boys, which suggests that these teenagers, like others in the GDR, are leading a typical or 'normal' life.

Yet, a melancholic voiceover is always lurking around the corner. At one point, the camera cuts to children aged eight to ten, showering, bathing and playing in the water, while a voiceover presents the film's first descriptions of domestic violence:

> My mom came in . . . and smoked a cigarette first. Then she started giving my little three-year-old brother a hard time, saying he'd better stop messing around or he'd get hit. He didn't listen and so he got hit . . . Then my mom kept on, this time with Marion – she's only half a year old – and my mom started messing with her. Marion suddenly started to cry in the living room, so I went in there and saw that my mom had

started beating Marion up, so I said to her, 'stop acting so crazy or you'll get a fat lip from me', and she just kept it up, so I punched her, then my grandpa started yelling at my mom, too.

As the camera cuts to a medium close-up of even younger children standing in a large shoe closet, looking directly into the camera, we hear Andrees ask: 'And why do you hit others?' His answer: 'Hmm, it's just natural. If you're cheeky you get slapped. That's what always happened to me, and to the others before me, so that's how it is with anyone... they'll keep on hitting others later on.' Andrees' use of voiceover thus foreshadows this naturalized violence as an almost certain future for the young people looking back at us on-screen. These children, having been officially rescued from the 'parental endangerment' (*Erziehungsgefährdung*) of their nuclear families, have been placed into new surroundings, but are unable to escape the violence that lives on in the social dynamics of the children in the home. This is underscored by the violence we see between young people on camera. In the shower, big boys shove their genitalia in the face of small boys. In the hall, one tween boy wrestles a girl into a corner and tries to shove something into her mouth while a group of boys watch calmly, some of them smiling. At an evening gathering, the blonde boy from the first set of interviews physically intimidates and grabs a girl. As she cowers and then acquiesces to his regressively violent overtures, three younger boys watch and smile.

Andrees' film ends with the children leaving the home for summer vacation. In the final scene, children and teenagers walk to the bus with their suitcases, some of them never to return. In their final home meeting prior to departure, the director of the home wishes those leaving for the summer a lovely vacation. For those who are of age and are departing for good, her words are a bit graver: 'I would like to say ... to all the pupils who are leaving us today, that we wish these pupils the very, very best in their future journeys in life, but I think we have to tell them though, it's up to each of you how your journey in life will be, whether it's positive or negative.' The director's emphasis here on individual rather than collective identity and responsibility leaves the viewer feeling less than hopeful. In this moment, it becomes quite obvious why *Heim* had to be shelved rather than shown as a supporting film for Gräf's feature film *P.S.* Gräf's uplifting message of individual perseverance learned in the bosom of the collective would have been untenable for viewers after witnessing the critical truths laid bare in Andrees' *Heim*.

Conclusion

In a recent essay collection, Cornelia Klauß and Ralf Schenk consider whether there was an *écriture feminine* in the DEFA.[19] For the most part, Klauß and Schenk summarize previous arguments about the women filmmakers of the DEFA: that women filmmakers' perspectives were one and the same as their subjects, as most of them focused on so-called 'women's issues' and, as a result, saw eye to eye with the subjects of their films; and that the residual patriarchal underpinnings of East German society meant that women were considered 'less politically mature' subjects whose questioning of East German social contradictions was 'more easily forgiven', such that they were more likely to be overlooked by censors.[20]

I would argue Klauß and Schenk's point even further: that assumptions about women's supposed political naivety made them authentic and trustworthy interlocutors not just for other women, but for East Germans generally, particularly for those who were marginally positioned via the social and political power structures in the GDR. This is a crucial aspect of these filmmakers' ability to construct authenticity in their documentaries. In each of the films discussed here, critical truths emerge because documentary subjects are willing to speak openly to the documentarian, who in turn renders the full complexity of their contradictory socialist lives. Moreover, because the documentary studios were more closely aligned with state ideologies and subject to more overt control and censorship than the feature film studios, documentaries were more likely to be perceived by the viewing public as ideologically suspect.

However, like their colleagues in the feature film studios, these last-generation women filmmakers' focus on seemingly apolitical positionalities – women, married couples, children and the elderly – enabled them to uncover the political in the personal. Misselwitz's study of Gundula Schulze uses voiceover monologue and extra-diegetic sound to comment on the ruptures between women's lived experiences and official ideologies of gendered beauty, painting a portrait of an artist whose work mirrors her own. In documenting the lives of three marriages, Tschörtner reveals the ways in which the public allocation of housing curtails the possibilities of personal happiness. Through predominant use of the talking-heads technique via medium and close-up shots, she documents the individual disappointment in her subjects' facial expressions as it directly relates to East Germany's inability to resolve the public/private distinction in the context of socialist marriage. In her film *In Our Old Age*, Tschörtner uses a variety of techniques that create an authentic document of collective loneliness: long, observational takes enable her subjects to speak of their abandonment without interruption, while editing and sound choices document the overt contradictions between official celebrations of the state – benevolent SED patriarchs cheered by the smiling masses – and the very real experience of elderly isolation. Similarly, Andrees' use of long, observational takes, the talking-heads technique, uninterrupted voiceover monologues and extra-diegetic sound poignantly depicts the orphanage in *Heim* as an institution that perpetuates (rather than prevents) the cycle of intergenerational violence. In documenting the socioideological contradictions and painful disappointments East Germans experienced in the care of its collective institutions, these filmmakers constructed authentic renderings of East German lived realities and enabled a critically truthful story of the GDR to emerge.

Jennifer L. Creech is Instructor of German at Oregon State University. Her research and teaching interests include late twentieth-century German literature, film and culture, porn studies, and Marxist and feminist theories. She is the author of *Mothers, Comrades and Outcasts in East German Women's Films* (Indiana University Press, 2016), and the co-editor (with Thomas O. Haakenson) of *How to Make the Body: Difference, Identity, and Embodiment: Visual Cultures and German Contexts* (Bloomsbury, 2022) and *Spectacle: German Visual Culture*, vol. 2 (Lang, 2015). She has also published on East German cinema, post-unification cinema and feminist pornography in *Seminar* and in the *Women in German Yearbook*.

Notes

1. Brian Winston, 'Documentary: I Think We Are in Trouble', in Alan Rosenthal (ed.), *New Challenges for Documentary* (Berkeley: University of California Press, 1988) pp. 21–33.
2. See Günter Jordan and Ralf Schenk (eds), *Schwarzweiß und Farbe* (Potsdam: Jovis, 1996). Elke Schieber opens her chapter on the 1980s by noting the persistence of these limitations evident in Karl Gass' opening statement at the National Festival for Documentary and Short Films in the GDR 1979, in which he quotes Rosa Luxemburg: '"There is nothing so harmful to the revolution as illusions; there is nothing so useful to it as clear, open truth..."

But this I know, it is one's duty, if one wants to teach the truth, to teach it wholly or completely; one must teach the truth clearly, without riddles, without reticence, without distrust in its power and usefulness . . . He who thinks of selling the truth all dolled up and wrapped like a chrysalis may well be truth's pimp, however: he was never her lover' (at p. 181). Unless otherwise stated, all translations are my own.
3. Elke Schieber, 'Im Dämmerlicht der Perestroika', in Jordan and Schenk, *Schwarzweiß und Farbe*, p. 186. The work of Gitta Nickel would be representative of the opposite trend. See also Eduard Schreiber, 'Zeit der verpassten Möglichkeiten 1970 bis 1980', in Jordan and Schenk, *Schwarzweiß und Farbe*, pp. 129–69.
4. Jennifer L. Creech, *Mothers, Comrades and Outcasts in East German Women's Film* (Bloomington: Indiana University Ppress, 2016), pp. 195–222.
5. See Joshua Feinstein, *The Triumph of the Ordinary: Depictions of Daily Life in the East German Cinema 1949–89* (Chapel Hill: University of North Carolina Press, 2002).
6. Creech, *Mothers, Comrades and Outcasts*, p. 97.
7. For an extensive analysis of the problem of the public/private distinction under socialism, see Susan Gal, 'A Semiotics of the Public/Private Distinction', *Differences: A Journal of Feminist Cultural Studies* 13(1) (2002), 77–95. For an in-depth analysis of how Gal's theory of the public/private distinction relates specifically to DEFA films about love and marriage, including a close reading of one such film, see Creech, *Mothers, Comrades and Outcasts*, pp. 31–34 and 61–83.
8. See 'Wohnungen der DDR: Altbau, Miete, Plattenbau, Wohnungsmangel', *MDR Geschichte*, 14 August 2020, https://www.mdr.de/geschichte/ddr/alltag/familie/wohnen-plattenbau-102.html, (retrieved 16 October 2022); Anke Domscheit-Berg, 'Familienpolitik in Ost- und Westdeutschland und ihre langfristigen Auswirkungen', *Heinrich Böll Stiftung*, 9 November 2016, https://www.boell.de/de/2016/11/09/familienpolitik-ost-und-westdeutsch land-und-ihre-langfristigen-auswirkungen (retrieved 16 October 2022); and 'Ehe und Familie' in the online exhibit 'Lebensstationen', Deutsches Historisches Museum, Zeughaus, Berlin, 26 March–15 June 1993, https://www .dhm.de/archiv/ausstellungen/lebensstationen/3_153.htm (retrieved 16 October 2022).
9. Here, Christel alludes to the myriad ways in which East German law stripped citizens of their parenting rights, particularly after revisions in 1965 to statutes governing the nuclear family in the Familiengesetzbuch (Family Legal Code) and the so-called Jugendhilfeverordnung (Youth Welfare Ordinance). I consider this issue in greater detail in my analysis of the last film under consideration, Tschörtner's documentary *Heim* (*Home*). See also 'Bericht zur Aufarbeitung der Heimerziehung in der DDR'.
10. Creech, *Mothers, Comrades and Outcasts*, p. 199.

11. Julia Lesage, 'The Political Aesthetics of the Feminist Documentary Film', *Quarterly Review of Film Studies* 3(4) (1978), 507–23.
12. 'Kollektiv', in *Pädagogisches Wörterbuch* (Berlin: DDR-Verlag Volk und Wissen, 1987), p. 202, available at: https://www.zdl.org/wb/wortgeschichten/Kollektiv (retrieved 28 May 2022).
13. See 'Sozialistische Arbeitsgruppe: *Kollektiv* im DDR-Sprachgebrauch', *Wortgeschichte zu Kollektiv – Kollektiv, Politik & Gesellschaft*, Zentrum für digitale Lexikographie der deutschen Sprache (ZDL), https://www.zdl.org/wb/wortgeschichten/Kollektiv (retrieved 28 May 2022). The primacy of the collective was so pervasive in the GDR that it actually persists to this day as an important aspect of familial identity for the generations born after 1989. See in particular Johannes Nichelmann, *Nachwendekinder: Die DDR, unsere Eltern und das große Schweigen* (Berlin: Ullstein, 2019); and Steffen Mau, *Lütten Klein: Leben in der Ostdeutschen Transformationsgesellschaft* (Berlin: Suhrkamp, 2019).
14. Interestingly, Petra Tschörtner worked on the film as Assistant Director to Andrees.
15. The GDR had three primary types of homes for children: *Normalheime*, *Spezialheime* and *Jugendwerkhofe*. Children assigned to the *Normalheim* were officially described as 'without family ties [and] socially endangered... without significant educational or behavioral difficulties; [and] children whose legal guardians were unable to fulfill their "caregiving duties" due to occupational activity, illness, or other reasons' ('Bericht zur Aufarbeitung der Heimerziehung in der DDR', p. 25).
16. The lack of transparency in East German child welfare and custody cases affected children, parents and the general public. Court proceedings occurred behind closed doors, and both parents and children could be removed from the courtroom according to the whims of the court. See 'Bericht zur Aufarbeitung der Heimerziehung in der DDR', p. 20.
17. The GDR was officially a 'sober' state: official doctrine actually described alcohol consumption as 'dem Sozialismus wesensfremd' (Kathleen Haack et al., 'Vom "wesensfremden Konsum" – Zum Umgang mit der Alkoholproblematik in einem DDR-Großbetrieb', *Psychotherapie, Psychosomatik, medizinische Psychologie* 72 (2022), 558–563; Thomas Kochan, *Blauer Würger: So trank die DDR* (Berlin: Aufbau, 2011); and Thomas Kochan, 'Alkohol und Alkoholrausch in der DDR', 2019, https://www.bundesstiftung-aufarbeitung.de/sites/default/files/uploads/files/2019-11/kochan_0.pdf (retrieved 12 January 2023). Yet, the East German population held the third highest position worldwide for alcohol consumption (Kochan, 'Alkohol und Alkoholrausch in der DDR'). Studies have, in fact, shown that 76 per cent of boys and 57 per cent of girls as young as 14 could be categorized as 'regular drinkers' (Margit Wiesner et al., 'Trajectories of Alcohol Use Among Adolescent Boys and Girls: Identification, Validation, and Sociodemographic Characteristics', *Psychology of Addictive Behaviors* 21(1) (2007), 62–75 [at 69]). As a result,

official media outlets swept the ever-growing problem of alcoholism under the rug and the SED tended to minimize the issue (Haack, Kochan 2011; and Erika Sieber, 'Alkoholmissbrauch und –abhängigkeit in der ehemaligen DDR und in den neuen Bundesländern', *Sozial- und Präventivmedizin* 43(2) (1998), 90–99).
18. I most certainly am not suggesting that alcoholism was always correctly or fairly used as a reason to strip parents of their rights. In fact, it has been shown that the wording in both the Familiengesetzbuch and the Jugendhilfeverordnung was vague at best, and the interpretation of the law, particularly of the concept 'Erziehungsgefährdung', which was one of the most common reasons given for removing children from their nuclear families, was based on official notions of collective rather than individual 'good'. See 'Bericht zur Aufarbeitung der Heimerziehung in der DDR', pp. 10–11, 17–18, and 25).
19. Cornelia Klauß and Ralf Schenk (eds), 'Die eigene Handschrift', in *Sie: Regisseurinnen der DEFA und ihre Filme* (Berlin: Bertz + Fischer Verlag, 2019).
20. Ibid., pp. 11, 12.

Select Bibliography

'Bericht zur Aufarbeitung der Heimerziehung in der DDR'. Arbeitsgemeinschaft für Kinder und Jugendhilfe. Berlin, 2012. https://www.agj.de/fileadmin/files/publikationen/Expertisen_web.pdf (retrieved 28 May 2022).

Domscheit-Berg, Anke. 'Familienpolitik in Ost- und Westdeutschland und ihre langfristigen Auswirkungen', *Heinrich Böll Stiftung*, 9 November 2016, https://www.boell.de/de/2016/11/09/familienpolitik-ost-und-westdeutschland-und-ihre-langfristigen-auswirkungen (retrieved 16 October 2022).

Feinstein, Joshua. *The Triumph of the Ordinary: Depictions of Daily Life in the East German Cinema 1949–89*. Chapel Hill: University of North Carolina Press, 2002.

Gramann, Ulrike. 'Sehnsucht adé: Begegnung mit Kurzfilmen von Petra Tschörtner und Helke Misselwitz', *Frauen und Film* 62 (2000), 125–28.

Haack, Kathleen et al. 'Vom "wesensfremden Konsum" – Zum Umgang mit der Alkoholproblematik in einem DDR-Großbetrieb', *Psychotherapie, Psychosomatik, medizinische Psychologie* 72 (2022), 558–63.

Jordan, Günter, and Ralf Schenk (eds). *Schwarzweiß und Farbe*. Potsdam: Jovis, 1996.

Klauß, Cornelia, and Ralf Schenk (eds). 'Die eigene Handschrift', in *Sie. Regisseurinnen der DEFA und ihre Filme*. Berlin: Bertz + Fischer Verlag, 2019, pp. 11–24.

Lesage, Julia. 'The Political Aesthetics of the Feminist Documentary Film', *Quarterly Review of Film Studies* 3(4) (1978), 507–23.

Mau, Steffen. *Lütten Klein: Leben in der Ostdeutschen Transformationsgesellschaft*. Berlin: Suhrkamp, 2019.
Nichelmann, Johannes. *Nachwendekinder: Die DDR, unsere Eltern und das große Schweigen*. Berlin: Ullstein, 2019.

PART III
Transnational Documentary

CHAPTER 8

East German Documentary Films by and about Sorbs

Andy Räder

For over a century, films have been created by and about the Sorbs, yet Sorbian filmmaking has consistently faced marginalization, both in the past and the present. In the sphere of documentary production, it is striking that there has been a greater emphasis on producing films *about* the Sorbs rather than *by* and *for* them (especially during the 1950s and 1960s). DEFA played a significant role in this, crafting documentaries that focused on Sorbian traditions, folklore while highlighting the alleged 'otherness' of this indigenous minority. However, these films often presented a distorted portrayal of Sorbian culture. Non-Sorbian directors, such as Hans-Günter Kaden, Kurt Stahnke, Erich Barthel, Werner Kreiseler, Heinz Müller, Armin Georgi, Gerhard Jentsch, Rolf Hofmann and the sole female director Maria Hohnstein, made these short films under the auspices of the DEFA-Studio für Wochenschau und Dokumentarfilme (DEFA Studio for Newsreel and Documentary Films) and the DEFA-Studio für Populärwissenschaftliche Filme (DEFA Studio for Popular Science Films). It was not until the 1970s and 1980s that Sorbian filmmakers began producing their own short films. These productions sought to capture various aspects of Sorbian daily life, history, and artistic and cultural expressions encompassing literature, theatre, the visual arts and music. Throughout these documentaries, questions surrounding Sorbian identity persistently emerge, reflecting the ongoing exploration of the Sorbs' sense of self.

This chapter examines the establishment of Sorbian filmmaking within German Democratic Republic (GDR) film institutions, the films' contributions to the development of Sorbian national identity, their primary thematic motifs, and the response of both the East German state and audiences. I use two documentary short films as examples: *Briefe – In Gedenken an Dr. Maria Grollmuß; Listy* (*Letters – In Memory of Dr. Maria Grollmuß; Listy*, 1985) and *Sokoł – P.S. ke kapitlej našich stawiznow/Sokol – P.S. zu einem Kapitel unserer Geschichte* (*Sokol – P.S. On a Chapter of Our History*, 1990), both directed by Toni Bruk, a Sorbian filmmaker. In *Listy*, the documentary tells the story of Marja Grólmusec (Maria Grollmuß), a Sorbian publicist and antifascist fighter who died in the Ravensbrück concentration camp in 1944. The film intertwines her personal suffering with images of her Sorbian homeland, her family's history and the official culture of remembrance in the GDR. *Sokoł – P.S. ke kapitlej našich stawiznow* also explores Sorbian resistance against the Nazi regime, focusing on the almost forgotten history of the Sorbian gymnastics association Sokoł. The documentary features interviews with former members and contemporary footage to chronicle the association's history until its forced dissolution in 1933. It presents the memory of Sokoł as an integral part of Sorbian identity.

To provide a comprehensive understanding of the cultural and historical aspects of the Sorbian minority in the GDR, I give a general description of the Sorbs and their film production to situate the significance of these films in the context of East German minority politics and Sorbian national identity, before I apply Roger Odin's semio-pragmatic approach as a theoretical framework for the analysis of the films. Odin's theoretical concept considers the historical context, the significance of individual protagonists and the effects on the audience. It goes beyond analysing the film text itself and considers how different audiences, including the Sorbian minority in the GDR, read and interpret the film, to eventually allow exploration of the cultural and societal impact of Sorbian filmmaking within the GDR.

The Sorbs and their Films

The Sorbs, a West Slavic ethnic group, originally settled in Upper and Lower Lusatia during the seventh and eighth centuries. Historically, they were often referred to as 'Wends', a term that was sometimes used derogatorily. However, today, 'Sorbs' is the more commonly used term, although in Lower Lusatia, the phrase 'Sorben/Wenden' is still used.[1]

Within the GDR, the Sorbs were the only officially recognized autochthonous minority. The GDR Constitutions of 1948 and 1968 guaranteed the rights of the Sorbian people.[2] While the East German minority policy officials focused on integrating and assimilating the Sorbian population into the socialist state, the Sorbs were granted a certain degree of autonomy in administration, education and culture. Bilingualism and the preservation of cultural practices were actively encouraged as part of the minority's protection.

One of the primary concerns for the Sorbian minority, both then and now, is the fear of losing their homelands to open-cast coal mining. This issue is closely tied to questions of identity, as the industrialization of Upper and Lower Lusatia led to significant German labour migration, particularly in brown coal (lignite) mining. Over the course of the twentieth century, more than 100 Sorbian villages were destroyed, and tens of thousands of Sorbs had to be resettled. The destruction of the natural landscape was accompanied by the loss of Sorbian identity, as the heritage and culture of the Sorbs could not be fully reconstructed in the new settlement areas. Consequently, one of the prominent themes in Sorbian artistic and cultural production revolves around the loss of their homeland and identity due to coal mining. Another crucial topic explored is the period of National Socialism, during which the Nazi government sought to assimilate the Sorbs, resulting in the arrest, imprisonment and murder of many Sorbian intellectuals. I will explore these subjects in more detail in my analysis of the films and offer a more comprehensive understanding of the Sorbian minority's struggles and experiences that highlights the challenges they faced in preserving their language, culture and identity in the face of significant sociopolitical and environmental changes.

During the early 1970s, there was growing support for Sorbian filmmaking, driven by various initiatives within the Sorbian cultural scene. These initiatives provided opportunities for Sorbian filmmakers to produce their own films. In 1971, the Arbeitskreis Sorbischer Filmschaffender (Working Group of Sorbian Filmmakers) was established, allowing several Sorbian cultural and creative workers to organize themselves. This working group joined the existing Sorbian groups dedicated to theatre, literature, music and the visual arts. In 1980, the Sorbian cultural anthropologist Toni Bruk established the Serbska filmowa skupina (Production Group Sorbian Film), which operated under the auspices of the DEFA-Studio für Trickfilme (DEFA Studio for Animated Films) in Dresden.[3] Its mission was to create two to three films each year that captured significant aspects of Sorbian history, culture and daily life. The members of the production group had access to the technical resources and production facilities of the Dresden studio. The initial films produced by the Sorbian production group were documentary shorts ranging from 10 to 30 minutes in length. These documentaries focused on showcasing the unique history, culture, language and way of life of the Sorbian minority. The headquarters of the production group were in Budyšin (Bautzen), which served as the cultural and political centre for Upper Sorbian activities.

The establishment of the Serbska filmowa skupina contributed to an increase in the production of live-action films at the Dresden studio. This institutionalized Sorbian film production in the context of the official minority policy in the GDR. However, despite being part of the DEFA Studio, the Sorbian production group faced marginalization in terms of geography, language and content. They received little attention from DEFA film studio officials and employees until the end of the production group and the GDR itself.

Additionally, Budyšin (Bautzen), the cultural centre of Sorbian activity, borrowed film equipment from the 'agra' film studio, which was under the administration of the Ministry for Agriculture, Forestry and Food Industry. This borrowing was made possible because Sorbian director and co-founder of the production group, Johannes (Jan) Hempel, worked at the 'agra' film studio in Leipzig-Markkleeberg.[4] These developments within the Sorbian cultural scene and the establishment of the Serbska filmowa skupina provided a significant boost to Sorbian filmmaking, allowing Sorbian filmmakers to access necessary resources and facilities to produce films that represented their history, culture and everyday experiences.

Despite having some degree of artistic freedom and the advantage of distance from major film centres like Dresden, Potsdam and Berlin, the filmmakers of the group still had to adhere to the ideological restrictions imposed by the communist state's minority policy. Film concepts had to be approved by both the DEFA-Studio für Trickfilme and the Hauptverwaltung Film (HV Film) of the Ministerium für Kultur (MfK – Ministry of Culture). The completed productions also went through an official acceptance and controlling process to ensure they aligned with the political and ideological agenda of constructing socialism. During the period from 1980 to 1991, an impressive total of over thirty Sorbian documentaries were produced, making it the most productive decade for Sorbian filmmaking in the GDR. Among these films, eight were co-productions with film studios from the Socialist Federal Republic of Yugoslavia, the Soviet Union, Czechoslovakia and Poland. This international collaboration expanded the reach of Sorbian cinema beyond national boundaries.

The documentaries covered a wide range of topics, focusing on various aspects of Sorbian life within East German socialism. They delved into Sorbian cultural heritage, exploring traditional customs, folklore and artistic expressions. Additionally, they shed light on contemporary Sorbian art, capturing the vibrant cultural scene of the minority group. Most of these documentaries took the form of portraits, highlighting individual Sorbian personalities or social groups. They aimed to provide insights into Sorbian life and traditions for non-Sorbian audiences, acting as a bridge of understanding between the Sorbs and the wider German society. Notably, these films navigated the question of Sorbian identity by incorporating a blend of both German and Sorbian languages, showcasing the linguistic and cultural fusion that characterizes the Sorbian community.

In this chapter, I analyse and compare the two Sorbian documentary films *Briefe – In Gedenken an Dr. Maria Grollmuß: Listy* and *Sokoł – P.S. ke kapitlej našich stawiznow / Sokol – P.S. zu einem Kapitel unserer Geschichte* in terms of their strategies and concepts of cinematic representation of Sorbian life, with a particular focus on the audience. These films were produced by Toni Bruk, the Sorbian filmmaker and founder of the production group, during the mid- to late 1980s. Their purpose was to provide insights into the group's production profile and to showcase the broad cultural-political mission of the Sorbian community.[5] The production group had four key guidelines for their films: first, they aimed to introduce the Sorbs in the context of the socialist present of the GDR, featuring artists, teachers, industry leaders and politicians; second, they focused on showcasing Sorbian cultural heritage and present-day art, introducing East Germans to Sorbian culture and its historical significance; third, they highlighted the social and political struggles of the Sorbs, portraying them as active participants in the German labour movement; and, finally, they explored the international relations, traditions and connections of the Sorbs with socialist countries.

However, these documentaries had limited viewership outside of Upper and Lower Lusatia, and even in the Dresden and Cottbus areas, they were rarely screened. Only a few films were included in the cinema programme of the Progress film distribution company and received limited broadcast on East German television. Most of the films were stored and distributed by Sorbian organizations or the production group itself, catering to interested individuals or institutions. Films that lacked German subtitles, such as *Sokoł – P.S. ke kapitlej našich stawiznow*, had limited appeal to German-speaking audiences. This restricted exposure to wider audiences contributed to the marginalization of Sorbian films and the challenges they faced in reaching a broader German audience.

Roger Odin's framework helps provide insights into the viewers' engagement with the films and addresses questions such as the viewers' role, differences in interpretation between Sorbs and non-Sorbs, opportunities for cultural exchange, and the authenticity of documentaries that actively engage with the everyday life of their protagonists.[6] According to semio-pragmatics, the enunciator in the medium of film is the speaker who directly addresses the viewer. While the audience is the target of the audiovisual expression in a documentary, Odin suggests that the meaning of a documentary is not solely inscribed in its text, but also emerges from its reception. Therefore, the production of meaning occurs both in the mode of production and in the mode of reading. Applied to Sorbian film, Odin's modes of reading films, the mode of fictionalizing and the mode of documentarizing, are influenced by two factors: the film text itself (the propositional structure of the documentary produced by the Sorbian production group) and the context in which the film is presented (for example, a screening in a Sorbian cultural institution). These circumstances significantly impact how viewers experience and understand a film. For example, watching a documentary with a thematic introduction at a Domowina-sponsored event predominantly attended by Sorbs would create a different viewing experience compared to watching the same film as part of a cinema programme for a DEFA feature film in an East German cinema, where the film's engagement with minority issues may not be a central consideration.[7]

By analysing the interplay between the film text and the context of presentation, this chapter explores how these factors shape the viewers' interpretations and experiences of Sorbian documentaries. This approach allows us to consider the role of the audience, the potential divergences in understanding between different viewers, and the implications of cultural exchange in the reception and meaning making of these films. Additionally, it makes it possible to investigate how the common communicative competence shared by the protagonists, filmmakers and audience members serves as a reservoir of modes for producing meanings and affects within the historical corpus of Sorbian minority documentary films from the 1980s.

Considering Bruk's background, experiences and dedication to Sorbian filmmaking, analysing his directorial choices and intentions will provide valuable insights into the films' propositional structures and their contributions to the broader mission of representing Sorbian culture, history and identity. Born in 1947, Toni Bruk immersed himself in Sorbian cultural organizations and worked for the Domowina after leaving high school. His interest in Sorbian cinema led him to research and establish the film archive in the Serbski dom (House of the Sorbs) and organize film screenings in Budyšin. Although initially rejected as a student at the Hochschule für Film und Fernsehen (HFF), he pursued cultural studies at the Karl Marx University in Leipzig, with a specific focus on Sorbian film. In 1984, he earned his Ph.D. from the Film and Television Faculty of the Academy of Performing Arts in Prague (FAMU). As a founding member of the Arbeitskreis Sorbischer Filmschaffender in 1971, Bruk played an instrumental role in the development of Sorbian filmmaking. He served as the director of the Serbska filmowa skupina at the DEFA-Studio für Trickfilme in Dresden from 1980 until its dissolution in 1992. During this period, he led the production group, overseeing the creation of numerous documentaries that shed light on Sorbian everyday life, culture and history. The dissolution of the production group prompted him to establish the Sorabia Film Studio in Budyšin, where he continued to contribute to Sorbian filmmaking. His subsequent works primarily consisted of short TV documentaries on various aspects of Sorbian life, as well as films for children and educational films for Sorbian schools. Bruk's extensive involvement in establishing and promoting Sorbian filmmaking in the GDR earned him recognition as the doyen of Sorbian film.[8] His contributions spanned the entire trajectory of Sorbian cinema, and his role as the director of the production group highlights his commitment to advancing Sorbian cultural representation through film.

Briefe – In Gedenken an Dr. Maria Grollmuß; Listy

The documentary *Briefe – In Gedenken an Dr. Maria Grollmuß; Listy* presents a portrait of Marja Grólmusec, a Catholic Sorbian woman who became a symbol of political resistance and suffering during the National Socialist era. The film, with a running time of 17 minutes, sheds light on the political conflict of conscience experienced by Grólmusec and the subsequent instrumentalization of her martyrdom by the East German state. Born in Leipzig in 1896, Marja Grólmusec was deeply committed to her Catholic faith and pursued a career as an academic, journalist, editor and teacher. She hailed from Radwor (Radibor), a Sorbian town in Upper Lusatia, where her father worked as a Sorbian teacher. With the rise of the National Socialist Party in Germany in 1933, Grólmusec went into hiding in Radwor and became involved in aiding refugees, acting as a courier between Germany, Czechoslovakia and Austria. Notably, she assisted the children of Max Seydewitz, who later became the first Prime Minister of Saxony, in their escape. In 1934, she was arrested by the Gestapo on charges of plotting to forcefully change the Reich's Constitution, a highly treasonable offense in the eyes of the Nazi regime. She was sentenced to six years in prison, initially serving her sentence at Zuchthaus Waldheim. In January 1941, she was transferred to Ravensbrück, a concentration camp for women, where she ultimately passed away on 6 August 1944.

The documentary delves into the life and experiences of Marja Grólmusec, highlighting her courageous acts of resistance against the National Socialists and her subsequent persecution and imprisonment. The film also explores the posthumous recognition and exploitation of her martyrdom by the East German state, further contextualizing her significance within the broader sociopolitical climate. Analysing the film allows for an examination of the cinematic representation of Grólmusec's life and the ways in which her story is framed and interpreted. It offers insights into the complexities of her experiences as a Catholic Sorbian woman and her enduring legacy as a symbol of resistance and sacrifice. Moreover, the documentary employs various narrative elements to create an authentic and emotional experience for the viewers. It taps into the existing Sorbian discourse of remembrance surrounding Grólmusec, presenting her as a highly religious Sorbian, a respected scholar and a heroic communist resistance fighter. This narrative aligns with the prevailing narrative of active Sorbian antifascist resistance against the National Socialist Party.

One of the prominent plot elements in the film is the depiction of Upper Lusatia's serene landscapes and natural settings. Through visually captivating shots, the film showcases the region's forests, meadows, ponds, lakes and deserted neighbourhoods. These images not only emphasize the beauty of nature but also evoke a sense of nostalgia. Grólmusec's letters, which are read aloud in the film, serve as a conduit for her personal memories and reflections. She fondly recalls the time spent with her sister at their parents' summer home, highlighting the connection between nature, family and the Sorbian way of life. Additionally, the film includes close-up shots that feature significant landmarks such as the church in Radwor, Grólmusec's father's birthplace. These visual cues serve to reinforce the viewer's association with the small Sorbian villages and their traditional communities. By emphasizing the vulnerability of these communities in the face of the impending catastrophe of the Second World War, the film aims to evoke a sense of empathy and emotional resonance within the audience. Through its careful use of narrative elements and visual storytelling, *Listy* aims to immerse the viewers in the tragic story of Marja Grólmusec. The film captures the essence of her personal experiences and the larger context of the Sorbian community's struggle during the turbulent times of the National Socialist era. By weaving together these elements, the documentary aims to create an authentic portrayal of Grólmusec's life and the historical backdrop in which it unfolded.

The second narrative line in *Listy* takes a dramatic turn as the focus shifts abruptly to the Ravensbrück concentration camp. This transition creates a stark contrast between the serene landscapes of Upper Lusatia and the harrowing reality of the camp. The change in rhythm and imagery aims to convey the immediate threat and terror faced by Marja Grólmusec and the other female prisoners. The sequence of images captures the grim atmosphere of the concentration camp, including photographs of cremation, toxic gas barrels, and depictions of captive women and camp life. These visuals serve as a powerful representation of the harsh conditions and suffering endured by the prisoners. The intention is to immerse the audience in the same sense of immediacy and fear that the inmates experienced, thereby eliciting a strong emotional response. The decision to shift the narrator's voice from an empathetic female Sorbian voice to a loud and aggressive masculine German voice when reading the death notification from the camp commandant is significant and reflects the power dynamics and the gendered roles associated with the historical context of the Sorbian minority. The perpetrators are portrayed as male, while the victims are predominantly female. This representation aligns with the prevalent historical perceptions of the Sorbian minority during that time. Furthermore, the documentary's use of images predominantly featuring women dressed in traditional costumes to portray Sorbian life suggests a deliberate focus on the cultural aspects associated with Sorbian identity. By highlighting traditional costumes and cultural practices, the filmmakers aim to reinforce the distinctiveness and resilience of the Sorbian minority in the face of oppression and adversity.

Overall, the juxtaposition of landscapes, concentration camp imagery and gendered narration in *Listy* aims to create a powerful cinematic experience that immerses the audience in the story of Marja Grólmusec and sheds light on the historical experiences of the Sorbian community during a tumultuous period. The suffering experienced by the concentration camp prisoners is brought into the present through contemporary footage of the Ravensbrück National Memorial. Bruk utilizes images such as prison cells, barred windows and a cell door to evoke the oppressive and claustrophobic environment of the camp. Additionally, the inclusion of Willi Lammert's sculptures 'Frau mit Tuch' and 'Frau mit abgeschnittenen Haar' (1956), Fritz Cremer's 'Müttergruppe' (1965) and pictures from the exhibition at the memorial further emphasize the historical context and the atrocities that took place.

The camera's movement towards Marja Grólmusec's portrait on the wall of victims signifies a moment of intimate connection between the protagonist and the audience. This moment serves as a rupture in the narrative, drawing attention to the personal experiences and struggles of Grólmusec and the countless other victims of the concentration camp. This poignant sequence is juxtaposed with images of the crematorium and emaciated prisoners, intensifying the emotional impact on the viewers. To establish the culpability for the suffering endured by the inmates, the camera moves along the 'Wall of Nations' before focusing on the sign for 'Deutschland' (Germany). This visual cue aims to emphasize the collective responsibility of the German nation for the horrors of the concentration camps.

In conjunction with these visuals, the voice of the female narrator reads a passage from a letter written by Grólmusec in Sorbian. In this letter, Grólmusec draws a parallel between her own situation and that of Joan of Arc:

> I think of my saint, the self-chosen patroness of confirmation Jeanne d'Arc. In the midst of depravity, despair, and betrayal, in a land that had fallen into insanity, she believed in the bright, auspicious virgin of the annunciation.

The combination of these elements in the documentary seeks to create a powerful and evocative portrayal of Grólmusec's story, highlighting the profound suffering endured by the concentration camp prisoners and emphasizing the historical and cultural significance of their experiences.

The third plot element focuses on the Sorbian Secondary School in Radwor, named 'Dr. Maria Grollmuß' in honour of the protagonist. The film presents footage of students in the classroom reciting parts of Marja Grólmusec's biography. These scenes, featuring the students providing lively information about Grólmusec, are praised for their natural and unrehearsed performances (see Figure 8.1).[9] In addition to the recitations, the documentary incorporates visual elements that complement the narration. It includes portraits of Grólmusec, as well as black-

Figure 8.1. Camera set up in the classroom to capture the school children's performances in Toni Bruk's *Briefe – In Gedenken an Dr. Maria Grollmuß; Listy* (1985). © DEFA-Stiftung/Foto: Lothar Schuster

and-white drawings created by the children under the guidance of Toni Bruk's brother. These drawings depict everyday life in a concentration camp, showcasing images of barbed wire, barred windows, interrogation rooms and prisoners gathered around Grólmusec's deathbed.

The documentary concludes with a positive portrayal of a new generation of Sorbian children. The ideological underpinning of the films suggests that these children will play a role in building East German socialism and shaping a promising future. The film presents scenes of children playing in the schoolyard and vibrant, colourful drawings inspired by the Young Pioneer song 'Immer lebe die Sonne' (Long Live the Sun). These drawings depict happy young pioneers wearing neckerchiefs, scenes of nature and elements of the landscape. By highlighting the involvement of children and their connection to the legacy of Marja Grólmusec, the documentary seeks to convey a sense of continuity and hope for the future. It presents a vision of the younger generation actively participating in the construction of an idealized socialist society in the GDR.

In the documentary *Listy*, three eyewitnesses are interviewed towards the end of the film, and their comments contribute to the exaggeration of Marja Grólmusec's reputation as a courageous and intelligent resistance fighter. However, one particular interview with Rosa Jochmann stands out due to a technical limitation. As Jochmann was living in Vienna and the Sorbian filmmakers were not allowed to travel to Austria, the conversation could only be recorded on audio. To overcome this limitation, Toni Bruk, the filmmaker, hired historian and Slavic expert Gero Fischer from Vienna to conduct the interview. The audio recording of the interview was then combined with photos of Rosa Jochmann, Grólmusec and the concentration camp.

The other two interviewees in the documentary are Fridolin Seydewitz, a lawyer and the son of Max Seydewitz, and Eva Lippold, an author. Their interviews, along with visual illustrations such as images of locations in the border zone depicting Lippold's escape to the Czech Republic, contribute to highlighting Grólmusec's suffering and emphasizing her significance for the Sorbian identity after the Second World War By placing Grólmusec alongside other East German antifascist and socialist heroes, Bruk aims to demonstrate the successful integration and assimilation of the Sorbs into the GDR state. Overall, these interviews and visual representations serve to amplify Grólmusec's role as a symbol of resistance and underscore her importance in shaping the Sorbian identity in the postwar period. Through her story, the documentary seeks to prove that the Sorbian community found its place within the larger framework of the socialist system.

The documentary utilizes multiple voices and narrators that alternate in various ways to convey its story. The opening credits do not provide explicit clues about the modes of documentarizing or the direct speaker. However, there is a brief reference to the Sorbian film title, which appears after one-and-a-half minutes without translation into German. According to Odin, this strategy suggests those who may be responsible for shaping the discourse surrounding the film. This includes the filmmakers themselves, as well as the eyewitnesses Rosa Jochmann, Fridolin Seydewitz and Eva Lippold, who influenced the production of meaning and may have been involved in screenings, introductions or audience discussions.

This mode of documentarizing creates a 'discursive space', as described by Odin, where a diversity of voices influences the communicative space of *Listy*. The film incorporates various stylistic elements that contribute to its journalistic nature, such as the use of different narrators, contemporary witnesses and experts, archival footage, photographs and children's drawings specifically created for the film. These elements reflect the film's multifaceted approach to storytelling. Notably, there is no single testifying individual who represents the viewers, such as a Sorbian director who would shape the mode of documentarizing. Instead, the DEFA-Studio für Trickfilme in Dresden, mentioned first in the credits, is likely perceived by the audience as the official authority behind this act of cultural and political enunciation.

It seems that the documentary was designed to align with the official narrative of resistance against Hitler's Germany and the socialist construction of the GDR. By focusing on a Sorbian individual biography and incorporating Sorbian themes and motifs throughout the film, the intention was to appeal to the Sorbian audience, allowing them to connect the martyrdom of the resistance fighter to their own Sorbian history. This portrayal also aimed to contribute to the majority society's collective memory and the founding myth of the GDR. However, it appears that outside of bilingual Lusatia, where the Sorbian language and culture are more prevalent, East German citizens did not have the same opportunity to engage with the film. Despite the existence of both a German-language and a Sorbian-language copy, the German-language version was not screened and remained stored at the Domowina for several years. This suggests that the film's impact and accessibility were limited to the Sorbian community and those with knowledge of the Sorbian language, while the broader East German population did not have the same exposure to the film.

It is striking that, in addition to the documentary film, there was only one biography written about Marja Grólmusec's life in the GDR titled *Sterne über dem Abgrund. Das Leben von Maria Grollmuß* (*Stars above the Abyss. The Life of Maria Grollmuß*) by Marja Kubašec (Maria Kubasch) in 1961.[10] Both the biography and the film portrait aimed to connect the history of the Sorbs with the myth of the antifascist foundation of the GDR through the narrative of Marja Grólmusec's suffering. A quote from Eva Lippold, the writer and eyewitness, at the end of the documentary further emphasizes this connection, stating that she is certain Marja would belong to them today, thus implying that Marja would be a part of the socialist GDR if she were alive. This suggests a deliberate cultural and political instrumentalization of Sorbian history and individual biographies by the East German cultural policy. The modes of production of meaning by the Sorbian filmmakers and the interpretative modes of the Sorbian audience created a space of communication that was assumed to be consensual, where the documentary was received and understood within a specific cultural and political context. This in turn reflects the extent to which the film was intended to reinforce a particular narrative and foster a sense of solidarity and identity among the Sorbian community within the GDR.

The cultural and political instrumentalization of *Listy* can be observed in the process of its official approval and subsequent modifications. The DEFA Studio management raised minor technical concerns about the documentary, but the HV Film approved it with objections. One objection was related to a negative statement made by a child regarding Leipzig's poor air quality, which Deputy Minister of Culture Horst Pehnert found unacceptable.[11] Pehnert demanded that the scene be cut from the film. This procedure was unusual, as the HV Film had approved very few films produced by the production group. It is noteworthy that Bruk complied with the request to remove the scene without criticism. However, he expressed his dissatisfaction in a formal letter to Pehnert, pointing out that Sorbian films were at a disadvantage compared to other DEFA films because they did not receive approval from the responsible governmental institution.[12] Bruk aimed to prevent Sorbian filmmaking from being relegated to a parallel culture within East German cinema. He sought equal treatment for this minority cinema in the GDR.

Sokoł – P.S. ke kapitlej našich stawiznow/Sokol – P.S. zu einem Kapitel unserer Geschichte

Despite the presence of German subtitles in almost all Sorbian documentaries, making them accessible to German audiences and state officials, these films were marginalized before and after the incident with *Listy*. It is worth mentioning that only one film, *Sokoł – P.S. ke kapitlej našich stawiznow*, released in 1990 and shot exclusively in Sorbian without subtitles, gained attention, but remained an exception within the broader context of Sorbian cinema. The short documentary – also directed by Toni Bruk – focuses on the Sorbian Sokoł Association and its legacy. Interestingly, the idea for a film about the Sokoł Association, provisionally titled 'Das Vermächtnis des Sokol' (The Legacy of Sokol), had been planned since 1982, with Konrad Herrmann initially intended as the director. However, filming could not commence until 1989. During the long gap between the initial planning and the actual filming, several challenges arose. The advanced age of the protagonists presented significant difficulties for the production team. Unfortunately, before shooting began in Lusatia, several members of the Sokoł Association had passed away, necessitating multiple revisions of the script to reflect these losses.[13]

The film project *Sokoł – P.S. ke kapitlej našich stawiznow* was part of a film-historical tradition of Sorbian filmmaking that dates back to the late 1920s. During that time, Herbert Cerna, a Lower Sorbian pastor and local historian, and the Czech director Vladimír Zmeškal embarked on documenting everyday life in the Sorbian villages of Lower and Upper Lusatia. These films marked the first original documentary recordings by Sorbian filmmakers, capturing the unique Sorbian/Wendish culture. Among the four silent short movies produced during this period, the last one, entitled *Hornja Łužica* (*Oberlausitz*, 1931), included footage of the Sokoł meeting of Lusatian Sorbians held in Radwor in 1927. Building on this historical context, the 1989 documentary focused on former members of the Sokoł Association, which was regarded as the most progressive organization within the Sorbian national movement. The Sokoł movement, functioning as a sports and cultural organization, played a significant role in the pursuit of national independence for Slavic minorities.[14] The Sokoł gymnastics movement was established in Prague in 1862 with the aim of promoting national unity among Slavic nations. Numerous Sokoł organizations emerged in various regions, including Lusatia, where the Sokoł Association served as an important platform for physical training and cultural activities, contributing to the preservation and advancement of Sorbian identity within the broader context of Slavic solidarity.

The Serbski Sokoł Association, founded in 1920, played a crucial role in promoting Sorbian nationalism and fostering a sense of Sorbian identity. The association organized annual Sokoł meetings in Lusatia from 1924 to 1931, providing a platform for Sorbian athletes to showcase their skills and participate in international Sokoł competitions held in various locations such as Prague, Skopje, Belgrade and Poznań. The Serbski Sokoł went beyond sports and encouraged political and cultural activities. They actively promoted cultural education among Sorbian children, including the establishment of a puppet theatre in Hrodźišćo (Gröditz) that aimed to familiarize them with the Sorbian language and culture. The association published the *Sokołske listy*, a songbook containing songs frequently sung by its members, which further fostered a sense of unity and camaraderie among the Sorbian community. However, the Serbski Sokoł faced repression and persecution under the National Socialist Party. In 1933, as part of the Nazi regime's measures to suppress the Sorbian minority, the association was forced to disband. The Nazis viewed the Sorbs as a foreign ethnic minority and sought to suppress their cultural and national identity.

More than half a century later, in Bronjo (Brohna), former Sokoł members came together to shoot the documentary, reminiscing about their time in the association. Prominent Sorbian painter and writer

Měrćin Nowak-Njechorński (Martin Nowak-Neumann), one of the founders of the Sorbian Sokoł Association in 1920, was among the participants, highlighting the enduring significance and impact of the Sokoł movement on the Sorbian community. The documentary *Sokoł – P.S. ke kapitlej našich stawiznow* incorporates various elements to portray the eyewitness testimonies and convey the history of the Sokoł sports movement. The framing narrative of the film revolves around a puppet theatre production featuring the hand puppets Kasper and Jan (Figure 8.2). This approach not only serves as a creative and engaging storytelling device but also pays homage to the Sokoł puppet theatre in Hrodźišćo. By using puppets and involving contemporary witnesses, the documentary humorously depicts key aspects of the Sokoł sports movement. The direct addressing of the protagonists and the inclusion of the audience in the action create a participatory and immersive experience. The film also incorporates authentic documents, historical film footage and photographs to support the eyewitness testimonies and provide a visual representation of the Sokoł movement.

Strikingly the entire film is shot in Sorbian without any subtitles. This decision to exclusively use Upper Sorbian was a result of the political transformation occurring between the fall of the Berlin Wall and German reunification. During this period, the control mechanisms of HV Film were not functioning effectively, particularly in relation to Sorbian films in Budyšin. The members of the production group took advantage of this situation to create a film specifically tailored for the Upper Sorbian audience, allowing for a more direct and intimate connection with the local community. The production of the documentary in Upper Sorbian reflects a unique opportunity facilitated by the changing political landscape, enabling the Serbska filmowa skupina to produce a film that directly addressed the Upper Sorbian community and showcased their language and culture. There is a notable emphasis on the cinematic mise-en-scène, particularly in the way in which documentary images are presented. The film begins and ends with shots of a film projector in the fictional present, projecting archival footage from the 1930 Allsokol meeting in Belgrade onto a screen. These images capture Sorbian gymnasts performing their disciplines in the stadium, providing a historical context, and setting the tone for the documentary.

Throughout the film, there are glimpses of the camera and dolly tracks in the hosts' garden where the former Sokoł members gather. These shots, along with occasional appearances of the production crew (though their specific roles are not identified), contribute to an understanding of the documentary's mode of production and documenta-

Figure 8.2. Shooting of the hand puppet scene in *Sokol – P.S. zu einem Kapitel unserer Geschichte* (1990). © DEFA-Stiftung/Foto: Jürgen Matschie

rizing. The presence of the camera and the production team highlights the process of capturing and documenting the testimonies and events. Moreover, the documentary incorporates a close-knit community of protagonists, including the contemporary witnesses and the production crew, who come together to remember and celebrate Sorbian history. They interact with each other in their own language, often dressed in traditional Sokoł costumes, symbolizing a confident representation of Sorbian identity within a reunified Germany. The focus is on their shared experiences and the preservation of Sorbian history rather than catering to a broader German audience or prioritizing accessibility to non-Sorbian viewers.

This approach reflects a sense of liberation from previous political and cultural constraints, allowing the Sorbian community to assert their identity and express themselves in their own language and cultural practices. The film creates a space where the Sorbian community can assert their history and celebrate their heritage, regardless of whether it is fully understood or accessible to the wider German public. The absence of subtitles for the speakers' names or roles contributes to the film's documentarized reading. For Sorbian viewers, the former Sokoł members are familiar personalities, except for Dušan Stanimirović, the expert on the Sokol movement from the University of Skopje in Macedonia. He is introduced by the narrator's voice as an expert before being questioned. The contemporary witnesses, including Lenka Meltke, Měrćin Nowak-Njechorński, Paul Greulich and Georg Frenzel, speak as private individuals and are filmed in everyday situations, sharing their personal memories.

Lenka Meltke, whose late husband was involved in the founding of a women's department at the Sokoł Association, discusses the challenges faced by Lower Lusatian Sorbs in the 1930s and presents memorabilia from the Sokoł. Měrćin Nowak-Njechorński talks about the forced dissolution of the Sorbian Sokoł Association, while Paul Greulich visits the deteriorating Strahov Stadium in Prague, where he participated in the Allsokol Meeting in 1932 as a member of the small Sorbian group of athletes. Georg Frenzel, the Mayor of Horka (Ralbitz), is portrayed as a dedicated advocate for sports in the region, upholding the 'spirit of the Sokoł.'

This ensemble of enunciators serves a direct statement function, progressively developing and solidifying throughout the documentary. The emphasis is on nostalgia and reflecting on their own history, as well as the subsequent suffering of the Sorbs during the era of National Socialism. Since the documentary adopts a narrative perspective from within the community, there is limited room for the viewer to critically engage with the statements and develop their own perspective. The documentary aims to evoke a sense of collective memory and reinforce a particular viewpoint rather than encouraging a critical dialogue with the audience. In addition, the absence of traditional opening credits also impacts on the interpretation of the documentary's modes of meaning production and documentarizing. The Sorbian film title appears after a two-minute performance by the Lusatian puppet theatre Šěrachow, which serves as a framing device for the documentary. Throughout the film, a narrator guides the audience, providing explanations and clarifications when necessary. The narrator acknowledges the construction of the enunciator as a presumed reality within the context of documentarized reading and references various individuals involved in the discourse.

Alfons Wićaz (Alfons Lehmann), a journalist and Slavist, wrote the scenario, which remained consistent throughout the documentary's production history despite changes in the director. The replacement of Konrad Herrmann, who was born and raised in Budyšin but is not Sorbian, is significant. Despite not speaking the Sorbian language, Herrmann was fascinated by Sorbian artists and intellectuals due to his own background. On the other hand, native Sorbian Bruk, whose mother tongue was Upper Sorbian and who had deep connections with Sorbian institutions and their representatives, was better equipped to address a Sorbian audience with this documentary. The Sorbian audience could identify with this film production as their own, as it was created, written, staged and performed for them. However, the language barrier prevented transcultural exchange between the dominant culture and the minority culture in the GDR and, after 1990, in unified Germany. Sorbian filmmakers relied on the audience's documentarized reading and, for the first time in the history of the Sorbian production group, an exclusive and pure Sorbian mode of meaning and affect in the communication space between the Sorbian sender and Sorbian receiver was possible.

Paradoxically, despite premiering in 1990 and receiving approval from the DEFA studio during the turbulent period between the fall of the Berlin Wall and reunification, the documentary never reached a Sorbian audience. Very few people were concerned with Sorbian filmmaking or documenting everyday Sorbian life during this chaotic time of transformation. The challenges of the post-reunification period affected the Sorbian population as much as the rest of East German society. The Lusatian Sorbs experienced transformation and marginalization twice: first as the only minority in the GDR and then as they had to share their status as an autochthonous national minority with the Danes in Southern Schleswig, the Frisians, and the German Sinti and Roma in the Federal Republic.

Conclusion

The 1980s witnessed significant developments in Sorbian cinema, with a range of films catering to both German and Sorbian audiences. The exploration of two films from the Serbska filmowa skupina during this period revealed the filmmakers' active efforts to engage and connect with Sorbian viewers, sometimes at the expense of non-Sorbian viewers. Despite occasional interference from governmental institutions like the HV Film, the filmmakers demonstrated a commitment to documenting socialist themes and prompting the Sorbian audience to see themselves in the narrative. Towards the end of the 1980s, there was a notable shift in Sorbian filmmaking, highlighting the importance of understanding and addressing a specific audience. *Sokoł – P.S. ke kapitlej našich stawiznow* exemplifies this shift, as director Bruk and his team aimed to create a film that was free from institutional influences and exclusively targeted the Sorbian audience. The documentary was produced entirely in Upper Sorbian, without subtitles, and sought to establish a communicative space rooted in the rich history and culture of the Sorbian minority. However, due to the challenges and upheavals during the post-reunification period, neither a Sorbian nor a German audience was able to experience the film. Overall, the 1980s were a pivotal time for Sorbian cinema, showcasing the filmmakers' determination to engage their audience and preserve Sorbian history and culture through the medium of film. While facing constraints and uncertainties, these filmmakers made significant contributions to the Sorbian film landscape, emphasizing the importance of tailoring their work to the specific needs and interests of the Sorbian community.

Andy Räder is Lecturer in Communication and Media Studies at the University of Rostock (Germany). His research interests are (East) German cinema and television, media history, minorities and marginalized film cultures, historical audience research, digital humanities and children's film. He holds a Ph.D. in media studies on the television director Ulrich Thein and GDR television drama. His latest publications include (co-authored with Grit Lemke) *Sorbische Filmlandschaften. Serbske filmowe krajiny* (Bertz + Fischer, 2024).

Notes

1. For this reason, I will use the term 'Sorbs' for both the Lower Lusatian Wends and the Upper Lusatian Sorbs.
2. The equality of the Sorbian minority was guaranteed in Article 11 of the GDR's very first Constitution of 1949: 'Foreign-language speaking people in the German Democratic Republic are encouraged to develop independently; in particular, they shall not be prevented from using their mother tongue in education, administration and judiciary' (Verfassung der Deutschen Demokratischen Republik, 7 October 1949, http://www.documentArchiv.de/ddr/verfddr1949 [retrieved 9 August 2022]). Article 40 of the 1968 Second Draft of the Constitution of the GDR specifies as follows for the Sorbian minority: 'Citizens of Sorbian origin in the German Democratic Republic have the right to cultivate their native language and culture. The right is supported by the state' (Verfassung der Deutschen Demokratischen

Republik, 6 April 1968, http://www.documentArchiv.de/ddr/verfddr1968 (retrieved 9 August 2022)).
3. Toni Bruk, 'Film', in Franz Schön and Dietrich Scholze (eds), *Sorbisches Kulturlexikon* (Bautzen: Domowina-Verlag, 2014), pp. 122–25. See also Toni Bruk, 'Die Sorben im Film. Zur Gründung der Produktionsgruppe sorbischer Film bei der DEFA', *Filmwissenschaftliche Beiträge* 80(2) (1980), 92–123.
4. Agra-Landwirtschaftsausstellung der DDR, Markkleeberg (= Sächsisches Staatsarchiv: Inventory 20314).
5. Protokoll der Beratung zur mittelfristigen thematischen Planung der Produktionsgruppe Sorbischer Film des DEFA-Studios für Trickfilme beim Stellvertreter des Ministers für Kultur, Dr. Friedhelm Grabe am 26.07.1985 (= BArch DR 1/24039).
6. For more on Roger Odin's semio-pragmatic approach, see Roger Odin, 'Pour une sémio-pragmatique du cinéma'. *Iris* 1(1) (1983), 67–82; Roger Odin, 'Sémio-pragmatique du cinéma et de l'audiovisuel. Modes et institutions', in Jürgen E. Müller (ed.), *Towards a Pragmatics of the Audiovisual. Theory and History* (Münster: Nodus, 1994), pp. 33–46; Roger Odin, 'Kunst und Ästhetik bei Film und Fernsehen. Elemente zu einem semio-pragmatischen Ansatz', *montage/av* 11(2) (2002), 42–57; Roger Odin et al., *Kommunikationsräume. Einführung in die Semiopragmatik* (Berlin: OA Books, 2019).
7. The Domowina is an umbrella organization of the Sorbs in Lusatia and represents the national interests of the Sorbian people.
8. Theresa Jacobs and Andy Räder, 'Ja mam sony za filmy. Za filmowcow žadyn són nimam. Ich habe Träume für Filme. Für Filmemacher habe ich keinen Traum. Zwiegespräche mit Toni Bruk von Theresa Jacobs und Andy Räder', in Grit Lemke and Andy Räder (eds), *Sorbische Filmlandschaften. Serbske filmowe krajiny* (Berlin: Bertz + Fischer, 2024), 230–52.
9. Studioabnahme von *Briefe – In Gedenken an Dr. Maria Grollmuß / Listy*, 18 December 1984. (= Sorbisches Institut, Kulturarchiv XXVII, 8712).
10. Maria Kubasch, *Sterne über dem Abgrund. Das Leben von Maria Grollmuß* (Bautzen: Domowina-Verlag, 1976).
11. Letter from Deputy Minister of Culture Horst Pehnert to director Toni Bruk, 13 February 1985, pp. 1–2 (= Sorbisches Institut, Kulturarchiv, DEFA-SFS 8711).
12. Letter from Toni Bruk to the head of the DEFA Studio for Animated Films Thomas Wedegärtner, 23 February 1985 (= ibid.).
13. Final Report on the Film *Sokoł – P.S. ke kapitlej našich stawiznow* (Prod. No. 555004) (= BArch DR 116/132).
14. Alfons Wićaz, 'Zur Geschichte der sorbischen Sokol-Bewegung (1920–1933)', in Diethelm Blecking (ed.), *Die slawische Sokolbewegung. Beiträge zur Geschichte von Sport und Nationalismus in Osteuropa* (Dortmund: Forschungsstelle Ostmitteleuropa, 1991), pp. 182–97 (at p. 182).

Select Bibliography

Bruk, Toni. 'Die Sorben im Film. Zur Gründung der Produktionsgruppe sorbischer Film bei der DEFA', *Filmwissenschaftliche Beiträge* 8(2) (1980), 92–123.
Final Report on the Film *Sokoł – P.S. ke kapitlej našich stawiznow* (Prod. No. 555004). (= BArch DR 116/132).
Jacobs, Theresa and Andy Räder. 'Ja mam sony za filmy. Za filmowcow žadyn són nimam. Ich habe Träume für Filme. Für Filmemacher habe ich keinen Traum. Zwiegespräch mit Toni Bruk von Theresa Jacobs und Andy Räder', in Grit Lemke and Andy Räder (eds), *Sorbische Filmlandschaften. Serbske filmowe krajiny*. Berlin: Bertz + Fischer, 2024, pp. 230–52.
Kubasch, Maria. *Sterne über dem Abgrund. Das Leben von Maria Grollmuß*. Bautzen: Domowina-Verlag, 1976.
Protokoll der Beratung zur mittelfristigen thematischen Planung der Produktionsgruppe Sorbischer Film des DEFA-Studios für Trickfilme beim Stellvertreter des Ministers für Kultur, Dr. Friedhelm Grabe am 26.07.1985. (= BArch DR 1/24039).
Schön, Franz and Dietrich Scholze. *Sorbisches Kulturlexikon*. Bautzen: Domowina-Verlag, 2014.
Wićaz, Alfons. 'Zur Geschichte der sorbischen Sokol-Bewegung (1920–1933)', in Diethelm Blecking (ed.), *Die slawische Sokolbewegung. Beiträge zur Geschichte von Sport und Nationalismus in Osteuropa*. Dortmund: Forschungsstelle Ostmitteleuropa, 1991, pp. 182–97.

CHAPTER 9

'Are These Pictures a Deception?'
Socialist Self-Reflexivity in the Cambodia Trilogy of Studio H&S

Martin Brady

Alongside sixteen films on Vietnam and nine on Chile, five films on Cambodia constitute the third substantial corpus of Walter Heynowski and Gerhard Scheumann, aka Studio H&S, on global conflict. Alongside two shorts – *Fliege, roter Schmetterling* (*Fly, Red Butterfly*, 1980) and *Exercises* (1981) – the corpus comprises the 'Cambodia Trilogy': *Kampuchea – Sterben und Auferstehn* (*Kampuchea – Death and Resurrection*) of 1980, *Die Angkar* (*The Angkar*) of 1981 and *Der Dschungelkrieg* (*The Jungle War*) of 1983.[1] Following the enforced dissolution of Studio H&S as a quasi-independent studio in late 1982, for political reasons to which I shall return, the final instalment of the trilogy was produced by DEFA. The reincorporation of the filmmakers into the state film studios is witnessed by a small sticky label on the front cover of the accompanying film protocol (*Montagebuch*), which reveals that 'Studio H&S' has been hastily pasted over with 'DEFA'.

Self-Clarification

Heynowski and Scheumann are not generally considered self-reflexive filmmakers, at least not when it comes to the subject matter of their films. In the five-DVD box set of twenty-four films released in 2014 by absolut MEDIEN only one, the earliest (*O.K.*, 1965), deals with the German Democratic Republic (GDR) directly, and even this short, about a woman who left the country legally in 1961 only to return a few years later, is more a reflection on the horrors of the Federal Republic of Germany (FRG) than a portrait of the GDR. Other works in the boxset, including those made after the dissolution of Studio H&S and associated travel restrictions were imposed on its directors, are more concerned with the legacy of Nazism in the FRG than with domestic matters. However, the abuse of cherished communist iconography by the Khmer Rouge in Cambodia in the mid to late 1970s forced Heynowski and Scheumann to confront uncomfortable questions about their own ideological position. The so-called 'Killing Fields' of Cambodia were, after all, the product of a system that adopted as its insignia the red flag and the hammer and sickle. Whilst this did not challenge Heynowski and Scheumann's ideological certitudes in any discernible way, it did compel them to engage in a protracted extrication of righteous and respectable Marxism-Leninism from its deformation and falsification by Pol Pot, Ieng Sary and others in Cambodia. As the directors put it in the interview that serves as an Introduction to the published script of *Die Angkar*:

> Research into the reasons was necessary, we had to pose the question as to how it could come about . . . We too, in the course of our work, had encountered disquieting facts. One such fact was that the murders in Kampuchea had been carried out under the sign of the hammer and sickle. This cannot be casually passed over by those of our generation, for whom the hammer-and-sickle flag raised over the Reichstag in Berlin in the last days of the war marked a turning-point in life. We had never felt so clearly that creative production is always also a matter of self-clarification. If one honestly seeks and questions, then all those will follow who have the same problems and questions as the seeker (*Angkar*, XII).[2]

'Self-clarification' (*Selbstverständigung*) may not embrace challenging the essential tenets of Marxism-Leninism, and it is certainly not a soubriquet for the contemporary poststructuralism or postmodernism of the capitalist West, but in the Cambodia films of Studio H&S, much more than in those addressing Vietnam and Chile, it does entail examining, critically and self-reflexively, the construction and dissemination of meaning. This includes reflecting on the construction, language(s) and the very apparatus of film itself. Whilst such an investigation of the *dispositif* of film is not unique to Studio H&S – it is also to be found in the more experimental films of Annelie and Andrew Thorndike, Jürgen Böttcher, Eduard Schreiber and others – it is rarely undertaken so openly and ideologically within DEFA. It is the perhaps surprising contention of this chapter that the Cambodia trilogy allows us to consider the work of Studio H&S within a tradition of self-reflexive essay(-istic) filmmaking that begins with the films of Alain Resnais, Chris Marker, Agnès Varda and Jean Rouch in 1950s France and remains a vital strand of contemporary filmmaking. Seen in this context, the films of Studio H&S still resonate today.

The Cambodia Trilogy as a Solidarity Present

Heynowski and Scheumann were commissioned to document the Killing Fields of Cambodia in January 1979. The resulting trilogy was to be a 'solidarity present' for the victorious Vietnamese who had defeated the Khmer Rouge on 7 January and who had also been the subject of Studio H&S's first major corpus of films on global conflict. In the words of a Politburo protocol of 23 January, the filmmakers were not only to demonstrate the brutality of the regime itself, but also to expose China's ideological complicity in and military support for Pol Potism, the 'hegemonic politics of the Peking leadership'.[3] This political programme was publicly expounded by the directors in an essay in *Neues Deutschland* in October 1980. It quotes the terms of their commission almost verbatim, noting that the Khmer Rouge 'after appropriate "consultation"', i.e. with China, 'had the Khmer people annihilated in their millions to make room for a branch of Peking in Indochina'.[4] Heynowski and Scheumann go on to denounce China on two further occasions in their essay: we learn about the 'campaign of destruction inspired by Peking' and that traditional Cambodian dance is alive once again, having survived a 'cultural revolution based on the Peking model'. The distinction between Pol Potist-Maoist 'communism' and the Marxism-Leninism of the Soviet Union and its allies, including the GDR and Vietnam, could scarcely be sharper.

However, the black-and-white distinction between good and bad communism – Heynowski would retrospectively define the latter as 'stone age communism'[5] – set out by the directors in their *Neues Deutschland* essay and fervently adopted in the first two films of the trilogy would soon turn out to be unexpectedly awkward. Thus, following the GDR premiere of Part One of the trilogy (*Kampuchea – Sterben und Auferstehn*), an enthusiastic review appeared in the same newspaper making no reference to China and its portrayal in the film as jointly responsible for the Killing Fields;[6] a week later, *Neues Deutschland* reported that the film had premiered in West Berlin as part of the campaign against the 1979 NATO Double-Track Decision, implying that it constituted a call for peace in the face of an escalating nuclear arms race;[7] a year later, in December 1981, the same paper reviewed the second instalment, as outspoken in its condemnation of Maoist aggression as its predecessor, and again making no mention of China.[8] In hindsight, these official responses to the Cambodia films reveal that a chasm had opened up between Studio H&S's damning condemnation of China and the GDR's strategic desire to avert attention from the complicity of a prospective political and, above all, economic partner.

As historian Hannes Riemann has convincingly set out in some detail, the Cambodia trilogy coincided with rapid changes in GDR foreign policy in relation to China.[9] The result was that whilst the first film was officially commissioned to uncover the truth about the Khmer Rouge and Chinese complicity in it, the second, *Die Angkar*, was unexpectedly denied a screening on GDR television and the third, *Der Dschungelkrieg*, was censored to expunge all explicit reference to Chinese aggression. Studio H&S had come up against an ideological barrier – unforeseen and beyond its control – in trying to tackle what Heynowski in 1982 termed the 'the great shock and also challenge' of violence in Cambodia.[10]

Cambodia 1: *Kampuchea – Sterben und Auferstehn*

The first part of the Cambodia trilogy, *Kampuchea – Sterben und Auferstehn*, presents a broad overview of the rise and fall of the Khmer Rouge, examines its ideology and collects testimony from its victims. It is a stocktaking of what Heynowski and Scheumann found on their arrival in post-Khmer Rouge Phnom Penh. Following a brief introductory episode heralding the victory of the joint forces of the Kampuchea United Front for National Salvation and Vietnam, there is a lengthy episode portraying the abandonment and devastation of the capital. This sequence opens with one of the more experimental passages in the film, a travelling shot through the deserted streets of the city filmed from the side window of a car and lasting almost two-and-a-half minutes. This haunting shot is accompanied by dramatically dissonant, minimal music by composer Reiner Bredemeyer, a melancholy and broken descending scale on the piano accompanied by occasional vocal outbursts that resemble screams of horror.[11] In experimental fashion, the episode ends, following interjected fragments of interview and commentary, with an unexpected freeze-frame as the camera captures the first sign of life spotted by the directors: a pair of pigeons disturbed by the passing car.

Freeze-framing is a device that is frequently used to draw attention self-reflexively to the constructedness of a film by depriving the image of the very thing that makes it cinematic in the first place: movement. Notable examples include the re-editing of the wedding party by Elizaveta Svilova in Dziga Vertov's Stalinist documentary *Chelovek s kino-apparatom* (*Man with a Movie Camera*, 1929), the vignette with the lakeside photographer in Robert Siodmak and Edgar G. Ulmer's Weimar feature *Menschen am Sonntag* (*People on Sunday*, 1930), a cyclist in Jean-Luc Godard's *Sauve qui peut (la vie)* (*Every Man for Himself*, 1980) and passengers on a ferry near the beginning of Chris Marker's essay film *Sans soleil* (*Sunless*, 1983).

For Roland Barthes, the still image, here figured in the form of arrested motion, is both 'a certificate of presence' and an 'agent of Death',[12] whilst according to Susan Sontag, a moving image is always connected to the present and a frozen one a *memento mori*, a tragic record of 'lives heading towards their own destruction'.[13] In freeze-framing, Heynowski and Scheumann draw attention not only to the lives lost to the cityscape of Phnom Penh, but also the cinematic apparatus of photographic reproduction itself. Less than a minute later the filmmakers underscore this remarkable gesture of self-reflexivity with an explicit authorial reflection on cinematography and the dangers of aestheticization: panning out rapidly from close-ups of flowering plants to wider frames embracing vestiges of destruction and decay, the voiceover notes: 'The agonising discovery that nature propagates its beauty even in this desert, thereby making us ever more keenly aware of the desert itself.'[14] And again, shortly after this observation, we are shown an image that is unmistakably a construction for the camera, and a provocatively ideological one at that: a *tableau vivant* of a portrait of Mao Zedong, representing Chinese imperialism and hegemonic expansionism, set alongside a can of Castrol GTX oil, unmistakably standing in for the US equivalent (Figure 9.1). Whilst this interjection leaves little to the imagination ideologically, it once again draws attention to the constructed nature of the cinematic image, to the filmic *dispositif*, in a way that is little short of experimental. Heynowski and Scheumann went on to make use of the self-reflexive *tableau* device repeatedly in the second and third instalments of their trilogy.

Towards the end of *Kampuchea – Sterben und Auferstehn*, the filmmakers use the device of the freeze-frame for only the second time in

Figure 9.1. Studio H&S, *Kampuchea – Sterben und Auferstehn*, 1980. © DEFA-Stiftung/Gerhard Scheumann

the film. Following some of the most disturbing footage across the trilogy – including a deep-freeze chest used as a makeshift guillotine that contains rotting human remains – Heynowski and Scheumann turn to testimony from the indoctrinated killers themselves, who impassively describe how they executed their fellow countrymen. In the case of a man who joined the regime on 5 September 1975, the voiceover notes that the murderer is 'a killer on the lowest rung of the Pol Pot hierarchy, a man without any sense of guilt because the clique indoctrinated him into believing that killing is a revolutionary task'. As these words are spoken, the footage freezes for eight seconds into what is, unmistakably, a *memento mori* of the perpetrator. Symbolically, at least, the film has 'captured' or more precisely immobilized – both emblematically and figuratively – a Khmer Rouge killer. A comparison can be drawn here to the still images of Heinrich Himmler used as evidence of his culpability in Alain Resnais' Holocaust documentary *Nuit et Brouillard* (*Night and Fog*, 1955).

In foregrounding the cinematic apparatus as an integral part of a political analysis, the devices metatextually deployed by Heynowski and

Scheumann demonstrate that Studio H&S is engaging in a very specific form of self-reflexivity, one that is fundamentally different from the kind to be found in the work of Siodmak and Ulmer, or Marker and Godard.[15] The intention is not self-reference per se, but rather metatextuality as a rhetorical tool or device, as an integral part of a self-reflexive engagement with socialism, with its language(s) and with how it can best be documented and communicated. Just as the filmmakers enlarge and pinpoint relevant details in textual and photographic documents through rostrum camera zooms, selective focus, highlighting and so forth – very much in the pedagogical manner pioneered in the Thorndikes' archive films – so they also construct meaning by arresting motion (freeze-framing) and, as we shall see in what follows, through an arsenal of rhetorical devices, including split-screen, animation and metatextual authorial reflection. To cite just one famous example that is contemporary with the Cambodia trilogy, the self-reflexivity that is integral to the strategies deployed by Studio H&S functions very differently from the oft-quoted opening sentence of Italo Calvino's 1979 postmodern novel *If on a Winter's Night a Traveller*, in which the reader is informed that they are 'about to begin reading Italo Calvino's new novel, *If on a Winter's Night a Traveller*'.[16] Put simply, whilst Calvino's self-reflexivity is a limitlessly recursive or centripetal *mise en abyme*, that of Studio H&S is centrifugal insofar as it opens out to a broader discourse on the (party) politics and ideology of (socialist) representation.

However, unlike its more self-reflexive, experimental sequel, *Kampuchea – Sterben und Auferstehn* for the most part uncovers evidence of the Killing Fields in the manner of straightforward communist reportage, with interviews and visual documentation relating the case histories of victims and perpetrators. As well as underscoring culpability by means of provocative juxtaposition – the Mao/Castrol GTX example is perhaps the most striking – the commentary also acknowledges that the atrocities unearthed are, at times, 'barely imaginable'. This is the first but by no means the last time in which the trilogy explicitly refers to the limits of (its own) representation. In so doing, Heynowski and Scheumann engage in a metadiscourse of the kind Resnais had pioneered in *Nuit et Brouillard*. Repeatedly the commentary of Jean Cayrol in that film – famously translated by Paul Celan for the West German version – draws attention to its own inadequacy in communicating the full horror, or rather the full truth, of the events that took place in the concentration and death camps of Nazi Germany, most directly in the case of the commentary accompanying images of products, including fertilizer and soap, purportedly made from the bodies of the murdered prisoners:

'mais on ne peut plus rien dire' (but one can say no more). However, whilst Heynowski and Scheumann are quite prepared, for maximum polemical impact, not only to show the most repulsive of imagery – such as the freezer and its contents mentioned above – but also to display a volume of the thoughts of Pol Pot in Chinese translation and with Chinese characters polemically superimposed in order to highlight the fatal contiguity of Khmer Rouge ideology and the 'pseudo-revolutionary teachings' of Mao's 'so-called Cultural Revolution', they also acknowledge, rather more circumspectly, that 'we must think carefully about concepts entirely new to us'. Towards the end of the film, they concede, again in the voiceover, that the images of victims and perpetrators do not, in and of themselves, provide ready insights. The directors conclude: 'We must continue to ask questions.'

Unlike its sequel, to which this chapter now turns, the first part of the Cambodia trilogy is relatively circumspect with its historical analogies beyond standard references to 'colonial exploitation' and American imperialism, although the secret police headquarters in Phnom Penh is labelled the 'Gestapo Headquarters' and there is an aside towards the end of the film, noting, as an unmistakable historical parallel, that 'Blood and Soil were united here once again'. Analogies of this kind were a weapon previously developed for the rhetorical arsenal of the Studio H&S's Vietnam films: for example, when H.B. Ringsdorf, one of the downed pilots interrogated in *Piloten im Pyjama* (*Pilots in Pyjamas*, 1967), protests that he was only following orders, he is reminded of the Nuremburg Trials. In a similar manner, *Die Teufelsinsel* (*The Devil's Island*, 1976) not only refers to Buchenwald and Bergen-Belsen, but also draws a direct comparison between revolutionaries incarcerated in Côn Sơn and Erich Honecker's imprisonment by the Gestapo in Nazi Germany.

Cambodia 2: *Die Angkar*

Reflecting in *Die Ankar* on the gruesome aftermath of the Cambodian massacres for a second time, the directors confront the paradox that the murderous regime – which they refer to as the 'Pol-Pot-Ieng-Sary-clique' to avoid any association with legitimate Marxism-Leninism – adopted as its standard a beloved communist symbol: 'hammer and sickle here, hammer and sickle there' (shots 54–55), as the voiceover reminds us. How are we to distinguish between the anticommunism of the Khmer Rouge and its ally Mao Zedong, and the healthy, progressive Marxism-Leninism of the GDR, Soviet Union and Vietnam? Just five minutes into the film, Heynowski and Scheumann pose the question in the following, strikingly direct terms:

> The symbol of the hammer and sickle is personally dear to us communists... And now the hammer and sickle together with this Pol Pot, the butcher of the Kampuchean people. A revolting juxtaposition, which we would rather have overlooked or even got rid of – if it hadn't been for those ideologues of imperialism who claim to have discovered in Pol-Potism a version of communism. This was a challenge we couldn't ignore. (Shots 41–45)

Agonizing with some candour over the thorny question of who does and does not have the right to adopt the emblems of Marxism-Leninism, *Die Angkar* gradually becomes a self-reflexive effort to extricate the hammer and sickle and the red flag from the hands of the Khmer Rouge, to separate ideological rectitude in the GDR, Soviet Union and Vietnam from its debasement in Cambodia and its ally China. As the directors put it in the interview quoted above, their task with the second part of the trilogy is to engage in a protracted act of 'self-clarification'. This means gaining insight into how the Killing Fields relate to political history at home. Thus, *Die Angkar* shows, by means of split-screen, violence in (Nazi) Germany and (communist) Cambodia side by side. Uniquely metatextual within the Studio's oeuvre, the film also painstakingly and self-reflexively deconstructs a Chinese-made Cambodian propaganda film discovered by the directors. *Die Angkar* asks questions, less than a decade before the end of the Cold War, about the nature of communist identity and ideology in the face of one of its most violent and murderous global manifestations. As Fred Gehler put it in a 1982 review of the film in the GDR journal *Film und Fernsehen, Die Angkar* is:

> a short but enduring lesson about the interchangeability of words, slogans, insignia, emblems, also about the seduction of surfaces, the relationship between 'simple' and 'complicated' truths. Finding the truth has not become easier – on the contrary.[17]

Although *Die Angkar* does not, as already noted, amount to evidence for the triumphant entry of poststructuralist enquiry into GDR documentary practice or theory, it does raise some thorny semiotic questions not found elsewhere in contemporary East German cinema by consistently adopting a self-reflexive approach to its own reportage and the presentation of documentary evidence.

Foregrounding the Apparatus

The first part of the trilogy had offered an overview of the rise and fall of the Khmer Rouge and was an immediate response to what Heynowski and Scheumann found when they were commissioned to visit and film post-Khmer Rouge Phnom Penh. As an exercise in further, detailed interrogation of the 'Organization', *Die Angkar* investigates the operation of the Tuol Sleng headquarters of the secret police, the aforementioned 'Gestapo Headquarters', known as 'Security Office 21' or 'S-21'. After a contextual introduction, including a definition of the term 'Angkar' (Organization) with recourse to a Khmer-English dictionary, Heynowski and Scheumann turn to the main body of documents that the film, in what amounts to a systematic self-reflexive gesture, will address: still photographs. In the abandoned rooms of Tuol Sleng, a former school, the directors found thousands of passport-size identity photos of victims and perpetrators along with piles of forms, reports, registers and lists. These form the main body of documents interrogated by the film along with paintings, drawings and effigies of Pol Pot discovered in an artists' studio attached to S-21.

The filmmakers use the technical devices that were available to them in the GDR – having taken crucial documents back home – to frame, highlight and challenge the material they find. Strips of bright light (in red and green) highlight relevant details in handwritten and printed texts, words are frequently superimposed onto photographs, and the rostrum camerawork is extremely varied and sophisticated in reproducing the identity photographs and other documents, even including digital counters for adding up the tally of victims. Individual photos are zoomed in and out, multiple images are captured with smooth tracking shots, relevant details are highlighted by selective focus, and images are juxtaposed using split-screen and superimposition. In its entirety, the film can be read as a compendium or primer of techniques for presenting documentary evidence, rather as had been the case with the Thorndikes' *Unternehmen Teutonenschwert* (*Operation Teutonic Sword*, 1958).

For example, six minutes into the film, there is a striking and polemical use of animation and colour choreography as it grapples with the multiple uses and abuses of the hammer and sickle emblem. The commentator explains: 'Hammer and sickle – and Pol Pot. Take one of Pol Pot's legacies, a heap of skulls, and take the hammer and sickle symbol used by Pol Pot, put them together and call it communism, and you have a disarmingly simple recipe from the cuisine of the Cold War' (shots 52–53). The film does precisely what is described: in a single, complex shot, the directors take a still image of a portrait of Pol Pot below a hammer and sickle emblem, superimpose a pile of skulls onto the bottom of this image and then, in a brief animation, extract the hammer and sickle from the red flag and transport it across the image onto the skulls. As the emblem is lifted from the red flag, it turns black, suggesting, presumably, that it has been drained of the genuine lifeblood of Marxism-Leninism. The shot then ends with a zoom in so that the black-and-white image of the hammer and sickle on the skulls entirely fills the screen. This is followed by alternating positive (Lenin and Vietnam) and negative (Mao Zedong and Pol Pot) historical deployment of the hammer and sickle emblem. The directors then summarize their conclusion from this primer in the use and abuse of emblems:

> So it has to be said: hammer and sickle here [Lenin], hammer and sickle there [Mao], hammer and sickle here [Vietnam], and hammer and sickle there [Pol Pot], the hammer and sickle can in this complicated world of today be displayed with quite different intentions. (Shots 54–58)

This insight, juxtaposing positive 'here's and negative 'there's, is accompanied by a fictional insert – Scheumann in an interview rather nicely terms such moments 'organization for photographic purposes'[18] – lasting a mere seven seconds. Hands enter the frame from the left and right to place a real sickle and a real hammer on top of one another on a bright red background (Figure 9.2). This literal-yet-iconic juxtaposition of hammer and a sickle is similar to the tableau of helmets constructed in 1954 for inclusion in Bertolt Brecht's *Kriegsfibel* (*War Primer*) using props from the Berliner Ensemble.[19] The difference is that Heynowski and Scheumann openly acknowledge the constructed nature of their image, as hands are seen carefully placing the tools on top of one another on the red background. Signs, the sequence implies, are not only constructions but can also be *de*constructed. Self-reflexivity here serves to demonstrate that meaning and truth – inseparable in the work of Studio H&S from ideology, as Olaf Möller has pointed out[20] – can, and indeed should, be assembled in a dialectical, materialist manner.

Ideological Deconstruction

The most striking case of iconographic or ideological deconstruction in *Die Angkar* is the film's engagement with a Chinese-produced propaganda film made in 1976 for the Khmer Rouge. In a further self-

Figure 9.2. Studio H&S, *Die Angkar*, 1981. © DEFA-Stiftung/Horst Donth, Winfried Goldner

reflexive gesture, one that is perhaps unique in GDR documentary, the directors systematically unpick this document. Initially, they do so in a series of strikingly materialist clips: they show the American Kodak Eastman Company film cans with Chinese lettering – neatly connecting two malevolent regimes once again – and also the test card images not normally projected to an audience that contain Chinese characters. The implication is that the filmmakers are engaging in forensic research and, in an ironically complimentary aside, they applaud the quality of the light and colour grading in the Chinese footage. The commentary here is quite remarkable:

> What is falsified here is the whole.
> When the German fascists were already carrying out their programme for the 'final solution of the Jewish question' – the extermination of the Jews – fascist directors and cameramen made a film for consumption abroad about the Theresienstadt concentration camp with the rather inviting title 'The Führer gives the Jews a town'. That particular project is the only thing comparable with this Chinese camouflage of the reality of the Pol Pot rule over Kampuchea.

> Against the background of facts available today these scenes are a self-condemnation. The fact that the Pol Pot regime was a regime of murder would today be denied only by obstinate Maoists – just as obstinate fascists to this day think they can deny the reality of the gas chambers of Auschwitz. (Shots 131–36)

At this point, the directors intercut an image of a smashed skull before returning to the Chinese film for a further sequence of four shots of Pol Pot visiting a cotton field. As the skull is interpolated, the self-reflexive gesture is expanded:

> This shot doesn't come from the Chinese film, but from our own camera. It was farming hoes that smashed them in. Whoever knows about this reality cannot watch this scene without horror. There were and there still are directors who are ready to render their employers their services as counterfeiters. (Shots 137–40)

The inference is clear: Studio H&S's forensic camera is deployed to uncover (unearth, both literally and metaphorically) visible evidence, and the Chinese-Cambodian propaganda film's camera is an apparatus to stage lies.

Uncovering evidence also entails drawing historical connections. Parallels are thus drawn repeatedly in *Die Angkar* to Nazi Germany: the flag hoisted on the Reichstag by the Red Army in 1945 already mentioned; barbed wire and the motto 'Arbeit macht frei' over the gate to Auschwitz; medical experiments in Nazi concentration camps; split-screens with victims of Nazi concentration camps on the left labelled 'Nazi concentration camp' and of the Khmer Rouge on the right labelled 'Angkar concentration camp'. Later on, a comparison is drawn between the barbarity of Pol Pot's guards and the SS-Einsatzkommandos, and towards the end, a sarcastic rhetorical question is asked as to whether Hitler was 'perhaps a socialist just because he called his political doctrine National Socialism' (shot 653).

While further detailed analysis of the film would reveal, for example, its repeated use of sequences of identity photographs of Khmer Rouge victims as *memento mori* in the sense used by Sontag, it is clear from the examples discussed here that *Die Angkar* is a primer in the use of visible evidence for ideological ends. To construct their argument and to denounce the misappropriation of the emblems of socialism by the Khmer Rouge, Heynowski and Scheumann consistently engage with the cinematic apparatus self-reflexively. In the case of the Chinese propaganda film and the regime's identity photos, material is systematically refunctioned or *détourned*, to use Guy Debord's term for the Marxist appropriation of existing documents.[21]

Cambodia 3: Deceptive Images in *Der Dschungelkrieg*

The third instalment of the Cambodia trilogy is a study of misinformation and false propaganda – the various ways in which the mismatched opponents of the legitimate People's Republic of Kampuchea (PRK), including surviving Pol Potists and followers of Norodom Sihanouk, attempted to destabilize the post-Khmer Rouge alliance during the early 1980s with what is now termed 'fake news'.

The film opens with a performance of guerrilla warfare staged for the visiting GDR filmmakers by Pol Potist insurgents, supporters of the so-called 'Democratic Kampuchea' in the Thai-Cambodian borderlands. Repeatedly, the filmmakers use the English-language term 'sightseeing' to disparage the charade presented to them. To uncover the real facts, we read in the opening credits, the GDR filmmakers had to resort to 'undercover means' (shot 5) and in the opening episode of the film, we are presented with a *tableau vivant* of their tools: a film camera and tape recorder. A little later, as the film crew travels through the jungle on the back of an elephant, the voiceover reminds us that such sightseeing tours are organized for 'political tourists [*Polit-Touristen*]' equipped with a 'camera, mike and notebook' (shot 36). The truth behind such simulations, the film demonstrates, can be uncovered – as with the Killing Fields in the first two instalments of the trilogy – by the ethical (counter)deployment of the cinematic apparatus. In a strikingly self-reflexive gesture underscoring the difference between the simulation and its unmasking, a still photograph is interpellated into the scene in the jungle that, the voiceover tells us, shows Studio H&S's own cinematographer and sound engineer seated on an elephant. Later on in the film, Heynowski and Scheumann introduce a town planner in the new PRK government who first appeared three years previously in *Kampuchea – Sterben und Auferstehn* and insert a photograph of themselves standing alongside him and his family in Phnom Penh in 1979.[22] Once again, self-reflexivity is used as a certification of authenticity.

A further *Spektakel* ('spectacle' or 'attraction') (shot 80) of false ideology is unmasked by the use, once again, of freeze-frame – a theatrical performance staged for foreign visitors to the region by the Pol Potists is slowed down to a freeze-frame by the filmmakers to reveal its constructedness and inauthenticity; in the words of the voiceover, the film will 'present and explain fragments' (shot 81) of the drama – that is, deconstruct it. In this instance, unusually, the slowing down of the sound along with the image even has a faintly comic effect, further debunking the masquerade staged for visiting Pol Pot 'guests' or 'sympathizers' (*Sympathisanten*) (shot 84).

Towards the end of *Der Dschungelkrieg*, which is for the most part more straightforward cinematically than the first two instalments of the trilogy, the filmmakers use footage of Vietnamese soldiers buying food with the local currency in Cambodia as incontrovertible visible evidence to refute the fake news of Vietnamese atrocities disseminated by 'Democratic Kampuchea': we see a soldier choosing a melon and handing a banknote to a market trader as the voiceover asks the following rhetorical question: 'Are these pictures a deception?' (shot 427). For Heynowski and Scheumann, they are clearly nothing of the kind: the footage candidly confirms an indisputable fact. This episode, towards the end of the trilogy, along with the others discussed above, highlights the parameters of Studio H&S's 'self-clarification' addressed in this chapter: their engagement with the cinematic *dispositif* can and should encompass self-reflexivity, but always in the service of ideological illumination.

Bracketing-out Bad Communism

The Cambodia trilogy is sometimes referenced in histories of GDR film not for its insights into the Khmer Rouge, but on account of its controversial reception and for the part it may have played in the demise of Studio H&S. In his notoriously critical paper delivered at the Fourth Congress of the Association of Film and Television Producers of the GDR in September 1982 – a document that swiftly led to punitive sanctions and the loss of independence for the studio – Scheumann, frustrated by the refusal of GDR television to broadcast *Die Angkar*, cited the film as an example of the problems facing GDR media:

> The reception of the film 'Die Angkar' has caused viewers to ask the documentarists why our media kept silent about Cambodia . . . The question is not what considerations may have brought this about, but about the trustworthiness of our media. In such cases documentary film must point out that this question is being directed to the wrong address.[23]

Earlier in the same document, Scheumann pointedly notes that documentary film cannot simply bow to 'diplomatic or economic contexts' and goes on to claim that 'if documentary film is used merely as a vehicle for everyday media politics it will degenerate [verkommen]'.[24] Put simply, Scheumann's point is that the search for truth in Cambodia cannot be subservient to *Tagespolitik* and, implicitly at least, that Chinese anger at the Cambodia films – which had led to a walkout by their delegation at a film festival in Bilbao[25] – should not be a reason for denying them airtime on East German television. As Rüdiger Steinmetz has noted, 'the subject matter fell within a period of changed foreign policy in the GDR towards China ... and it was viewed as no longer opportune for television'.[26]

The Cambodia trilogy is exceptional in H&S's vast catalogue. The filmmakers' certainties confront uncomfortable facts in the abuse of communist ideology and iconography by the Khmer Rouge and its supporters. The directors' description of *Die Angkar* as '[a kind of] optimistic tragedy' (*Angkar*, XII) – optimistic insofar as it ends with liberation from Pol Pot, tragic in terms of the death toll and suffering – suggests the contradictions. As the directors noted in the interview for the screenplay publication of that film: 'Our film "Die Angkar" is not designed simply as a recording of historical facts. Every documentary film which is not only a straightforward report should seek and display the lessons to be learned from its subject matter' (*Angkar*, XIII). For Heynowski and Scheumann, meaning has to be constructed.

For 'Communist film-makers' (*Angkar*, XIII), these lessons were uncomfortable, and the untypically long passages without commentary in the opening sequence of *Kampuchea – Sterben und Auferstehn* and the roll calls of victims in *Die Angkar* may be read as textual, or rather structural, evidence of this. Interviewed in 2003, Heynowski went so far as to admit that Stalinist atrocities and domestic Marxism-Leninism could not be entirely 'bracketed-out' in the Cambodia cycle; he even surmised that an awareness of the potential implications of the films at home may have contributed to the treatment of the Studio in the wake of Scheumann's speech.[27] What is clear is that what the directors found in Cambodia – both in terms of the human cost of the Khmer Rouge regime and the documentary, frequently photographic evidence it left behind – encouraged them to work more searchingly, more personally and more self-reflexively than had hitherto been the case. Looking back, Heynowski concluded that with their Cambodia films they had 'pushed the limits of what was possible' in the GDR.[28] In the volume *Schwarzweiß und Farbe*, Elke Schieber concludes that *Die Angkar* is not only 'one of the most important and convincing works' of Studio H&S, but also that 'nothing is hushed up, even if it could damage their own ideology and political position'.[29]

The Limits of Representation

A roll call of photographs of victims in *Die Angkar* accompanied by the funeral march from Frédéric Chopin's *Piano Sonata No. 2*, the only music deployed by the filmmakers, is a particularly striking example of 'words failing' in the manner addressed by Jean Cayrol in *Nuit et Brouillard*. At times across the trilogy, the directors seem genuinely lost for words when faced with the extreme cruelty of the Khmer Rouge and they repeatedly feel the need to engage self-reflexively with their own practice, not least when confronted by the Cambodian regime's widespread abuse of still and moving images. This reveals a personal, quasi-auteurist dimension to the work of Studio H&S, one that Scheumann was himself at pains to stress in his 1982 paper: 'In fact, documentary film is never reality itself, but always a subjective image of the objective world and to that extent related to the fictional genres of art. The author is just as present in documentary film as in feature films.'[30]

Whilst the Cambodia trilogy and the Studio that made it fell victim to Scheumann's mundane 'diplomatic contexts' and what Riemann deems a simple 'change in *political conditions*' in the GDR,[31] the films themselves remain relevant to ongoing debates on the use and abuse of visible evidence on screen, not least because, as *Neues Deutschland* noted in its enthusiastic review of *Die Angkar*, the filmmakers were courageous enough to ask 'penetrating questions'.[32] These questions are not restricted to matters ideological or historical, but go to the heart of what constitutes a cinematic *dispositif*. In their manifest socialism and in their self-reflexivity, the films of the Cambodia trilogy transcend the *Tagespolitik* of the GDR and the internecine skirmishes of its media to pose penetrating questions about the cinematic apparatus itself and the manifold ways in which it can be instrumentalized.

Martin Brady is Emeritus Reader in German and Film Studies at King's College London. He has published on European film (Huillet & Straub, documentary, GDR cinema, Brechtian and experimental film and Wenders), music (Schönberg, Dessau, Larcher and Krautrock), philosophy (Adorno), literature (Böll, Handke, Jelinek and Honigmann), Jewish exile architects, the visual arts (Beuys and Kiefer), disability, foraging and ordinariness.

Notes

1. This chapter evolved, in part, out of an essay written for the volume *Violence Elsewhere 1: Imagining Distant Violence in Germany 1945–2001*, edited by Clare Bielby and Mererid Puw Davies (Rochester, NY: Camden House, 2024). The discussion that follows returns to examples cited in that piece, which focused on the second film of Studio H&S's trilogy (*Die Angkar*) and was principally concerned with the relationship between the GDR, Cambodia and China. I am very grateful to Progress (Berlin) for allowing access to *Der Dschungelkrieg* and to Anna Drum (Dresden) for locating material for this research during the COVID-19 pandemic.
2. Studio H&S, *Die Angkar*. Berlin: Studio H&S, 1981, p. XII. Here and in what follows, the commentary and English translations for the first and third parts of the Cambodia trilogy are taken from the published protocol books listed in the Bibliography. These volumes include full translations of the scripts and introductory interviews with the directors into English and French, and short resumés of the films in Khmer, Russian and Spanish. References to these volumes within the text relate to shot numbers, in the case of scripts, and page numbers (Roman numerals) with the short title '*Angkar*' in the case of the interview in the *Angkar* protocol book. *Die Angkar* has 684 shots, while *Der Dschungelkrieg* has 615.
3. Hannes Riemann, *Eine Herausforderung an jeden Kommunisten: Die Khmer Rouge, der III. Indochinakrieg und Kambodscha im Fokus von Dokumentarfilmen des Dokumentarfilmstudios H&S (1979–1983)*. Erfurt: TKG, 2011, p. 42. I am very grateful to Hannes Riemann for providing a PDF of this volume when the publisher was unable to supply a copy. Pagination follows Riemann's document. See also Hannes Riemann, 'Geschichtsbilder in Kambodscha', *ASPuZ*, 21 June 2008, https://www.bpb.de/shop/zeitschriften/apuz/31131/geschichtsbilder-in-kambodscha (retrieved 6 July 2022).
4. Walter Heynowski and Gerhard Scheumann. 'Das Lächeln der Apsara: Impressionen aus Kampuchea', *Neues Deutschland*, 11 October 1980, p. 11.
5. Christiane Mückenberger, Ingrid Pross and Anne Richter (eds). *Das Prinzip Neugier: DEFA-Dokumentarfilmer erzählen*. Berlin: Verlag Neues Leben, 2012, p. 87.
6. Henryk Goldberg, 'Auch aus dem Zorn wächst Kraft für die Zukunft: "Kampuchea: Sterben und Auferstehn" von H & S', *Neues Deutschland*, 13 November 1980, p. 4.
7. Anon., 'Kampuchea-Film wurde in Westberlin aufgeführt', *Neues Deutschland*, 18 November 1980, p. 4.
8. Henryk Goldberg, 'Ein Film, der anklagt und bohrende Fragen stellt: "Die Angkar", eine Arbeit aus dem Studio H & S', *Neues Deutschland*, 16 December 1981, p. 4.
9. Riemann, *Eine Herausforderung an jeden Kommunisten*.
10. Quoted in ibid., p. 44.

11. In an effective rhetorical twist, this descending scale will be inverted to a rising one at the very end of the film, where the focus is on liberation as the peace agreement is signed between Vietnam and Cambodia in January 1979. Encouraged by Paul Dessau, Bredemeyer (born to a German family in Colombia in 1919) moved from West Germany to East Berlin in 1954 and composed prolifically for the concert hall (around 300 works), film and theatre (a further 300 compositions). He died in Berlin in 1995. See https://reiner-bredemeyer.de (retrieved 18 October 2022).
12. Roland Barthes, *Camera Lucida*. London: Vintage Classics, 2000, pp. 87, 92.
13. Susan Sontag, *On Photography*. London: Penguin, 1979, pp. 15, 70.
14. Translations from *Kampuchea – Sterben und Auferstehn*, for which there are no subtitles or published script (see n 2 above), are by the current author.
15. For a discussion of Heynowski and Scheumann's technique of 'foregrounding the device' in their Vietnam cycle, see Nora Alter, 'Excessive Pre/Requisites: Vietnam through the East German Lens', *Cultural Critique* 35 (1996–97), 39–79 (at pp. 64–65).
16. Italo Calvino, *If on a Winter's Night a Traveller*, trans. W. Weaver. London: Vintage, 1998, p. 3.
17. Schenk, Ralf. *Studio H&S: Walter Heynowski und Gerhard Scheumann: Filme 1964–1989*. Berlin: absolut MEDIEN, 2014 (DVD booklet), p. 27.
18. Walter Heynowski, Robert Michel and Gerhard Scheumann, 'Werkstattgespräch Studio H&S 4./5. April 1977', in Robert Michel (ed.), *Arbeitshefte 27: Dokument und Kunst: Vietnam bei H&S*. Berlin: Akademie der Künste der Deutschen Demokratischen Republik, 1977, pp. 93–135 (at p. 108).
19. Bertolt Brecht, *Kriegsfibel*. Frankfurt am Main: Zweitausendeins, 1968, no page numbers.
20. 'The separation of propaganda and documentation is alien to Walter Heynowski and Gerhard Scheumann, bourgeois nonsense to believe that there is such a thing as objective truth. A truth, i.e. an opinion, is something one has to fight for; truth has to be created' (quoted in Schenk, *Studio H&S*, p. 13).
21. See, for example, Guy Debord and Gil J. Wolman, 'Methods of Detournement', in Ken Knabb (ed. and trans.), *Situationist International Anthology*. Berkeley: Bureau of Public Secrets, 1981, pp. 8-14.
22. On a number of occasions in *Der Dschungelkrieg*, Heynowski and Scheumann quote briefly from the previous parts of the trilogy.
23. Tilo Prase and Rüdiger Steinmetz, *Dokumentarfilm zwischen Beweis und Pamphlet: Heynowski & Scheumann und Gruppe Katins*. Leipzig: Leipziger Universitätsverlag, 2002, p. 157.
24. Ibid.
25. Riemann, *Eine Herausforderung an jeden Kommunisten*, p. 81.
26. Prase and Steinmetz, *Dokumentarfilm zwischen Beweis und Pamphlet*, p. 150.
27. Mückenberger, Pross and Richter, *Das Prinzip Neugier*, p. 88.

28. Ibid.
29. Schieber, Elke. 'Im Dämmerlicht der Perestroika 1980 bis 1989', in Günter Jordan and Ralf Schenk (eds), *Schwarzweiß und Farbe* (Berlin: Jovis, 1996), pp. 180–233 (at p. 220).
30. Prase and Steinmetz, *Dokumentarfilm zwischen Beweis und Pamphlet*, p. 56.
31. Riemann, *Eine Herausforderung an jeden Kommunisten*, p. 104.
32. Goldberg, 'Ein Film, der anklagt und bohrende Fragen stellt', p. 4.

Select Bibliography

Alter, Nora. 'Excessive Pre/Requisites: Vietnam through the East German Lens', *Cultural Critique* 35 (1996–97), 39–79.
Anon. 'Kampuchea-Film wurde in Westberlin aufgeführt', *Neues Deutschland*, 18 November 1980, 11.
Barthes, Roland. *Camera Lucida*. London: Vintage Classics, 2000.
Brecht, Bertolt. *Kriegsfibel*. Frankfurt am Main: Zweitausendeins, 1968.
Calvino, Italo. *If on a Winter's Night a Traveller*, trans. W. Weaver. London: Vintage, 1998.
Debord, Guy, and Gili J. Wolman. 'Methods of Detournement', in Ken Knabb (ed. and trans.), *Situationist International Anthology*. Berkeley: Bureau of Public Secrets, 1981, pp. 8–14.
Goldberg, Henryk. 'Auch aus dem Zorn wächst Kraft für die Zukunft: "Kampuchea: Sterben und Auferstehen" von H & S', *Neues Deutschland*, 13 November 1980, 4.
———. 'Ein Film, der anklagt und bohrende Fragen stellt: "Die Angkar", eine Arbeit aus dem Studio H & S', *Neues Deutschland*, 16 December 1981, 4.
Heynowski, Walter, and Gerhard Scheumann. 'Das Lächeln der Apsara: Impressionen aus Kampuchea', *Neues Deutschland*, 11 October 1980, 11.
Heynowski, Walter, Robert Michel and Gerhard Scheumann. 'Werkstattgespräch Studio H&S 4./5. April 1977', in Robert Michel (ed.), *Arbeitshefte 27: Dokument und Kunst: Vietnam bei H&S*. Berlin: Akademie der Künste der Deutschen Demokratischen Republik, 1977, pp. 93–135.
Mückenberger, Christiane, Ingrid Pross and Anne Richter (eds). *Das Prinzip Neugier: DEFA-Dokumentarfilmer erzählen*. Berlin: Verlag Neues Leben, 2012.
Prase, Tilo, and Rüdiger Steinmetz. *Dokumentarfilm zwischen Beweis und Pamphlet: Heynowski & Scheumann und Gruppe Katins*. Leipzig: Leipziger Universitätsverlag, 2002.
Riemann, Hannes. *Eine Herausforderung an jeden Kommunisten: Die Khmer Rouge, der III. Indochinakrieg und Kambodscha im Fokus von Dokumentarfilmen des Dokumentarfilmstudios H&S (1979–1983)*. Erfurt: TKG, 2011.
Schenk, Ralf. *Studio H&S: Walter Heynowski und Gerhard Scheumann: Filme 1964–1989*. Berlin: absolut MEDIEN, 2014 (DVD booklet).

Schieber, Elke. 'Im Dämmerlicht der Perestroika 1980 bis 1989', in Günter Jordan and Ralf Schenk (eds), *Schwarzweiß und Farbe* (Berlin: Jovis, 1996), pp. 180–233.
Sontag, Susan. *On Photography*. London: Penguin, 1979.
Studio H&S. *Die Angkar*. Berlin: Studio H&S, 1981.
———. *Der Dschungelkrieg*. Berlin: DEFA-Studio für Dokumentarfilme, 1983.

CHAPTER 10
Polycentric Images of Africa in East German Documentary Film

Sebastian Heiduschke

Documentary film played a critical role as the German Democratic Republic (GDR) jumped at the chance to assert itself as an independent nation entering into diplomatic relationships in the early 1950s with the increasing number of sovereign African nations.[1] East German documentary film production followed a similar trajectory of celebrating state-sponsored solidarity with African nations and its peoples by supporting the Socialist Unity Party (SED) government's Africa policy of establishing a political presence in the postcolonial and anticolonial landscape. Later on, documentary cinema carried out Cold War politics in the 1970s and gradually withdrew from African topics in the 1980s.[2] If one ignores Hans Kubisch's popular science film *Wildbahn Afrika* (*Hunting Ground Africa*, 1956) shot for the DEFA-Studio für populärwissenschaftliche Filme (DEFA-Studio for Popular Science Films), or occasional footage from Africa in early DEFA *Der Augenzeuge* newsreels of 1947, the two East German documentaries Hans Dumke's *Das Gesicht des neuen Afrika* (*The Face of the New Africa*, 1960) and Konrad Herrmann's *Dort, wo die Sonne schnell versinkt* (*Where the Sun Sets Quickly*, 1994) bookend more than 100 East German nonfeature films about Africa made during a span of thirty-four years.[3]

Most of the documentaries depict political relations between the GDR and independent, postcolonial African nation states, along with a display of images of peoples, their living situations, and their cultural customs and traditions exemplified in music, dance, theatre and fashion. Three of them – Joachim Hellwig's *Der schwarze Stern* (*The Black Star*,

1965) about Ghana, *Hirde Dyama* (Moussa Kémoko Diakité and Gerhard Jentsch, 1971) about Guinea and *Grüße aus Maputo* (*Greetings from Maputo*, Lisa and Joachim Hadaschik, 1979) about Mozambique – form the core of this chapter as typical examples of imagery, iconography, narrative style and sound design of the corpus.[4] My readings of these films situate them in the context of African cinemas and explore how, once one ignores their German voiceover, these works can function as Afrocentric narratives.

Previous studies about East German documentaries questioned the authenticity and reality of their content (Hodgin), positioned the depiction of the Global South in the films against the backdrop of politics and history (Shen and Slobodian), read Blackface and racism in them as chiffres of a proletarian internationalism against Western imperialism (Piesche), proposed them as white reassurance narratives (Decker) and, in this volume, argue for the instrumentalization of the Black body in East German documentary film (Layne, see Chapter 10).[5] My chapter approaches Africa in East German documentaries from a different angle as I consider the corpus of East German documentary films about Africa by way of engaging with imagery, iconography, narrative style and sound design. It bypasses Eurocentric methodologies that read Africa through the lens of (East) German cinema, foreign politics or postcolonial history. Instead of othering Africa and its peoples, an approach that positions their lives depicted on celluloid at the centre of a white, Eurocentric and largely male gaze, my goal is to situate these East German Africa documentaries in the traditions and environments of African cinema. Informed by the theories of Ella Shohat and Robert Stam (2014) and inspired by Olivier Barlet (2000), as well as recent research published in Kenneth Harrow and Carmela Garritano's *A Companion to African Cinema* (2019), I look at the three films from polycentric vantage points in order to acknowledge the films' intellectual agency not as East German products, but rather as paradigms of Africa's postcolonial, national cinemas.[6]

One advantage of a polycentric approach lies in the systematic unthinking of film analysis that draws on the work of European theorists, as these Eurocentric discourses 'exclude specific voices, aesthetics and representations' and 'produce the non-European world for Europe'.[7] European or rather Western models of thought and analysis suggest Western superiority in creating art forms, and the 'non-West provides unsigned raw materials to be refined by named Western artists and legitimated by powerful Western institutions which retain the power to establish the canon and define what qualifies as "art"'.[8] Polycentrism is thus a way of guarding against the 'monopolization of cultural power' without ignoring the visual evidence of a colonial past in a postcolonial environment.[9] Similar to Kenneth Harrow's study *Trash: African Cinema from Below* (2013) that approaches postcolonial contemporary African feature film regarding issues of power and trash, I also use an approach free from 'conventional cinema readings of dominant western forms of commercial or auteur cinema', not out of ignorance, but purposefully as a way of counteracting an interpretation of the films as depicting a Global South.[10] When read through the lens of polycentrism, the three East German documentaries are no longer proselytising products of an autocratic system pursuing pictorial navel-gazing, but they tell stories of African tradition, resilience and success.

As suggested earlier, the key issue in adopting such an approach is the removal of the German voiceover when analysing the documentary. Ignoring the East German vernacular shifts the 'audible … shape' of the documentaries and upends the documentary voice, moving it from an East German '*representation* of the world' closer towards an African '*reproduction* of reality – as contentious as this expression may be'.[11] Tenaciously ignoring political subtexts found in these voiceovers allows us to sharpen our focus as we now pay attention to the *mise-en-scène*, to costumes, to colours and contrasts, to cinematography and editing techniques, and to what Vlad Dima has termed the 'aural spaces' of African cinema: ambient soundscapes, music, rhythm and dance.[12] Dima reminds us that African cinema connotes much more than simply films produced in the four dominant languages: Arabic, English, French and Portuguese. In addition to hundreds of tribal languages and local dialects spoken in nation states whose political borders are mere remnants of random demarcation by colonial powers, illiteracy and languages existing only in oral form render the use of subtitles impossible.

As much as taking note of Anglophone, Francophone, Lusophone and Arabophone films helps to contextualize tropes depicted on the screen, the German voiceover serves as a mnemonic aid to situate the subject matter in documentaries about Africa historically, but skews our perception and compels us to read the images in ways that are predetermined by the voiceover and thus by a German understanding of events. The polycentric approach in this chapter, on the other hand, pairs the visual information with traditions of African cinema, i.e. images familiar to an African eye, such as costumes, *mise-en-scène*, camera angles and movement, but also the function of dance, rhythm and movement, patterns of sound and music and melody instead of the spoken word, along with a different concept of time and temporality than that to which many Western viewers might be accustomed. Seen from such vantage points, viewers are suddenly able to discover how African cinemas create a new type of space, combining sound, noise and song, and how they pair them with visual information to supplant colonial and neocolonial traditions. Taking this approach allows us to perceive East German documentary films about Africa as contributions to a large corpus of cinema that has shaped an entire continent during its struggle for independence.

African Consciousness: Senghorism and *Négritude*

Joachim Hellwig's *Der schwarze Stern* is an early East German documentary about a young, newly independent African nation.[13] Hellwig co-authored the script with his long-time colleague Hans Oley who acted as associate director and head of production at the DEFA-Studio für Wochenschau und Dokumentarfilme (DEFA Studio for Newsreels and Documentary Film). In his search for a reliable newsreel and documentary cinematographer who would be able to shoot the film in the West African Republic of Ghana, Hellwig turned to the experienced Wolfgang Randel, who at this time had already compiled an impressive list of films as director of photography at DEFA. *Der schwarze Stern* has a running time of 36 minutes and was filmed using ORWO 35 mm colour film stock, a rather unusual practice for East German documentary film in the 1960s, where black-and-white film stock was prevalent and standard practice, but one almost certainly made possible by bringing in Oley as scriptwriter.

The documentary opens with an establishing shot of an engraved double-page portrait from the Mercator-Hondius Atlas of 1619, showing the Dutch Geert de Kremer (Gerardus Mercator) and the Flemish-Dutch Joost de Hondt (Iodocus Hondius), two white, male cartographers from the sixteenth century well known for their maps of the world. The camera zooms in onto a globe positioned on a table before a dissolve reveals a historical map of Africa from the same Atlas. We see another zoom, this time onto the location of modern-day Ghana in the northwestern portion of Africa, this time followed by a glance at paintings of explorer ships presumably from the same book. The historic sequence only lasts 46 seconds, before the camera cuts to the cockpit of a Ghana Airways plane, showing first the Ghanaian captain, then the flight attendant in the cabin announcing the plane's imminent arrival to the capital city Accra. When the plane touches down, we observe a group of mostly

Black passengers – predominantly dressed in colourful traditional garments – who are disembarking from the plane and boarding a modern shuttle bus. What follows are wide shots and pans across Accra's clean cityscape, orderly motorized traffic consisting of cars, trucks and busses driven by Ghanaians, a low-angle shot of a Ghanaian traffic police officer in a crisp white uniform (see Figure 10.1), the juxtaposition of urban high-rises and colonial buildings with single-floor residences along unpaved roads that are simple and well preserved, the camera following Ghanaian judges in long black robes and white wigs walking through a city park and into a government building, and a pan across a group of children congregating in small groups on the patio of a school building while reading from books.

This collocation of colonial and postcolonial elements during the opening sequence offers an authentic view of Ghana's capital in a style known in African cinema as Senghorism. The Senegalese cultural theorist Léopold Sédar Senghor co-founded the concept of *Négritude* to explain why emotion dominated the African cultural system as 'it is their emotive attitude towards the world which explains the cultural values of the African... Their religion and social structure, their art and literature, above all, the genius of their languages'.[14] Senghor further proclaimed that postcolonial African culture ought not to be freed from Western influences, but that legitimizing African autonomy would only become possible through the amalgamation of these influences with precolonial traditions to form a new, contemporary culture. Thus, the uniforms of the personnel working for Ghana Airways, and even more so the long robes and wigs of the lawyers and judges, no longer invoke colonial times, but rather connote a sovereign Ghana controlled by Ghanaians. Images of Ghanaians occupying positions that used to be exclusively a white person's domain create a sense of unity, belonging and pride among domestic Ghanaian audiences, particularly as the subjects on screen look, dress and behave in ways that represent diverse facets of Ghana since its 1957 independence from British rule.[15] The choice of camera angle also suggests respect. The traffic police officer becomes a figure of authority, the close-up of the airline captain's alert face exhibits his expertise, and the pans through residential areas and the business district alike evince admiration in a well-organized infrastructure. Ghanaians, the camera suggests, have made this country their own in the eight years since independence that had passed at the time of filming.

White people throughout the documentary are few and far between, be it a computer technician training his Ghanaian colleague or an East German politics teacher introducing herself and her lecture topics on Karl Marx by writing her name and book titles on the chalkboard.

Figure 10.1. Orderly traffic, controlled by a Black police officer in a white uniform in Joachim Hellwig's *Der schwarze Stern* (1965). ©DEFA-Stiftung/Horst Donth, Winfried Goldner

These moments are brief and immediately contrasted with Blackness as an integral part of *Négritude*, as a university chemistry lecture by a Ghanaian professor immediately follows the computer training, and a political speech given by the Ghanaian university dean in front of a large student crowd directly succeeds the sequence with the East German teacher as a way to mitigate the presence and significance of white people in an otherwise Black space. Even a representation of whiteness in the form of the East German containership *Rhön Rostock* is framed and accompanied visually with Ghanaians working on and around the ocean. Before we see the containership for the first time, we encounter a dozen Ghanaian fishermen at dawn pushing their long rowboat into the ocean and then paddling through the choppy water towards the open seas. While the *Rhön Rostock* manoeuvres through the waters of Tema Harbour, it appears that it can only do so under the guidance of a Ghanaian tugboat. In this instance, a water dolly shot positions the tugboat at the foreground of the frame and partially covers our view of the containership. An extended sequence of almost four minutes follows detailing how Ghanaian workers unload livestock, cars and other commodities destined for Ghana from the containership. Tradition, such as the fishing vessel, and innovation, in the form of the tugboat coordinating international trade, blend together at this moment, suggesting the benefits of co-existence between the old and the new that created opportunities for Black Ghanaians who are now equal to the white people they used to depend on.

The fishermen sequence is also noteworthy due to a German voiceover of speeches and texts by Ghana's first President, Kwame Nkrumah.[16] *Der Schwarze Stern*'s soundtrack follows the principles of direct cinema, as it dispenses with a narrator and ambient music in favour of synchronous ambient sounds and diegetic dialogue, circumspectly mixed by two of DEFA documentary studio's sound specialists, Heinz Dinter and Ingrid Schernikau. Although the subject matter of the German voiceovers might appear important as they relate directly to the on-screen images, little would be lost from the narrative if Dinter and Schernikau had cut the passages of Nkruma's inauguration speech given in English as the country's first President while we see the archival colour film footage from 1957 on screen. The pictures tell the story, just as in another sequence, when we see images from an elementary school with a teacher providing instruction in a local dialect, without the need for any subtitles or other aids to help us understand the content of the diegetic conversation. Throughout the entire film, diegetic voices and voiceovers alike enhance the narrative, but they neither function as its most dynamic component, nor are they necessary for our comprehension of the events taking place on screen. Rather, they serve as acoustic adornments and complement the visual information, regardless of the language on screen being Ghana's *lingua franca* English, one of the local dialects, or a German-language version of Nkruma's texts. Spoken by Helmut Karl Piontek and Helmut Müller-Lankow, two of East Germany's most recognized voices due to their frequent appearance in theatre, film, television and the synchronizations of foreign films, the few German passages are not didactic but poetic in nature. The low pitch, raspy timbre and composed speed of both voices create a comforting experience even for viewers without any German knowledge in a manner typical of the way African cinemas utilize soundtrack:

> It is thus sound that breathes life into the neocolonial town and city, spaces that are traditionally rife with colonial visual markers such as buildings, clothes, signs, and posters written in the colonisers' language. A different kind of space is thus born, out of sound, out of noise and song, and it is a space that pairs itself with the visual neo-colonial town and city, not in order to complete it (as one would imagine given the traditional relationship between image and sound in cinema – a symbiotic enterprise, as it were), but rather in order to supplant it.[17]

The cultural principles of Senghorism prevail in sound and *mise-en-scène* to such an extent that *Der schwarze Stern* could be confused for a contemporary documentary produced by the Ghana Film Industry Corporation. After Ghana's independence in 1957, the company that had emerged from the British Gold Coast Film Unit was nationalized, along with the entire film production and distribution under the leadership of Kwameh Nkrumah. Editing and processing facilities for 16 mm and 35 mm film were set up locally to discontinue the previous practice of sending the negatives abroad.[18] A shortage of trained Ghanaian directors could not be remedied right away; the Gold Coast Film Unit employed white filmmakers only, while Ghanaians would be relegated to assistant positions at most. Even after independence, only a few local professionals such as King Ampaw would head abroad to train in Europe and return home to work in the Ghana film industry, while foreigners still directed the bulk of films.[19] Nonetheless, filmmakers such as German-born Sean Graham hit the appropriate tone in terms of style and content in films like *Freedom for Ghana* (1957) and other documentaries of that time listed in the Ghana Film Industry Corporation's production catalogue *Films We Have Produced*, the Ghana Central Film Library's catalogue *Films from Ghana 1962* and an updated library catalogue from 1971/1972.[20] East German documents and publications not only show that the GDR was well aware of Ghana's film production, but also prove that the DEFA-Studio für Wochenschau und Dokumentarfilme, and therefore Hellwig and especially Oley, had access to original film footage from Nkrumah's inauguration publications and to his books.[21] Their script and the final version of *Der schwarze Stern* imitated the cinematic fabric of Ghanaian documentaries so well that one could mistake it as a Ghana Film production of those years.

African Storytelling: *Griots*, Music and Dance

While Hellwig's documentary imitates Ghanaian cinema, *Hirde Dyama* (1971), co-directed by East German Gerhart Jentsch and Guinean Moussa Kémoko Diakité, does not need to masquerade as an African documentary because it is a co-production proper between DEFA and Guinea's national film studio Sily-Cinéma. Shot on ORWO colour stock to bring out the vibrant costume colours and filmed on 35 mm film stock, *Hirde Dyama* has a running time of 24 minutes. It is the second part of a two-part documentary series about Guinea, following *Guinea heute* (1971). Both parts reinforced the strong cultural ties between the two nations that started after a 1968 'DDR Filmwoche' in Guinea, and political ties when the GDR opened its embassy in 1970, coincidentally the same year as the inaugural Hirde Dyama cultural festival that lent its name to the documentary.

A collective DEFA and Sily-Cinéma crew collaborated on *Guinea heute* and *Hirde Dyama*, and released them in the GDR in the space of three months. Both films have a similar structure: sequences toggle between various regions of Guinea depicting their distinctive features in terms of agricultural or industrial production, and then juxtapose cultural performances typical of these regions. With a dominant focus on cultural performances that are strung together in a seemingly illogical order, *Hirde Dyama* very likely appeared highly repetitive and confusing to Western viewers. Also repetitive to their ears were probably the drumbeats that accompany dances and seem to be without obvious beginnings or endings, and xylophones, whistles and bells that produce dissonant chords and puzzling melodies.

However, seen from the perspective of an African viewer, *Hirde Dyama* is a wonderfully crafted African documentary, its form and content reminiscent of storytelling in the style typical of a *griot*, itinerant storytellers who would move around Western Africa and entertain with a combination of music, dance, song and theatre.[22] As early as its opening sequence, *Hirde Dyama* pleases African viewers in particular when it shows a female singer perform a song about a free Guinea. Accompanied by a male musician playing the kora, a traditional twenty-one-string instrument reminiscent of a combination of lute and harp, the musicians showcase all the typical features of African music. They utilize microtonal shadings, chromatic chords and polyphony, along with melodic repetition that intensifies with each iteration. We also see Guinean faces before the camera cuts once more to the musicians, while the song continues as the final credits in French and German roll across the screen. Throughout the film, we see only Black Guineans, apart from foreign ambassadors and guests shown when the camera pans across the opening speech given by Guinea's President Ahmed Sékou Touré as he explains the purpose of the festival as bearing testimony to the rich traditions of African cultures and art, and to dynamically promote this culture and art in the present day. These visual and aural arrangements invite the Black African – not the European – viewer to identify as the target audience, something that is even further accentuated by the decision not to translate or explain the film title.

Not only the festival but also the film itself advanced Guinean culture. *Hirde Dyama* is both a crucial contribution to African film history and an excellent example of Guinea's commitment to establish a national film production apparatus free from postcolonial structures. Guinea set up its own infrastructure immediately after independence and formed Sily-Cinéma in 1958 to produce, distribute and exhibit nationally. As early as 1960, the country had built its own 16 mm production facilities, and after 1966 no longer used foreigners to direct documentary films, but funnelled a portion of the revenue from domestic productions and exhibition of imported films to fund the education of Guinean film directors.[23] This strategy proved to be successful. Costa Diagne's film *Hier, aujourd'hui, demain* (*Yesterday, Today, Tomorrow,* 1968) won the Joris Ivens Prize at the Leipzig film festival, and *Hirde Dyama* won Second Prize in 1972 at FESPACO, Africa's biggest film festival that only accepts films by African filmmakers and that are mainly produced in Africa. The official festival documents list only Moussa Kémoko Diakité as the director and Sily-Cinéma as the production studio, whereas the names 'Gerhart Jentsch' and 'DEFA' do not appear at all. This is quite curious, since Guinea did not yet have 35 mm production facilities or equipment at that time, East German names clearly appear in the opening credits, and the film might have been screened with the German voiceover. Perhaps the most logical possibility for this oddity is the FESPACO rule of selecting only African films.

Regardless of these inconsistencies, by awarding this prize, the jury acknowledged how *Hirde Dyama* performed and preserved African culture in its appropriate presentation of visual, aural and oral traditions. For instance, when the Bembeya Jazz National ensemble with their singer Aboubacar Demba Camara – declared Africa's top vocalist by the BBC[24] – takes to the stage, viewers are exposed to jazzy interpretations of historical chants originally sung by the cavalry of West African popular hero Almamy Samory Touré, who fought and died in a battle against French colonizers. The music is a distinctive African variation of jazz music, combining trumpets and saxophone with bongos and the xylophone. Demba Camara sings traditional melodies with the same microtonality we already encountered in the documentary's opening song. In this instance, the jazz combo's performance perfectly illustrates the standards of African music: open-endedness instead of a linear musical structure, opposition instead of harmony, repetition-as-intensification instead of variation and musical key change: 'in the Africanist perspective each repeat is different than the one that went before, is shaped by the one that went before, and predicates the one that will follow'.[25]

Demba Camara's singing, accompanied by his swaying body and by expressive gestures, also presents a familiar environment to an African, and particularly a Guinean, audience. Body movement is inseparable from music, and African polycentric and polyrhythmic dancing was and still is used as an expression of freedom and liberation among Africans.[26] Western audiences of *Hirde Dyama* might also have been and still be confused by an abrupt transition from the jazz combo to a Guinean ballet performance about the heroic tales of freedom fighter Alfa Yaya Mayudo, while audiences familiar with these histories and traditions perceive this as a smooth and logical bridge from one dance spectacle to another. To them, the three-minute-long sequence performed by the famous ballet ensemble Les Ballet Africaines allegorizes Mayudo's struggles against French colonists on a stage instead of performing subversively during the times of occupation.[27] Polyrhythmic and polycentric actions on stage and film include the dancers moving from more than one focal point, while their spines bend in interaction with head, pelvis and bent-legged postures (see Figure 10.2). Regardless of their age, dancers display high affect coupled with ephebism – a display of youthfulness and agility – to deliver a fast-paced sequence of dance patterns showing flexibility and intensity as they dance across the stage.[28]

Altogether, the structural concept behind *Hirde Dyama* is designed to appeal to viewers who understand the dance patterns and musical tropes, who spot the historical and cultural contexts behind costumes and protagonists, and who recognize the singers, dance troupes and ensembles on screen. The documentary thus goes beyond the recording and archiving of these practices. It lends a voice to Guineans and provides them with the opportunity to organize sights and sounds according to their customs instead of being silenced by Western filmmakers. As an African film, *Hirde Dyama* creates a spatiotemporal sphere that includes history, collective imagery and characteristics of orality in griot style that brings a cinematic Guinea to Guineans.

Kuxa Kanema: (Re)Claiming African Narratives

Grüße aus Maputo could be understood as an antipode to *Hirde Dyama* due to its ostensibly political message and objective to report about Erich Honecker's official visit to Mozambique. Lisa and Joachim Hadaschik, two fervently political filmmakers, co-wrote and co-directed the 15-minute documentary as part of their work for Camera DDR, a production group founded in 1968 by DEFA and the East German Foreign Ministry to create short documentaries with content of interest to foreign audiences (see Chapter 2 in this volume). No expenses were spared: the Hadaschiks employed two of DEFA's most experienced cinematographers with Günter Breßler, who had worked on many *Augenzeuge* and *Kinobox* newsreels, and Manfred Gronau, a long-time cinematographer for both Hadaschik and on the set of Barbara and Winfried Junge's *Golzow* documentaries. Joachim Hadaschik's position as head of Camera DDR

Figure 10.2. Ballet performance featuring polyrhythmic dancing in Moussa Kémoko Diakité and Gerhard Jentsch's *Hirde Dyama* (1970). ©DEFA-Stiftung/F. Thoms, H. Sylla, W. Bogdanow et al.

allowed the crew to take the best equipment available to DEFA at that time and the best film (most likely the latest NC 3 ORWO 35 mm colour film stock that allowed capturing vivid colours outdoors in order to optimize the picture for television broadcasts). On the one hand, the film's structure appears rather conventional: sequences of work and leisure activities from Mozambique dominate the first part, while an extensive documentation of the official reception in honour of Honecker's official visit rounds out the second half. Using the methods of Western theorists to analyse *Grüße aus Maputo* would result in classifying it as a visual ode to the GDR's efforts to showcase international solidarity with a young African nation.

A polycentric approach, on the other hand, provides the opportunity to ponder how this documentary would contribute to *Kuxa Kanema*, Mozambique's variant of the newsreel. After the country's independence in 1975, its newly formed government tasked the recently established national cinema service Instituto Nacional de Cinema (INC) with dual roles. The INC was asked to set up a distribution network that would reach even remote areas of the country where cinema was unknown, and to produce weekly newsreels that would depict the intense social, political and cultural activities, and convey a positive image of a united and free Mozambique. In order to overcome the challenging lack of a cinematic infrastructure with only a few movie theatres in bigger cities that were exclusively playing imported feature films, but also to answer the question of accommodating multiple languages in addition to the colonial Portuguese, the INC mounted Soviet film projectors on trucks that hauled the newsreels from village to village for nightly screenings, and introduced the entire nation to the (to them) modern medium. *Kuxa Kanema* or 'birth of the image' was deemed a fitting designation to express the significance of this operation. Since none of the Mozambican vernaculars had a name for the newsreel genre yet, Kuxa Kanema became the *nom de guerre* of Mozambique's weekly newsreel programme.[29] These newsreels had the difficult mission of developing a sense of common identity among people from different backgrounds who were speaking a wide variety of languages. They had to be crafted in ways that offered paths of identification with the new nation, serve as mirrors of urban and rural societies, reflect common problems and offer solutions, and show that a postcolonial Mozambique was going to bring progress and prosperity to everyone without the ability to fall back on spoken language.

Read alongside these cornerstones, *Grüße aus Maputo* appears like a manifest filmed with the intent to showcase a fledgling Mozambique to its residents. Following the opening credits and the display of a map of Europe that shows the position of a black-red-and-yellow coloured GDR on the continent, the camera zooms out until both Europe and Africa are visible, and then zooms in, this time in Africa, where we see a clearly designated Mozambique. The image initially only reveals the contours of the country on the right and a black dot with the word 'Maputo' marking the capital city next to it. The flag of Mozambique's liberation movement FRELIMO – since independence also its national flag – fades in on the lower left of the screen. In the upper-left corner of the screen, the words 'Saudações de Maputo' appear in a white font and are then replaced with the German translation, 'Grüße aus Maputo'. This juxtaposition of Mozambique's shape, its flag and the words in its *lingua franca* Portuguese renders visible the ideal of Kuxa Kanema to communicate a common national identity through the delivery of familiar images. Mozambicans without access to formal education and thus unable to decipher the letters or identify the shape of their nation would probably have recognized the FRELIMO flag from the independence struggles or from previous films. Others could have communicated the various elements on screen and their meaning to fellow audience members.[30]

Mediating the film by Mozambicans is also what Kuxa Kanema hoped to achieve among the population. Regardless of content, films such as *Grüße aus Maputo* served as an occasion to gather in communities and to recapitulate, discuss and interpret the images that had

Figure 10.3. Visualized ideals of Kuxa Kanema in Lisa and Joachim Hadaschik's *Grüße aus Maputo* (1979). ©DEFA-Stiftung/Günter Bressler, Manfred Gronau.

unfolded to audiences. For instance, the film places images of modern housing in Maputo alongside the shacks and huts in rural areas, but shows that the residents in either location are Mozambicans. Juxtapositions such as this presented opportunities for the viewers to discuss these images, to assure themselves that economic prosperity was now accessible for more parts of the population, and that life conditions had been improving since independence. Other potential discussion topics might have been the presentation of urban life as an option to those interested in furthering their education. On multiple occasions, the camera captures all sorts of students assembling in one classroom: mothers carrying their babies in slings learn to read and write next to eight-year-old children, and students of all genders attentively follow their instructor in what appears to be a college classroom. Education, so the message goes, is the bond for a new Mozambique.

Reflection and identification also take place explicitly through the selection of the framing narrative. A school-aged boy attending the secondary school Escola Secundária Francisco Manyanga leads the documentary as narrator. We see him only four times, i.e. in the beginning of the film, at the end and twice more throughout the narrative. However, his voice accompanies and structures the entire film as a Portuguese voiceover. The boy portrays his home country, Mozambique, and reports about the changes that have occurred since independence four years earlier. When he breaks down the fourth wall as he addresses the audience directly and looks straight into the camera, he acts not only as an oral storyteller, but he also does so as an African storyteller. Hearing a voice that sounds native and seeing a face that looks like other Mozambicans provide additional levels of acceptance. The boy serves as an embodiment of a new generation growing up free, educated and conversant with performing in front of a camera. With his youthfulness, he personifies what Manthia Diawara identified as the exuberance, joyfulness and verve of the oral tradition African cinema was known for.[31]

In fact, vitality and ebullience prevail in most of *Grüße aus Maputo*, be it in those moments when children swim in the ocean, when dance troupes perform modern and traditional dances in Western or African costumes, or during a four-minute-long series of sequences that present the celebrations during Honecker's visit. Slower sequences, such as the images of the sun setting on the horizon or elephants and giraffes wandering through the forest steppe, come alive with the help of non-diegetic traditional sounds played with drums, whistles and sticks. The vivid colour schemes of nature, but also of the murals located in Maputo's national history museum appear even more nuanced due to the high-quality cameras and expensive colour film stock.

Familiar moving images in colour coupled with diegetic and non-diegetic sounds echoing the tones of Mozambique shape a film that educated and entertained simultaneously. Curiously, *Grüße aus Maputo* executes the ideals of Kuxa Kanema better than similar films produced in Mozambique. For instance, the seminal 1977 documentary *25*, directed by Celso Luccas and José Celso Martinez Corrêa, and co-produced by the ICN played in the Director's Fortnight competition in Cannes. The 130-minute film about the process of Mozambican independence likely resonated more with an international than a domestic audience due to its length, complexity and narrative structure. *Grüße aus Maputo* places the narrative in African hands as it operates with simple but effective tools that allow African rural and urban viewers to identify with the protagonists, to find their own lives and their environments, and to feel informed regardless of their current level of education.

Conclusion

When read as Afrocentric narratives in the contexts of African cinemas, East German documentaries imitate methods, theories and traditions that originated in those regions. African discourses are identifiable to domestic audiences, unique pictorial languages blend colonial and postcolonial characteristics to form new visual languages, and sonic layers reflect the diverse aural environments of a rich and multifaceted continent. They contributed to film corpora at moments in time when national cinemas were still developing, and they provided models for observation and quality standards African filmmakers were able to study. East German filmmakers were willing to collaborate, to share knowledge without looking down or pontificating, and often enough, the East German documentaries are of superb visual and technical quality.

It is possible that the DEFA directors filming in Africa did not necessarily intend to create their films according to the traditions of African cinemas, and yet it appears that they observed closely, operated carefully and provided ample space for African peoples to express themselves and to showcase their regional customs and traditions. Not only is the absence of white people striking, but also how the films tell stories of success, of perseverance, of strength of character and of pride in their stories. Once the biggest obstacle – the German voiceover – is removed from the analysis, East German films even tackle what many African films have a difficult time with – they are often able to address the fundamental causes of social stratification due to colonialism by showcasing the accomplishments of African nations since their independence.

Certainly, not all East German Africa films lend themselves to polycentric readings, but even films such as Andreas Dresen's 1989 documentary *Jenseits von Klein Wanzleben* (*Far from Klein Wanzleben*) about the daily life of an East German Friendship Brigade in Zimbabwe or Kurt Stanke's playful *Unter der Sonne Ägyptens* (*Under the Egyptian Sun*, 1956) about performance tests for the new East German Trabant and Wartburg car models offer worthwhile observations and lack an overtly politically red hue that a contemporary viewer might expect. It would also be interesting to take a contrastive look at the other side of the Iron Curtain and inquire how West German cinema about Africa compares to its East German counterparts. What might happen if we applied a similar polycentric approach is a fascinating question.

Film studies has yet to contextualize East German cinema in relation to Africa, in German as well as in English, and future projects could look at notes, memos and other material documents available in the German Bundesarchiv and their equivalent archives in African countries. These and other projects would benefit from critical inquiries about the value of Eurocentric approaches. Unique perspectives and innovative vantage points often yield new and more profound insights, which might stimulate our future understanding of East German documentary cinema.

Sebastian Heiduschke is Professor of World Languages and Cultures at Oregon State University. His film publications include the books *East German Cinema: DEFA and Film History* (Palgrave, 2013 in English, 2019 in a Japanese edition), *Re-imagining DEFA: East German Cinema in Its National and Transnational Contexts* (co-edited with Seán Allan, Berghahn Books, 2016), as well as essays in *Camera Obscura*, *Feminist German Studies*, *German Studies Review*, *Monatshefte* and various edited collections.

Notes

1. Ulf Engel and Hans-Georg Schleicher, *Die beiden deutschen Staaten in Afrika – Zwischen Konkurrenz und Koexistenz 1949–1990* (Hamburg: Institut für Afrikakunde, 1998).
2. Ilona Schleicher and Hans-Georg Schleicher, *Die DDR im südlichen Afrika – Solidarität und kalter Krieg* (Hamburg: Institut für Afrikakunde, 1997); Christian Kleinschmidt and Dieter Ziegler (eds) *Dekolonisierungsgewinner: Deutsche Außenpolitik und Außenwirtschaftsbeziehungen im Zeitalter des Kalten Krieges* (Boston: De Gruyter, 2018); Gareth Winrow, *The Foreign Policy of the GDR in Africa* (Cambridge: Cambridge University Press, 1990); Ulrich van der Heyden (Ed.), *Die DDR und Afrika – Zwischen Klassenkampf und neuem Denken* (Münster: Lit, 1993).
3. A search of Progress Film's database yields 114 documentaries along with 137 newsreels of *Der Augenzeuge* and *Kinobox* covering aspects of Africa.
4. All titles and filmographic information follow the online database of the DEFA Stiftung, https://www.defa-stiftung.de/filme/filme-suchen (retrieved 9 November 2021).
5. Nick Hodgin, 'Alternative Realities and Authenticity in DEFA's Documentary Films', in Marc Silberman and Henning Wrage (eds), *DEFA at the Crossroads of East German and International Film Culture: A Companion*, (Boston: De Gruyter, 2014), pp. 281–303; Qinna Shen and Martin Rosenstock (eds), *Beyond Alterity: German Encounters with Modern East Asia* (New York: Berghahn Books, 2014,) pp. 94–114; Quinn Slobodian (ed.), *Comrades of Color*, (New York: Berghahn Books, 2015); Peggy Piesche, 'Irgendwo ist immer Afrika… "Blackface" in DEFA-Filmen', in AntiDiskriminierungsBüro (ABD) Köln and cyberNomads (eds), *The BlackBook. Deutschlands Häutungen* (Frankfurt am Main: IKO, 2004,) pp. 286–91; Philip Decker, 'Screening White Reassurance: Insecurity and Redemption in Four German Africa Films', *Oxford German Studies* 51(2) (2022), 161–85.
6. Olivier Barlet, *African Cinemas: Decolonizing the Gaze* (London: Zed Books, 2000).

7. Ella Shohat and Robert Stam, *Unthinking Eurocentrism: Multiculturalism and the Media* (New York: Routledge, 2014), p. 18.
8. Ibid., p. 365.
9. Ibid.
10. Kenneth Harrow, *Trash: African Cinema from Below* (Bloomington: Indiana University Press, 2013), p. 3.
11. Bill Nichols, *Introduction to Documentary* (Bloomington: Indiana University Press, 2010), p. 68, emphasis in original.
12. Vlad Dima, 'The Aural Life of Neo-colonial Space', in Kenneth Harrow and Carmela Garritano (eds), *A Companion to African Cinema*. Hoboken, NJ: Wiley-Blackwell, 2019, pp. 176–93.
13. I would like to thank Progress Film in Berlin for providing access to digitized versions of the films I discuss in this article.
14. Léopold Sédar Senghor, *Les Fondements de l'Africanité ou Négritude et Arabité* (Paris: Présence Africaine, 1967), p. 35.
15. See Achille Mbembe, *On the Postcolony* (Berkeley: University of California Press, 2001), p. 55.
16. The passages translated into German are from Kwame Nkrumah, *Africa Must Unite* (New York: Praeger, 1963) and Kwame Nkrumah, *The Autobiography of Kwame Nkrumah* (Edinburgh: Nelson, 1957).
17. Dima, 'The Aural Life of Neo-colonial Space', p. 176.
18. Manthia Diawara, *African Cinema: Politics & Culture* (Bloomington: Indiana University Press, 1992), pp. 5–6.
19. Keyan Tomaselli, 'African Cinema: Theoretical Perspectives on Some Unresolved Questions', in Imruh Bakari and Mbye B. Cham (ed.), *African Experiences of Cinema* (London: BFI, 1996), pp. 165–74 (at p. 170). See also http://www.colonialfilm.org.uk/production-company/gold-coast-film-unit (retrieved 9 February 2022). King Ampaw trained in East and West Germany as well as in Austria. His connections helped him act alongside Klaus Kinski and also co-produce Werner Herzog's *Cobra Verde* (1987).
20. https://archive.org/details/GhanaFilmIndustryCorporationFilmsWeHaveProduced/, https://archive.org/details/FilmsFromGhanaAccraCentralFilmLibrary1962 and https://archive.org/details/CatalogueOfFilmsGhanaCentralFilmLibrary1971–72 (retrieved 9 February 2022). See also Jennifer Blaylock, 'Cinema in Transit', https://cinemaintransit.wordpress.com (retrieved 9 February 2022).
21. Albert Wilkening, Heinz Baumert and Klaus Lippert (eds), *Film: Kleine Enzyklopädie* (Leipzig: VEB Bibliographisches Institut, 1966), pp. 673–78; 'Maßnahmeplan 1964 für Afrika', 23 January 1964, p. 5 (= SAPMO BArch DY 30/IV A 2/20/1975).
22. See, for example, Lizbeth Malkmus and Roy Annes, *Arab and African Film Making* (London: Zed Books, 1991).
23. Diawara, *African Cinema*, pp. 54–78.

24. Frank Tenaille, *Music Is the Weapon of the Future: Fifty Years of African Popular Music* (Chicago: Chicago Review Press, 2002), p. 32.
25. Brenda Dixon Gottschild, *Digging the Africanist Presence in American Performance: Dance and Other Contexts* (Westport: Greenwood Press, 1996), p. 8.
26. Rex Nettleford, 'Foreword', in Welsh Asanta (ed.), *African Dance: An Artistic, Historical, and Philosophical Inquiry* (Trenton: Africa World Press, 1996), pp. xiii–xviii (at p. xvi).
27. Tracy Snipe, 'African Dance: Bridges to Humanity', in Welsh Asanta (ed.), *African Dance: An Artistic, Historical, and Philosophical Inquiry* (Trenton: Africa World Press, 1996), pp. 63–77 (at pp. 70–71).
28. Dixon Gottschield, *Digging the Africanist Presence*, p. 7.
29. Camillo de Souza, 'State Initiatives and Encouragement in the Development of National Cinema: Mozambique', in Imruh Bakari and Mbye B. Cham (eds), *African Experiences of Cinema* (London: BFI, 1996), pp. 128–31.
30. Ibid., p. 128.
31. See Manthia Diawara, 'Popular Culture and Oral Traditions in African Film', *Film Quarterly* 41(3) (1988), 6–14.

Select Bibliography

Bakari, Imruh, and Mbye B. Cham (eds). *African Experiences of Cinema*. London: BFI, 1996.
Barlet, Olivier. *African Cinemas: Decolonizing the Gaze*. London: Zed Books, 2000.
Diawara, Manthia. 'Popular Culture and Oral Traditions in African Film', *Film Quarterly* 41(3) (1988), 6–14.
Dima, Vlad. 'The Aural Life of Neo-colonial Space', in Kenneth Harrow and Carmela Garritano (eds), *A Companion to African Cinema*. Hoboken, NJ: Wiley-Blackwell, 2019, pp. 176–93.
Harrow, Kenneth, and Carmela Garritano (eds). *A Companion to African Cinema*. Hoboken, NJ: Wiley-Blackwell, 2019.
Shohat, Ella, and Robert Stam. *Unthinking Eurocentrism: Multiculturalism and the Media*. New York: Routledge, 2014.
Van der Heyden, Ulrich (ed.). *Die DDR und Afrika – Zwischen Klassenkampf und neuem Denken*. Münster: Lit, 1993.
Welsh Asanta (ed.). *African Dance: An Artistic, Historical, and Philosophical Inquiry*. Trenton: Africa World Press, 1996.
Winrow, Gareth. *The Foreign Policy of the GDR in Africa*. Cambridge: Cambridge University Press, 1990.

CHAPTER 11

East Germany's Anti-racist Politics and Black Abjection in Documentary Film

Priscilla Layne

Throughout its forty-year existence, the international politics of the German Democratic Republic (GDR) were heavily invested in aligning the country with so-called 'Third World nations' to gain more allies in the fight against capitalism – a politics often conveyed through film. When one specifically considers the documentary footage produced by GDR filmmakers about Africa, one notes very different techniques depending on whether the goal was to inform the East German public about notable topics or condemn the Federal Republic of Germany (FRG) for its imperialist relationship towards Africa.

In this chapter I argue that in the case of documentaries made with the intention of shaming the FRG, there is a more pronounced focus on displaying brutalized Black bodies, including those of starving children or executed political rivals. To that end, I will compare three different East German documentaries from the 1960s and 1970s: Ella Ensink's *Abschied von Afrika* (*Farewell to Africa*, 1961), Walter Heynowski's *Kommando 52* (*Commando 52*, 1965) and Günter Weschke's *Apartheid – No!* (1974). I argue that these documentaries about Africa are never *really* about Africans, but are using Africans to make the West look bad and demonstrate how progressive the GDR is. Sometimes this instrumentalization of Africans happens in the form of offering close-ups of anonymous, suffering, mutilated and murdered Black bodies, which is the case in both *Kommando 52* and *Apartheid – No!*. Meanwhile, the documentaries that are meant to be entertaining and not *overtly* political, such as represented by *Abschied von Afrika*, do a poor job of maintaining a critical stance on neocolonialism. Such educational films emphasize Africa's importance as a place for conservation and continue the colonial tradition of depicting Black people as an 'undifferentiated collective, devoid of individuality, memory, or psychological depth'.[1]

Despite these differences, I believe all three films participate in Black abjection. Darieck Scott defines Black abjection as:

> a judgment animating arguments and rhetoric in both currents in which the history of peoples in the African diaspora – having been conquered and enslaved and then, post-Emancipation, being dominated by colonial powers or by homegrown white supremacists – is a history of humiliating defeat, a useless history which must be in some way overturned or overcome.[2]

Thus, when we consider these three films – *Abschied von Afrika*, *Kommando 52* and *Apartheid – No!* – regardless of whether they are overtly political or educational films, and regardless of whether they show images of mutilated and murdered Black bodies or not, all three documentaries instrumentalize oppressed Black bodies for East German purposes, never allowing us to hear directly from Black subjects or see Black people as agents of social or political change. And this is why they participate in Black abjection.

Arguably, the tension between disavowing and reaffirming race in these films reflects the ambivalent relationship of the GDR towards this issue. While on the one hand, the SED regime rejected the idea of separate races as a fallacy propagated by capitalism, on the other hand, racialized people were not portrayed or treated as equals to white East Germans, an ideology Quinn Slobodian describes as Socialist chromatism: racialized people are represented, but *white* people are shown as being in charge, creating a paternalist relationship.[3] As Sara Pugach notes: 'The GDR was more a site of ambivalence and inconsistency than tolerance when it came to questions of race.'[4] In this chapter I argue that what we can see from these three documentaries is that by focusing on racialized people as worthy of pity and in need of a white saviour, East German racial politics failed to stress them as *agents*, ultimately participating in a process of Black abjecting, turning Black bodies into pawns in an ideological battle between East and West Germany.

Abschied von Afrika (1961)

Produced in 1961, *Abschied von Afrika* was directed by Ella Ensink and focuses on the expertise of Hans Schomburgk (1880–1967), who at the time was renowned as an ethnographic filmmaker who had been directing so-called 'ethnodramas' since the 1920s. Ensink's film career spanned Nazi Germany (1933–45) and the only other films she directed or co-directed in the GDR was the documentary featuring Paul Robeson, Joris Ivens' *Lied der Ströme* (*The Song of the Rivers*, 1954) and *Mein Kind* (*My Child*, 1956), a short film featuring scenes of loving mothers from all over the world, which was made in cooperation with the Women's International Democratic Federation.

Schomburgk's biography and career situate him as an implicated subject, to borrow Michael Rothberg's term, vis-à-vis the African subjects he filmed. His interest in Africa – its landscapes, people and animals – betrayed an attitude common among white European modernists in the early twentieth century. As Christian Rogowski writes, people like Schomburgk and fellow explorer Carl Hagenbeck produced 'exotic adventure films' that had an 'often unconscious, colonialist dimension (typical) of early Weimar German fictional feature films'.[5] He may have found Africa an enticing place to shoot films and may have been motivated by a desire to educate the public about this vast continent, but this did not mean he did not harbour racist views towards Africans. As Rogowski notes: 'Films such as those directed by Schomburgk or produced by Hagenbeck help cement racially biased stereotypes concerning the supposedly natural moral and intellectual superiority of whites and the concomitant inferiority of blacks.'[6]

Schomburgk, who identified as German Jewish, had a successful military career in Africa, having served as a sergeant-major in Rhodesia (now Zimbabwe). At the time of his military service, Schomburgk was actually convicted of physical assault causing the death of natives, which resulted in his dismissal from service.[7] Schomburgk remained in Africa, traversing several colonies from hunting elephants in German East Africa to being credited as the first European to explore 'the dark hinterlands of Liberia'.[8] His first foray into filmmaking was sponsored by Duke Adolf Friedrich zu Mecklenburg (1873–1969), who, following Germany's loss of its colonies after signing the Treaty of Versailles, 'cofounded the Übersee-Filmgesellschaft in Berlin' with Schomburgk. Langbehn writes that Schomburgk 'cleverly cut corners by editing his pre-war African location footage into adventure stories filmed on the outskirts of Berlin, yet Übersee-Film folded after only three full-length features, and Schomburgk returned to lecture tours and documentary film'.[9] Yet like many German Jews who had served in the military prior to the Nazis' seizure of power, his commitment to German colonialism, his recognition as an explorer and his military service did not save him from Nazi persecution. As Gerlinde Waz writes, Schomburgk refused to join the Nazi Party and was openly critical of Hitler's war, which made the discovery of his Jewish maternal grandmother a convenient reason for the Nazis to act against him.[10] Schomburgk was banned from filmmaking and the Nazis re-edited, redubbed, and redeployed 'his' films for their propaganda purposes – with his name removed from the credits.

Abschied von Afrika is the least overtly propagandistic of the three documentaries I will discuss. It falls squarely in the category of a documentary intended to entertain and inform an East German public about Africa. The film was released in both the GDR and the FRG in different cuts.[11] *Abschied von Afrika* does not engage with overtly political topics, failing even to take a critical stance vis-à-vis neocolonialism. In fact, there is even a tinge of colonial longing in its framing, photography and narrative. The documentary is framed as an opportunity to accompany Schomburgk on his last trip to Africa. In that sense, it follows the style of a nature or ethnographic film, which has the intention of sharing 'expert' knowledge with its viewers and offering them a unique look at life in a different part of the world. As opposed to the more overtly political nature of the other two documentaries I will discuss, which deal more explicitly with Apartheid, racism and neocolonialism, this film has a much lighter tone, particularly due to how much of it showcases the unique flora and fauna on the continent. It begins with whimsical, instrumental music accompanying the credits, followed by an establishing shot of the film's expert, Schomburgk, an elderly white man whose authority on the subject is established both by the shelves filled with books to his right and the array of African artifacts decorating the wall behind him; everything from wooden fertility statues to a framed painting of a lion. This mise-en-scène conveys the kind of colonial attitude one might not expect in a film meant to promote solidarity with African countries. The voiceover informs us that these 'trophies' and artwork serve to remind Schomburgk of his many expeditions.

The narrator introduces Schomburgk as an 'explorer, hunter, writer, sitting at home in Munich'. Despite Schomburgk's residence in the FRG, East German audiences were quite familiar with his work. He was received as a reasonably progressive Imperial German whose heyday was in the cosmopolitan Weimar Republic, but whose Jewishness made him a victim of the Nazi regime. It is this reputation that made him and his films so hugely popular in the GDR. In fact, three years prior to this film, Schomburgk directed his own film *Hans Schomburgk – Mein Abschied von Afrika* (*My Farewell to Africa*, 1958), which would have been instantly recognizable to East German viewers. In his heyday Schomburgk directed films with such titles as *Eine Weisse unter Kannibalen* (*A White Person among Cannibals*, 1921), *Das letzte Paradies* (*The Last Paradise*, 1932) and *Die Wildnis stirbt* (*The Wilderness Is Dying*, 1936), which was his last film before *Abschied von Afrika*.

The narrator describes Schomburgk's relationship to Africa in colonial terms; it is the 'hot continent' that would not let him go – a line that feminizes Africa, while simultaneously turning the continent into a lustful woman, pursuing Schomburg.[12] Such phrases recall the racialized 'colonial fantasies' Susanne Zantop criticized, such as how Africa was frequently depicted as the dark, mysterious continent, home to women who would lust after white men.[13] As the camera zooms in on Schomburg's collection of African artefacts, the music switches to Indigenous, traditional music, evoking a sense of exoticism. This editing further establishes his authority over Africa by literally having him draw on a map, an action that recalls such colonial events as the Berlin Conference, when several European powers, including the then German Empire led by Bismarck, met to divide up Africa into colonies.[14]

At first, *Abschied von Afrika* adopts the guise of an ethnographic or nature film, with its shots of how the Atlantic and Indian Oceans come together in the south, and shots of seals swimming and lounging at Mossel Bay in South Africa, along with proclamations like 'Africa, sunlit continent'. As Tobias Boes has argued, this is a rhetorical move common of German-language nature films of this era. Africa is portrayed as a place for conservation, and the human struggles are pushed into the background.[15] In this way, *Abschied von Afrika* is a curious mixture of romantic, exotic tropes, combined with a few critical observations about the political reality of South Africa. Whenever the film adopts a stance of 'informing' viewers about historical facts, the narrator takes an uncritical approach vis-à-vis colonialism, such as the statement 'A stone that Dutchmen put down in 1630 was the first post office' or the more ambiguous comment 'City names as import items. Reminiscent of inglorious chapters in colonial history', which is accompanied by shots of local, South African places named after Berlin – for example, a highway named 'N2 Berlin' and a café called 'Berlin Tea Lounge'. There are also shots of the Victoria Falls in Zimbabwe, referred to in the film as Rhodesia, accompanied by the following statement: 'Long before the Englishman Livingston discovered this beautiful natural phenomenon for the whites in 1855, the waterfall was already called Mosi-oa-Tunya by the Africans. The sounding white smoke.' Thus, the narrator acknowledges that the country had a history and its own names for things before the British arrived. But there is no direct condemnation of British colonialism, nor does he question what the implications are of naming this waterfall after the Queen of England.

There are also moments when the film recalls ethnographic and feature films from the Nazi period, which used the African continent as an exotic location for escapist narratives or as part of a larger argument for why Germany should recover of its colonies. In Nazi propaganda films, Black *female* bodies in particular were often put on display, a practice one can observe in a film like *Quax in Afrika* (filmed 1943–44, released in 1947). Images of Black women and girls' nude bodies served to reaffirm Nazis' belief in their superior civilization, while also offering them tantalizing, sexual fantasies.[16] In *Abschied von Afrika*, there are remnants of this film grammar when Indigenous communities are filmed. In one scene, while the narrator explains the differences between female and male clothing, and why the people do not need as much material as in Europe, a camera lingers on a young woman, tilting slowly upwards and focusing on her bare breasts. A similar close-up of a woman's breasts is included in a shot when we see a Ndebele woman helping construct and adorn a building. There, the camera frames her breasts, arms and the colourful bracelets she is wearing.

While the political reality of Black South Africans takes a back seat in *Abschied von Afrika*, there are a few brief moments where the film acknowledges colonial crimes, though they are still framed primarily of educational importance. For example, when the camera focuses on a *kraal* – a village of huts surrounded by a stockade that functions as a kind of refrigerator, the narrator casually explains that in the past, 'this was the last centre of defence of the warlike Zulus against the cruel colonialists. This is where their supplies were stored'. Although the narrator points out that the colonialists were *cruel*, modifying Zulus with *warlike* makes it unclear who the initial aggressors were.

Interspersed with scenes of rural life are shots of the bigger cities, allowing the audience to marvel at just how modern South Africa has become. Indirectly, the narrator acknowledges that all this wealth has come from the mines which can be seen in the background, as the camera pans across the high-rises in the foreground, accompanied by peppy jazz. The narrator's statement, 'the lords of the large metropolis reside in the shopping centres and high rises, built from Africa's gold' is accompanied by shots of white men and women marching through the streets, either shopping or heading to work. In stark contrast to *Apartheid – No!*, which I will discuss later, in *Abschied von Afrika* there is no reflection about the fact that only South Africa's white citizens can enjoy these leisure activities like going to the movies and surfing. The film does show some scenes of the poverty in the segregated Black neighbourhoods; but these amount to little more than shots of naked South Africans, such as the image of a little boy without either trousers or underwear standing in a dusty landscape among other children. Even though there is a vague reference to the apartheid system, only the banks and businessmen are indicted.

An obvious example of this is provided by a sequence of Black women collecting water from fountains as we are told how precious a resource water is (see Figure 11.1). Above them, a sign indicates that these fountains are 'Fonds du Bien-être Indigène', which means that these fountains are designated for the Indigenous, suggesting that elsewhere there are fountains only for whites, indicating the apartheid system. But the narrator never draws attention to what the sign means. Instead, he focuses on the fact that these faucets are a rarity, and that a lot more must be done to make life here more modern and therefore more comfortable, and to provide basic services 'which are already

Figure 11.1. In this shot from Ella Ensink's *Abschied von Afrika* (1961), Black South African women collect water from an outdoor tap. The sign above them reads the 'fountains are designated for the Indigenous', an example of the apartheid system. © DEFA-Stiftung/Karl Breselow, Klaus Phillip

taken for granted elsewhere'. This is an indication of the general tone of the film. While apartheid is visually present in the everyday, the film does not criticize ordinary white South Africans for helping to uphold the system. Instead, the East German viewers are, paradoxically, invited to identify with the white people in the film. When the voiceover attests to how close to nature people live and how danger, in the form of wildlife, can easily seep indoors, the potential victims of such dangers are shown to be not the Indigenous inhabitants, but rather a white mother and her young son. Thus, white East Germans are encouraged to adopt a colonial gaze, and wonder how white people *like them* can manage living in such an environment. The film's generalized reference to inequality is quickly brushed over with the narrator's comments that these problems will only be conquered when 'the poor and backwards way of life will change' thanks to 'the development of Africa's young nation state'. Thus, rather than focusing on the inequality that is created by this white supremacist system, the suggestion is that the *rural* parts of the country just need to be modernized and catch up with the rest of the world.

Kommando 52 (1965)

Kommando 52 is a critique of West German imperialism by examining the participation of West German mercenaries during the so-called Congo Crisis, a period of political upheaval and conflict between 1960 and 1965. As Christian Bunnenberg writes, 'roughly thirty-six of such soldiers were recruited to fight on the side of the Congolese central government against the so-called Simbas . . . for most of the Germans, deployment began in "Commando 52" – led by captain [Siegfried] Müller. They started from the capital of the province Coquilhatville [today Mbandaka] and were supposed to liberate the province Équatorial'.[17] For most West German newspapers, Müller and his Commando 52 were ideologically fighting on the right side. And they uncritically reported on the group's activities, including interviewing Müller's wife in their Hessian house. The West German media frenzy surrounding Müller naturally presented an excellent opportunity for East German critics. In their view, Müller and his men's activities demonstrated the Federal Republic's role as a 'stooge for American imperialism'.[18]

In *Kommando 52* Heynowski relies on techniques of montage developed by earlier Soviet filmmakers like Dzhiga Vertov and Sergei Eisenstein, manipulating footage shot by the West German *Stern* reporter

Gerd Heidemann to make his intended argument. The narrator of the film is particularly important since we hardly have any diegetic sound. Instead, we see Heidemann's footage, with Heynowski's narration. Due to the source of the images, we cannot charge Heynowski with taking such exploitative pictures of Congolese victims of this war. However, he made the choice as to which images to use and how to edit them together, as well as what type of narration to include. Thus, in order to better understand how *Kommando 52* participates in Black abjection for the political purposes of the GDR, we must consider *how* the film is constructed and what kinds of ideological arguments Heynowski is making.

Heynowski accomplishes much merely through editing, zoom and transitioning. For example, when the narrator claims that Moïse Kapenda Tshombe – Patrice Lumumba's political opponent and the man thought responsible for his assassination – has purchased white mercenaries for his struggle for power, this is visually conveyed by zooming in on a picture of Tshombe and a white mercenary and using a fade to white technique, effectively erasing Tshombe so that the focus is the white mercenary (see Figure 11.2). But some evidence of Tshombe remains, like a ghost, so that we are aware on whose behalf the mercenaries operate. The fact that foreign interests are at play in this conflict is also conveyed when one of the mercenaries claims that 'we may be serving under a foreign flag, but we have the same aims as the Federal Republic. The fight against Bolshevism'.

We are told that many Germans are among them. Although there are other Western Europeans represented, Heynowski is most interested in emphasizing West German involvement. We get several close-ups of footage and photographs of men, as the narrator runs off a list of German names. Only once do we get real proof of their nationality in the form of a passport. The fact that the narrative repeatedly remarks that the mercenaries are speaking German – 'richtig Deutsch' (real German) – relays that these men are not foreign conscripts serving under a German commander; rather, they are themselves German nationals who come from the Federal Republic and that is why – unlike the GDR – the FRG is a fascist and imperialist state.

Throughout the entire film, there is a constant tension between authenticity and a constructed narrative. There are several techniques Heynowski uses to insist, for example, that the footage we are seeing is authentic and that it came from a West German. Several things are at stake vis-à-vis its authenticity. If we believe the footage is real, then we know that Heynowski is not just making up claims about the Federal

Figure 11.2. In this shot from Walter Heynowski's *Kommando 52* (1965), through editing, Tshombe slowly fades out, leaving the focus on the West German mercenaries who are fighting on his behalf. © DEFA-Stiftung/P. Hellmich, H. Donth, T. Billhardt.

Republic for the purpose of propaganda. Emphasizing the authenticity of the footage also removes some responsibility for the brutal images we see. Heynowski is not the person who killed these people, and he also was not sick enough to photograph it. But he is now presenting us with these images, as uncomfortable as they may be, to do something good, namely to expose West German involvement in an unjust and brutal war. But to convince the audience of this authenticity, he must often withhold information. The film begins *in medias res*. In the frame we see several photographic materials for developing film. A male voice states: 'I have just learned that the plane will fly to Leopoldville to find out what is happening to our supplies.' We are not given any context for who is speaking. Our disorientation is made greater by the fact that the framing excludes all parts of the person standing before the photography materials. We do not even see their hands; rather, the image of the dead man seems to magically appear as the chemicals in the developing tray are washed back and forth. It is only when a letter is blended in and superimposed over the image of a corpse that it gradually becomes clear that what we are listening to is a letter written by 'Hans', the dead man in the photograph who has been shot. Hans describes his role as a photo reporter, but the filmmakers refer to him as a mercenary. This letter is also included in a companion book to the film entitled *Kannibalen* published by Verlag der Nation in East Berlin in 1967. While the book primarily focuses on Müller and his activities in Congo, it is clear from the beginning that the authors are trying to draw an explicit link between Müller, the Federal Republic and Western imperialism more generally. In one photo that spans two pages, for example, we see three soldiers wearing West German fatigues, standing behind barbed wire and holding machine guns. On page 18, which shows the left side of the picture, a soldier is seen from his right profile, standing in front of a white sedan that is facing the camera with the driver side door open. On page 19 we see the right-hand side of the photo with the other two soldiers. The soldier in the background appears to just be standing guard, looking down the road, while the soldier in the foreground is standing over and threatening a man who is wearing a dark suit and kneeling on the ground. It appears that this man in the suit was driving the car in the photo and the soldiers have stopped him, but we do not know who the man is or why he has been stopped. The caption of the photo, printed above on page 19, states that the Vietnam War might seem far away, but West German special units are already practising for the so-called 'dirty war'.[19] The propaganda is clear, as we have no knowledge of who is in this photo, or where or when it was taken. The licence plate on the car begins with ZW, which might refer to Zweibrücken. While the soldiers' uniforms betray their country, we are not told why the man kneeling is being detained and what his fate will be.

Returning to the letter, Hans writes that he is supplying the recipient with several films he has shot in Congo. This suggests that the person developing the film materials is someone from the team at the DEFA-Studio für Wochenschau und Dokumentarfilme. But the truth is that this is *not* how Heynowski got hold of the film material to which Hans refers; he obtained the footage thanks to a contact at the West German magazine *Stern* (Ernst Petry), who supplied him with material from the *Stern* reporter Gerd Heidemann. Heidemann had corresponded with Müller for years and had 'taken photos in Congo on 16 mm film'.[20] In addition to this footage, Heidemann also had 'recordings of conversations with Tschombe, Captain Müller and other West German soldiers'.[21] Allegedly, in order to use the materials, Heynowski had to agree that they would not be used as propaganda against the FRG.[22] Heynowski's way of getting around this agreement was to 'conceptualize the project as such, to assume, that we had received all of the footage from the Congolese Liberation Movement. In the Congo, all the photos, tapes, recordings and newspaper clippings were found on a dead Tschombé soldier'.[23] The true identity of the letter writer, 'Hans', and the origins of the film material he hints at may remain blurred, but their function is to impart a sense of 'authenticity' to the account that Heynowski's film delivers.

In the film, the narration starts halfway through the letter at the point where 'Hans' mentions sending some of the last film he has shot.

He states that 'apart from the Mission Church I also photographed a shot Mulele'. The term 'Mulele' refers to the men fighting for Pierre Mulele, who was the Minister of Education in Lumumba's cabinet. When we see this unidentified Black man lying on the ground, face down and presumably dead, from the letter, we hear the following remarks: 'Our hero David killed him; the third he has shot like this.' The initial picture from the film is also included in the book in a much clearer form.

All the mechanisms which Heynowski employs at the start of the film to both authenticate the photos and distance himself from them reveal the moral gymnastics necessary to engage in 'pornotroping'[24] – reducing Black people to mere flesh, stripping them of personhood and making them into the object of violent impulses – while still positioning oneself as being on the right side of history. In this manner, not only is the brutality of the mercenaries' activities the focus, but the filmmakers also draw attention to the very process of documenting these atrocities. We are in fact encountering several layers of a story. Mercenaries shot this man, and a West German journalist photographed his body, but not the act of killing. And now it would appear that someone from the East German film team is developing those photographs. By interposing so many levels between the viewer and the horrific action depicted in the film, the filmmaker offers a critique not just of the mercenaries' actions, but also of the West German journalists and their complicity in the events depicted. The tone of the letter does not seem at all appropriate for the subject matter. Hans seems not only detached from and uncritical of the violence he has witnessed, but also to lack any sympathy for the Congolese victim. He mentions the 'dead Mulele' among other items he has photographed like a missionary church. He labels the mercenary who shot the man a hero. His racist disrespect for the Congolese is reflected in a close-up of the letter showing a drawing Hans made beside his name: it is apparently a Black man's face, wearing rings in his ears and nose, and with two spears crossed beneath him. This is the German stereotype of the African savage. Juxtaposing this close-up with a shot of four Congolese men staring straight into the camera enacts a return of the gaze. But this shot demonstrates precisely what is wrong with this documentary. Although the filmmakers' intentions may have been to focus on West Germans' crimes in Congo and make an argument about a continuation between Nazi Germany and the FRG, to make this argument, the East German filmmakers themselves are guilty of stripping the Congolese of their identities and using them as an anonymous mass of victims who are useful for their fungibility. The film cuts from Hans' letter to an alleged close-up of his body, laid out with a hood over its head.

The narrator claims that Hans was shot by freedom fighters before he could send his letter. The film then cuts to a close-up of Hans, sitting among the mercenaries. The camera zooms in on the gun he is holding and the camera hanging around his neck. After zooming in, the mercenaries in the background are blended out, as the background fades to white. By focusing in on Hans in this way, the East German filmmakers present a critique of the complicity of photojournalism in imperialist conflict, a critique that is rearticulated in the narrator's dry observation: 'His days of shooting people – and photos are over.'

The narrator informs us that when the liberation fighters captured Hans, they also captured his 16 mm film. In this manner, Heynowski attempts to further establish how he allegedly got a hold of Hans' roll of film and his letter. This false narrative makes the short film appear like an exposé, revealing atrocities that might have otherwise gone unseen, or perhaps might have been printed uncritically in some Western magazine. Thus, the film becomes yet another commodity over which people are fighting in this postcolonial struggle, much like the fight over 'evidence' and 'truth.' By inserting themselves into the narrative, the DEFA film team positions themselves as people who are going to reveal the truth and shed light on what is happening in Congo. This places the focus on why the film is important and not *how* is it constructed. The reality is that by presenting us with numerous images of faceless, nameless Congolese victims of violence, Heynowski is exploiting violated Black bodies to critique West German involvement in the conflict.

Although the documentary does not include any interviews with the Congolese liberation fighters, the filmmakers attempt to give the victims a voice by showing us evidence of their names and reading quotes from the Mouvement National Congolais (MNC) literature they have on them. We are told that every member of the MNC carries a book with him, in which it states that they are fighting against colonial exploitation and for the unity of men around the world. Such information is clearly an attempt to create sympathy for the Congolese MNC and convince East German viewers that they share the same ideology and are on the right side of the fight.

Kommando 52 was released at a time when exploitation cinema often relied on excessive violence to lure reluctant moviegoers back to the cinema, now that television sets had become more ubiquitous.[25] Films like the blaxploitation classic *Shaft* (1971) and the sexploitation classic *Deep Throat* (1972) were very popular, grossing $12 million and $18 million at the box office respectively. As Callum Waddell points out, 'the exploitation film *shows* what the Hollywood film *hides*', which frequently included showcasing scenes of violence and focus on authenticity, 'leaving little to the imagination'.[26] Yet, *Kommando 52*'s documentary style makes it more similar to the 'mondo films' of the era, like the Italian films *Mondo Cane* (1962) or *Africa Addio* (1966), the latter of which had such exploitative scenes of violence in Africa that African students in West Germany protested against its screening at theatres.[27] In a similar vein, *Kommando 52* exposes the brutality of the mercenaries' actions by showing footage of executions and torture.

In addition to the way in which it highlights violence and authenticity, what *Kommando 52* also shares with exploitation films are similar aesthetic techniques: voiceover, 'freeze frames, rapid zooms, and extreme close-ups' as well as 'a collage of disparate footage'.[28] What arguably differentiates *Kommando 52* from these Western European films is its socialist, anti-imperialist ideology and the argument that the film is necessary to reveal hidden truths about West Germany. While most exploitation films interpolate the viewer as a voyeuristic, intrusive figure to re-create the subversive nature of 'bygone twenty-four-hour inner-city theatres/drive ins with other people',[29] Heynowski wants the viewer to be an intrusive figure in a political sense, uncovering the bad deeds of the Federal Republic of Germany. Waddell states that 'the auteur of the exploitation film is neither the director nor the producer but rather the market itself',[30] but in the case of *Kommando 52*, Heynowski's vision and Socialist politics make the film conform to his overall oeuvre of uncovering oppression in the Global South. Unfortunately, his attitude of Black abjection decided that showcasing the corpses of Black bodies would be more effective than allowing Congolese people to speak for themselves.

Apartheid – No! (1974)

The documentary *Apartheid – No!* takes a very different approach from either of the previous documentaries discussed in this chapter. In contrast to *Abschied von Afrika*, it was clearly made with a more pronounced political agenda. And while both *Kommando 52* and *Apartheid – No!* set out to inform viewers of the oppression occurring in parts of Africa, the focus of *Apartheid – No!* is not so much the revelation of crimes committed by Western, imperialist governments, but rather the (allegedly) progressive politics of the GDR in respect of combating apartheid. Produced thirteen years later than *Abschied von Afrika*, it reflects a shift in East German politics towards a more overt condemnation of the South

African regime for its system of apartheid. This shift may have been informed by several actions on the part of the United Nations, including Resolution 1761 (1962), which condemned apartheid, and the Crime of Apartheid Convention, which was held in 1973.

At the very start of the film, an English intertitle informs us that this is a 'film report on the meeting of the UN Special Committee on Apartheid held in Berlin, the capital of the GDR'. The significance of this meeting being hosted for the first time not only in a socialist country but also in Berlin, 'the capital of the GDR', was not lost on East German viewers and is evident in a propagandistic tone that borders at times on the triumphalist. In this way, while *Abschied von Afrika* appeared to largely be an entertaining film that sought to bypass the political, the aim of *Apartheid – No!* was, at least in part, to legitimize East Germany as a world power with valuable contributions.

Like *Kommando 52*, this film uses a range of aesthetic devices to sway the audience. The beginning of the film is framed as showing the viewers how Africa, a 'long-suppressed continent', is now moving towards progress thanks to the benefit of socialism. Africa's progress is highlighted through an animation of a dark map of Africa as, one by one, African nations appear on the grey map in a darker shade of grey, outlining the borders of each state, while a date appearing in the bottom left-hand corner indicates when each state gained independence. In this way, the film aligns with the Négritude movement's assertion that the rise of the independent nation state was the path to liberation. The map begins with outlines of Ethiopia, Libya and Egypt in 1951, followed by Morocco, Tunisia and Sudan in 1956, until the date shows 1965 and thirty-five countries have coloured in the continent almost completely. Due to the tones of the black-and-white film, the countries that are independent appear to form one solid, black piece. Again, this recalls arguments made by Négritude's leading thinkers, such as Aimes Cesaire and Léopold Sédar Senghor, that nationalism and Black identity go hand in hand. By using this animation and play with colour, our eyes are automatically drawn to the parts of the map that remain light grey in the southern region – what is today Angola, Namibia, South Africa, Mozambique and Zimbabwe. This is the quarter of the continent, as the narrator informs us, that is still under foreign, colonial rule. Several of these countries – Angola, Namibia and Mozambique – benefited from East German solidarity politics, sending apprentices, students and, in the case of Namibia, the children of freedom fighters to the GDR for education and work training.[31] But as scholars like Pugach, Slobodian and Mike Dennis and Norman LaPorte have pointed out, this East German solidarity that invited Africans to the country for a short time did not mean they did not face racism and exploitation in the GDR.

Apartheid – No! in particular singles out South Africa as a 'bulwark of imperialism'. Shooting in Pretoria, the film's cinema verité style juxtaposes two sides of South African society and does so in a way that is more blatantly political than *Abschied von Afrika*. On the one hand, we see symbols of modern life such as high-rises, busy traffic and bustling crowds going to work and shopping in stores, but on the other hand, we see South Africa's Black residents living in destitute shanty towns. Shots of the camera tilting up to reveal massive high rises are juxtaposed with close-ups of evidence of the countries whose business with South Africa helps fund these operations, such as Great Britain. These shots are contrasted with anonymous masses of Black South Africans. The cameraman is eager to uncover all South Africa's dirty little secrets. We see a glimpse of the message 'Europeans Only' (Slegs vir Blankes) written on a bench, shortly before a white man sits down and leans back, covering the message with his body. Unlike *Abschied von Afrika's* lack of critique vis-à-vis ordinary white South Africans, here the message conveyed is that white South Africans both benefit from this system of apartheid and they do not want to show it to the outside world. We see these words 'Slegs vir Blankes' re-created on many different signs, at bus stops and the train station. This kind of racial discrimination is associated with the past. The narrator informs us that it is as if time stood still there. But while the East German filmmakers were right to uncover the inhumane and oppressive conditions in South Africa, there is no attempt at self-reflection on the conditions of Black people in East Germany. The film is ultimately propaganda because rather than honestly engaging with race in the GDR for a comparative analysis with South Africa, the GDR is held up as a model example where racism has been eliminated and time has not *stood still.*

Although *Apartheid – No!* and *Kommando 52* arguably have similar political aims – condemning the actions of the West, the former is not as blatant in its exploitation of brutalized Black bodies to make a point. As opposed to *Kommando 52*, there are very few scenes of actual violence. Usually there is a focus on the perpetrators – shots of dozens of white South African police carrying batons – and their actions, like documentation of lists of those to be executed, close-ups of women (presumably wives and mothers) crying and shots of rows of coffins. But there is an occasional shot of dead and injured Black South Africans lying in the street, as well as masses of anonymous, Black people suffering from poverty and oppression who are juxtaposed with South Africa's modern architecture and veneer of respectability.

To further associate the GDR's political ideology with Africans' fight *against* colonialism and *for* independent nation states, we see Socialist Realist artwork: paintings of crowds of workers who disappear in the masses, with only a few individuals outlined with detailed facial expressions, carrying flags that, due to the black-and-white film, only appear dark, but that one could imagine are red. But unlike the Socialist chromatism Quinn Slobodian identifies in GDR artwork, in this case Black people – men and women – are foregrounded. As the camera zooms out on a panel of African leaders speaking, we see a giant Social Realist mural of an African woman breaking her chains, standing before an array of streamers that from afar can be taken for a flag. The symbol of breaking chains is significant, as the narrator draws a connection between colonialism in Africa and politics in Europe by pointing out the connections between Portugal's activities overseas and its fascist dictatorship. Yet despite this single mention of Portugal, the focus of the film is South Africa. South Africa's description as a 'stronghold' for right-wing reactionism and a bulwark for imperialism is a warning to East German viewers. If colonialism in Africa has ties to Europe, it is dangerous to have any 'stronghold' of fascism in the world, including in South Africa.

The GDR as Socialist Ideal

What is striking about *Apartheid – No!* is that only the first third of the film focuses on scenes from South Africa. With much of the film focusing on the GDR and its progressive, anti-racist society, *Apartheid – No!* is therefore a further example of how these East German documentaries instrumentalize Africa to tell a self-congratulatory story about the GDR. For a short while, the film briefly references anti-apartheid protests around the world: Australia, Norway and the Soviet Union. But after just a few minutes of footage from a meeting about world peace in Moscow, the film transitions to political activity in the GDR. This is introduced in a medium close-up of the *Fernsehturm* surrounded by high-rise buildings – the picture of modern progress; in a voiceover, the narrator announces we are in 'Berlin, the capital of the German Democratic Republic'. A subsequent shot with a low camera angle looking up to several GDR flags waving in the wind helps to solidify the patriotic sentiment these shots are meant to convey to East German viewers. The subject of the remaining twenty minutes of the documentary is a meeting of the UN's special committee against apartheid, founded in 1962. This meeting is taking place during an international solidarity week with Africa, which is meant to showcase the GDR's commitment to African nations fighting against imperialism.

An example of the GDR's solidarity is a scene where we see Albert Luthuli, a South African freedom fighter, and a representative of the African National Congress, visiting a brigade at a state-owned factory for chemical production in Berlin. The narrator informs us that 'The Berlin workers are describing to him how they organize solidarity in their daily work' and they have also named their brigade after South African freedom fighter Alba Blue Tully; an example of the performative solidarity on the surface that often hid anti-Black racism happening in everyday life in the GDR. We also see a member of the anti-apartheid special committee visiting the Herder-Institut at the Karl-Marx-Universität in Leipzig, where not only GDR citizens are present, but also African students in front of a statue of Lumumba. By naming this institute after Herder, the GDR aligns itself with those few German idealist thinkers who opposed slavery and colonialism.[32]

At the Herder Institute, we never actually hear from the African students about what their lives in the GDR are like, which suggests that the state was not really interested in their experiences or their opinions, and that this event is just for optics.[33] The only people who are allowed to speak are officials. We hear about how students 'from young nation states' and 'from the ranks of freedom movements' are allowed to study for free in the GDR. And Pugach notes that 'African students were not simply pawns of Cold War politics. Degrees obtained overseas could bring heightened status at home, and study in the GDR was sometimes the first step to travel and settlement elsewhere, often in the West'.[34] In the documentary, we hear that already, hundreds of thousands of young people from Africa, Asia and Latin America have successfully completed their studies there. This statement is followed by a close-up of an African student in class, giving an answer in fluent German. We are told that the knowledge they acquire will be helpful to the oppressed in these struggles in their fight to liberate their people. Thus, the second half of the documentary becomes an advertisement for how progressive and anti-racist the GDR is. The GDR is presented as a racial utopia for all the people visiting from 'oppressed' countries, but in order to do so, the reality of anti-Black racism and colonial thinking in the GDR has to be covered up. The film ends with Hermann Axen, secretary of the Central Committee of the leading Socialist Unity Party, who claims that although the GDR is one of the newest members of the UN, it has long fought against racism, apartheid and racial discrimination since its founding: 'For national freedom, against imperialism...'

What these three documentary films demonstrate is that while East German filmmakers frequently critiqued imperialism and racism in Africa during the Cold War, *how* this critique is conveyed often depended on the documentary's purpose for GDR audiences. *Abschied von Afrika* is presented as an informational, educational documentary and, as such, limits its comments about South African apartheid. But even in the documentaries that are more blatantly critical, the purpose of the propaganda pushes Black experience to the margins. In the case of *Kommando 52*, the goal is to indict West Germany for its contribution to imperialism and the atrocities committed by its citizens in the Congo. In the case of *Apartheid – No!* the goal is to demonstrate how anti-racist East German society is. But in the case of all three documentaries, we never hear directly from Black subjects, nor do we see Black people as agents of social or political change – they are either filmed as (dead) victims of violence, anthropological curiosities who have not yet been brought into the modern world or subjects whose stay in the GDR has modernized them. The clear message is that Africans' struggles can only become legible to East Germans if and when they are framed within a narrative East Germans can understand. On the one hand, that is a narrative of Socialist Realism, but on the other hand, it is a narrative about Blackness informed by racist images and beliefs going back to the colonial period.

Priscilla Layne is Professor of German, African, African American and Diasporic Studies at the University of North Carolina, Chapel Hill. She is author of *White Rebels in Black: German Appropriation of Black Popular Culture* (University of Michigan Press, 2018) and co-editor of *Minority Discourses in Germany since 1990* (Berghahn Books, 2022).

Notes

1. Christian Rogowski, 'The "Colonial Idea" in Weimar Cinema', in Volker Max Langbehn (ed.), *German Colonialism, Visual Culture, and Modern Memory* (New York: Routledge, 2010), pp. 220–238 (at p. 236 n. 26).
2. Darieck Scott, *Extravagant Abjection: Blackness, Power, and Sexuality in the African American Literary Imagination* (New York: New York University Press, 2010), p. 4.
3. Quinn Slobodian, 'Socialist Chromatism: Race, Racism, and the Rainbow in East Germany', in Quinn Slobodian (ed.), *Comrades of Color: East Germany in the Cold War World* (New York: Berghahn Books, 2015), pp. 23–40 (at p. 24).

4. Sara Pugach, 'African Students and the Politics of Race in the German Democratic Republic', in Slobodian, *Comrades of Color*, pp. 131–56, (at p. 132).
5. Rogowski, 'The "Colonial Idea" in Weimar Cinema', p. 221.
6. Ibid., p. 226.
7. Paul von Schoenaich, '"Major" Schomburgk', *Deutsch-Ostafrikanische Zeitung*, 8 April 1914.
8. Paul von Schoenaich, 'Hans Schomburgk', *Afrika Nachrichten*, 31 May 1923.
9. Langbehn, *German Colonialism*, p. 223.
10. Gerlinde Waz, 'Auf der Suche nach dem letzten Paradies: Der Afrikaforscher und Regisseur Hans Schomburgk', in Hans-Michael Bock, Wolfgang Jacobsen and Jörg Schöning (eds), *Triviale Tropen: exotische Reise- und Abenteuerfilme aus Deutschland, 1919–1939* (Munich: Text+Kritik, 1997), pp. 95–110 (at p. 107).
11. Ibid., p. 108.
12. See Sander Gilman, *On Blackness without Blacks: Essays on the Image of the Black in Germany* (Boston: G.K. Hall, 1982); and Michael Kater, *Different Drummers: Jazz in the Culture of Nazi Germany* (New York: Oxford University Press, 2003).
13. Susanne Zantop, *Colonial Fantasies: Conquest, Family and Nation in Precolonial Germany, 1770–1870* (Durham, NC: Duke University Press, 1997).
14. For more on the Berlin Conference, see Robbie Aiken and Eve Rosenhaft, *Germany: The Making and Unmaking of a Diaspora Community, 1884–1960* (Cambridge: Cambridge University Press, 2013), p. 7.
15. Tobias Boes, 'Political Animals: Serengeti Shall Not Die and the Cultural Heritage of Mankind', *German Studies Review* 36(1) (2013), 41–59.
16. Priscilla Layne, '"Don't Look So Sad Because You're a Little Negro": Marie Nejar, Afro-German Stardom, and Negotiations with Black Subjectivity', *Palimpsest* 4(2) (2015), 179–81.
17. Christian Bunnenberg, '"Die Roten haben mich als Zielscheibe ausgewählt": Der (west)deutsche Söldner "Kongo-Müller" im DDR-Dokumentarfilm', in Michael Wedel, Barton Byg, Andy Räder, Sky Arndt-Briggs and Evan Torner (eds), *DEFA International. Grenzüberschreitende Filmbeziehungen vor und nach dem Mauerbau* (Wiesbaden: Springer Verlag, 2013), pp. 165–82 (at p. 168).
18. Ibid., p. 166.
19. Walter Heynowski and Gerhard Scheumann, *Kannibalen: ein abendländisches Poesiealbum in Selbstzeugnissen vorgelegt von Heynowski & Scheumann* (Berlin: Verlag der Nation), 1967, p. 19.
20. Ibid., p. 170.
21. Ibid., p. 177.
22. Bunnenberg, '"Die Roten haben mich als Zielscheibe ausgewählt"', p. 172.
23. Heynowski, cited in *Kannibalen*, p. 172.
24. For 'pornotroping', see Hortense Spillers, 'Mama's Baby, Papa's Maybe: An American Grammar Book', *Diacritics* 17 (1987), 65–81.

25. Callum Waddell describes the 1960s and 1970s as being the height of American exploitation film, while acknowledging that the phenomenon was present internationally in Italy, the FRG and the UK. See Callum Waddell, *The Style of Sleaze: The American Exploitation Film, 1959–1977* (Edinburgh: Edinburgh University Press, 2018), pp. 5–6.
26. Ibid., p. 186.
27. Niels Seibert, *Vergessene Proteste: Internationalismus und Antirassismus 1964–1983* (Münster: Unrast, 2008).
28. David Ray Carter, 'It's Only a Movie? Reality as Transgression in Exploitation Cinema', in John Cline and Robert G. Weiner (eds), *From the Arthouse to the Grindhouse: Highbrow and Lowbrow Transgression in Cinema's First Century* (Lanham: Scarecrow Press, 2010), pp. 297–315 (at pp. 247 and 249).
29. Waddell, *The Style of Sleaze*, p. 187.
30. Ibid., p. 189.
31. See Peggy Piesche, 'Black and German? East German Adolescents before 1989: A Retrospective View of a "Non-existent" Issue in the GDR', in Leslie A. Adelson (ed), *The Cultural After-life of East Germany: New Transnational Perspectives*, (Washington DC: AICGS, 2002), pp. 37–59. See also the documentary films *Die Ossis von Namibia* (*The East Germans of Namibia*, 2010) and *Omulaule heißt schwarz* (*Omulaule means Black*, 2006). See also white German artist Birgit Weyhe's graphic novel about Mozambicans in the GDR, *Madgermanes* (Dresden: V&Q, 2016).
32. For a discussion of Herder's anti-imperialist views, see John K. Noyes, *Herder: Aesthetics against Imperialism* (Toronto: University of Toronto Press, 2015).
33. For more information about the experience of African students in the GDR, see Sara Pugach, 'African Students and the Politics of Race in the German Democratic Republic', in Slobodian, *Comrades of Color*, pp. 131–56.
34. Ibid., p. 134.

Select Bibliography

Bunnenberg, Christian. '"Die Roten haben mich als Zielscheibe ausgewählt": Der (west-) deutsche Söldner "Kongo-Müller im DDR-Dokumentarfilm"', in Michael Wedel, Barton Byg, Andy Räder, Sky Arndt-Briggs and Evan Torner (eds), *DEFA international: Grenzüberschreitende Filmbeziehungen vor und nach dem Mauerbau*. Wiesbaden: Springer, 2013, pp. 165–82.

Gilman, Sander. *On Blackness without Blacks: Essays on the Image of the Black in Germany*. Boston: G.K. Hall, 1982.

Heynowski, Walter, and Gerhard Scheumann, *Kannibalen: ein abendländisches Poesiealbum in Selbstzeugnissen, vorgelegt von Heynowski & Scheumann*. Berlin: Verlag der Nation, 1967.

Musser, Charles. 'Utopian Visions in Cold War Documentary: Joris Ivens, Paul Robeson and Song of the Rivers', *Cinémas* 12(3) (2002), 109–53.

Slobodian, Quinn. 'Socialist Chromatism: Race, Racism, and the Rainbow in East Germany', in Quinn Slobodian (ed.), *Comrades of Color: East Germany in the Cold War World*. New York: Berghahn Books, 2015, pp. 23–39.

Steinmetz, Rüdiger. 'Heynowski & Scheumann: The GDR's Leading Documentary Film Team', *Historical Journal of Film, Radio and Television* 24(3) (2004), 365–79.

Zantop, Susanne. *Colonial Fantasies: Conquest, Family and Nation in Precolonial Germany, 1770–1870*. Durham, NC: Duke University Press, 1997.

PART IV
Documenting Alterity

CHAPTER 12

Ein Tagebuch für Anne Frank (A Diary for Anne Frank, 1958)
The GDR's Answer to Alain Resnais' Nuit et Brouillard (Night and Fog, 1956)?

Elizabeth Ward

From the outset, images of the Holocaust were instilled with a pedagogic and political purpose in East German productions. The thirty-seven-minute documentary *Todeslager Sachsenhausen* (*Death Camp Sachsenhausen*, 1946), commissioned by the Soviet Military Administration in Germany (SMAD) and filmed by DEFA, was the first German film to examine National Socialist crimes[1] and adopts an interpretative framework that quickly came to dominate presentations of National Socialist crimes in official memory discourses in the German Democratic Republic (GDR).[2] In the GDR, National Socialism was understood to be the consequence of a political and economic system of oppression that could reassert itself again in the future. In speeches by political and state officials, in newspaper features, school textbooks and museum exhibitions, fascism was not considered to be exclusively synonymous with National Socialism; rather, it was framed as *a* manifestation of fascism, which could return in the future if the prerequisite political and economic structures remained intact. Through this interpretive framework, the Second World War was framed as a political and an ideological rather than primarily a national war,[3] which in turn facilitated the presentation of the East German state and its citizens as both the working-class victims of, and antifascist victors over, National Socialism.[4] As the party of the self-designated workers' and farmers' state that counted several leading antifascists among its political elite, the Socialist Unity Party (SED) leadership thus proclaimed that 'the first socialist state on German soil' had irrevocably broken the triangulation between capitalism, fascism and militarism.[5] By contrast, it was asserted that the capitalist Federal Republic had not only failed to dismantle the political and economic structures that had given rise to National Socialism, but had also facilitated the often seamless rehabilitation of former National Socialist functionaries to new positions of power.

Attempts to expose such individuals – most notably Hans Globke, the Chief of Staff of the German Chancellery under Konrad Adenauer – gained traction in the late 1950s and 1960s.[6] These efforts were pursued on multiple fronts, including in political speeches, newspaper features and in the controversial *Braunbuch* (*Brown Book*), a publication listing the names of thousands of individuals in the Federal Republic who, it was claimed, were 'responsible for Nazi and war crimes' and 'not only remain[ed] unpunished, but also occup[ied] leading positions in the economy, state, military and police, in educational establishments as well as in publishing houses and the mass media'.[7] During this period, documentary films also played a key role in the GDR's indictment of the Federal Republic of Germany (FRG), with over fifty feature and television documentaries examining links between the National Socialist past and (overwhelmingly) the West German state in the present made between 1956 and 1965 alone.[8]

Joachim Hellwig's 1958 documentary, *Ein Tagebuch für Anne Frank* (*A Diary for Anne Frank*) exemplifies both the politicization of Holocaust memory in the GDR during this period and the particular role played by documentary film in developing what one publication at the time termed 'a way of thinking' that is 'constantly related to the historical mission of our Republic' more broadly.[9] Indeed, a 1969 publication described Hellwig's historical films as 'examples of the importance of scholarly thinking in political journalism – not only in terms of their preparation, but also in terms of their themes and methods' through their 'Marxist examination of the fascist past and neo-fascism', an approach that comes to the fore in *Ein Tagebuch für Anne Frank*.[10] Using photographs, court documents and film footage (including extracts from *Todeslager Sachsenhausen*), Hellwig seeks to demonstrate how the perpetrators of the Holocaust occupied influential positions in West German politics and business, and often enjoyed considerable wealth.

The opening minutes of the film create the impression that Jewish victimhood will be the primary concern in *Ein Tagebuch für Anne Frank*. The film opens with a voiceover of a young girl who announces: 'This is the girl whose diary is read all over the world. This is Anne Frank', as onscreen we see a photograph of children in a school classroom and then eight portraits of Anne Frank. However, a male narrator then directs the audience's attention away from the global resonance of her diary and towards the film's political purpose by stressing: 'But what Anne Frank could not write about and what a play cannot show needs to be revealed.' The first four-and-a-half minutes of the film are dominated by images of Anne Frank and Jewish victims, with footage and discussion of them comprising 74 per cent of the screen time. However, from the moment the narration links Jewish concentration camp prisoners to German industry and forced labour, the focus in the film shifts. From this point onwards, discussion of Jewish victimhood comprises only 19 per cent of the film, with the rest of the running time dedicated entirely to revealing the postwar fates of National Socialist perpetrators now living in the Federal Republic. In each case, the film establishes the individuals' actions during the Third Reich through documents (which are shown on screen), followed by photographs or film footage revealing their lives in the Federal Republic. On multiple occasions, the narrator emphasizes the international origin of the material and, by implication, thereby places the candid camera footage of West German targets commissioned by the East German filmmakers on an equal footing with material filmed by, for instance, American and British war correspondents. The film closes with a return of the voiceover of the young girl who, over a photograph of Anne Frank, announces:

> You were their victim, Anne Frank. But your murderers are back in the West German part of our homeland [*Heimat*]. For you, the horror was nameless. We know their names. We know that they would do the same thing again if we do not stop it.

As is typical of DEFA Holocaust documentaries of the late 1950s and 1960s, the political and ideological positioning of *Ein Tagebuch für Anne Frank* is explicit from the outset. The seventeen-minute-long film is a clear attempt to conflate its own offering with, and to profit from, the popularity of Frances Goodrich and Albert Hackett's 1955 stage play adaptation *The Diary of a Young Girl* (in German: *Das Tagebuch der Anne Frank*), and George Stevens' 1959 Hollywood film. However, despite the foregrounding of the fifteen-year-old girl in the title, Anne Frank herself remains a marginal figure in the East German documentary with footage of or about her comprising just 12 per cent of the film in total. Even if we broaden the focus to include footage of or about Jewish persecution, the amount of screen time – five minutes and fifty-five seconds – is significantly lower than the amount of time dedicated to the perpetrators (ten minutes and forty-three seconds or 61 per cent of the film's running time). The disparities in screen time alert us to the real focus of the film. Hellwig's film brings together archival material to support the central tenet of the film that not only were the perpetrators of National Socialism to be found in the Federal Republic, but that they also now occupied the governmental offices and executive boardrooms of West German politics and industry.

At this point, it is important to stress that it would be highly misleading to view DEFA Holocaust documentaries as little more than unquestioning, affirmative filmic appendages of SED politics. DEFA may have been a state-owned film studio and the parameters for discussing the National Socialist past were certainly clearly delineated in the GDR. However, neither discussions of, nor films about, Jewish persecution and the Holocaust were suppressed or considered undesirable in the GDR. In both documentary and feature film, directors and screenwriters engaged with the Holocaust and Jewish persecution throughout the history of the GDR in ways which did address alternative and underdiscussed experiences that often did not otherwise receive a national platform.[11] However, during the late 1950s and early 1960s, there was a clear shift in East German documentary and feature film to plots and subject matter that more closely aligned with state-led attacks against the Federal Republic. As this chapter will argue, *Ein Tagebuch für Anne Frank* is at once an extraordinary and yet also representative East German Holocaust documentary. It is undoubtedly an extraordinary documentary in relation to the resources dedicated to the film of a *Nachwuchsregisseur* (young director) in the hope that the international interest in the figure of Anne Frank would allow DEFA – and, by extension, the GDR – to expand its efforts to expose the rehabilitation of former National Socialist perpetrators in the Federal Republic among audiences outside its own borders. Yet, at the same time, it remains a representative film in terms of how Holocaust memory was politicized in the GDR in the late 1950s and 1960s. It is precisely the tension created by shaping an explicitly political film according to dominant domestic frames of reference while simultaneously attempting to achieve international resonance beyond the GDR's borders that renders *Ein Tagebuch für Anne Frank* such an interesting example of East German Holocaust documentary film.

Filmic References from at Home and Abroad

Joachim Hellwig first broached the subject of an Anne Frank documentary in 1956. At this point, the most notable work on Hellwig's filmography was Annelie and Andrew Thorndike's 1956 documentary *Du und mancher Kamerad* (*The German Story*), on which Hellwig had worked as an assistant director. Indeed, Hellwig was repeatedly described as a 'student of Thorndike' in reviews for *Ein Tagebuch für Anne Frank*.[12] The Thorndikes' film is a particularly important point of reference in relation to how Hellwig both approaches his historical subject matter and uses documents: *Du und mancher Kamerad* draws on archival documents to create a direct line between the National Socialist past and the Federal Republic in the present.[13] This same approach is used in *Ein Tagebuch für Anne Frank*, where the mixture of textual, photographic and in some instances moving-image documents is designed not simply to inform, but crucially to guide the spectator through the desired reading of the film. This desired reading is underpinned by a strategy of exculpation through inculpation, whereby responsibility for the crimes of the National Socialist past is displaced onto the Federal Republic in the present. In an interview in 1962, Hellwig described his role as 'a type of criminal investigator, state prosecutor and historian all in one'.[14] While documents are never falsified, this approach removes any space for critical self-reflection on an individual or a collective level, and instead frequently presents the GDR as the political, ideological and even moral counterweight to the 'capitalist fascist' Federal Republic.

The Thorndikes' films unquestionably inform the strategy pursued by Hellwig in *Ein Tagebuch für Anne Frank*. At the same time, in order to understand how Hellwig presents his material so as to shape and direct audience readings, it is first helpful to place Hellwig's film alongside a non-East German documentary that never actually received a general cinematic release in the GDR, but that serves as an important point of reference for *Ein Tagebuch für Anne Frank*, namely Alain Resnais' 1956 documentary *Nuit et Brouillard* (*Night and Fog*).[15] The production of *Ein Tagebuch für Anne Frank* and the planned release of *Nuit et Brouillard* ran in parallel in the GDR. Hellwig's film entered pre-production just weeks after DEFA acquired a copy of Resnais' film, and both films were submitted for pre-release approval within weeks of each another. However, the relationship between the two films extends beyond production schedules. Hellwig was in repeated contact with Olga Wormser, who served as a historical advisor for *Nuit et Brouillard* and in July 1958, Hellwig secured the agreement of Wormser and Alain Resnais to use all unused material from *Nuit et Brouillard* in *Ein Tagebuch für Anne Frank*.[16] At this point, it is important to stress that the various pre-release reports attached to *Ein Tagebuch für Anne Frank* make no reference to the French documentary, and there is no evidence to suggest that the East German film was designed to replace or replicate *Nuit et Brouillard*. Rather, by placing these two films in dialogue with each other, we are afforded a deeper understanding of how Hellwig shapes his material and why an explicit political positioning was central to the approval of the film by DEFA.

There was every intention of releasing *Nuit et Brouillard* in the GDR, one suspects in no small part because of the international controversy caused by the West German government during the Cannes Film Festival in 1955.[17] DEFA Außenhandel first expressed interest in acquiring the film in August 1956. Although a German-language translation had already been commissioned by the West German government,[18] officials at HV Film expressed reservations about using the translation, having been cautioned by Hanns Eisler (who had composed the music for *Nuit et Brouillard*) that it would be prudent to compare the West German text with the original.[19] HV Film consequently instructed DEFA to undertake a comparison and, upon so doing, DEFA's Studio für Synchronisation discovered that the West German translation had made key changes to the original text such as translating 'Big industry is interested in this endlessly renewable workforce' as 'Industrial planning shows interest in this inexhaustible reservoir' which, it was argued, deliberately downplayed the link between fascism and capitalism.[20]

The following year, an East German translation was commissioned and here the GDR's dominant frame of reference vis-à-vis the presentation of the National Socialist past comes through clearly: 'Nazi', for instance, is translated as 'fascist oppressors' ('faschistische Menschenschinder').[21] By August 1958, an East German translation of the original French narration had been approved and recorded. However, upon viewing the finished film, HV Film determined that the release of the East German narration should be dependent on the addition of a prologue and an epilogue, ostensibly to make the film longer and thus better suited for the matinée programme, but tellingly also in order to 'reinforce to audiences the message of the resolve to fight (Kampfentschlossenheit)' through the addition of 'existing archive material that convincingly shows today's struggle against West German imperialism', which in turn was to 'emphasize the role of the GDR in the struggle against neo-fascism and militarism in West Germany in particular'.[22] This instruction is particularly interesting given that it directly contradicts a particular strength of the film that was singled out by HV Film two years earlier when considering DEFA Außenhandel's request to purchase it, namely that 'the film dispenses with all verbose commentary and lets the authentic footage speak for itself'.[23] Work began on preparing the additional material in November 1958, but was never completed and the East German version of *Nuit et Brouillard* was only screened to selected audiences, such as at film clubs.[24] While the film's production files provide no definitive answer as to why the request for additional material was never fulfilled, the reason why DEFA did not commit the additional resources to creating new material for the French documentary film may well have been pragmatic: domestic films were already in production. If HV Film's main criticism of *Nuit et Brouillard* was the open form of the film, then no such concerns could have been harboured about the studio's domestic productions, the closed form of which explicitly guides the viewer towards the desired reading.

Shaping an East German Anne Frank Film

The decision to make a documentary about Anne Frank must, of course, also be considered a response to the popularity of the stage play and subsequent publication of *The Diary of a Young Girl*. Sylke Kirschnick's excellent study on the legacy of Anne Frank in the GDR reveals both the genuine public interest in the experiences of the fifteen-year-old Jewish girl and how this popularity was then harnessed by political and cultural officials.[25] The stage adaptation of *The Diary of a Young Girl* first appeared in German theatres in October 1956, just one year after the play made its Broadway debut. In a highly unusual move, the German-language adaptation premiered simultaneously in eight theatres in the Federal Republic, West Berlin, the GDR, Austria and Switzerland.[26] The East German premiere was staged at Dresden's Theater der Jungen Generation where Anne Frank was played by the twenty-six-year-old actor Ruth Schroeder.[27] The Dresden staging of the play unlocked a 'wave of performances' across the GDR,[28] and public interest in Anne Frank was further bolstered by the East German publication of *Das Tagebuch der Anne Frank* by Union Verlag in 1957, a publication house particularly known for its religious-themed works.[29]

By studying reviews of the play, Kirschnick has revealed an important shift in how it was framed in the East German press during this period, from initial – although admittedly 'vague' – acts of 'self-reflection, moral admissions of guilt and confessions of shame' that potentially 'still linked the East Germans to the National Socialist past' to explicit ideological attacks against the Federal Republic. The politicization of the figure of Anne Frank meant that she quickly acquired a 'symbolic function' that served as a means not only of condemning the actions of perpetrators during the Third Reich, but crucially also of exposing the rehabilitation of such figures in the Federal Republic.[30] *Ein Tagebuch für Anne Frank* is an explicit contribution to such efforts, but at the same time Hellwig develops the 'symbolic function' of the figure of Anne Frank further.[31] Not only are 'Anne Frank's murderers' revealed to be living in the Federal Republic,[32] but the film also seeks to present the GDR as Anne Frank's *Heimat* had she survived Bergen-Belsen concentration camp by repositioning Anne Frank within the GDR's antifascist imaginary.

Given the film's focus on the perpetrators above the fifteen-year-old victim, we may well be inclined to ask why DEFA and Hellwig chose to use her name in the title at all. After all, it was far more common during this period for condemnatory compilation documentary films to carry the name of the perpetrator or the associated criminal case.[33] However, archival documents make it clear that the filmmakers had identified clear advantages to using Anne Frank's name. Commercial considerations were certainly at play. In February 1958, Hellwig commented that it was to be assumed that 'a large part of [the film's] political effectiveness' would 'depend on the extent to which it could be released at the same time as the Hollywood film and exploit Hollywood publicity for our film'.[34] However, the advantage was not only commercial; there were clear political motivations as well. The similarity of the East German film title *Ein Tagebuch für Anne Frank* to the German-language title of George Stevens' Hollywood film (*Das Tagebuch der Anne Frank*) also appears to have been motivated by a desire to obfuscate the real focus of the film for the international market in a way that the working title *Anne Frank and Her Murderers* would never have achieved. This strategy certainly caused alarm among West German officials. Having seen a copy of the film at the Presse- und Informationsamt der Bundesregierung (Federal Press and Information Office), officials at the West German Chancellery and the Foreign Office became increasingly concerned that the film would be screened abroad, especially in the United States, where, one official claimed, audiences were far more 'receptive to this kind of pseudo-political cinematic machismo'.[35] As a result, the Foreign Office wrote to its representatives at sixty-three embassies, seven legations, thirty-four Consulates General, sixty-one consulates and six representatives of international organizations (including the United Nations and NATO) to instruct them to report any attempts to release the film in their respective countries.[36]

In its final version, *Ein Tagebuch für Anne Frank* only focuses on Anne Frank explicitly for two minutes in its seventeen-minute running time. However, earlier versions of the screenplay did feature Anne Frank far more prominently. Originally *Ein Tagebuch für Anne Frank* contained a framing device whereby the film was to open with a young actor (named Anne II in the screenplay) returning home, having learned that she was to play Anne Frank on stage. The film then closed with the actor vowing: 'I want to say everything that you could no longer say, Anne Frank. I want to say that there is no point in just going into hiding [*untertauchen*] – you must rise.'[37] The call to resistance through the overt antifascist positionings of the legacy of Anne Frank has been removed from the final film, although part of the final monologue is still present in a significantly truncated form. The removal of the framing device appears to have been motivated by two factors: first, DEFA expressed continued unease at the legal implications of any dramatization of Anne Frank's life,[38] lest they infringe the copyright of *The Diary of a Young Girl*;[39] and, secondly and seemingly more pressingly, the filmmakers and studio officials were resolute that the film was to be 'antifascist, but not anti-German'.[40]

Despite the film's clear focus on the perpetrators as murderers above Anne Frank as victim, the figure of Anne Frank still performs an important function in the film through the attempt to use her as a means of legitimizing the GDR. In January 1958, *Das Tagebuch der Anne Frank* premiered at East Berlin's Deutsches Theater with the sixteen-year-old Kati Székely in the role of Anne Frank and Wolfgang Heinz as Otto Frank, and a recording of the performance was broadcast on East German television in the same year. In *Ein Tagebuch für Anne Frank*, Székely is the voice of the young girl at the start and end of the film, and Heinz provides the film's narration. As one of the most celebrated actors in the GDR, Heinz – far more than Székely, who was making her film debut – would have been known to many East German audience members, if not from his voice, then certainly through mention of his name in subsequent reviews of *Ein Tagebuch für Anne Frank*. It is here that the film's casting choices gain particular significance. First, by casting Székely, the film places its politicized presentation of Anne Frank in dialogue with the official, authorized staging of her life in both the stage play and the diary by creating a direct line of continuity between the official work (the stage play) and the unofficial work (Hellwig's film). Second, by casting Heinz as the film's authoritative narrator who guides the audience through the politicized presentation of the perpetrators' actions in the past and their lives in the present, the film indirectly seeks to harness the figure of Otto Frank for its postwar attack on the Federal Republic.

Constructing a Narrative

Plans for *Ein Tagebuch für Anne Frank* date back to 1956, when Joachim Hellwig presented possible ideas for his next film. The ideas were certainly eclectic, ranging from a documentary that sought to present hunting as a *Volkssport* to a film provisionally titled *Berlin, dich werde ich doch erobern* (*Berlin, I Will Conquer You*), an 'often grotesque' Berlin film about a young woman who becomes acquainted with Berlin while learning to drive. The fourth entry on the list is a film titled *963 Tage sind ein Leben* (*963 Days Are a Life*) and it is here that we find the first mention of an East German Anne Frank film.[41] Seeking to demonstrate its domestic relevance, Hellwig argued that 'it should be the duty of antifascist German filmmakers to take up this problem, especially at the present time'. Whereas in the Federal Republic, 'the "fate" of Anne Frank is more or less put down as regrettable or pitiable, her hatred as understandable', this film would show 'the full truth and indeed today by Germans – and this can only be done by us'.[42] Strikingly, however, just a few months later, the film was rejected for 'political reasons'. The report made it clear that:

> we would be misjudging the mission of documentary film today if, as suggested in the exposé, we were to turn the subject into a backward-looking film that would ultimately be nothing more than a general statement about humanity.

Specifically, the film was to demonstrate how:

> Anne Frank's murderers are still living in the Federal Republic today and can live under the conditions there as upright citizens and, under certain circumstances, in high political positions.

In this way, DEFA's film about Anne Frank was to 'become an indictment of these murderers: then it would have a politically correct and topically combative note'.[43]

The filmmakers were nonetheless permitted to continue to develop the project on the understanding that the film team accentuate the political message of the film in the present and source appropriate documentary evidence to expose the perpetrators' past actions. The further politicization of Anne Frank's fate that unfolded over the subsequent months is most immediately reflected in the change of title. Now carrying the working title *Anne Frank und ihre Mörder* (*Anne Frank and Her Murderers*), the project clearly remained an important film for the studio despite its initial rejection. Indeed, the resources dedicated to the film were remarkable. Hellwig undertook a series of trips to Moscow, Auschwitz, the Federal Republic and the Netherlands to locate material. The filmmakers worked with nine East German institutions, including the Supreme Court and the Ministry for State Security ('Stasi').[44] During this period, Hellwig also established contact with Otto Frank via Lin Jaldati, a Dutch Jewish artist living in East Berlin who had met Anne Frank in Westerbork camp and at Bergen-Belsen.[45] In a document written a month after their meeting, Hellwig reported that Otto Frank felt unable to participate in the film due to his obligations towards the Hollywood feature film and because he refused to see Anne Frank's name used for 'one-sided political goals'. Undeterred, Hellwig stressed that:

> Frank's statement does not change anything about our project, especially since we do not want to make a film *about* Anne Frank, but rather one about her murderers. The Anne Frank myth that has been created still seems to us to be a favourable level from which we can spread our consistent antifascist stance.[46]

Nevertheless, the film subsequently received an indirect blessing from Otto Frank when he confirmed that he raised no objections to the use of pre-agreed passages from the diary in the film.[47] Twelve months later, the filmmakers submitted a new version of the screenplay. Although the committee praised the fact that 'the political line is undoubtedly correct', doubts remained regarding the 'limited' amount of material the filmmakers had been able to access. The filmmakers were again encouraged to expand their range of perpetrators (to include, for example, Hans Globke) in order to prove 'in documentary form that the criminals of the past are once again in good standing today and have a share in power'. Should this happen, the report concluded, 'the film, using Anne Frank's diary as its platform, can make a decisive contribution to one of Germany's most pressing problems' by providing 'a response to the Western cult of Anne Frank, which, at least as far as its promotion by the state is concerned, is nothing other than hugely hypocritical'.[48]

The filmmakers had already expressed frustration with the difficulties they encountered in securing archival material. In April 1958, Hellwig travelled to Moscow in the hope of accessing material and 'incriminatory material' (*Belastungsdokumente*) from the archive of Goebbels' papers. However, upon arriving in Moscow, he learnt that the material he sought was held at the Russian Interior Ministry, which led him to suspect he would not, in fact, be able to access it in the time available. Strikingly, Hellwig reported that the reason given to him as to why the Soviet authorities were reluctant to share material was the desire not to 'interfere with its policy toward the Federal Republic'.[49] An indication of the importance DEFA and state officials placed in the film – which by this point had already been criticized twice for its insufficient amount of condemnatory material – is reflected in the direct intervention of Walter Ulbricht, who, albeit in an almost word-for-word copy of a letter already sent by DEFA to the Central Committee's Foreign Policy Department one week earlier,[50] appealed to the Central Committee of the Communist Party of the Soviet Union for assistance.[51] However, Hellwig's return to Moscow in July 1958 proved to be little more successful than his previous visit: he reported that only material already submitted to the Nuremberg Trials had been made available to the film team, which had 'no value in the context of our film' as it '[does] not incriminate the SS murderers'.[52]

By the end of 1958, the final version of the film had been submitted to the studio and HV Film for approval. This time, the film was praised for allowing audiences 'to recognize the essence of today's Bonn state and to see through its democratic façade'.[53] The pre-release reports also point to a second important way in which *Ein Tagebuch für Anne Frank* seeks to use the figure of Anne Frank: in his report, the head of HV Film argued that the film showed audiences 'the real background of the "fate" of Anne Frank, *which even she herself could not recognize*'.[54] While substantively vacuous, the assertion that Anne Frank had not been aware of the significance of the capitalist fascist forces that would result in her murder in 1945 nonetheless alerts us to the role of documenting socialism in this film. As much as *Ein Tagebuch für Anne Frank* is unquestionably an outward-facing production concerned with the inculpation of leading political and business figures in the Federal Republic, it also seeks to embed Anne Frank within a socialist or, more specifically, an East German tradition. The film not only resolutely avoids any insinuation that the perpetrators of the Holocaust may also live and work in the GDR, but it also positions the country as the natural home of Anne Frank had she survived.

Plans were made for an international press conference to be held in February 1959 and sixty copies of the film were ordered, the highest number for any DEFA documentary film in the first quarter of 1959. The fifty-four-page press booklet prepared to accompany the film provides an interesting insight into how the film was presented to the invited guests at the premiere. Of the seventeen different pieces included in the press notes, only five directly or indirectly discuss the film; the other twelve entries are dedicated to political attacks against individuals, organizations and companies in the Federal Republic.[55] However, the most revealing piece of marketing came in the form of a double-sided pamphlet by Progress Film-Verleih with a photograph of Kati Székely on one side and text written by the actor on the reverse. In the text, Székely discusses how, prior to being cast as Anne Frank, she lived in the United States and that ever since arriving in the GDR aged fifteen, she had wanted to play Anne Frank, even though she initially spoke no German. The decision to publish a pamphlet written by Székely is odd. After all, Székely never appears on screen as Anne Frank – we only ever hear her voice. Nor is there any indication in the film itself of Székely's original intertextual function – that is, there is no suggestion in the film that she is playing the part of an actor cast in the role of Anne Frank or indeed that at the time of the film's release, she was playing such a role on stage. Instead, the link between Székely and the figure of Anne Frank is established paratextually through interviews and in the Progress Film-Verleih pamphlet. The motivation behind Székely's text nonetheless becomes clear in the final paragraph. Having urged audiences to 'think of Anne's desperate eyes, of her love for life and for people' when they 'see my eyes fixed in horror on the gruesome events in this film', Székely becomes the voice of authority and authenticity by insisting: 'I have seen with my own eyes the documents of their shame upon which this film is based. They are the truth and nothing but the pure truth!'[56]

This dual strategy of distancing perpetration while integrating victimhood is evident in the film itself. The candid camera footage used in the film captures not only key industrial targets in the West, but also repeatedly frames them in such a way as to reinforce the link between the individuals and the West German state. In one key sequence, Albert Konrad Gemmeker, the former commandant of Westerbork concentration camp, is photographed walking alongside election posters for the CDU (see Figure 12.1). As much as the film relies on the impact of the visual evidence, what we hear is also of key importance. At the start of the film, for instance, we are specifically told that Anne Frank was born in Frankfurt am Main – a biographically verifiable fact, of course, but also evidence of the smaller, perhaps more subtle ways in which the film seeks to reinforce the link between Anne Frank's persecution and the Federal Republic, or rather between finance capital, fascism and the Federal Republic.

Figure 12.1. The former commandant of Westerbork concentration camp, Albert Konrad Gemmeker, walks alongside CDU election posters in Joachim Hellwig's *Ein Tagebuch für Anne Frank* (1958). © DEFA-Stiftung/Waldemar Ruge

In contrast to *Nuit et Brouillard*, *Ein Tagebuch für Anne Frank* unquestionably seeks to achieve a closed form – that is, a desired reading facilitated by both the selective use of archival material and the filmic presentation of this material. This is accomplished by interweaving an alternative model of behaviour in the past and present. One of the first instances of this occurs in the first third of the film, when, by means of a single photo of Anne Frank shown in extreme close-up and a dramatized audio clip (again, possibly a reflection of the need to avoid any dramatic filmic re-enactment), the film collapses the 761 days of the original title to just 74 seconds as the film covers the arrest and deportation of the Franks. We hear a car screeching to a halt, the sound of footsteps and then banging on a door, a girl screams and then we hear a gunshot. The narrator pointedly tells us: 'This is how it was.' At this point, the film begins to differentiate between a projected 'they' (*sie*) and 'the persecuted' (*die Verfolgten*). Visually, the photographs of the 'many . . . [who] resisted in Holland' are contrasted with the images of the Jewish victims who we see in positions of submission: undergoing arrest with raised hands, looking out of deportation trains.[57] We are told that: 'They forged identity cards for the persecuted. They formed resistance groups. They armed themselves. They learned to use weapons. They followed the Allied operations. They printed pamphlets. They alerted the population. They went on strike.' With each repetition of 'they', the 'persecuted' fall further into the background as the focus moves to the resistance.

A photograph included in the montage of resistance activities acquires particular importance in this sequence. The film's poster and opening shot depict a wall, on which the film's title is written as if it were a handwritten message. The choice of this backdrop initially appears entirely without context, since at no point in Anne Frank's life does an exterior brick wall connote a specific experience or event. However, the image of a wall with writing does appear at one crucial point in *Ein Tagebuch für Anne Frank*: in celebration of the resistance. In one of the selected images of resistance in the film, we see a photograph of a political message – 'leest de waarheid' (read the truth) – written on a wall in Amsterdam as part of a montage of photographs of the Dutch resistance (see Figure 12.2).[58] Placed in this context, the decision to restage the image for the film's poster and opening image can be understood as an attempt to place *Ein Tagebuch für Anne Frank* in dialogue with acts of raising public consciousness against fascism. Indeed, this very idea was emphasized by Hellwig in an interview in 1962 in which he specifically discusses *Ein Tagebuch für Anne Frank*, when he argued that 'exposing the causes of wars and the conspiracy of the Kaiser's and Hitler's generals against peace has always been in the interest of the working class' and so doing had 'become one of the best traditions of journalism in Germany'. Here, Hellwig specifically cites examples such as broadcasts by the antifascist radio station Deutscher Volkssender, the distribution of leaflets and pamphlets 'under the eyes of the Gestapo', and the *Spartakusbriefe* (*Spartacus Letters*). However, continued Hellwig, 'it was only in our Republic that this great line of tradition could be extended to the mass medium of film'.[59] Viewed in this context, the poster and opening shot of *Ein Tagebuch für Anne Frank* can be understood as further attempts both to align the film with forms of antifascist resistance and to position Anne Frank's legacy in an antifascist context.

While the first third of the film appears more concerned with resistance than persecution, and the second third more interested in perpetration than victimhood, the final third finally appears to address Anne Frank's death and legacy, but does so by situating her legacy firmly within the GDR. In the final moments of the film, Kati Székely's voiceover returns, and she addresses Anne Frank directly:

Figure 12.2. In Joachim Hellwig's *Ein Tagebuch für Anne Frank* (1958), viewing the truth is positioned as the successor to 'reading the truth'. © DEFA-Stiftung/ Waldemar Ruge

> You were their victim, Anne Frank. But your murderers are back in the West German part of our homeland [*im westdeutschen Teil unserer Heimat*]. For you, the horror was nameless. We know their names. We know that they would do the same thing again if we do not stop it.

In the film's final lines, the differentiation between 'we' and 'they' continues, but this time it is reconfigured to separate the GDR from the Federal Republic. Not only does the 'we' place Anne Frank in a connotative community with the GDR, but the appeal to 'our homeland' in 'the West German part' of the country marks a striking claim to a German cultural and territorial shared past, but one that is also devoid of any sense of collective responsibility. Indeed, according to Hellwig, the young actor providing the voiceover was only able to 'discover the full truth' about Anne Frank because 'she lives in a state in which there is no fascism and no racial hatred'.[60] In the late 1950s, projections of perpetration, responsibility and guilt in DEFA documentary could be summed up, to borrow a line from the film's press notes, as: 'The murderers are blossoming again in the west of our homeland' ('die Mörder mausern sich wieder im Westen unserer Heimat').[61]

Conclusion

Ein Tagebuch für Anne Frank uses the persecution of Jews and the murder of Anne Frank to reaffirm the GDR's criticisms of the Federal Republic found in both contemporaneous political documentaries and political discourse in the late 1950s. There can be no doubt that the film instrumentalizes the murder of Anne Frank for political attacks in the present. Jewish victimhood is subordinated to presentations of the perpetrators and there is no attempt to grapple with state-driven or socially prevalent antisemitism. The incorporation of an explicit interpretative framework was central to approval of the film, a point that is evident from both the film's production files and from the successes and failures of contemporaneous productions, not least *Nuit et Brouillard*. The overt criticism of the Federal Republic in *Ein Tagebuch für Anne Frank* has nonetheless also obscured a second important aspect of the film, namely how in the film's final lines and in the paratextual framing of the film, Anne Frank becomes a figure aligned with, and integrated into, the antifascist values of the GDR.

There can be little doubt that *Ein Tagebuch für Anne Frank* fulfils the aims of revealing the postwar lives of National Socialist perpetrators in the Federal Republic. However, the wider long-term impact that DEFA sought to achieve by ensuring that this was 'heard and understood far beyond the borders of our GDR' was overwhelmingly frustrated: the film was screened in the United Kingdom and the Netherlands, but only after initial bans on account of the film's charges against individuals were overturned.[62] *Ein Tagebuch für Anne Frank* received the main prize at the 1960 Leipziger Kurz- und Dokumentarfilmwoche, but it is hard to conclude that the decidedly muted international resonance constituted a success for DEFA, especially considering the resources dedicated to the film. Hellwig argued that the effectiveness of the film could be seen 'in the judgement of friends and adversaries'.[63] His assessment is correct, but for reasons other than the ones he intended. *Ein Tagebuch für Anne Frank* is not just framed by the political – and politicizing – discourse of its country of production; it is ultimately constrained by it.

Elizabeth Ward is a film historian specializing in German cinema. She is an akademische Mitarbeiterin at the Europa-Universität Viadrina, Frankfurt Oder and a Marie Skłodowska-Curie Actions Fellow at the University of Leipzig. Her research specialisms include East German cinema, Cold War German cinema and contemporary historical film. Her recent publications include the monograph *East German Film and the Holocaust* (Berghahn Books, 2021) and the volume *Entertaining German Culture. Contemporary Transnational Television and Film* (co-edited with Stephan Ehrig and Benjamin Schaper, Berghahn Books, 2023).

Notes

1. Elke Schieber, *Tangenten: Holocaust und jüdisches Leben im Spiegel audiovisueller Medien SBZ und der DDR 1946 bis 1990* (Berlin: Bertz + Fischer Verlag, 2016), p. 12. For more on *Todeslager Sachsenhausen*, see Günter Agde, 'Falls zusätzliche Aufnahmen gewünscht werden...', in Klaus Marxen and Annette Weinke (eds), *Inszenierung des Rechts: Schauprozesse, Medienprozesse und Prozessfilme in der DDR* (Berlin: Berliner Wissenschafts-Verlag, 2006), pp. 121–39; Danny Pinto, '"They Saw Their Guilt on Screen": *Death Camp Sachsenhausen* (1947) and the Plasticity of Authenticity', unpublished manuscript (University of Chicago, 2023).
2. 'Official' is used here to denote the presentation of the past in public discourse by politicians and state officials, as well as in schools and in museums.
3. Manuela Gerlof, *Tonspuren. Erinnerungen an den Holocaust im Hörspiel der DDR, 1945–1989* (Berlin: De Gruyter, 2010), p. 32.
4. Elizabeth Ward, *East German Film and the Holocaust* (New York: Berghahn Books, 2021), pp. 1–2.
5. Erich Honecker, 'Die DDR tritt in ihr fünftes Jahrzehnt', *Neues Deutschland*, 6 October 1989.
6. Hans Globke had written a legal commentary to the 1935 Nuremberg Race Laws. He was convicted in absentia of war crimes and crimes against humanity by the Supreme Court of the GDR.
7. Albert Norden, *Braunbuch. Kriegs- und Naziverbrecher in der Bundesrepublik: Staat, Wirtschaft, Armee, Verwaltung, Justiz, Wissenschaft,* (Berlin: Staatsverlag der Deutschen Demokratischen Republik, 1965), p. 8.
8. Based on the findings of Schieber, *Tangenten*, pp. 126ff.
9. Rolf Liebmann, Evelin Matschke and Friedrich Salow, *Filmdokumentaristen der DDR* (Berlin: Henschel Verlag, 1969), p. 5.
10. Rolf Liebermann, 'Joachim Hellwig', in ibid., pp. 75–92 (at p. 75).
11. For more on this, see Ward, *East German Film and the Holocaust*.
12. For instance, 'Ein Tagebuch für Anne Frank', *Deutsche Film-Korrespondenz*, 10 March 1959; Gottfried Paulsen, 'Anne Frank in West und Ost. Ein USA-Film nach dem Tagebuch', *Die Zeit*, 3 April 1959.
13. The format of the condemnatory compilation film was subsequently developed into a series of documentary films between 1957 and 1962, collectively known as the 'Archive sagen aus' series, which focused on former National Socialists now living in the Federal Republic. For more on these films, see Helen Hughes' chapter in this volume and Judith Keilbach, 'Archive sagen aus. Zum Stellenwert von Filmdokumentation in den Filmen von Andrew und Annelie Thorndike', in Hilde Hoffmann and Jörg Schweinitz (eds), *DDR Erinnern, Vergessen. Das visuelle Gedächtnis des Dokumentarfilms* (Marburg: Schüren, 2009), pp. 133–53.

14. Joachim Hellwig, 'Auf der Leinwand verurteilt', *Wochenpost*, 10 November 1946.
15. The film was screened at the 1956 Leipziger Kultur- und Dokumentarfilmwoche and at a closed screening at the Akademie der Künste. It was also approved for screenings by organizations such as the Komitee der Antifaschistischen Widerstandskämpfer (Committee of Antifascist Resistance Fighters).
16. Joachim Hellwig, 'Bericht über die Aussprache mit Frau Prof. Olga Wormser', 17 July 1958 (= BArch DR 118/2115).
17. For more on the scandal, see Jörg Frieß, 'Das Blut ist geronnen. Die Münder sind verstummt? Die zwei deutschen Synchronfassungen von *Nuit et Brouillard* (1955)', *Filmblatt* 28 (2005), 40–58; Knud Breyer and Oliver Dahin, *Filmmusik zu/Film Music* to Nuit et Brouillard (Wiesbaden: Breitkopf & Härtel, 2014); Sylvie Lindeperg, *Nuit et Brouillard: Un film dans l'histoire* (Paris: Jacob, 2007); Ewout van der Knaap, *Nacht und Nebel. Gedächtnis des Holocaust und internationale Wirkungsgeschichte* (Göttingen: Wallstein Verlag, 2008).
18. For more on the commissioning of the West German versions of the commentary, see Breyer and Dahin, *Filmmusik zu/Film Music* to Nuit et Brouillard.
19. Verband deutscher Komponisten und Musikwissenschaftler, Letter to HV Film, 21 March 1957 (= BArch DR 1-Z/13450).
20. In the original, the writer of the report has underlined the words 'big industry' (*Grossindustrie*) and 'industrial planning' (*Industrieplanung*). DEFA Studio für Synchronisation, Letter to HV Film, 28 February 1957 (= BArch DR 1-Z/13450).
21. Frieß, 'Das Blut ist geronnen', p. 53.
22. HV Film, 'Zusatzprotokoll zum Protokoll Nr. 0357/58', 22 September 1958 (= BArch DR 1-Z/13450).
23. HV Film, 'Protokoll Nr. 555/56', 6 August 1956 (= BArch DR 1-Z/13450).
24. Ibid., p. 56. The East German version was also screened at the Leipziger Kultur- und Dokumentarfilmwoche in 1965 and 1966. See Frieß, 'Das Blut ist geronnen', p. 56. Breyer and Dahin have also highlighted that the film was broadcast as part of a season of 'Films against Fascism' in September 1974 when commentary was read by the actor Erwin Geschonneck, best known for his antifascist resistance roles; see Breyer and Dahin, *Filmmusik zu/Film Music* to Nuit et Brouillard, p. xxxviii. For more on the limited release of the film in the GDR, see Lisa Schoß, *Von verschiedenen Standpunkten. Die Darstellung jüdischer Erfahrung im Film der DDR* (Berlin: Bertz + Fischer, 2023), p. 197.
25. As Kirschnick reminds us, while the play was unquestionably a public hit, the number of performances staged in the late 1950s should not be seen solely as a reflection of popular demand; performance schedules were al-

ways agreed with cultural officials, who could intervene to shape the repertoire on both a thematic level and in respect of individual plays. Sylke Kirschnick, *Anne Frank und die DDR: Politische Deutungen und persönliche Lesarten des berühmten Tagebuchs* (Berlin: Ch. Links Verlag, 2009), p. 50.
26. Ibid., p. 38.
27. Ibid., pp. 38–39.
28. Ibid., p. 45.
29. A German-language translation had appeared in the Federal Republic two years earlier in March 1955. Ibid., pp. 63 and 71.
30. Ibid., p. 45.
31. Ibid. It is important to stress that *Ein Tagebuch für Anne Frank* is by no means the only film to project a political identity onto the figure of Anne Frank. As Barbara Kirshenblatt-Gimblett and Jeffrey Shandler have discussed, the presentation of Anne Frank's life and diary as 'paradigmatic' and 'transcending the particulars of her circumstances' has repeatedly allowed filmmakers to reshape not only the figure who appears on screen during the period of the Franks' hiding between 1942 and 1944, but also the message projected onto her suffering and fate for postwar audiences. See Barbara Kirshenblatt-Gimblett and Jeffrey Shandler (eds), *Anne Frank Unbound: Media, Imagination, Memory* (Bloomington: Indiana University Press, 2012), pp. 1–22 (at p. 5).
32. Joachim Hellwig, Günther Deicke and Hans Möhring, 'Ein Tagebuch für Anne Frank. Ein Dokumentarfilm-Drehbuch', 10 February 1958 (= BArch DR 118/11597).
33. For example: *Unternehmen Teutonenschwert* (*Operation Teutonic Sword*, 1958), *Der Fall Heusinger* (*The Heusinger Case*, 1959), *Mord in Lwow* (*Murder in Lwow*, 1959), *Die Affäre Heyde-Sawade* (*The Heyde-Sawade Affair*, 1963) and *Globke heute* (*Globke Today*, 1963).
34. Joachim Hellwig, 'Zur Produktion des Dokumentarfilms *Anne Frank und ihre Mörder*', 14 February 1958 (= BArch DR 118/2115).
35. Stellvertretender des Staatssekretärs des Bundeskanzleramts an das Auswärtige Amt, 'Betrifft: Film *Ein Tagebuch für Anne Frank*', 17 September 1959 (= PA AA, B 95 Ref 605/IV6/487).
36. Auswärtiges Amt, 'Betr.: Sowjetzonaler Film *Ein Tagebuch für Anne Frank*', 28 December 1959 (= PA AA, B 95 Ref 605/IV6/487).
37. The verb 'untertauchen' is ambiguous here. It could equally be translated as 'to go underground' or 'to go into hiding'. Hellwig, Deicke and Möhring, 'Ein Tagebuch für Anne Frank'.
38. Dramaturgie, 'Stellungnahme zum Szenarium *761 Tage sind ein Leben*', 30 March 1957 (= BArch DR 118/3002).
39. *Ein Tagebuch für Anne Frank* may assiduously avoid any explicitly fictional restagings of her life, but as I have argued elsewhere, the character of Ruth Mamlock in Konrad Wolf's 1961 film *Professor Mamlock* is imbued with several intertextual references to Anne Frank. See Elizabeth Ward, 'Zur strategi-

schen Aneignung der Anne-Frank-Figur in Konrad Wolfs *Professor Mamlock* (1961)', in Peter Seibert, Jana Piper and Alfonso Meoli (eds), *Anne Frank: Mediengeschichten* (Berlin: Metropol-Verlag, 2014), pp. 54–62; and Ward, *East German Film and the Holocaust*, pp. 85–87.
40. Stab Hellwig, 'Zu Stoff und Gestaltung', no date (= BArch DR 118/3002).
41. The title is a reference to how many days the Franks were in hiding. This number is, in fact, incorrect and the title was modified just a few months later to *761 Tage sind ein Leben*.
42. Joachim Hellwig, Letter to the Dramaturgie, 1956 (= BArch DR 118/3877).
43. Szenarienkommission, 'Stellungnahme: *761 Tage sind ein Leben*', 22 May 1957 (= BArch DR 118/3002).
44. Stab Hellwig, 'Arbeitsplan und Versuch einer Disposition', 1957 (= BArch DR 118/2116).
45. Kirschnick, *Anne Frank und die DDR*, p. 83.
46. Emphasis in original. Stab Hellwig, 'Ergebnis der ersten Reise', 31 October 1957 (= BArch DR 118/2115).
47. Otto Frank, Letter to Joachim Hellwig, 2 April 1958 (= BArch DR 118/3003).
48. Dramaturgie, 'Stellungnahme der Dramaturgie zu dem Drehbuch', 28 February 1958 (= BArch DR 118/2115).
49. Joachim Hellwig and Joachim Stellmacher, 'Bericht über die vierte Reise für den Film *Anne Frank und ihre Mörder* vom 10.–19.4.1958 nach Moskau', 21 April 1958 (= BArch DR 118/2115).
50. DEFA Studio für Wochenschau und Dokumentarfilme, Letter to the Central Committee's Foreign Policy Department, 11 June 1958 (= BArch DY 30/3752).
51. Walter Ulbricht, Letter to the Central Committee Communist Party of the Soviet Union, 18 June 1958 (= BArch DY 30/3752).
52. Joachim Hellwig and Joachim Stellmacher, 'Bericht über die Reise für den Film *Anne Frank und ihre Mörder* vom 6.–12.7.58 nach Moskau', 21 July 1958 (= BArch DR 118/2115).
53. Filmproduktion, 'Einschätzung des Dokumentarfilms *Anne Frank*', 12 December 1958 (= BArch DR 1-Z/3170).
54. Emphasis added. HV Film, 'Einschätzung', 12 December 1958 (= BArch DR 118/3003).
55. Progress Film-Verleih, 'Presseheft zum DEFA-Dokumentarfilm. *Ein Tagebuch für Anne Frank*', 1959 (= BArch FILMSG 1/35975).
56. Progress Film-Verleih, '*Ein Tagebuch für Anne Frank*', 1959 (= BArch FILMSG 1/35975).
57. The original German uses 'Holland', not 'the Netherlands'.
58. *De Waarheid* was also the name of a communist resistance newspaper during the German occupation of the Netherlands.
59. Hellwig, 'Auf der Leinwand verurteilt'.
60. Joachim Hellwig, 'Darüber spricht man nicht … in Bonn', 22 December 1958 (= BArch DR 118/11597).

61. Erwin Kohn, 'Presseheft: Im Gedanken an Anne Frank', 1959 (= BArch FILMSG 1/35975).
 62. No author, 'Gleitwort zu einem Film', 24 February 1959 (= BArch DR 118/3003).
 63. Hellwig, 'Auf der Leinwand verurteilt'.

Select Bibliography

Ebbrecht, Tobias, Hilde Hoffmann and Jörg Schweinitz (eds). *DDR Erinnern, Vergessen. Das visuelle Gedächtnis des Dokumentarfilms*. Marburg: Schüren, 2009.
Gerlof, Manuela. *Tonspuren. Erinnerungen an den Holocaust im Hörspiel der DDR, 1945–1989*. Berlin: De Gruyter, 2010.
Kirschnick, Sylke. *Anne Frank und die DDR. Politische Deutungen und persönliche Lesarten des berühmten Tagebuchs*. Berlin: Ch. Links Verlag, 2009.
Liebmann, Rolf, Evelin Matschke and Friedrich Salow. *Filmdokumentaristen der DDR*. Berlin: Henschel Verlag, 1969.
Marxen, Klaus, and Annette Weinke (eds). *Inszenierung des Rechts: Schauprozesse, Medienprozesse und Prozessfilme in der DDR*. Berlin: Berliner Wissenschafts-Verlag, 2006.
Schieber, Elke. *Tangenten. Holocaust und jüdisches Leben im Spiegel audiovisueller Medien SBZ und der DDR 1946 bis 1990*. Berlin: Bertz + Fischer Verlag, 2016.
Ward, Elizabeth. *East German Film and the Holocaust*. New York: Berghahn Books, 2021.

CHAPTER 13

A Woman's Work?
Women Soldiers, Masculinities and Binary Panic in Documentaries of the East German Army

Tom Smith

The Nationale Volksarmee (National People's Army [NVA]) was among East Germany's most avowedly masculine institutions, but it would be a mistake to presume that it was therefore the preserve of cis men. The East German armed forces employed women in uniformed and civilian roles from the beginning, and there were queer and trans people in the ranks, especially under conscription from 1962. Yet in its self-presentation, the NVA strongly associated military service with masculinity and cis male bodies, rarely grappling publicly with what it meant for women to serve in uniform. Of around a dozen DEFA features focused on the NVA, none shows a woman in military uniform. Women appear as wives and girlfriends, mothers and sisters, restaurant proprietors and in other civilian roles. Where they appear in uniform, it is usually as nurses outside the military. By contrast, nonfiction films from various genres do depict women in NVA uniform. These documentaries, newsreels and training films aimed to normalize women's presence within the armed forces and targeted both an NVA audience and a wider public. Most of these films position women's military jobs as work like any other, but to counter this move away from gendering military jobs, they also overemphasize and stereotype women's femininity to minimize any unsettling effect on military masculinities and their association with cis men.

In this chapter, I analyse sequences from the NVA's *Armeefilmschau* (*Army Newsreel*, 1961–89), documentaries from the Armeefilmstudio (Army Film Studio [AFS]), the DEFA documentary *Gabi – Vermittlung Platz 12* (*Gabi – Switchboard Position 12*, 1985) and the independent film *Neugier und Bewährung* (*Trying and Prevailing*, 1988) by amateur filmmakers Filmgruppe 82 based within the AFS. Inspired by trans theories, I explore what I term 'binary panic', especially in the official productions of DEFA and the AFS. These films and newsreels constantly foreground and reinforce binary gender in ways that reveal it to be under pressure. The films show that women influenced how masculinity developed in the NVA, embodied military masculinities themselves and forced cis male comrades to reflect on what masculinity meant in the army. Filmmakers were interested in this question too, especially in *Neugier und Bewährung*, which may explain why the NVA withdrew this amateur film. While these films never move beyond the binary, they do highlight its inadequacies. Masculinities and femininities collide, mix and overlap in the gender practice of the women NVA members shown on screen.

Filming Women and Binary Gender

Although the Armeefilmstudio has received less attention than other East German documentary film studios, it offers considerable insight into how East German institutions enlisted nonfiction film.[1] The AFS was established on 31 December 1960 along the model of Poland's Czołówka studio and Army Film in Czechoslovakia. High-ranking military figures and politicians saw film as a solution to problems facing the fledgling army: high desertion rates, declining recruitment and poor education infrastructure.[2] The AFS, later also called Filmstudio der NVA, was based in Berlin-Biesdorf under the purview of the propaganda section of the Ministry for National Defence.[3] In this respect it stood apart from other studios, yet especially in the early years its around one hundred staff depended on equipment loaned from DEFA.[4] Most AFS workers were civilians, but some were in military roles, and its director until 1987, Walter Helbig, was a Colonel. Many of the studio's editing staff were women and isolated productions were directed by women, but overwhelmingly men took responsibility for directing and camerawork. The output of the Armeefilmstudio is one of few corpora documenting the presence of women soldiers in the NVA, but these films rarely reflect on the positionalities of the men who made them or involve women soldiers in the creative process. Yet, in the sense used by Vinzenz Hediger and Patrick

Vonderau, these are 'films that work', and which provide insights into the NVA and its institutional concerns.[5] In particular, in these depictions of women soldiers, the status of military masculinities emerges as a central anxiety that shapes and challenges assumptions about the gender binary.

Around half the studio's productions were training films for internal use, but as the NVA saw the potential for films to promote military service, the significance of documentaries increased. These were explicitly propaganda documentaries screened at internal training events and for the public, including at events for Berlin schoolchildren and on television.[6] Beginning in 1961, the AFS also produced a newsreel, the *Armeefilmschau*, initially with a small number of instalments, increasing to twelve per year from 1963.[7] Each contained up to fourteen segments, marking significant anniversaries or news events. Most segments document everyday life in the NVA for an internal audience, but some were licensed to East German cinemas for screening before a feature or to television news.[8] Depictions of women in civilian or military roles are more common in newsreels than in AFS or DEFA documentaries, reflecting a dissonance between women's significant presence in the army's everyday life and its investment in preserving the link between military service, masculinity and cis male bodies.

One early *Armeefilmschau* for International Women's Day in 1962, for example, celebrates women's contributions, overlaying a man's voiceover on shots of women working in kitchens and messes and in a mailroom. Only the mailroom worker is in military uniform, and all are smiling as they work. The voiceover upholds a distinction between stereotypes of femininity and masculinity in military roles: 'They provide for the soldiers' home comforts [*leibliches Wohl*], and they work in positions of responsibility.'[9] The newsreel associates women with food, wellbeing and support functions, and depicts them in a caring, maternal light. Despite reference to 'positions of responsibility', no senior women are shown, and the roles depicted are co-extensive with careers commonly held by women in early 1960s civilian society.[10] In fact, women's roles were more diverse: they served across the NVA and its forerunner, the Kasernierte Volkspolizei (Garrisoned People's Police [KVP]), most commonly in communications and administration, as educators, technical or medical staff, in kitchens and in cultural roles.[11] Even at this early stage in the NVA's development, there were women officers in senior positions.[12] Yet this newsreel shows that in 1962, the NVA preferred to envision women in conventionally feminine occupations and civilian clothes.

Women only entered the NVA as volunteers, unlike men, who from 1962 were overwhelmingly conscripted. Women served as officers or noncommissioned officers (NCOs), either on a short-term basis (*auf Zeit*) for three to ten years or as career soldiers. The 1962 Conscription Law contained provisions for women to be conscripted 'to medical, veterinary, dental, technical or to another special occupation in the National People's Army'.[13] These restrictions applied to conscription during full mobilization only, and women could – and did – volunteer as career soldiers across other roles. But the law gives a snapshot of which roles were envisioned for women. The legal text takes for granted women's presence in the NVA, although it preserves a distinction between 'women' and 'male citizens' ('männliche Bürger') that suggests differential access to the privileges of citizenship.[14] From the early 1980s onwards, changes to regulations allowed for women to be recruited more widely to officer and NCO training, ostensibly under the same conditions as men, and the 1982 Military Service Law removed the 1962 restrictions on conscription.[15] In their 1985 study, Christiane Lemke and Gero Neugebauer describe a conflict that typifies the NVA's attitudes. As the gulf between recruitment figures and targets widened, the NVA needed to accept women and offer them real prospects, yet they continued to insist that certain masculine-coded occupations be reserved for men.[16] As in its newsreels, the NVA's regulations assert and uphold a binary concept of gender that links military service and masculinity to cis male bodies, even as the actual presence of women in military uniform put pressure on these assumptions.

To assert this gendered image of military service, the NVA's films focused on depicting civilian women, emphasizing their femininity and support for their partners and husbands. AFS documentaries often created an image of women as soldiers' brides, as in *Soldatenhochzeit* (*A Soldier's Wedding*, 1964), or faithful partners, as in *Meiner ist bei den Soldaten* (*My Boyfriend's a Soldier*, 1975).[17] Christine Eifler has documented similar trends in NVA magazines, emphasizing the clichés and misogyny in depictions of women as always supportive and in need of protection.[18] By presenting women as men's partners, military film asserted structural heterosexuality. Filmgruppe 1982 even made erotic films starring women civilian employees for private use, including by NVA officers.[19] These structures placed women soldiers in an impossible place amongst binary oppositions between masculinity and femininity, military and civilian, protection and vulnerability. This gendered structure directly affected their lives, with many first-hand accounts describing sexual advances from other soldiers as well as physical and verbal abuse while wearing uniforms outside the barracks.[20]

As part of a wider campaign to normalize women's contributions to traditionally masculine working environments, AFS filmmakers present them as workers in a job like any other, attempting to sidestep the more disruptive question of what it meant for military masculinity for women to work for the NVA.[21] Often filmmakers preferred to show women civilian workers. The documentary *Hier ist mein Platz* (*This Is My Place*, 1979) focuses on an artillery range and especially mechanic and technician Sieglinde Johannimann. A man's voiceover introduces Johannimann, unlike her male colleague, with her marital status as a divorced mother of three.[22] Besides this nod to expectations around femininity, the film centres on Johannimann's skilled work. It emphasizes the severe working conditions and shows Johannimann's work being appreciated by her comrades. The documentary does briefly address the hardships that women faced, with Johannimann describing how her colleagues give her dismissive nicknames like Raketenliese, which combines the name Liese, a belittling slang term for 'woman', with a pun on 'Rakete', meaning literally 'missile', but also used by men for an attractive woman. Johannimann herself is confident and no-nonsense, framing herself as just one of the workers: 'Everyone's trying their best and I'm just doing the same.' On the one hand, the film pays relatively little attention to Johannimann's status as a woman in a male-dominated context, portraying her as experienced, professional and well integrated in the collective. Yet, on the other hand, repeated references to her family show the work being done by the filmmakers to reinforce her femininity, as if her confidence, technical expertise and camaraderie risk unsettling the NVA's binary understanding of masculinity and femininity.

Binary Panic

In these examples of women depicted in civilian roles, films are at pains to emphasize stereotypically feminine aspects of their lives. When women appear in uniform, this anxiety around images of military women becomes a more pronounced panic about the stability of the gender binary. Many *Armeefilmschau* newsreels emphasize women's femininity to create military femininities in line with binary gender. The April 1965 instalment, for example, celebrates women soldiers across the socialist world, with a montage of wireless operators, parachutists and women in military headquarters alongside uniformed women queuing to adjust their hats in a mirror, pushing prams and changing from combat boots into high heels.[23] Their shoes are shown in close-up, cutting out their faces, depersonalizing the portrayal and exaggerating feminine stereotypes. The montage is set to a Czech pop song, sung on screen by a uniformed man surrounded by smiling women soldiers, with lyrics including disparaging stereotypes about women being obsessed with their appearance.[24] Women soldiers most frequently appear in the final newsreel segment, which was reserved for a 'light-hearted topic'. In this case, a last-minute exercise meant that no NVA soldiers were available to film as planned with singer Volkmar Böhm, who was to be described with mock envy as a 'cock in the henhouse'.[25] Instead, a substitute film was found from the Czechoslovak Army Film studio and dubbed.[26] Although the voiceover praises women's contributions, the light-hearted tone depends on the edit and song lyrics playing on an artificial disconnect between feminine stereotypes and women's military uniforms. The short montage thus reinforces a clearly delineated gender binary where the voiceover's praise of women's professionalism is outweighed by feminine stereotypes.

Trans theories are helpful for understanding these anxieties around the binary of masculine and feminine. Theorists have often emphasized the potential for trans experiences and perspectives to challenge normative structures and imagine alternative understandings of identity, bodies and gender. Jack Halberstam argues, for example, that by loosening assumptions around gender, we can reimagine embodiment and identity:

> When logic that fixes bodily form to social practice comes undone, when narratives of sex, gender, and embodiment loosen up and become less fixed in relation to truth, authenticity, originality, and identity, then we have the space and the time to imagine bodies otherwise.[27]

By investing in the link between masculinity, military service and cis male bodies, the NVA – like many other militaries – perpetuated the fixed relationship between 'bodily form' and 'social practice' that Halberstam describes. The AFS films go to great lengths to feminize and often trivialize the contributions of women soldiers, to foreclose any military gender practice that might unsettle gender norms. In fact, these depictions of people of other genders in uniform suggest that military masculinities were influenced by a diverse range of bodies and gender practice.

Even when portrayals of women soldiers are less trivializing and take their authority seriously, the films' awkwardness around the gender binary remains. For example, the June 1972 *Armeefilmschau* profiles Lieutenant Colonel Dr Gudrun Anacker, a military doctor and party secretary. A voiceover introduces her, using the generic masculine 'Parteisekretär' over a medium close-up in dress uniform.[28] Her head tilted to one side and her half-smile show her listening attentively, while her shirt, tie and ornate epaulettes signal her rank and authority. The voiceover says that she has served in uniform for almost eighteen years, meaning she joined the NVA's predecessor, the KVP. Anticipating an incredulous male audience, the voiceover asks: 'but where and who does she command? Which branch [*Waffengattung*] does she belong to?' On 'Waffengattung', the camera cuts to Anacker in a white coat taking a patient history, shot over the bare shoulder of her younger male patient. The cut seems designed to assuage anxieties about a high-ranking woman by showing her fulfilling an unarmed role. Even though medicine was also a male-dominated profession in East Germany, the voiceover emphasizes its conventionally feminine aspects: 'Lieutenant Colonel Dr Anacker doesn't order "about turn" or "forward march" but rather says sympathetically, "How are you feeling?"' This emphasis on care and empathy contrasts with Anacker's dispassionate questions and responses, a disconnect that is even more striking than in earlier newsreels because we hear Anacker's own words. *Armeefilmschau* creators here relativize the professionalism of a doctor who had achieved one of the highest ranks held by a woman in the NVA, implicitly showing anxiety about what it meant for a woman to hold such a senior uniformed role.

I term this anxiety 'binary panic', by analogy with 'homosexual panic' as deployed in Eve Kosofsky Sedgwick's early work. This homophobic psychological diagnosis postulated a pathological condition that hindered men's control over their violent reactions to the presence of gay men. Courts have used 'homosexual panic' as grounds to acquit or mitigate sentencing of men charged with assault, and a comparable defence of 'trans panic' has also been used to defend perpetrators of transphobic violence, suggesting they had reduced capacity because their cisheterosexuality was threatened.[29] Sedgwick argues that the defence disguises the structures of binary gender and normative heterosexuality as individual psychology, and that appropriating the term could 'dramatize, render visible, even render scandalous' the overlap between the psychological and structural forces that perpetuate and defend norms.[30] My interest is less in the psychology of men threatened by women in uniform than in how their responses shape military masculinity, reinforce gender binaries and directly affect women, queer and trans folks in the NVA. As Ian Barnard has argued, trans panics are broad, unspecific anxieties about the gender system taken out, often violently, on trans folks, 'aimed at or resulting in the rehabilitation and stabilization of binary sex-gender systems'.[31] The AFS shows similar panic about reinforcing binary gender, although it is activated not by trans people, but by people the NVA presumes to be cis women. I prefer the phrase 'binary panic' for this panicked recourse to gender stereotypes prompted by images of women in military roles. This binary panic highlights the instability of military masculinity and the role that people of all genders play in shaping it.

The most acute episode of binary panic in the NVA's history came after the 1982 Military Service Law provided for conscription of women during full mobilization. The law codified changes that were already in process, as the NVA opened more career paths for women around 1980, but the clause on conscription brought widespread publicity to questions around military service for women. The idea of women being conscripted, especially rumours that nurses in Mecklenburg had been called for medicals and issued military IDs, triggered the founding of a feminist peace movement Frauen für den Frieden (Women for Peace) and a petition protesting the Military Service Law.[32] On both sides, the debate mobilized ideas about the gender binary. Ministry spokesmen insisted that women would not enter combat units or other stereotypically masculine roles, while Women for Peace wrote that they 'see military service for women not as an expression of equality, but in contradiction with their femininity [Frau-Sein]'.[33] Their petition crafted a principled rejection of militarism in the language of binary gender, to appeal to men in East Germany's political and military structures. The military's reaction to the debates in 1982 was not just to reassert women's position as workers as they had in previous decades, but to emphasize their femininity more directly.

The *Armeefilmschau* encapsulated this binary panic with its item advertising new uniforms for women in December 1982. The new uniforms were exhibited at NVA headquarters in Strausberg before being rolled out in 1983, and an *Armeefilmschau* team led by NCOs Hans Werner and Dieter Behrend developed an 'entertaining' segment to mark the occasion.[34] The segment opens with a man in camouflage lying in the undergrowth looking through binoculars. The film cuts away to signs reading 'Fashion '83' and 'New uniforms for female NVA members', and shows the man joined by a woman in similar camouflage. AFS productions recruited actors from the army where possible, but as the uniforms were only available in sample sizes, the filmmakers hired five models.[35] In the opening, the model smiles at the camera, walks towards it and poses. Her confident expression and eye contact with the lens break with the realist aesthetic of other newsreels, while the binoculars also playfully signal that the uniforms and film were targeting a straight male audience. These techniques signal a more self-aware, even self-ironic approach than usual for the *Armeefilmschau*. The end of the segment also gently mocks the film's artifice and low-budget production. A shot of a woman walking in a winter overcoat in the snow zooms out to show two models circling a man on a ladder as he throws fake snow over them. Two more models in the background are laughing, enabling viewers to feel like all are in on the joke. These touches also ironize the film's limitations, especially the limited timeframe that meant producers had no time to seek out the desired weather conditions and instead filmed most of the segment indoors.[36]

The uniforms themselves demonstrate how the NVA extended its panic about representing military masculinity to women's bodies. Skirts were reshaped, waists cinched and various other alterations made to differentiate women's uniforms. These changes were more noticeable in dress uniforms, which feature most in the *Armeefilmschau* fashion show. The focus on dress uniforms suggests that these changes sought to influence image rather than functionality and to separate military masculinity visually from women's bodies. One former trainee officer, Anna Fröhlich, remembers differences in how their uniforms were perceived:

> In our eyes, the uniform was unattractive. But the male trainee officers often saw things differently. When we were wearing our skirts and blouses, they thought we looked pretty fit [*knackig*]. Comfort, materials, cut – none of it was ideal.[37]

Fröhlich suggests that men were the real audience for these new uniforms, and her description supports the newsreel in suggesting that the changes were part of a broader attempt to emphasize women's femininity and bolster binary gender.

The segment's use of humour makes it hard to interpret: light-hearted newsreel segments were common, but women themselves are rarely so prominent in shaping the humour as the models in this fashion show. Unlike the 1965 segment, where a man's ironic and sexualizing voiceover was to be added over footage of women in uniform, the uniform segment depends on the models' acting for levity. A sexualizing and misogynist tendency remains evident, with Werner's team foregrounding the uniforms' aesthetic over practicality and little disguising the fact that their models were not soldiers. In the second scene, for example, the camera slowly scans up a uniform from the large black combat boots to the collar. This shapeless brown combat uniform is on a mannequin and behind it a woman in a blue-grey dress uniform and black soft cap grins and gives an exaggerated wink. The joke here is presumably that the combat uniform should lead viewers to expect a male soldier. Yet instead of wearing this uniform herself, in a way that might unsettle those expectations, the actor emerges from behind wearing a smart dress uniform. She spins, showing her blue-grey collared dress belted at the waist. This set-up highlights the contrast between her overtly feminine attire and the combat uniform. Her extravagant wink, like other ironic moments, renders the subject matter unserious. Though this acting trivializes the work of women soldiers, it also creates space for the models to take pleasure in irony and draw attention to their own exaggerated performances. Their exaggerated acting is out of place even among the lighter *Armeefilmschau* segments, and by seeming to be in on the joke, they potentially redirect the newsreel's humour at the military's stuffy seriousness. The AFS files do not include any comments on the newsreel's reception, but as the audience will not have consisted entirely of committed cis male soldiers, the self-irony may have made a welcome change from the NVA's usual self-seriousness.

Disrupting the Gender Binary

In the period after 1982, women soldiers attained greater attention on screen within and beyond the AFS, including on television news.[38] The DEFA Studio for Documentary Film produced a short film following a soldier and telegraph operator entitled *Gabi – Vermittlung Platz 12*, directed by Uwe Belz.[39] The Filmgruppe 1982, made up of employees of the AFS but working separately from it, made a more substantial documentary of around thirty minutes, *Neugier und Bewährung*.[40] Director Dietmar Schürtz and cinematographer Kurt Hartig followed a group of women training in the Border Guard and interviewed them about their experiences. This film had the cooperation of the Perleberg Officers' Academy and the Border Guard, and the team had access to film the soldiers at various stages up to their swearing-in ceremony. Yet *Neugier und Bewährung* was withdrawn, with Schürtz's AFS superiors taking what they believed to be Schürtz's only copy and locking it away. The AFS files do not document the film or its withdrawal, but it suggests that women's increased visibility as soldiers remained controversial into the late 1980s. Schürtz has since screened the film and it was the subject of 1993 and 2009 documentaries by Süddeutsche Zeitung TV following up with the soldiers depicted.[41] *Gabi – Vermittlung Platz 12*, on the other hand, was released in East German cinemas, albeit infrequently, as a short before feature films.[42] The women in these films present themselves as professionals invested in their training and inhabit their uniformed roles confidently, often showing greater ease in uniform than in civilian clothes. While in *Gabi* the women are largely separate from other soldiers, *Neugier und Bewährung* shows a rare mixed-gender environment and comes closest of all these films to unsettling the gender binary.

Binary panic is still in evidence in these films, most noticeably in the framing and mise-en-scène of the interviews with Gabi Arzt, an NVA telegraph operator in Thüringen. After an interview with Gabi and her colleague Carmen about their qualifying exams, in which they discuss how rigorously their typing skills are assessed, the camera cuts abruptly to an interview in Arzt's room at home. The tone suddenly changes: in Figure 13.1, she is being interviewed about the soft toys surrounding her. 'Presents, mostly', she explains. The interviewer asks who gave her the presents and misidentifies the penguin in the shot as a duck. With a

Figure 13.1. Interview with Gabi Arzt surrounded by soft toys. Still from Uwe Belz's *Gabi – Vermittlung Platz 12* (1984). © DEFA-Stiftung/Peter Sbrzesny

smile and an awkward laugh, Arzt corrects him and holds the penguin up to the camera. She is framed by net curtains and shelves full of knick-knacks, a marked change from the austere furnishings of the telegraph room. This interview is presumably designed for characterization, but it is jarring to move directly from her explanations of technical skills to a discussion of soft toys. This effort to depict her as childlike is echoed in the film's explanatory text, which to this day describes her as a 'young girl', despite her being at least eighteen at the time of filming.[43]

Despite gestures that infantilize and exaggerate soldiers' femininity, Arzt and her comrades, as with Johannimann and other women in AFS productions, present themselves as proud professionals. Repeatedly, women soldiers describe enlisting to attain qualifications and advancement prospects. In Arzt's own words, now in uniform just after she has taken the oath and formally joined the NVA:

> I think for me it's a job like any other, just here you [*man*] happen to wear a uniform and are a member of the army [*Armeeangehöriger*]. You [*man*] have a job to do just like a worker in industry [*ein Arbeiter im Betrieb*].

By emphasizing her career, Arzt attempts to normalize the presence of women in uniform. Her words also push back against the NVA's efforts to reinforce a gender binary. She consciously emphasizes her experiences as ungendered using 'man' and the generic masculine 'Armeeangehöriger' and 'Arbeiter'. Even though we do not see her or Carmen in exercises with male trainees, she does not describe women soldiers as isolated, but makes a point about all army careers. She articulates her place within the military as an individual seeking skills and career advancement, and shaping the institution in ways that are not limited by her gender.

Arzt's attempt to find language to talk about her career choices outside of the NVA's gender binaries draws attention to the instabilities of military gender and to filmmakers' attempts to resolve them. Arzt's words work against the film's editing and mise-en-scène that exaggerate stereotypical aspects of femininity. This portrayal of a soldier who confidently exudes both conventional femininity and a professionalized, uniformed military femininity that does not fit so easily into binary gender places the binary itself in the foreground, raising the question of what happens when femininities and masculinities overlap or are no longer easily separable. As trans theorist Marquis Bey writes in their discussion of what trans studies mean for our understanding of subjectivity:

Figure 13.2. Mixed-gender training exercise at the Unteroffiziersschule Perleberg, c. 1988. Screen capture from *Neugier und Bewährung*. © Dietmar Schürtz, used with permission

Worked through the knowledges produced via trans studies subjectivity becomes an open question that is unsettled, flickered, and self-determined via asking itself the question of itself.[44]

These are all cis-authored films that presume cisness in their subjects, unlike the trans theories Bey is discussing, but they repeatedly ask questions of the gender binary. The filmic techniques often attempt to control the gendered subjectivities being presented, while women's interviews and self-presentations insistently keep the question open, allowing flickers of identification across the binary. The workings of binary gender are even more visible the more strongly it is asserted as part of the military's binary panic, and such an open question allows for many possible less settled responses.

The binary is most clearly unsettled in depictions of women in combat training in *Neugier und Bewährung*, suggesting why in AFS and DEFA productions women are rarely shown with weapons or in combat uniforms. Shots like that given in Figure 13.2 frequently draw attention to the instability, overlap and mutual dependence of masculinities and femininities. It is part of a long montage of a mixed training exercise combining men's and women's platoons. It is often impossible to distinguish soldiers' faces in these sequences, much less make assumptions about their gender. As in this shot, their uniforms are nearly identical, and the focus is not individual characterization, but skill and efficiency.

Hartig occasionally shoots close-ups of faces recognizable from interviews, but in long shots and group shots, uniforms obscure rather than emphasize bodily differences. Unlike the models in dress uniforms in the 1982 newsreel, these women are in combat uniforms throughout, except at formal ceremonies. The robust and shapeless uniforms prioritize not gender differences or soldiers' femininity, but function: the film shows their determination and skill in overcoming obstacles, with the physical obstacle course standing in for the metaphorical hurdles of training. The fact that gender becomes indistinguishable when training for combat exercises, the most conventionally masculine of military activities, challenges the unthinking binary division of military labour between genders. In Bey's terms, such shots 'ask the question' of the binary's usefulness.

Neugier und Bewährung also demonstrates explicitly how women shaped understandings of masculinity within the NVA. The filmmakers ask men about training in a mixed gender setting and their answers show that serving alongside women forces them to reflect on their own position and their gendered assumptions. One trainee describes his expectations being challenged:

> Even when it's just guys together, it spurs you on when someone's doing more, but when it's a *girl* [sic] doing more, then it gets to you so much that you really put your back into it.[45]

Training with women affects how he understands his masculinity. He is forced to accept that his cishet masculinity does not guarantee that he will hold his own. As their platoon leader says, there are few significant differences in their physical abilities: 'the girls are basically just as resilient as the boys'. The trainee's suggestion that women spur him on demonstrates the significant effect that mixed-gender competition could have on masculinity within the troops. He goes on to start generalizing: 'but otherwise, girls in the unit, well. . .'. At this point, the woman behind him, who has been smiling and listening, suddenly gives him a warning glare, opening her eyes wide and turning her mouth down sternly. Her expression is a reminder that many women soldiers endured abuse and harassment and she could be preparing for him to say something offensive. Or it could be a sign of a comradely relationship that she can offer a warning or intervene if he oversteps. Either way, in moments like this, women actively shape the NVA's gender norms and men reflect on their own masculinities in response to women enacting and embodying military roles. This scene is one of the most powerful reminders that, however rare women in uniform may be compared to the ubiquity of male soldiers in East German film, culture and society, people of all genders were always engaged in shaping what masculinities and femininities meant in the GDR, with women negotiating and leaving their mark on masculinities in significant ways.

Conclusion

The NVA's films and publications always emphasized the link between military service, masculinity and cis male bodies, but this link is rarely as clear as in these representations of women soldiers. The most explicit aims of the AFS films were to boost morale, contribute to education or promote a positive image of military service in East German society. Yet depictions of NVA soldiers also shape how military masculinities are understood. Across the AFS's output and DEFA's military-focused films, depictions of male-presenting soldiers naturalize cis male bodies as the sole site where military masculinities are developed and negotiated. This gendered project is common to most modern militaries, and the assumptions around military masculinity mean this work is often effortless, unconscious and barely visible.[46] The link is so unquestioned that women hardly ever appear in military uniform on film in the GDR, despite their small but significant presence across branches, regiments and military occupations. In documentaries and newsreels that do depict women soldiers, the work to emphasize the gender binary is not only visible but central to the films' creation. By explicitly asking what it is like to serve in a masculine institution as a woman, and implicitly what it means when the boundary between femininities and masculinities begins to blur, these films foreground the instability of binary gender, the work that goes into sustaining it and the binary panic around images of uniformed women.

These films' interest in the gender binary shows that women did influence military masculinities in the NVA. Whilst this influence is clearest in *Neugier und Bewährung*, the broader AFS and DEFA examples also show how the presence of women in the NVA caused filmmakers to address and reinforce the military's gender order that equated the military with masculinities and cis male bodies. Portrayals of cis men soldiers also shaped military masculinities in the NVA in complex ways, but, as Jack Halberstam argues and as the AFS films show, we learn most about masculinity where it leaves cis male bodies.[47] The NVA's films do not acknowledge the presence of trans soldiers or civilian workers, but those the army hailed as men or women will have included people of other genders. Jayne-Ann Igel, for example, who was conscripted herself, later created a masculine-presenting protagonist in *Unerlaubte Entfernung* (AWOL, 2004) whose military service is shaped by disorientation, self-distance and bodily dysphoria.[48] Trans women like Igel were often conscripted after 1962 and there is some evidence that trans soldiers or civilian workers were known to superiors.[49] Though the AFS films do not acknowledge the existence of soldiers like Igel's protagonist or Igel herself, their binary panic reveals the often imperceptible representational work that goes into bolstering binary gender.

The gender binary never disappears in these films. Despite scenes in *Neugier und Bewährung* where gender assumptions are blocked or confused by the homogeneous appearance of a mixed-gender training unit, all these films focus on women and presume binary gender and the cisness of their subjects. Most commonly, the NVA's newsreels diminish the professionalism of women soldiers, fixate on stereotypes of femininity and use humour or characterization to reinforce gender hierarchies. Yet these films are not entirely without self-awareness, as in the 1982 newsreel showcasing new uniforms for women. It is possible to imagine how women soldiers might have received such a film differently from its intended male audience: whether focusing more on what the new uniforms would be like to wear, sharing wry smiles at generalizations or camp pageantry, or shooting a warning glare at male comrades like the trainee in *Neugier und Bewährung*. More fundamentally, by making the work involved with sustaining binary gender visible and audible, the films foreground moments when gender is questioned or obscured. For example, *Neugier und Bewährung* features two scenes with the trainee NCOs dancing, once just the women together on base and once in a local nightclub. Even in the nightclub, where there are men present, two women dance together, with great concentration and apparent joy. Moments like this capture intimacy and closeness between the women and suggest that, despite the hardships of the NVA, they were engaged in building communities, support structures and forms of agency within such a masculine – and masculinist – institution.

Women's negotiations of East German military institutions could be fraught, both for them and for the NVA's norms. Many suffered abuse and harassment in the NVA and were materially affected by the violence used to reinforce binary gender. Yet their presence influenced how masculinities were shaped and negotiated, requiring the NVA to make visible the work needed to sustain the gender binary. These films show that military women forced men – from fellow recruits to filmmakers and the command structure – to consider what masculinity meant. In many ways, the command structure had to acknowledge women's role embodying military masculinities and take steps to reassert binary gender, with direct effects on discipline, policies and the NVA's self-presentation. When this binary is most strongly asserted, the unsettling effects of women's influence on masculinities are clearest, so that the military in these documentaries ends up, in Marquis Bey's terms, asking itself the question of itself.

Tom Smith is Senior Lecturer in German at the University of St Andrews. His research focuses on masculinities and on queer and trans German studies, including from the GDR and the period since 1990. His book, *Comrades in Arms: Military Masculinities in East German Culture*, was published by Berghahn Books in 2020. He is one of the Arts and Humanities Research Council's and the BBC's New Generation Thinkers, and regularly presents his work on BBC radio.

Notes

With thanks to Dietmar Schürtz, colleagues at the Bundesarchiv in Berlin and Freiburg, Kerstin Lommatzsch at Progress, Linda Söffker at the DEFA Foundation and Jörg Möhring at MDR for access to materials and permissions.

1. Thomas Maulucci analyses the Foreign Ministry Films in a similar vein in Chapter 2 of this volume.
2. Matthias Rogg, '"Filme von der Fahne": Das Armeefilmstudio der Nationalen Volksarmee der DDR', in Bernhard Chiari, Matthias Rogg and Wolfgang Schmidt (eds), *Krieg und Militär im Film des 20. Jahrhunderts* (Munich: Oldenbourg, 2003), pp. 611–34 (at pp. 614–15); Werner Patzer, 'Die personelle Auffüllung der NVA', in Wolfgang Wünsche (ed.), *Rührt euch! Zur Geschichte der NVA* (Berlin: edition ost, 1998), pp. 363–90 (at p. 366).
3. Ralf Gründer, '". . .sie wollen Deinen Ehrendienst stören": Indoktrination und tausendfacher Aufruf zum Brudermord durch das Armeefilmstudio der Nationalen Volksarmee der DDR', *Zeitschrift des Forschungsverbundes SED-Staat* 19 (2006), 136.
4. Rüdiger Wenzke, *Ulbrichts Soldaten. Die Nationale Volksarmee 1956 bis 1971* (Berlin: Links, 2013), p. 562.
5. Vinzenz Hediger and Patrick Vonderau (eds), *Films That Work: Industrial Film and the Productivity of Media* (Amsterdam: Amsterdam University Press, 2009).
6. Rogg, 'Filme von der Fahne', pp. 627–28.
7. On East German newsreels, see Reinhild Steingröver's chapter (Chapter 3) in this volume.

8. See e.g. 'Filmzulassung Armeefilmschau', 6 April 1987 (= BArch DR 1-Z/2577).
 9. *Armeefilmschau*, 2/1962, 'Frauen an unserer Seite'. (= BArch B108352/1–1). All translations are mine.
10. On women's employment in East Germany, see Anna Kaminsky, *Frauen in der DDR* (Berlin: Links, 2017).
11. Christiane Lemke and Gero Neugebauer, 'Frauen und Militär in der DDR', *Deutschland Archiv* 18 (1985), 416–18.
12. Ibid., 415–16. See the profile of Iris Wittig in Reinhard Brühl et al., *Armee für Frieden und Sozialismus: Geschichte der Nationalen Volksarmee der DDR* (Berlin: Militärverlag der DDR, 1985), p. 125.
13. Gesetz über die allgemeine Wehrpflicht (Wehrpflichtgesetz) vom 24. Januar 1962, *Gesetzblatt der Deutschen Demokratischen Republik* 1 (1962), 2–6, §31.
14. Edna Levy explores women soldiers' relation to citizenship in the Israeli context: 'Women Warriors: The Paradox and Politics of Israeli Women in Uniform', in Sita Ranchod-Nilsson and Mary Ann Tetreault (eds), *Women, States and Nationalism: At Home in the Nation?* (London: Routledge, 2000), pp. 196–214.
15. Uwe Markus, *Frauen in der NVA* (Berlin: Phalanx, 2020), p. 32; Gesetz über den Wehrdienst in der Deutschen Demokratischen Republik (Wehrdienstgesetz) vom 25. März 1982, *Gesetzblatt der Deutschen Demokratischen Republik* 1 (1982), 221–29, §3.5.
16. Lemke and Neugebauer, 'Frauen und Militär in der DDR', 415 and 418.
17. *Soldatenhochzeit* (D039), dir. Manfred Tzschaksch, Armeefilmstudio, 1964 (= BArch B103991–1); *Meiner ist bei den Soldaten* (D240), dir. Heinz Killian, Armeefilmstudio, 1975 (= BArch B105206–1). See Matthias Rogg, *Armee des Volkes? Militär und Gesellschaft in der DDR* (Berlin: Links, 2008), pp. 404–7.
18. Christine Eifler, '". . .es schützt Dich mein Gewehr": Zu Frauenbildern in der NVA-Propaganda', in Zentrum für Interdisziplinäre Frauenforschung (ed.), *Unter Hammer und Zirkel. Frauenbiographien vor dem Hintergrund ostdeutscher Sozialisationserfahrungen* (Pfaffenweiler: Centaurus, 1995), pp. 269–76; Christine Eifler, '"Ewig unreif": Geschlechtsrollenklischees in der *Armeerundschau*', in Simone Barck, Martina Langermann and Siegfried Lokatis (eds), *Zwischen 'Mosaik' und 'Einheit': Zeitschriften in der DDR* (Berlin: Links, 1999), pp. 180–88.
19. See Lutz Rentner and Otto Sperlich (dirs), *Pornografie – Made in GDR?*, Video MDR 100171015, *MDR Zeitreise*, ARTE, 2 February 2007, 11:15 pm.
20. For example, Diary of a trainee officer, 16 July–5 December 1990 (= Deutsches Tagebucharchiv, Emmendingen, DTA 1350/056); Petition by a trainee officer to the SED, 26 October 1988, fols 148–51 (= BArch DY 30/1169).
21. See Kaminsky, *Frauen in der DDR*, pp. 76–81.
22. *Hier ist mein Platz* (D290), dir. M. J. Blochwitz, Armeefilmstudio, 1979 (= BArch B105247–1).
23. *Armeefilmschau*, 4/1965, 'Filmnotizen' (= BArch B108416–1).
24. With thanks to Barbora Krausová for help with the Czech.

25. 'Text für Armeefilmschau 4/65', fols 39–41 (at fol. 41) (= BArch DVP 3–3/1543).
26. Prokoll der Studioabnahme der Armeefilmschau 4/65', fols 42–43 (at fol. 42) (= BArch DVP 3–3/1543).
27. Jack Halberstam, *Trans*: A Quick and Quirky Account of Gender Variability* (Oakland: University of California Press, 2018), p. xii.
28. *Armeefilmschau*, 6/1972, 'Militärarztin' (= BArch B108986–1).
29. See Ian Barnard, *Sex Panic Rhetorics: Queer Interventions* (Tuscaloosa: University of Alabama Press, 2020).
30. Eve Kosofsky Sedgwick, *Epistemology of the Closet* (Berkeley: University of California Press, 1990), p. 21.
31. Barnard, *Sex Panic Rhetorics*, p. 68.
32. See Ingrid Miethe, *Frauen in der DDR-Opposition: Lebens- und kollektivgeschichtliche Verläufe in einer Frauenfriedensgruppe* (Opladen: Leske + Budrich, 1999). Petition published as Frauen für den Frieden, '"Wir fordern Recht auf Verweigerung": DDR-Frauen protestieren gegen das neue Wehrdienstgesetz', *Der Spiegel* 36 (1982), 49. Members recall the Mecklenburg rumour in interviews: Almut Ilsen and Ruth Leiserowitz (eds), *Seid doch laut! Die Frauen für den Frieden in Ost-Berlin* (Berlin: Links, 2019), 23, 39, 54.
33. Frauen für den Frieden, '"Wir fordern Recht auf Verweigerung"'.
34. *Armeefilmschau*, 12/1982, 'Uniform' (= BArch B109577–1). See 'Konzeption für *Armeefilmschau* 12/1982', fol. 3 (= BArch DVP 3–3/12672).
35. Hans Werner and Dieter Behrendt, Aktennotiz, 11 October 1982 (= BArch DVP 3–3/12689).
36. Ibid.
37. Anna Fröhlich, 'Ich bin generell gegen Krieg und gegen Waffen', in Markus, *Frauen in der NVA*, pp. 87–105 (at p. 93).
38. *Aktuelle Kamera*, 28 November 1986, 'Festveranstaltung 40 Jahre Grenztruppen' (= Deutsches Rundfunkarchiv, Potsdam-Babelsberg, DRA-B AC14026/1); *Aktuelle Kamera*, 4 May 1988, 'Meeting der Waffenbrüderschaft mit mongolischer Militärdelegation' (= DRA-B OVC3799/1).
39. *Gabi – Vermittlung Platz 12*, dir. Uwe Belz, DEFA, 1985.
40. For more on Filmgruppe 82 and amateur cinema, see Ralf Forster, *Greif zur Kamera, gib der Freizeit einen Sinn: Amateurfilm in der DDR* (Munich: text+kritik, 2018), pp. 380–85.
41. 'Die NVA-Frauen: Die Lebenswege dreier Soldatinnen der DDR', *Süddeutsche Zeitung TV*, VOX, 14 November 2009, 11.00 pm.
42. For example, '1985 im Kino', *Neues Deutschland*, 9 July 1985, p. 7; 'Im Kino ab Freitag', *Berliner Zeitung*, 21 January 1986, p. 8.
43. See the description on the DEFA Foundation website: 'Gabi – Vermittlung Platz 12', *DEFA-Stiftung*, Filmdatenbank, https://www.defa-stiftung.de/filme/filme-suchen/gabi-vermittlung-platz-12/ (retrieved 8 April 2024).
44. Aren Z. Aizura, Marquis Bey, Toby Beauchamp, Treva Ellison, Jules Gill-Peterson and Eliza Steinbock, 'Thinking with Trans Now', *Social Text* 145 (2020), 131.
45. *Neugier und Bewährung*, dir. Dietmar Schürtz, Filmgruppe 82, c. 1988.

46. For example, Ruth Seifert and Christine Eifler (eds), *Gender und Militär: Internationale Erfahrungen mit Frauen und Männern in Streitkräften* (Königstein/Taunus: Helmer, 2003).
47. Jack Halberstam, *Female Masculinity* (Durham, NC: Duke University Press, 1998), p. 2. On military masculinities more broadly, see Tom Smith, *Comrades in Arms: Military Masculinities in East German Culture* (New York: Berghahn Books, 2020).
48. Jayne-Ann Igel, *Unerlaubte Entfernung* (Basel: Engeler, 2004), p. 85.
49. Stasi reports contain isolated references to trans women in an NVA context that misrepresent them as 'homosexual', e.g. Bundesbeauftragter für die Unterlagen des Staatssicherheitsdienstes der ehemaligen Deutschen Demokratischen Republik (BStU), Berlin, MfS HA I 19698.

Select Bibliography

Eifler, Christine. '". . .es schützt Dich mein Gewehr": Zu Frauenbildern in der NVA-Propaganda', in Zentrum für Interdisziplinäre Frauenforschung (ed.), *Unter Hammer und Zirkel: Frauenbiographien vor dem Hintergrund ostdeutscher Sozialisationserfahrungen*. Pfaffenweiler: Centaurus, 1995, pp. 269–76.

———. '"Ewig unreif": Geschlechtsrollenklischees in der *Armeerundschau*', in Simone Barck, Martina Langermann and Siegfried Lokatis (eds), *Zwischen 'Mosaik' und 'Einheit': Zeitschriften in der DDR*. Berlin: Links, 1999, pp. 180–88.

Forster, Ralf. *Greif zur Kamera, gib der Freizeit einen Sinn: Amateurfilm in der DDR*. Munich: text+kritik, 2018.

Halberstam, Jack. *Female Masculinity*. Durham, NC: Duke University Press, 1998.

Lemke, Christiane, and Gero Neugebauer. 'Frauen und Militär in der DDR', *Deutschland Archiv* 18 (1985), 411–26.

Markus, Uwe. *Frauen in der NVA*, Berlin: Phalanx, 2020.

Rogg, Matthias. '"Filme von der Fahne": Das Armeefilmstudio der Nationalen Volksarmee der DDR', in Bernhard Chiari, Matthias Rogg and Wolfgang Schmidt (eds), *Krieg und Militär im Film des 20. Jahrhunderts*. Munich: Oldenbourg, 2003, pp. 611–34.

Smith, Tom. *Comrades in Arms: Military Masculinities in East German Culture*. New York: Berghahn Books, 2020.

CHAPTER 14

The Queer Cipher in East German Documentary
In Sachen H. und acht anderer (*In the Matter of H. and Eight Others, 1972*) and Queer Activist Super 8 Films

Kyle Frackman

The 1970s were a significant period for queer rights and visibility in the German Democratic Republic (GDR). The 1968 official decriminalization of male homosexual sex was one event in a public and private media landscape of film, television, photography, radio and periodicals that reflected slowly changing moral attitudes and uses of technologies. This chapter analyses two film examples of queer reality in that media landscape – one within official structures and the other in private. The first example, Richard Cohn-Vossen's *In Sachen H. und acht anderer* (*In the Matter of H. and Eight Others*, 1972), depicts court proceedings following an assault on presumed homosexuals near Kollwitzplatz in Berlin.[1] What follows in this film is a sustained thirty-minute analysis of the ostensible subject: juvenile delinquency. Why did these young men and others like them engage in unacceptable – or what was sometimes called 'antisocial' – behaviour? Sparked by the initial assault, the subject of citizens' responsibility to one another and the collective runs throughout the film as the viewer is encouraged to consider degrees of social belonging. This chapter's second example is a collection of subversive Super 8 films presenting East German queer life of the 1970s. Statistics, humour and irony contribute to the activist filmmakers' use of a private medium to describe the context of the Homosexuelle Interessengemeinschaft Berlin (HIB) (Homosexual Interest Community of Berlin), the first organized queer liberation group in the GDR. The filmmakers in both examples use queerness as a means of communicating something greater about life in the GDR.

This chapter attends to uses of queerness and what they might tell us about public and private film in this context. In *What's the Use?*, Sara Ahmed theorizes the techniques of 'use', how things are used and what these uses – proper or otherwise – can mean or do. One way to think of a use is, Ahmed writes, as 'an instrumental relation', when something becomes a 'utensil', 'when it is used in order to do something'.[2] Use can be limited by requirements or shaped by instructions.[3] Use can also deviate from these and other expectations by taking a form other than those foreseen or by being useful to unplanned users, in which case it might become 'queer use'.[4] Queer uses have radical potential for effecting change and subverting dominant prescriptions for action or behaviour.

The examples I discuss here show queerness being used for two seemingly related but actually opposed objectives. In the first example, Cohn-Vossen's film, queerness appears, however briefly, as a means of interrogating social behaviours (i.e. juvenile delinquency) and communicating societal expectations to the viewers. A queer viewer recognizes the objectifying appearance of the queer component for its incidental quality, while also identifying with the unhappiness provoked by the anti-queer assault.[5] The second example, the private amateur films, come from distinctly queer perspectives, using information and methods associated with that standpoint. The HIB films constitute an opportunity for deeper queer identification and communication, as they illustrate both the absurdities of heteronormative prejudices and the potential of queer community. Whereas *In Sachen H. und acht anderer* concentrates on how civil society structures should respond to nonconformity, the activist films demonstrate how nonconforming individuals can respond to governing structures in society. To put it another way, the divergent uses of queerness – one for the state and one for the community – demonstrate control or possibility. In this chapter, I argue that queerness is used as a cipher, a stand-in or vehicle, to support the aims of the filmmakers. The cipher's functions change depending on the user and their intended use. Cohn-Vossen's film uses queerness as a vehicle for measuring majority societal cohesion. The Super 8 films use queerness to promote cohesion in a minority community. Below I will discuss the metaphor of the cipher before analysing its uses in *In Sachen H. und acht anderer* and then the amateur activist films.

The Cipher and East German Documentary

The term 'cipher' connotes a figure whose appearance has both more and less meaning than what is immediately apparent. Perhaps most prominent among a cipher's definitions is that of a code, as in a 'cipher telegram' or 'deciphering' encrypted data. More comprehensively, the *Oxford English Dictionary* lists seven definitions of the word 'cipher' relating to terms for 'void', 'to be empty' and the symbol 'zero'.[6] What the word's uses have in common is symbolic meaning as stand-ins for, or references to, something else.[7] Two definitions are important for my examination of queerness within the GDR. The first is a use of the cipher to describe 'a person who fills a place, but is of no importance or worth, a nonentity, a "mere nothing"'.[8] Like a '0' or the void of the word's origins, this cipher describes a placeholder, a figure, object or value that one deploys as an object without assertive, characteristic properties. This cipher can be a floating signifier, amenable to being attached to various signifieds depending on the interpreter. The second key definition refers to a covert communication system (or the key to this system).[9] Here too, the cipher becomes a means to create a different value. Where an object has 'no weight, worth, or influence', it can also be manipulated for other purposes – indeed, even for other meanings, as in the case of 'a message in code'.[10]

The cipher embodies different possibilities in the state-sponsored and private films. *In Sachen H. und acht anderer* exploits the queerness cipher to address a complex subject that is only tangentially related to homosexuality, namely juvenile delinquency and crime. Although the film implies that it is the victims' sexuality that is the underlying cause for both the assault and the ensuing legal process, this assumption is undermined almost as soon as it is raised. Since the role of sexuality and gender identity in the incident is simply referred to and not developed, it remains both a catalyst for discussion of social dynamics and an undeciphered figure that persists as something unexplained or inexplicable. The Super 8 HIB films, by contrast, wield the queerness cipher in its specifically East German context to support activist purposes. If the state-sponsored documentary instrumentalizes queer people as a means of understanding social troubles, then the HIB documentaries focus on that very process of instrumentalization to offer a critique of GDR state attitudes towards homosexuality. Queer people are presented as an assertive structuring force that reveals the determination of the activist filmmakers and their audacious use of nonfiction cinema. The amateur films proceed with the knowledge that the structures of state authority have at best limited accurate information about nonconforming embodiments of sexuality and gender. From this presumption, they take advantage of the cipher to foster community and express unique qualities of GDR queerness.

The films selected for analysis share some characteristics in terms of their use of the media and cinematic conventions. They also shed light on relationships between queer people and the East German state. The films illustrate the entanglement of media practices and political representation. Read in juxtaposition, they emphasize the mutual incomprehensibility of two distinct modes of communication. *In Sachen H. und acht anderer* reflects the contemporary distaste in the GDR for concentrating on marginalized or other identity-based groups (and the then recent decriminalization of homosexual acts in 1968 did not change this reality). The HIB films use cinematic techniques to depict a socialist society in which queer people are accepted as part of the collective.

In Sachen H. und acht anderer

Richard Cohn-Vossen's film depicts the consequences of youth criminality and inadequate social integration by focusing on a specific court case, which began with an anti-queer element. In its first few minutes, the narrator briefly describes the particulars as shots pan and cut between various spectators:

> A municipal district court in March of '72. The lawyers. The relatives and acquaintances. Their sons, brothers, [and] colleagues, surrounded individual passers-by, beat them bloody, [and] robbed them – all because one of them said that, unlike them, they were homosexuals.

Thus, the assailants in the case perceived a minority gender/sexual identity among multiple individuals, who then became their targets. Whatever attributes the perpetrators may have recognized among the victims, if any, also marked the targets as members of an objectionable and vulnerable group. For the assailants, the targets' queerness and weakness became a means to reach material gain.

The narrator's brief mention of the targets' homosexuality is the subject's only appearance in the film. One does not learn on what basis the assailants believed the targets were homosexual or, for that matter, whether the victims were homosexual or had homosexuals among them. Whether the targets were homosexual, or the 'homosexuality' is a substitute for weakness is irrelevant. Implicit in the accused's reasoning is the heteronormative logic that homosexuals are either easy targets for or deserving of such an attack on account of their group membership and susceptibility. The basic elements of the incident are clearly laid out. What remains for the film is to provide information about what may have led to this result. While the film communicates the social viewpoint that the assault and robbery are offensive to the civil order, the (at least partial) inspiration for the attack – the targets' homosexuality – is set aside as soon as it is mentioned. This dismissal is notable, given the court's concerted efforts to ascertain the perpetrators' motivation, but is perhaps to be expected for a taboo topic. It is remarkable that the judge and even the perpetrators themselves are incapable of definitively explaining, however many suggestions there might be, who is responsible for the event and why it occurred. Nonetheless, one conclusion to which the film leads the viewer is that giving up on any (hetero-conforming) member of society is unacceptable. The queerness cipher has served its purpose, in this case facilitating the examination of another phenomenon.

The avoidance of homosexuality in *In Sachen H. und acht anderer* is symptomatic of the majority GDR perspective on queerness in various forms: inconspicuousness and a lack of group identification are best. With the quick mention of the assailants' reasons, the film dismisses the underlying causes of the attack that were already known. Nick Hodgin has observed that documentary films from the GDR offer an important perspective on the GDR 'as much for what they show us of the East German life (and how they show it) as for what they do not show'.[11] Here, the empty vessel of the cipher – the lurking question of queerness's actuality – is filled by the official purpose of diagnosing problems with social cohesion and conformity. An example of anti-queer violence becomes normal or unworthy of further engagement. As Eric A. Stanley has argued, in such a situation the law becomes 'one of [the] methodologies of [harm's] proliferation' rather than a means to 'relief from such harm'.[12] In other words, in the film's logic the assailants' anti-queer motivation is not the important part of the story; rather, juvenile non-conformity and its social links deserve the audience's attention. With its concentration on juvenile behaviour, the film's presentation of context is enough to make the queer viewer suspicious. The state apparatus that prevents or discourages queer cohabitation, organized gathering, erotic expression and much public representation now shows concern about anti-queer violence. However, the social concern arises not because of the anti-queer element, but rather because of the perpetrators and what they might say about socialist society.

Over its nearly thirty minutes, *In Sachen H. und acht anderer* encapsulates the crime by presenting moments of social context as well as legal argument, testimony and sentencing. Beyond some establishing shots of Berlin apartment buildings, the documentary comprises primarily footage of the court proceedings to tell a story of a group's actions set amid urban life. Court scenes are intercut with shots of children playing – including play-shooting each other with toy guns and sticks – and both sullen and cheerful teenagers spending time around a park in Berlin. In the courtroom are nine young men between sixteen and twenty years old, whose faces and voices are visible in the film, who were responsible for the 'rowdy' behaviour at the root of the court proceedings.

Through its narration, cinematography and soundtrack, the film draws attention to its mediated observation. Cohn-Vossen illustrates lines of affiliation between and around particular groups of people (the accused, a teacher, a mother), including those in the milieu around Kollwitzplatz and an assumed like-minded audience, creating an illustration of a complex network of expectations and behaviours. The opening musical soundtrack, with lone strums of a guitar, and the voice-over narration by Felicitas Ritsch already produce an ominous effect as the short documentary begins its brief examination of a criminal occurrence that is at once both extraordinary and normal. The narrator implies that the viewer will feel the unease of being brought past the limits of someone else's privacy and into a disturbing situation. Any intrusive discomfort one might feel is necessary, the narration argues, because society must look at what has happened and examine its causes. However, what is also clear is the strangeness or 'foreignness' of what is to be discovered.

Individuals try throughout the film to explain what happened and why, turning the court and thereby the film into a means of reflecting on the possible interpretations of the circumstances. The catalyst – the queerness of the victims – is left unexplored. Crucially, the interpretations revolve around the question of responsibility and causation, pointing to at least three aggravating aspects that contributed to the underlying crimes: society, locations and groups. The state and other support structures have tried to address young people's needs, a defence lawyer argues, but the accused needed the help of society, which did not arrive soon enough. One of the young men's teachers asserts that everyone is responsible for what becomes of young people. Even the scene of the crime, Kollwitzplatz itself, might be partly to blame. The defence contends that the square and its park, where young people gathered and heard loud music (often from Western radio stations), constitute the primary common factor of influence among the accused, who have differing home and life circumstances. Another thread of explanations focuses on groups. The defence argues that one individual went along with the group's assault because he was unable to stand up for himself in the group of bullies.

Asking about responsibility for the crime becomes one way to avoid the meaning of the crime itself and any significance of the targets. Filmmaker Eduard Schreiber has written that this short documentary shows 'disturbed family relationships, faults of the parents and school, and the carelessness of society'.[13] Yet the figures in the film and the narration spend considerable time trying to provide a response to what the narrator articulates as an extended central question: 'Who controls their minds? The school? Their parents? And whose mass media?' This formulation about the perpetrators' actions is intriguing for the way it expresses a belief in external control or manipulation. Instead of providing information on what would seem to be a salient cause, various constituencies (prosecution, defence, witnesses, parents, teacher, victim) offer possible explanations for what occurred.

Early responses to such questions uncover the accused's desire to live what was sometimes called an 'antisocial' life, one without proper contribution to society. Officially, antisocial behaviour was prohibited by the GDR's legal code and comprised an individual's failure to meet their social obligation to work and earn an income if they were able to do so.[14] The judge asks one defendant what he liked about sitting in the square, listening to music and not doing anything else. 'A carefree life', he replies. Many times, the judge asks the accused questions such as 'Why did you strike them? Were you threatened by someone? Did someone tell you to hit them?' Crucially, the role of group dynamics is clear in some of the defendants' responses:

> I hit their face with my fist . . . I walked on and thought that the others would be coming along. Then I turned around and saw that the others were hitting the man over and over.

Another extensive line of questioning from the judge, abbreviated here, lays bare more of the underlying dynamics of the incident: 'Why did you also hit him? How do you explain the fact that you hit someone without actually knowing why? You didn't have a reason?' Two defendants offer seemingly banal responses to these questions that are also salient in a consideration of queerness at the social level: 'because the others were hitting them' and 'I don't want to exclude myself from such a large group if someone has something going. Otherwise, you don't look very good'. These young men become exemplary in a negative fashion – illustrating undesirable qualities in socialist society as well as a contributing factor to criminality.

The accused have deviated from expected norms, which enabled them to follow their, in a way, queer failing desire for something else ('a carefree life', amounting to their social failure). These young men are unable or unwilling to obey society's compulsion towards productivity. In so doing, the accused participate in another life structure, pursuing a different reward, and ironically have an unseen affinity with the queer targets of their assault. While *In Sachen H. und acht anderer* uses community scenes and children's play (with toy weapons) to illustrate how the perpetrators might have deviated from the right track, it simultaneously evokes what Jack Halberstam has called 'the wondrous anarchy of childhood', 'disturb[ing] the supposedly clean boundaries between adults and children, winners, and losers'.[15] The accused have not only become violent; they have also rejected aspects of '[h]eteronormative common sense', which expects successful societal integration in areas like 'advancement' and 'family'.[16] Moreover, the perpetrators' comments about the attack reveal that a significant contributing factor to their behaviour was their friends' behaviour. Such peer imitation is not surprising, but, in this context, it is a further illustration of the young men's failure to reach some degree of fulfilment in socially approved ways (e.g. job performance, family life and appropriate organized activities).

The perpetrators' selection of the victims is not incidental, as the film's depiction might lead one to believe. It is crucial for these young men's position within a society of compulsory heterosexuality. As Judith Butler writes: 'Heterosexual genders form themselves through the renunciation of the possibility of homosexuality.'[17] The assailants demonstrate that they have understood the code of compulsory heterosexuality and its rejection of other gender and sexual expression by using it for financial and social gain. The young men's expectations of heteromasculine behaviour also reorient the one accused man who had been called a 'mama's boy'. This perpetrator avoids exclusion by responding to the other men's code, what Ahmed has called 'enter[ing] the "contract" of the social bond'.[18]

The film's treatment of the inciting cause, namely violence against gender/sexual nonconformity, illustrates the queer's position as the archetypal cipher: the nonentity of no importance. Despite the attempts to find other causes, the case of H. and eight others is rooted in gender and sexual trouble – an omnipresent but veiled cipher. The underly-

The Queer Cipher in East German Documentary • 315

Figure 14.1. The judge extensively questions the accused, mediating information for both the legal case and the viewer in Richard Cohn-Vossen's *In Sachen H. und acht anderer* (1972). © DEFA-Stiftung/Christian Lehmann, Rudolf Schemmel

ing element of bias in the crime, namely the selection of targets based on gender or sexuality is a central structural component of this event. The vulnerability of a marginalized minority became an occasion for the crime in question. It was the targets' status as 'homosexuals' that prompted the hooligans to assault them in search of money they could steal. Here, one witnesses multiple simultaneous instances of enciphering and deciphering. Indeed, all aspects of the incident relate to codes of behaviour in one way or another: whether it is through the assault or the antisocial resistance to proper socialist life. However, the extreme nature of their enactment goes too far for the legal system, and the case is an instrument of reorienting them to a proper comprehension of both socialist living standards and anti-queer moderation.

Activists' Super 8 Films

Amateur and private films were beneficiaries of developing technology and changing social policy that enabled and encouraged more widespread use of still and motion picture cameras as well as other media technologies like audio recording. Laws promulgated in 1957 and 1976 regulated how film could be used in both the professional and amateur arenas.[19] Especially via the 1959 Bitterfeld conference, which launched the so-called Bitterfelder Weg (Bitterfeld Way) and set goals to expand the appeal of and representation in the arts, the state encouraged diverse voices to join the effort to update contemporary socialism by contributing to socialist art. An example of these efforts arose in the 1960s, when the monthly television programme *Greif zur Kamera, Kumpel!* (*Grab a Camera, Mate!*) offered advice and inspiration for amateur filmmakers. At least in part due to state sponsorship of equipment and supplies, exhibitions, prizes, hobby groups and workplace film production, and the influence this support fostered, much amateur filmmaking in the GDR was inclined towards the 'collectively organized and communally oriented'.[20] Indeed, in a way, the HIB's films, focusing on and oriented towards a group or collective, although with officially objectionable intentions for minority recognition, could be said to correspond to the regime's goals.[21]

One of the most noteworthy LGBTQ+ groups in East German history – alongside the 1980s association Lesben in der Kirche (Lesbians in the Church) – is the HIB. This group of lesbians and gay men (mostly the latter) first coalesced in 1972–73 and drafted a charter for the organization in 1975, a period that coincides with multiple important moments in queer GDR history.[22] The HIB had two primary functions: as a social and support network and as an activist and advocacy group.[23] The HIB practised its activism in several ways, usually trying to imagine LGBTQ+ people's integration into East German socialist society. In the late 1960s, queerness in the GDR had changed from a criminal to a medical and social concern, which affected how homosexuality entered public discourse and how public themes in turn appeared in queer artistic critique and humour. The 1970s was the era of Erich Honecker's 'no taboos' speech as well as an official wider redefinition of 'culture' to reflect depictions of a 'breadth and diversity of all possibilities' for fostering creativity.[24]

Among the HIB's archival artefacts are several Super 8 films gathered by Bodo Amelang, a telecommunications technician in the GDR and HIB member.[25] Amelang corresponded with official bodies in the GDR, like the Ministry of Justice and the People's Police, and periodicals like *Das Magazin* and *Wochenpost*, in addition to his involvement with the production of the Super 8 films, all of which feature his camerawork. Undated or dated variously in 1976 and 1977, the films range in length from one to twenty minutes and illustrate numerous parts of LGBTQ+ life in East Berlin, including various HIB activities. Several films depict HIB outings, like a 1976 spring excursion to the suburb Schmöckwitz and a late spring party in 1977. Other films parody the opportunities for queer people to gather in places like bars and gay men's use of public washrooms for sexual connections. The longest and most complex of the Super 8 films is director Michael Unger's *Auf der Suche nach dem Glück* (*In Search of Happiness*, 1977), a twenty-minute exploration of the unremarkable abnormality of queer lives in East Berlin comprising primarily excerpts from shorter Super 8 films. The HIB's campy film takes queerness, what had constituted the repurposed cipher in Cohn-Vossen's film, and uses it as a crucial means of community building, a code to be understood by the initiated.

Thinking communally but targeting a more private audience, the HIB's Super 8 films represent a clear voice in creative production that focuses on LGBTQ+ people. Moreover, these films confront the notions of public and private that policed queerness in the GDR and enforced the state's conservative morality – what had been partly responsible for the awkward avoidance of gender/sexual circumstances in *In Sachen H. und acht anderer*. Instead of positing queerness as a minor detail, the Super 8 films place queer experience at the forefront. Indeed, the camp sensibility demands attention. The films were not meant for consumption by the general GDR public; instead, they contributed to the organization's mission to act as a social and support network by speaking to like-minded viewers through a shared vocabulary and rhetorical style. In one of the few scholarly mentions of the films, historian Josie McLellan has written that they 'demonstrate how important style and humour were to [the HIB's] tactics'.[26] Amelang's voiceovers make use of restrained delivery, subtle irony and wit as they sometimes mimic public media or state-sponsored film while providing information and contributing to a unique portrayal of queer life, which also deftly satirizes the GDR regime and life in East Germany.[27] To illustrate the short films' method of foregrounding of queer experience and their contrast with *In Sachen H. und acht anderer*, I will discuss sequences from multiple HIB films, including the longer compilation film *Auf der Suche nach dem Glück*.

The HIB took its inspiration from a film directed by the West German filmmaker and activist Rosa von Praunheim that had done much for the LGBTQ+ movement in both the Federal Republic of Germany (FRG) and the GDR. Praunheim's film *Nicht der Homosexuelle ist pervers, sondern die Situation, in der er lebt* (*It Is Not the Homosexual That Is Perverse, But Rather the Society in Which He Lives*, 1971/72) had inspired the HIB by delivering a message about joint action and personal involvement, which were crucial for the future of queer liberation. The slogans at the end of the film ('Raus aus den Toiletten, rein in die Straßen. Freiheit für die Schwulen!', 'Out of the toilets! Into the streets! Freedom for gays!') – became programmatic for would-be LGBTQ+ activists in the FRG and the GDR.[28] *Nicht der Homosexuelle ist pervers, sondern die Situation, in der er lebt* focuses mostly on a fictional story and the ironic depiction of gay men's lifestyles as redolent of vapid, promiscuous insignificance. The conspicuousness of the recorded dialogue, which is dubbed and not synchronized with the film's action, underscores the importance of voice and narration, which it shares with the HIB films.

Auf der Suche nach dem Glück conveys the message that homosexuals are numerous, part of the diverse socialist community and sufficiently different to deserve separate attention, but not perversely abnormal. This is an elaborate film project, with many shooting locations, camera positions, edits and uses of (nondiegetic) sound, including voiceover and several additions of music. In its first few minutes, *Auf der Suche nach dem Glück* establishes its location in Berlin through static, panning and zoomed shots from and of Alexanderplatz, before the voiceover narration declares: 'This is the centre of Berlin, our Alex.' Footage of pedestrians, shoppers, passers-by and individuals lounging in the sunshine offers a tranquil overview of the people passing through this location. An orchestral soundtrack featuring piano and harp evokes serenity and wonder. The many people become the background for a central objective of the film as the voiceover continues to highlight queer experiences as part of East German experience itself. The voiceover declares:

> No one is concerned about what brings the many people to Alex and what they do there ... Who would know that every fifteenth person is a so-called homosexually inclined person. Homosexuals are a minority, but not so few that they could be ignored. However, almost no one knows anything about them. In public, they behave inconspicuously in order not to be conspicuous.

The various shots – including one extreme long shot of minuscule people taken from the television tower or the ground-level long shots of women and men walking or sitting – put the masses on display, implying that any of these individuals or pairs could be homosexuals.

The film self-consciously inserts itself into public discourses of gender and sexuality, deciphering details about queerness for an imagined broader audience. Following a sequence of on-screen text (title, crew and production details), these everyday scenes are accompanied by more exposition. The film will not delve into the origins of homosexuality, the narrator says – too many people do that already without sufficient experience or knowledge. Rather: 'The film would like to help provide information to dismantle prejudices. Prejudices create problems that we cannot solve alone.' The narration's overview makes clear that the film is carrying out an educational function while also delivering a critique of how gender, sexuality and homosexuality had been discussed in East German media. With its representational observations about the makeup of the queer community, *Auf der Suche nach dem Glück* also anticipates the project later assumed by the 1988 state-sponsored short documentary *Die andere Liebe* (*The Other Love*), directed by Axel Otten and Helmut Kißling.

Another section of *Auf der Suche nach dem Glück* focuses on public understandings of sexuality and gender nonconformity as they appear in magazines, newspapers and government correspondence. The film provides a succinct but effective demonstration of the workings of media and activism. This three-minute sequence is a selected summary of (mostly) public discussions of homosexuality or LGBTQ+ gender concerns. Showing an ongoing dialogue about sexuality that often occurred out of public view, examples from the *Wochenpost*, *Junge Welt*, *Das Magazin*, *Freie Welt* and *Für Dich* as well as correspondence from the Council of Ministers and the Ministry of Justice illustrate the multiple lines of communication surrounding these media stories. Close-ups, zooms and stop-motion animation concentrate on articles in these publications, one of Amelang's own letters to the editor, and letters received in response. Praunheim's film had influenced Amelang to write to *Junge Welt*, a daily newspaper, lauding the attention-grabbing demonstration of West Germany's openness and the ability to address a minority's problems.[29] The correspondence later inspired a positive article in the publication, according to the narration. Letters to and from media outlets show the efforts to adjust the perspective on sexuality and gender that was prevalent in public. Amelang's voiceovers give brief summaries of relevant points from the articles and offer ironic interpretations of the events. By making these articles the focus of attention, Amelang performs the opposite of what he finds in most media portrayals. Not only does queerness become a primary object of attention, but it also gains a positive treatment through Amelang's action and interaction with a media outlet. This example demonstrates both the effect of activism and the interactive, mutable nature of discourses of gender and sexuality.

The final example is a separate short film about three minutes long that is excerpted in *Auf der Suche nach dem Glück*. This longer version of the footage available in the archive '1. Mai: Wir sind dabei!' ('1 May: We're taking part!') places queer people directly at the centre of political and national symbolism. As its title suggests, '1 May' concentrates on festivities for the International Workers' Day in 1977 and HIB members' participation in the large-scale celebrations in Berlin. The first twenty seconds establish the location and subject of the film. "1 May" opens with a close shot of a 'Men' sign above a public washroom before zooming out and panning slightly to an extreme long shot of a loitering group of men and the on-screen text '1 May 1977'. As the film proceeds, the title 'We're taking part!' appears on the opposite side of the screen just before a cut to a medium-long shot of the group (Figure 14.2).

The short sequence has introduced several serious and ironic components that summarize the LGBTQ+ past and present. The 'Men' sign and the reference to the public washroom both show who will be the focus of the film (i.e. the queer 'men' of HIB) and draw the audience into the humorous tone that underlies most of the film by conjuring up a location of sex and social connections and a long-time hotspot of queer men's sexual activity. The shots of the gathered men have a dramatic effect too, as they set the stage for what will follow. As in other Amelang films (e.g. *Berliner Kneipen* [Berlin Bars, 1976]), the handheld long shot mimics observation and surveillance, while here showing the film's main characters in a kind of huddle that evokes conspiratorial thinking. The HIB participation in the festivities as a group performatively evinces the presence of queer people in the GDR – in this case limited to gay men – and had been previously explicitly disallowed. According to Peter Rausch, one of the HIB's founders who appears in the May Day film and assistant director of *Auf der Suche nach dem Glück*, in an effort to explain the male-centric display, a lesbian contingent was already active elsewhere.[30] The ordinary phrase 'We're taking part!' with the exclamation mark – which, in this case coupled with the establishing conspiratorial shot, exudes both incredulity and excitement – becomes extraordinary as it also labels the HIB's prohibited group participation in the parade.[31] Unlike Amelang's other short films, '1 May' has no added voiceovers. Instead, it resembles a propagandistic newsreel by combining visuals of the celebrations – including demonstrations, parades, a military procession, crowds milling about and the parade's review stand with Erich Honecker waving at the demonstrating masses – with spirited German and Russian music, beginning with dignified and serious brass instruments that accompany the 'Men' sign and then the huddling group.

The Queer Cipher in East German Documentary • 321

Figure 14.2. HIB members gather conspiratorially before their participation in the 1 May celebrations in Michael Unger's *Auf der Suche nach dem Glück* (*In Search of Happiness*, 1977).

Although they are but one example of the HIB's relationship to media, and it is impossible to address their full range in this article, the Super 8 films of 1976–77 are a remarkable example of LGBTQ+ efforts both to demonstrate their presence and to improve their position within the GDR. *Auf der Suche nach dem Glück* demonstrates creative engagement with the realities of public and private LGBTQ+ representation. Over its twenty minutes, the film's arc progresses from the prevalence of homosexuality to LGBTQ+ people's inability to integrate affection into their public lives, how LGBTQ+ people spend leisure time, and closing thoughts about the pervasive societal damage caused by prejudices. Using a variety of media samples, the HIB's Super 8 films illustrate both the seriousness of the HIB's political actions and the role cinematic media can play in the representation or revelation of the queer cipher. As Josie McLellan has observed, the year of the decriminalization of homosexual acts in the GDR (1968) did not mark a large turning point in LGBTQ+ people's self-understanding, queer activism or consciousness raising.[32] However, the HIB's filmic production is part of what McLellan called a 'revolution from below', in which progressive changes in social views of gender and sexuality 'happened from the bottom up'.[33] In this way, *Auf der Suche nach dem Glück* anticipated and heralded both activist work in the early 1980s and state-sponsored media discourses of the late 1980s.

Conclusion

The 1970s turned out to be both transformative and disappointing in the area of LGBTQ+ rights in the GDR. Although the primary antihomosexual law had recently been abolished, queer people still faced many obstacles in their public and private lives. Praunheim's film *Nicht der Homosexuelle ist pervers, sondern die Situation, in der er lebt* had galvanized LGBTQ+ people in the GDR, sparking demonstrations of activist fervour while encouraging greater group identification among queer women and men. That campy film encouraged viewers to think about the characters' (and their own) voices as they determined what they could use to improve their lives and political situation. The arrival of Praunheim's film coincided with the creation of *In Sachen H. und acht anderer*, which turns queerness into a means for examining a separate social problem. Then HIB members privately used Super 8 films to assert their presence in the GDR, illustrate their creativity and critique official misunderstandings of gender and sexuality that excluded them from society.

Earlier in this chapter, I invoked Sara Ahmed's theorization of 'use' and what it could reveal about the functions of queerness in GDR documentary films. How did the two films at the centre of analysis use queerness in their depictions of GDR life? *In Sachen H. und acht anderer* and *Auf der Suche nach dem Glück* share their deployment of a cipher in order to reach their objectives. The examples above illustrate that the queer cipher's characteristics and uses can and will change depending on whether they are being used to support or subvert conformity.

The films discussed in this chapter, both state-sponsored and private, show how the queer cipher can be used for the purposes of the norm or for queering the norm. Both films address themes of queerness and related concerns from divergent perspectives. On the one hand, *In Sachen H. und acht anderer* shows queerness to be a means of allowing a court and community members to find causes of social disintegration while ignoring an underlying form of it (anti-queer bias and violence). Although the film establishes the queer element as a cipher and non-entity, a queer-focused reading of the case turns it instead into a cautionary tale about modes of representation, outsiders' belonging and the possibilities of media. On the other hand, the Super 8 films, which are marvellous examples of queer media, shortly preceded the state-facilitated dismantling of the HIB. In these films, a world materializes in which the protagonists understand queerness and demonstrate how it can contribute to both to its own world making and the dominant, conventional society around it.

Kyle Frackman is Associate Professor of German and Nordic Studies at the University of British Columbia. His research is situated in nineteenth to twenty-first-century queer German media studies. His publications include *Classical Music in the German Democratic Republic. Production and Reception* (co-edited with Larson Powell, Camden House, 2015), *Gender and Sexuality in East German Film. Intimacy and Alienation* (co-edited with Faye Stewart, Camden House, 2018), *Coming Out* (Camden House, 2022), *Queer Temporality and Possibilities in German Studies*. Special issue of *Monatshefte* 114(3) (co-edited with Ervin Malakaj, 2022) and *Queer Time and Contemporary German Cinema*. Special issue of *The Germanic Review* 97(4) (co-edited with Ervin Malakaj, 2022).

Notes

1. Unless otherwise indicated, all translations from German are my own.
2. Sara Ahmed, *What's the Use? On the Uses of Use* (Durham, NC: Duke University Press, 2019), p. 6.
3. Ibid., pp. 26–29.
4. Ibid., p. 199.
5. Sara Ahmed, *The Promise of Happiness* (Durham, NC: Duke University Press, 2010), pp. 88–90.
6. 'Cipher | Cypher, n.', in *OED Online* (Oxford: Oxford University Press), https://www.oed.com/view/Entry/33155 (retrieved 17 May 2022).
7. Doris Zeilinger, 'Doctrine of the Ciphers Intercursions among Zeropoint-Utopia-Core', trans. Rainer E. Zimmermann, *Philosophies* 6(2) (2021), 44; https://doi.org/10.3390/philosophies6020044.
8. 'Cipher | Cypher, n.'.
9. Ibid.
10. 'Cipher', *Merriam-Webster.com Dictionary*, https://www.merriam-webster.com/dictionary/cipher (retrieved 17 May 2022).
11. Nick Hodgin, '"Only One Noble Topic Remained: The Workers." Sympathy, Subtlety and Subversion in East German Documentary Films', *Studies in Eastern European Cinema* 6(1) (2015), 49–63 (at 53).

12. Eric A. Stanley, *Atmospheres of Violence. Structuring Antagonism and the Trans/Queer Ungovernable* (Durham, NC: Duke University Press, 2021), p. 5.
13. Eduard Schreiber, 'Zeit der verpassten Möglichkeiten', in Günter Jordan and Ralf Schenk (eds), *Schwarzweiß und Farbe: DEFA-Dokumentarfilme 1946– 1992* (Berlin: Jovis, 1996), pp. 128–79 (pp. 137–38).
14. Birgit Wolf, *Sprache in der DDR: Ein Wörterbuch* (Berlin: De Gruyter, 2013), p. 12.
15. Jack Halberstam, *The Queer Art of Failure* (Durham, NC: Duke University Press, 2011), p. 3.
16. Ibid., p. 89.
17. Judith Butler, *The Psychic Life of Power. Theories in Subjection* (Stanford: Stanford University Press, 1997), p. 21.
18. Sara Ahmed, *The Cultural Politics of Emotion* (Edinburgh: Edinburgh University Press, 2004), pp. 106–7.
19. 'Verordnung über Lizenz- und Zulassungspflicht im Filmwesen', *Gesetzblatt der DDR*, 15 January 1976, p. 103.
20. John Lessard, 'Hypnagogic Mothers: Gender, Amateur Film Labor, and the Transmissive Materiality of the Maternal Body', in Kyle Frackman and Faye Stewart (eds), *Gender and Sexuality in East German Film: Intimacy and Alienation* (Rochester, NY: Camden House, 2018), pp. 22–41 (at p. 27).
21. Amateur filmmaking was officially intended to connect an individual to a group like a club or 'Filmzirkel'. See Ralf Forster, *Greif zur Kamera, gib der Freizeit einen Sinn: Amateurfilm in der DDR* (Munich: Edition Text + Kritik, 2018), p. 453.
22. Peter Rausch, 'Seinerzeit, in den 70ern', in Wolfram Setz (ed.), *Homosexualität in der DDR: Materialien und Meinungen* (Hamburg: Männerschwarm Verlag, 2006), pp. 153–60 (at pp. 153–54); Samuel Clowes Huneke, *States of Liberation: Gay Men between Dictatorship and Democracy in Cold War Germany* (Toronto: University of Toronto Press, 2022), p. 155.
23. Josie McLellan, *Love in the Time of Communism: Intimacy and Sexuality in the GDR* (Cambridge: Cambridge University Press, 2011), pp. 121–22.
24. Erich Honecker, 'Zu aktuellen Fragen bei der Verwirklichung der Beschlüsse unseres VIII. Parteitages', *Neues Deutschland*, 18 December 1971; Kurt Hager, 'Zu Fragen der Kulturpolitik der SED', *Neues Deutschland*, 8 July 1972, p. 7; Regine Schiermeyer, *Greif zur Kamera, Kumpel! Die Geschichte der Betriebsfotogruppen in der DDR* (Berlin: Ch. Links Verlag, 2015), pp. 238–42. For more on these cultural developments and their relationship to queer cultural production, see Kyle Frackman, 'Homemade Pornography and the Proliferation of Queer Pleasure in East Germany', *Radical History Review* 142 (2022), 93–109.
25. See the biographical note in Kristine Schmidt and Schwules Museum, *Findbuch Bestand Bodo Amelang* (Schwules Museum, September 2013), p. 2 (= Schwules Museum Archive, Berlin: Bestand Bodo Amelang). Some of the films are published on YouTube on the channel hosted by the Sonn-

tags-Club e.V., a centre for LGBTIQ people in Berlin: https://www.youtube.com/c/SonntagsClubeVLGBTIQZentrumBerlin/featured (retrieved 20 March 2024).
26. Josie McLellan, 'Glad to Be Gay behind the Wall: Gay and Lesbian Activism in 1970s East Germany', *History Workshop Journal* 74(1) (2012), 105–30 (at 121).
27. Josie McLellan has also compared Amelang's voiceovers with those of Volker Eschke in Praunheim's film. See McLellan, 'Glad to Be Gay', 121.
28. Erik N. Jensen, 'The Pink Triangle and Political Consciousness: Gays, Lesbians, and the Memory of Nazi Persecution', *Journal of the History of Sexuality* 11(1) (2002), 319–49 (at 324).
29. Teresa Tammer, 'In engen Grenzen und über die Mauer: Selbstbilder und Selbstbehauptungsstrategien der Homosexuellen Interessengemeinschaft Berlin (HIB) 1973–1980', *Österreichische Zeitschrift für Geschichtswissenschaften* 29(2) (2018), 132–52 (at 143–44).
30. HIB participation in May Day activities in 1976 was monitored by the Ministry for State Security (Stasi) with at least one informer. See Marthias [sic!] Köster, 'Aktivitäten der Gruppe zum 1. Mai', 29 April 1976, 66 (= Schwules Museum Archive, Berlin, HIB, Nr. 1).
31. This exclamation had previously been used in West Germany by members of the Homosexual Action West-Berlin (HAW) to signal LGBTQ+ participation in leftist demonstrations (including May Day), not always to positive effect. See Elmar Kraushaar, '"Nebenwidersprüche": Die neue Linke und die Schwulenfrage in der Bundesrepublik der siebziger und achtziger Jahre', in Detlef Grumbach (ed.), *Die Linke und das Laster. Schwule Emanzipation und linke Vorurteile* (Hamburg: MännerschwarmSkript-Verlag, 1995), pp. 142–78 (at p. 149).
32. McLellan, 'Glad to Be Gay', 107.
33. McLellan, *Love in the Time of Communism*, p. 9.

Select Bibliography

Frackman, Kyle. 'Homemade Pornography and the Proliferation of Queer Pleasure in East Germany', *Radical History Review* 142 (2022), 93–109.
Huneke, Samuel Clowes. *States of Liberation: Gay Men between Dictatorship and Democracy in Cold War Germany*. Toronto: University of Toronto Press, 2022.
Hodgin, Nick. '"Only One Noble Topic Remained: The Workers". Sympathy, Subtlety and Subversion in East German Documentary Films', *Studies in Eastern European Cinema* 6(1) (2015), 49–63.
Lessard, John. 'Hypnagogic Mothers: Gender, Amateur Film Labor, and the Transmissive Materiality of the Maternal Body', in Kyle Frackman and Faye

Stewart (eds), *Gender and Sexuality in East German Film: Intimacy and Alienation* (Rochester, NY: Camden House, 2018), pp. 22–41.

McLellan, Josie. *Love in the Time of Communism: Intimacy and Sexuality in the GDR*. Cambridge: Cambridge University Press, 2011.

Rausch, Peter. 'Seinerzeit, in den 70ern', in Wolfram Setz (ed.), *Homosexualität in der DDR: Materialien und Meinungen*. Hamburg: Männerschwarm Verlag, 2006, pp. 153–60.

Wolf, Birgit. *Sprache in der DDR: Ein Wörterbuch* (Berlin: De Gruyter, 2013).

PART V
The Presence of the Past: Reconstructing the Socialist Imaginary

CHAPTER 15

The Socialist City and Utopian Temporality in Halle-Neustadt Documentaries

Stephan Ehrig

Aufbau (construction) was a key term in the political lexicon of the German Democratic Republic (GDR) during the first two decades of its existence, and one that signified both the rebuilding of war-damaged cities and towns as well as the creation of a socialist society in which the social and the spatial forming were intricately linked. Architectural symbolism and semantics are ubiquitous in the discourse of the *Aufbau* years of the 1940s and 1950s. While the Free German Youth organization (FDJ) sang 'Bau auf, bau auf . . . für eine bessere Zukunft' (Let us build, let us build, for a better future), in 1951 Kurt Liebknecht, the then President of the GDR's newly inaugurated Building Academy, the Deutsche Bauakademie (DBA), stated that:

> The question of German architecture plays a significant role in the consciousness-raising of our people because architecture is the art of designing our cities and villages with the greatest societal effort in such a way that the . . . architectural ensembles and buildings embody the optimism of our social order.[1]

Thus, right from the start, architecture and planning were conceived as primary building blocks upon which to found the GDR's political self-conception.

It is not surprising, therefore, that the urban and industrial redevelopment of the GDR received enormous media and cultural attention that reflected not only party-political propaganda but critical voices as well. Documentary films and their textual counterpart, the reportage, played a pivotal role in documenting and commenting on this construction process, often exploiting both their text-image-hybridity and their transmediality by blurring the distinction between objective fact-based reporting and subjective storytelling.

In this chapter, I will investigate the different strategies employed by documentary films to establish the futuristic-utopian imaginary of the classless, socialist city during the construction of Halle-Neustadt. In contrast to the bias towards the contemporary in both fictional and nonfictional text-based responses to the socialist city, documentaries such as Wolfgang Bartsch's 1968 documentary *Gestern und die neue Stadt* (*Yesterday and the New City*), the TV documentaries *Der Mensch muss auch wohnen: Bilder über das Leben in Halle-Neustadt* (*People Must Have Homes, Too: Images of Life in Halle-Neustadt*, 1974) and *Halle-Neustadt – die Stadt der Chemiearbeiter* (*Halle-Neustadt – City of Chemical Workers*, 1975) propagated a pacifist, futuristic vision of an imagined socialist state that employed International Style modernist architecture and consumer goods to showcase its social and economic progressiveness both internally and externally. Accordingly, these films represent not only a general aesthetic shift from the grand socialist realist narratives of the Ulbricht era to the more subjective everyday perspectives under Honecker, mirroring social life, class structures, gender relations and individual political utopias, but also a temporal reconfiguration from futuristic ideals to contemporary everyday life perspectives.

Construction Site Documentaries and the 'Socialist Imaginary'

As Peter Zimmermann has shown, *Aufbau* films dominated documentary films in the 1940s and 1950s in an attempt to support the rebuilding of the country and the societal transformation towards socialism propagandistically. However, while in terms of sheer quantity, documentary films on these topics dominated the studio's output in this period, Zimmermann goes on to argue that the more critical and experimental tendencies in literature and film from the 1960s onwards make such films look increasingly outdated and misplaced.[2] Key examples of early *Aufbau* documentaries include Kurt Maetzig's *Berlin im Aufbau* (*Rebuilding Berlin*, 1946), Joop Huisken's *Potsdam baut auf* (*Rebuilding Potsdam*, 1946) or Andrew Thorndike and Karl Gass' *Der Weg nach oben. Der Film zum 1. Jahrestag der DDR* (*The Way Up*, 1950), which all feature rebuilding efforts out of the rubble and are delivered with triumphant voice-over narratives.

After the building of the Berlin Wall in 1961, documentary filmmakers were granted more liberties regarding their portrayal of work and everyday life scenes. The impact of the 'Bitterfelder Weg' (Bitterfeld Way) – a movement designed to encourage the involvement of ordinary members of the working classes to become actively involved in artistic production – and even more so the shift towards television broadcasting – which was seen as a significant medium in reaching the masses – marked a popular increase in documentary film. DEFA and TV documentary makers enjoyed significant freedoms by virtue of their permanent full-time contracts, which in turn meant that they had more time to research and plan, shoot, and edit than their mostly freelance colleagues in the Federal Republic of Germany (FRG), and cinematographers and editors often had significant creative influence on the finished product. All this is reflected in the films themselves, which benefited from the use of sophisticated camerawork and high-quality post-production facilities.[3] In a manner resembling that which Erhard Schütz has identified in East German reportage literature, some documentary films employ a 'specific mode of representation that oscillates between an accentuated objectivism of facts and a persuasive subjectivation' in the spectrum of media-specific formal elements.[4] In particular, documentaries focusing on new towns and construction sites of the 1950s and 1960s foreground the ideological and symbolic value of building for a socialist society, and many of them stage the construction site as the very embodiment of the utopian project itself, and as a spatial-cybernetic midwifery for the New Human.[5] As such, these films constitute a productive historical source for an exploration of what Maria Brosig has termed 'das Haus des Sozialismus' (the house of socialism),[6] a 'model metaphor for the GDR imagery' within what, following the philosopher Ernst Cassirer, might be termed a specific 'order of meaning' (Sinnordnung) and a 'semantic sub-realm' (Subsinnwelt) within the East German cultural imaginary.[7] Specifically, I want to read these films as mediators between the architectural and ideological masterplans on the one hand, and the different gendered, aesthetic and social meanings attached to the built environment by its various agents (architects, builders, residents, artists) on the other. In doing so, I seek to apply urban sociologist Martina Löw's dialogical concept of 'spacing', i.e. constructing, building or locating buildings and architecture, and so in this case, the architectural masterplan and architectural narrative of a new town and the material shape of that new town's built environment becomes the stimulus of critical assessment. Löw combines this concept of 'spacing' with what she terms 'operations of synthesis', i.e. processes of perceiving, imagining and remembering that built environment depending on specific context and defined by class, gender and milieu-specific schemes.[8] Applying this model to construction-site documentary films, I argue that they represent a way of making sense of the radical modernist restructuring of the built space in the GDR and its socialist imaginary[9] that encapsulates both the dialogical process between the ideological grand narratives of the futurist socialist utopia and the plurality of citizens and residents. At the same time, it adds a contemporary and often more critical perspective on the part of the user. Within the sociological epistemology of documentary filmmaking, the narrative techniques employed seek to capture the development of the new socialist societal experiment to document not only the status quo, but also the *quo vadis* of the utopian project.

From the late 1950s onwards, many documentaries placed a particular emphasis on the development of socialist new towns. The concept of building the socialist city was a highly symbolic aspect of GDR nation building that combined two elements: on the one hand, the cultural trope of utopian and ideal cities/states that merged Marxist teleology with modernist planning principles, and fuelled the notion that political utopias could, quite literally, be built as symbolic space.[10] On the other hand, urban social development projects such as Ebenezer Howard's garden city, the regional planning and social housing experiments of the 1910s and the interwar years, and Clarence Perry's early twentieth-century model of the neighbourhood unit all contributed to the notion that the design of the built environment could make an impact on societal functions and social relations (an idea that was embraced by liberal, communist and fascist societies alike).[11] The international New Town movement of the 1960s represented the apotheosis of this concept, and modernist mass housing was on the point of becoming the most widespread architectural scheme of the twentieth century.[12] These new towns and large estates were conceived in a planning euphoria and in the context of an ideological and economic rivalry on both sides of the Iron Curtain that itself was inspired by a belief in the interconnection of vision and plannability and in the active role of the state.[13] In the GDR, modernism was embraced as socialist internationalism after 1955, when Khrushchev initiated the Soviet-wide order of industrialized building following Stalin's death, thereby ending a decade of architectural Socialist Realism.[14]

Planning was also one of the ideological foundations of the East German imaginary and perceived as a rational, egalitarian and teleological vision of a new spatial arrangement. In this teleological logic, state-socialist planning sought to transform society in its totality, to encompass and reshape all existing social systems. Accordingly, the overriding aim was to create a qualitatively better future – through *Vergesellschaftung* (socialization) – and to ensure that complete control was fully embedded into both the propagandistic plan and central planning, even if, in most cases, these goals were only partially realized.[15] As Peter Caldwell has noted, in state socialism the planning process primarily operates on both a mythical and a technical level.[16] While the aspiration for complete control of the entire societal system was a pretence that was never realized in practice, the myth of the planned technological transformation of the world in the name of a qualitatively better future and a qualitatively new human lay at the very heart of the socialist state's claim for legitimacy.

In line with the logic of teleological planning, the postwar internationalist imaginary conceived of these new cities as all-encompassing megastructures and as machines that quintessentially merged technological futurism, grandeur and power, egalitarian mass society and total rationalism.[17] Moreover, as Rosemary Wakeman notes, the idealized socialist city operated within a specific ideological framework: they were new because they were planned and 'therefore avoided the incoherency and bourgeois cosmopolitanism of the capitalist city'; they were linked to heavy industry, they would give workers the right to the city and its public realm, and they would represent the spatial site of a new socialist generation that would grow up in peace and happiness.[18]

Halle-Neustadt: The Socialist City

The four socialist new towns built in the GDR – Stalinstadt/Eisenhüttenstadt (1950), Hoyerswerda (1957), Halle-Neustadt (1964) and Marzahn-Hellersdorf (1977) as a new, self-sufficient district of Berlin – represent four evolving approaches to urbanism spanning several distinct eras. Each attempted to improve on the mistakes of the past. Halle-Neustadt (literally 'Halle new town') was constructed to serve as the socialist city of chemical workers (Sozialistische Stadt der Chemiearbeiter) for the Leuna and Buna chemical plants and was built to house 100,000 inhabitants to the west of the regional capital Halle. Designed to be a new type of ideal city that could easily be copied, it was a clear symbol of Walter Ulbricht's post-1961 ambitions to modernize the GDR on a grand scale and highlight the state's social and economic progress. Within the futurist mindset of the state's so-called scientific-technological revolution, the task of the former Bauhaus student and chief planner of Neustadt Richard Paulick was to 'combine economic efficiency, practicability and beauty in harmony', which in reality meant little more than lowering construction costs while at the same time improving urban quality. This was supposed to be achieved by concentrating the social infrastructure, high-density building, and the application of technical innovation in a designated city centre.[19] Construction started in 1964. At the ceremony for laying the cornerstone, the Party Secretary for Halle, Horst Sindermann, outlined the sociopolitical and urbanist aims as follows:

> For us, it is not only about brighter and more attractive flats where people feel at home. In the City of Chemical Workers, we want to create living conditions that provide its residents with quality free time, with the time and leisure for their intellectual and cultural development, and with a form of urban living that holds out the prospect of happiness for all. In this way, we endeavour to make the past disappear.[20]

Accordingly, Neustadt was propagated as the quintessential socialist new town championing the ahistoricality of modernist architecture as a revolutionary, antifascist tradition of building that reflected the needs of classless mass society, which could provide an answer both to the social question and the German-German ideological competition by improving the housing conditions of the working class.[21]

As showcased in all the photographs and documentary films on Neustadt, particular prominence was given to public art as a distinctive and colourful stimulus for social engagement, and art of this kind was regarded both as an identity marker for a socialist city as well as a counter to criticisms of monotony.[22] The artworks were designed to support the 'development of socialist personalities and to document the international role of the first socialist state of the German nation in a representative way', while the modernist spatial environment was designed to help 'spatially organise the socialist way of life, stimulate its further development and mirror the socialist image of humanity by means of architecture, creating an interdependency through which the people build the city and through which the city builds the people'.[23]

However, most of the planned landmark buildings such as the 'chemistry tower' and the concert hall were scrapped after Paulick retired in

1968, and, as Michael Ostheimer notes, many of the anthropological and cultural initiatives underpinning of the planning process were drastically changed in the early years to make way for more affordable construction. Such decisions were at odds with the central demands of communist anthropology and, instead, reduced the individual to an object within the masterplan.[24] As with so many of the GDR's political and social ambitions, instead of working towards their long-term implementation, the SED simply declared the socialist new towns – then and there – to be the embodiment of sociopolitical goals that, originally, were seen as distant goals in the future.

Sindermann's speech also reveals the initial highly futuristic aspect of Halle-Neustadt's tabula rasa experiment, for which he commissioned many reportages and documentary films that were supposed to capture the ideological sub-realm and imbue it with cultural meaning. Ostheimer sees the role of these texts and films as, on the one hand, compensating for the lack of technological and economic resources by adding a cultural layer in the form of an elevated mythopoetic; on the other hand, they genuinely fulfil a legitimizing synchronization of technological and social development by connecting both unequal spheres through storytelling and through a symbolism that suggests agency for the planners, builders and residents involved.[25] In the case of Halle, especially during the 1960s, these documentaries and reportages endeavoured to deliver both, but ultimately, they moved away from more propagandistic grand narratives and towards more empirically focused, polyphonic approaches.[26] In their introduction, the authors of the 1969 Neustadt reportage *Städte machen Leute* (*Cities Make the Man*) foreground their desire to look beyond conventional declarations of political intent:

> Halle-Neustadt, the most recent city in our republic, is supposed to be a socialist city, but what defines a city as socialist? ... It is impossible to imagine an urban construction project of this size, so dedicated to the specific needs of the working people, under different societal conditions. But – is that all there is to it? What makes a city a *socialist* city? ... The coexistence of human beings, the people themselves who dwell in this city, whose very lives form the today and tomorrow of this city. So, is Halle-Neustadt already something that can call itself a socialist city? ... Perhaps the city itself, its being and becoming, can give us the answer.[27]

This core quest for what really defines socialist life is reflected in both the more ideological and propagandistic works commissioned (which focus on fulfilling the city's aspirations) as well as the more sociologically minded, observational works (which monitor the status quo). While by definition, the reportages leave more space for the author's individual and subjective perspective with regard to the grand narrative of Marxist teleology, the documentaries explore their narrative in different media-specific approaches. Alongside the different films highlighting the local chemical plants in Leuna and Buna,[28] and the relation of modernist Neustadt to the medieval university city Halle on the other bank of the Saale River,[29] I focus on three productions in particular: Wolfgang Bartsch's *Gestern und die neue Stadt* (1968), *Der Mensch muss auch wohnen* (1974) and *Halle-Neustadt – die Stadt der Chemiearbeiter* (1975). All three stage a pacifist, futuristic vision of an imaginary socialist state whose internationalist architectural and consumerist style represents the GDR's progressive attitude in respect of social and economic affairs both at home and abroad. The documentary filmic techniques fulfil two central functions: in the Ulbricht era up until 1971, they contribute to the futuristic teleological utopia of the construction site; and after 1971, following Honecker's explicit focus on everyday life, they establish a contemporary sociological interest in, and polyphonic representation of, the growing city through its diverse users.

Aufbau: Spacing and Propaganda

The very title of Wolfgang Bartsch's *Gestern und die neue Stadt* frames Neustadt as a socialist postwar peace project rising from the ruins of fascism, in a similar vein to Sindermann's appeal to the city's futurist ahistoricality. As Emily Pugh has noted, socialist regimes often presented images of home, belonging and national identity via architecture, urban planning and design:

> [Using] representational architecture, such as model homes or cityscapes shown in propaganda films, authorities offered images of the prosperous present they had created and of the progressive future promised to those who lived under their leadership.[30]

In 1968, all these tropes are assembled in Bartsch's 25-minute film, produced for the DEFA documentary studio: a continuous voiceover narrates over stark black-and-white expressionist imagery of a kind similar to that in Gerald Große's photographs in the reportage *Städte machen Leute*. We see young families moving into their new homes, working mothers appreciating the childcare and shopping facilities within the housing complex, and children pondering their ideas about the city twenty years into the future, all of which presents an unambiguous vision of a caretaker state providing peace and social stability for the future. These images of everyday life and finished streetscapes are cut against scenes from the urban planning and construction process in a way that foregrounds the enormous effort undertaken for this showcase socialist city. Yet the enthusiastic male voiceover does not simply remain in the present and future: one scene presents the line manager of a chemical plant telling his apprentices his personal life story, encompassing key historical events between 1918 and 1945. Supported by historical footage, we see the inflation and poverty of the 1920s and 1930s, the heroic efforts of the German Communist Party (KPD) and finally the new town as an example of better and healthier living conditions in the GDR. In another sequence, the voiceover comments 'A new town, but not without history. For it has the histories of all those who move here and of all those who built it' – a statement the viewers are encouraged to accept as truth, since it is the voiceover narrator who delivers it and none of the protagonists get to voice their perspectives themselves. Neustadt's masterplan narrative, in short, is built on the memory of the struggle of the working class and is already delivering on changing society for the better in a bright socialist future, which is typical for propagandistic films of this sort.

However, the most symbolic image is a close-up of Robert Hilscher's sculptural fountain *Taubenflug* (*Doveflight*), the first work of public art to be erected in the initial phase of the housing complex completed in 1966. In the frame, the doves dynamically make their way upwards, against a backdrop of construction cranes and the rising tower blocks of the city. The message is clear: the unity of the modernist new town, together with advances in science, technology, social progress, art and pacifism, will lead the GDR into a glorious future. In 1984, the doves were even incorporated into the city's coat of arms, where they represent peace surrounded by a series of chemical symbols referencing the city's core industry.[31] With this imagery, Bartsch's film provides a distinct example of the more propagandistic *Aufbau* period under Ulbricht, where the nation-building narrative is combined with a strict teleological view of communism and is predicated on a radical concept of worker's rights and the legacy of the communist party with its clear antifascist mandate.

In a similar vein, the 1975 documentary *Halle-Neustadt – die Stadt der Chemiearbeiter*, produced in colour for the Ministry of Construction by the DEFA-Studio für Kurzfilme (DEFA Studio for Short Films) and written and directed by Kurt Barthel, presents Halle-Neustadt with a similar expository voiceover 'from above', but with a particular focus on the building and planning process and its protagonists. Set largely to organ music composed by another iconic representative of Halle – Georg Friedrich Händel – the 23-minute film explores why the new town is so important. Starting with historic Halle's architectural heritage representing the fortresses of feudalism (along with images of the Moritzburg and Giebichenstein castles) as well as its humanist legacy (Schinkel's main university building), Barthel's voiceover explains that, previously, industry provided the industrialists with villas and their workers with unhygienic tenements. The socialist city of Neustadt will rectify this historical injustice by providing equal comfort for the physical and mental fulfilment of all classes, especially the workers. Here too, much of the film is devoted to explaining the masterplan, the architectural concept of the city and its design, and presenting the key decision makers: Diana Lang, the first mayor of the city, leading a city council of which a third of the members are chemical plant workers, and discussing better living conditions and commissioning more public art. Seven years after Bartsch's film and with more buildings and infrastructure in use, the focus of the narrative slowly shifts from *Aufbau* to everyday life (*Alltag*), while at times employing an observational mode of fast cutting between street scenes filled with pedestrians and children in playgrounds on the one hand, and public artworks and murals on the other. As the voiceover explains, 'the face of a city is shaped three times: by the planners, who design it, the workers, who build it, and by citizens, who appropriate it' – a synthesis of architecture and art combined with the habitualizing routines and spatial appropriations of the city's inhabitants. Overall, Barthel's narration frames the city in the image of a giant *Wohnmaschine* (*unité d'habitation*) designed to keep the factories afloat and the workers happy and healthy. Yet, through its focus on the building, planning and administrative sphere of the city's aspirations and the inclusion of Barthel's voiceover narration, the film still largely operates within the *spacing* aspect of Neustadt's architectural logic and ambitions to demonstrate its origins as a propagandistic showcase for the state's successes.

Ankunft: Polyphonic Everyday Life

A third documentary, *Der Mensch muss auch wohnen – Bilder über das Leben in Halle-Neustadt*, was entrusted in 1974 to the regional television broadcaster, Studio Halle and overseen by the district politician Horst Sindermann. The 32-minute colour film was produced by a large collective[32] and is highly representative of Honecker's 1971 *Wohnungsbauprogramm* (housing programme) initiative, albeit clearly more invested in exploring the *Alltag* (everyday life) in the new town – a shift also triggered by Honecker both culturally and politically.

Despite being produced by a regional TV station, the film is much more ambitious both technically and in terms of its narrative structure. Using minimal expository voiceover, the film is structured around live interviews with different residents. The interviews are conducted in the residents' homes and are interspersed with observational footage focusing on minute details, capturing street scenes, children, couples and the producers' spatial impression mixed in with information from the interviews. This *dérive* style cinematography and editing creates a vibrant urban buzz through its fast cut combination of helicopter flights over the city – almost identical footage is used, albeit to a lesser effect in Barthel's *Stadt der Chemiearbeiter* – and shots depicting the busy street life at ground level (see Figure 15.1). Set to jazz, modern rock music and various pop songs, the film is loosely organized around three chapters dealing with three different protagonists in interview format.

Figure 15.1. Aerial shots highlighting the masterplan model view. *Der Mensch muss auch wohnen – Bilder über das Leben in Halle-Neustadt* (Wolfgang Bartsch, 1974). © DRA

The first, *Über eine große Familie* (*About a Large Family*), features an interview with the Braune family who have been living with their seven children in a three-bedroom apartment since 1973. Kurt works in the Buna plant while Karin works part time as a receptionist in Halle. They have been married for twelve years, but she still picks him up from the train every single day. Having moved from a large tenement flat, Karin admits that she did not like the new apartment at all and at first refused to move in, but despite the still limited size she appreciates the low rent and the warm running water in the bathroom for her children. While listening to Frank Schöbel's hit song 'Schreib es mir in den Sand' (1972) on the radio, the couple describes how the community in the building was very friendly to begin with, but then became more distanced when they learned about the couple's seven children. Having more than two children continued to be frowned upon and Karin feels stigmatized.

The second chapter, *Über eine Frau aus der Kaufhalle* (*About a Woman in the Supermarket*), interviews Uschi Dröse, deputy manager of the largest supermarket with 104 staff, of whom only two are men, set to the German version of Abba's 'Waterloo' (1974). Asked about her impression of the people of Halle-Neustadt, she smiles and says: 'They are a little spoiled. They can do all their shopping in one place and for that reason have a lot of leisure time and time for their families.' A title card then displays the question: 'What is extraordinary about this city?' Here too, the voiceover frames the dialogue:

> At first sight, Neustadt looks pretty much like any other new development. However, an attentive observer will notice what the difference is: where else can you find an entire city made for just one industrial sector, where healthcare, educational, leisure and shopping facilities are built at the same time as residential buildings? . . . where can you find a city without chimneys, where every flat has a bathroom, where dark courtyards are unknown? In this city, time plays a vital role, especially free time. That is why every family has guaranteed childcare. That's why the commute is shortened by a new express train line. That's why all shopping facilities can be reached within minutes. Some impressive facts! Good conditions for good living. But what really matters is how people actually live here.

The concluding chapter, *Über die Leute vom Block 603* (*About the People from Block 603*), focuses on the community during a children's party hosted after a so-called 'subbotnik', the voluntary collective work effort that customarily took place on a Saturday. Herr Klöppel, head of the house administration of 261 residents is happy that most inhabitants took part, 'even if there are also those who wish to remain unattached'. Herr Fiebig, a student, is happy that he can easily afford the 87-mark rent for his two-bedroom flat on his scholarship. Frau Hoppe, one of the few grandmothers in Neustadt, is helping her children's family by taking care of a flower patch outside the house and claims to have adapted very easily to living in the city. Herr Kortyn works 12-hour shifts in Leuna and uses his free time for his garden allotment, which, he maintains, is all he needs to make him happy. Herr Kiesel has just become father to his second child – the sixty-first on the block. The sequence closes with a group shot of all the residents of the block.

It is striking that, while clearly attempting to present Neustadt as a success story of the GDR's socialist experiment, here the expository mode of the ideological masterplan that is used as a framing device in the two other documentaries recedes into the background; instead, the filmmakers are more concerned with presenting a genuine interaction with the newly arrived residents and to explore how they perceive and appropriate the new city. As Pugh has argued, during the 1970s, filmmakers had a particular interest in the relationships between place and community and – like many architects at the time – focused on daily life in prefabricated developments in order to explore how best to build a community and represent identity. Considering the day-to-day lives of residents was also seen as a way of confronting the 'problem of monotony' in these buildings and developing methods to counteract it.[33]

However, the most striking feature of the documentary is not the inclusion of interviews, but rather the two-minute sequence[34] that follows the first interview and that perfectly encapsulates the dynamic between the masterplan narrative (and residents' perception of the city) on the one hand, and Löw's 'spacing' and 'operations of synthesis' on the other. Through a series of fast cuts set to dissonant electronic-organ tunes, the camera engages in what the viewer experiences as a nauseating play of images featuring the endless uniformity and oversized proportions of the buildings' facades in accelerated speed. Juxtaposed with drive-through and flyover shots that highlight the masterplan models of the architects, the film seeks to convey the sheer enormity of an endeavour that is not only awe-inspiring but also symptomatic of the modernist monotony of such developments. Once the dissonant tunes and accelerated editing has reached a climax, the sequence ends with a title card asking 'Why does this city exist and who is it for?', before cutting to ground-level shots of people sunbathing on the lawns set to relaxed guitar music. This, in turn, is intercut with close-up shots of the manifold displays of public art, murals and sculptures, creatively cross-cutting the shapes of mural mosaic sunflowers to birds eye views of the circular kindergarten architecture (see Figure 15.2).[35] The voice-over then provides its own answer to the question: the aim of the city is to solve the contradiction between the essentially backward living conditions of workers and the increasingly modern technology to be found in factories, and to propose a modern urban solution to the evolving demands of contemporary socialist industrialization.

Apart from privileging the residents' voices, there is also a clear shift in cinematography and editing. Peter Zimmermann has shown that, especially as a result of the international programming of the International Leipzig Documentary Festival, direct cinema, cinéma vérité and nouvelle vague became important influences for young documentary filmmakers. In particular, the unbiased camera observation and the use of an original soundtrack often comprising interviews with citizens made it possible to present an unfiltered social perspective 'from below' instead of an ideological voiceover articulating a propagandistic masterplan.[36] This stylistic shift was further supported by the technological progress of on-shoot sound recording which allowed the interviewees to express their opinions freely on location. *Der Mensch muss auch wohnen – Bilder über das Leben in Halle-Neustadt* showcases a strong sociological interest in the appropriation of the city and finds a playful – almost poetic – cinematographic and narrative form for it by combining (and mildly subverting) the logic of expository masterplan 'spacing' with images of art and everyday life. This is combined with interviews to bring about a visualized and narrativized 'operation of synthesis' – the residents attempt to make sense of, and attachment meaning to, their built environment. Aesthetically speaking, this in turn represents the larger process of self-questioning and identity formation of the residents' *Ankunft* (arrival) period in which they reflect on the extent to which the promises of the futuristic masterplan are actually coming to fruition in the here and now.[37]

Most notably, the approach here is strikingly similar to its sister project, the montage-style reportage *Städte machen Leute. Streifzüge durch eine neue Stadt* (*Cities Make People. Expeditions through a New Town*, 1969) by the collective involving Werner Bräunig, Peter Gosse, Jan Koplowitz and Hans-Jürgen Steinmann. Michael Ostheimer suggests that the collective's writings demonstrate a genuine desire for individual fulfilment within the futuristic temporality of what he describes as the utopian chronotopos in Halle-Neustadt, which, in stark contrast to the collective mentality of the state's planning totality, is only par-

Figure 15.2. Mural mosaic *Gaben der Völker* (*Gifts of the People*), designed by Martin Hadelich (1968) from *Der Mensch muss auch wohnen – Bilder über das Leben in Halle-Neustadt* (Wolfgang Bartsch, 1974). © DRA

tially framed.[38] It is this very contrast – between the state's spatial and social planning euphoria in the 1960s and the cultural concerns about creating a liveable environment for a diverse population – that is the primary issue for those writers and filmmakers observing the construction site.[39] *Der Mensch muss auch wohnen – Bilder über das Leben in Halle-Neustadt* juxtaposes the logic of the 'spacing' (the architectural masterplan imposed 'from above', its ideological societal aspirations, and futuristic *Aufbau* temporality) and the residents' and the filmmakers' 'operations of synthesis' (footage of pedestrian perspectives, street life, individual interviews and a contemporary *Ankunft* temporality). In so doing, the documentary proves that, to a significant extent, the city does work, but it also highlights the fact that the socialist experiment is itself also a construction site insofar as it requires an ongoing discussion 'from below' involving a diverse range of contributors. Together, the logic of spacing' and the 'operation of synthesis' make up the basic dichotomy of the GDR's ideological and cultural sub-realm of *Aufbau/Alltag*.

Aufbau Spacing and *Alltag* Synthesizing

All three films discussed above demonstrate that the utopian repertoire of ideas encapsulated in the building of Neustadt was subject to multiple mediations. Despite their different perspectives, all of the films seek to make sense of the reciprocal process of how the city shapes its people and is, in turn, shaped by them – a process that Erhard Schütz has described in the context of East German reportage literature as one of 'oscillating between the accented objectivism of facts and persuasive subjectivism'.[40] The cinematic and narrative framing, I have argued, should be understood as a process of cultural production that adds cultural meaning to an architectural and urbanist debate in a way that resembles what Löw, operating in a sociological paradigm, describes as 'spacing' and 'operations of synthesis'. Within the GDR's ideological sub-realm of *Aufbau*, these works, analogically, oscillate between the utopian and futuristic horizon of expectation and the contemporary real existing socialist horizon of experience in an attempt to synthesize it.

Der Mensch muss auch wohnen in particular goes to considerable lengths to mediate between, on the one hand, the architectural vision and ideological aspiration of the city, and on the other hand, a curiosity regarding the genuine experience of the city coupled with an epistemological interest in finding out whether the urbanist experiment (as a case study for the GDR's socialist project as a whole) is working. The shift from voiceover to interviews – from an expository 'top-down' master's voice to a more inclusive and diverse 'bottom-up' polyphony – represents a temporal shift between the futuristic, teleological *Aufbau* of the Ulbricht years, towards the contemporary-focused, *Ankunft* years in the early Honecker period of the 1970s and its focus on everyday life and individual responses. Like that in the cultural sector that includes both DEFA cinema and literary production, this shift also represents an attempt to bring two competing Marxist aesthetics in the GDR into dialogue with each other. On the one hand, we have a more doctrinaire concept of Marxist modernism that, in its most utopian version, not only envisaged a total reshaping of mass society on a global scale, but also provided the fertile soil of the ideological grand ideas of the twentieth century. This version of Marxism, favoured by Georg Lukács in particular, shaped an aesthetic that promoted Socialist Realism with its optimistic heroes, mass scenes and grand narrative arches, and is identifiable in the voiceover narration and impressive total shots of the construction site in all three documentaries.[41] On the other hand, the combination of these grand narratives with the polyphonic, multiperspectival experiences provided by interviews, *derive*-style street scenes and a focus on everyday life functions as an embodiment of the other major Marxist aesthetic movement in the GDR, namely the dialectical approach, theorized by Hans Mayer and championed by the likes of Anna Seghers, Christa Wolf and Brigitte Reimann,[42] that engages constructively and critically with the ideological masterplan through the inclusion of compelling subjective perspectives, coupled with a focus on the contradictions of everyday life. The synthesis attempted by *Der Mensch muss auch wohnen* reflects an aesthetic programme that seeks to combine the architectural grand vision with the plurality of individual experiences – at least insofar as this was permitted by the censorship apparatus. With its supposed 'objectivity', the medium of documentary film was able to capture this dialectic by depicting the lived experience of reality through an – at times – ambiguous form of societally critical engagement. All three documentaries discussed in this chapter demonstrate how documentaries served as a pragmatic – but often ambiguous – cinematic genre within the socialist imaginary of the GDR and one that engaged in a sociological questioning of both the status quo as well as the *quo vadis* of real existing socialism.

Stephan Ehrig is Lecturer in German at the University of Glasgow. His research focuses on interdisciplinary approaches to East German cultural production pre- and post-1990, as well as on nineteenth to twenty-first-century literature, theatre and film. He is the author of *Der dialektische Kleist* (Transcript, 2018) and is co-editor (with Marcel Thomas and David Zell) of *The GDR Today. New Interdisciplinary Approaches to East German History, Memory and Culture* (Peter Lang, 2018), *Exploring the Transnational Neighbourhood. Integration, Community, and Cohabitation* (with Britta C. Jung and Gad Schaffer, Leuven University Press, 2022) and *Entertaining German Culture. Contemporary Transnational Television and Film* (with Benjamin Schaper and Elizabeth Ward, Berghahn Books, 2023).

Notes

The work on this chapter was made possible due to research funding provided by the Irish Research Council under grant number GOIPD/2018/61.

1. Alexander Karrasch, *Die 'nationale Bautradition' denken. Architekturideologie und Sozialistischer Realismus in der DDR der Fünfziger Jahre* (Berlin: Gebr. Mann, 2015), p. 13. All translations in this chapter are my own.
2. Peter Zimmermann, *Dokumentarfilm in Deutschland. Von den Anfängen bis zur Gegenwart* (Bonn: bpb, 2022), p. 231.
3. Ibid.
4. Erhard Schütz, 'Rückblick auf die Reportage unter gelegentlicher Rücksicht auf Kisch, Kommunismus und DDR', *Non Fiktion. Arsenal der anderen Gattungen* 2 (2022), 13–38 (at 13–14). All translations are my own unless otherwise stated.
5. Peer Pasternak, *Zwischen Halle-Novgorod und Halle-New Town. Der Ideenhaushalt Halle-Neustadts* (Halle/Saale: Der Hallesche Graureiher/Institut für Soziologie, 2012), pp. 52–54.
6. Maria Brosig, 'Das "Haus des Sozialismus". Ästhetische Stellungnahmen im literarischen Feld der DDR anhand von Architektur und Städtebau', in Ute Wölfel (ed.), *Literarisches Feld DDR. Bedingungen und Formen literarischer Produktion in der DDR* (Würzburg: Königshausen & Neumann, 2005), pp. 75–88 (at p. 75).
7. Silke Steets, *Der sinnhafte Aufbau der gebauten Welt. Eine Architektursoziologie* (Berlin: Suhrkamp, 2015), p. 113.
8. Martina Löw, *The Sociology of Space* (New York: Palgrave Macmillan, 2018), pp. 134–36.
9. For my use of the term 'socialist imaginary', I draw on the work of Charles Taylor and Seán Allan's recent expansion thereof. As Allan has noted in his use of the socialist imaginary for DEFA, the concept lends itself to a wider exploration of East German political and aesthetic discourse that goes beyond closed academic and political circles. Accordingly, Allan uses the term 'socialist imaginary' to focus on the way in which ordinary people 'imagine' socialist society and seek to articulate this not in theoretical documents, but rather in terms of a set of images, stories, legends and other cultural products, including literature and film. See Seán Allan, *Screening Art: Modernist Aesthetics and the Socialist Imaginary in East German Cinema* (New York: Berghahn Books, 2019), p. 4.
10. Rosemary Wakeman, 'Was There an Ideal Socialist City? Socialist New Towns as Modern Dreamscapes', in Jeffry M. Diefendorf and Janet Ward (eds), *Transnationalism and the German City* (New York: Palgrave Macmillan, 2014), pp. 105–24 (at pp. 105–6).
11. Rosemary Wakeman, *Practicing Utopia. An Intellectual History of the New Town Movement* (Chicago: University of Chicago Press, 2016), pp. 20–46.

12. Florian Urban, *Tower and Slab. Histories of Global Mass Housing* (New York: Routledge, 2012), p. 1.
13. Lena Kuhl, 'Zwischen Planungseuphorie und Zukunftsverlust. Städtebau in Ost und West am Beispiel von Halle-Neustadt und Wulfen (1960–1983)', in Thomas Großbölting and Rüdiger Schmidt (eds), *Gedachte Stadt – Gebaute Stadt. Urbanität in der deutsch-deutschen Systemkonkurrenz 1945–1990* (Cologne: Böhlau, 2015), pp. 85–118 (at pp. 85–86).
14. Elmar Kossel, *Hermann Henselmann und die Moderne. Eine Studie zur Modernerezeption der DDR* (Königstein im Taunus: Langewiesche Nachfolger, 2007), p. 181.
15. Tobias Zervosen, *Architekten in der DDR. Realität und Selbstverständnis einer Profession* (Bielefeld: Transcript, 2016), p. 41.
16. Peter Caldwell, 'Plan als Legitimationsmittel, Planung als Problem: Die DDR als Beispiel staatssozialistischer Modernität', *Geschichte und Gesellschaft* 34(3) (2008), 360–74 (at 361).
17. Sonja Hnilica, *Der Glaube an das Große in der Architektur der Moderne. Großstrukturen der 1960er und 1970er Jahre* (Zurich: Park Books, 2018), pp. 5–49.
18. Wakeman, 'Was There an Ideal Socialist City?', pp. 105–6.
19. Kuhl, 'Zwischen Planungseuphorie und Zukunftsverlust', pp. 85–89.
20. Ibid., p. 90.
21. Michael Ostheimer, *Leseland. Chronotopographie der DDR- und Post-DDR-Literatur* (Göttingen: Wallstein, 2018), p. 116.
22. Frank-Peter Jäger, 'Den neuen Menschen in lichterfüllte Räume führen', in Hans Engels (ed.), *DDR-Architektur* (Munich: Prestel, 2019), p. 11. See also Thomas Flierl (ed.), *Bauhaus Shanghai Stalinallee Ha-Neu. Der Lebensweg des Architekten Richard Paulick 1903–1979* (Berlin: Lukas Verlag, 2020); Anja Jackes, *Halle-Neustadt und die Vision von Kunst und Leben: Eine Untersuchung zur Planung architekturbezogener Kunst* (Berlin: De Gruyter, 2021); Matthias Hunger, *Sozialistisches Wohnkonzept und Wohnungsbau in der DDR: Das Beispiel Halle-Neustadt* (Hamburg: Diplomica, 2000); Martin Maleschka (ed.), *Baubezogene Kunst DDR. Kunst im öffentlichen Raum 1950 bis 1990* (Berlin: DOM Publishers, 2019).
23. Quotes by Flierl und Henselmann from Jackes, *e-Neustadt und die Vision von Kunst und Leben*, p. 89.
24. Ostheimer, *Leseland*, p. 117.
25. Ibid., p. 118.
26. Reportages include: Jan Koplowitz's *Die Taktstraße. Geschichten aus einer neuen Stadt* (*The Assembly Line: Stories from a New City*, 1969) and the collective reportage *Städte machen Leute. Streifzüge durch eine neue Stadt* (*Cities Make People: Expeditions through a New City*, 1969) involving Werner Bräunig, Peter Gosse, Jan Koplowitz und Hans-Jürgen Steinmann. Literary works include Rainer Kirsch's *Heinrich Schlaghands Höllenfahrt* (*Heinrich Schlaghand's Descent into Hell*, 1973); Jan Koplowitz's novel *Die Sumpfhüh-*

ner (*The Swamp Hens*, 1979); Hans-Jürgen Steinmann's novel *Zwei Schritte vor dem Glück* (*Two Steps Short of Luck*, 1987); and Edith Bergner's children's book *Das Mädchen im roten Pullover* (*The Girl in the Red Jumper*, 1974).
27. Ostheimer, *Leseland*, p. 128.
28. *Werke in Deutschland* (*Factories in Germany*, dir. Karl Gass, 1954), *Der Sekretär* (*The Secretary*, dir. Jürgen Böttcher, 1967), *Die dritte Generation* (*The Third Generation*, dir. Heinz Müller, 1972), *Die Mamais* (*The Mamais*, dir. Jürgen Böttcher, 1974), *Freizeitkünstler* (*Leisure Artists*, dir. Regina Sommermeyer, 1982) and *Die Karbidfabrik* (*The Carbide Factory*, dir. Heinz Brinkmann, 1988).
29. *Halle – wie es war – und wie es ist* (*Halle – How It Was – and How It Is*, dir. Erwin Kreker, 1948), *Wenn wir schreiten Seit an Seit* (*When We March Side by Side*, dir. Götz Oelschlägel, 1958) and *Optimistische Reportage* (*Optimistic Reportage*, dir. Harry Hornig, 1962).
30. Emily Pugh, *Architecture, Identity, and Politics in Divided Berlin* (Pittsburgh: University of Pittsburgh Press, 2014), p. 10.
31. Pasternak, *Zwischen Halle-Novgorod und Halle-New Town*, p. 49.
32. The end credits name Elke Zonsarowa, Peter Heese, Günter Lefass, Christian Träger, Gerd Pielert, Marianne Höhn, Irina Nebelung, Olaf Böttcher, Jürgen Hiemer, Kurt Böwe, Katharina Weigel, Eberhard Teichgräber and Dieter Seidel, without distinguishing their roles in the production.
33. Pugh, *Architecture, Identity, and Politics in Divided Berlin*, p. 146.
34. https://youtu.be/86DpEgOunPg?t=711, at 11:52–14:03 (retrieved 26 May 2022).
35. For more details on public art in Neustadt, see J.R. Jenkins, *Picturing Socialism: Public Art and Design in East Germany* (London: Bloomsbury, 2021), p. 111. For a discussion of the symbolism of the sunflower and the circular buildings, see Stephan Ehrig, 'Circular Utopia(s): Alfred Wellm's *Morisco* and the Socialist City', in Michael G. Kelly and Mariano Paz (eds), *Forum for Modern Language Studies* 1 (2023), Special Issue: *Urban Utopics. Writing the City in the Light of Utopia*, 123–39.
36. Zimmermann, *Dokumentarfilm in Deutschland*, p. 233.
37. The period was named after Brigitte Reimann's socialist realist novel *Ankunft im Alltag* (*Arrival into the Everyday*, 1961).
38. Ostheimer, *Leseland*, pp. 120, 128.
39. Ibid.
40. Schütz, 'Rückblick auf die Reportage', 13.
41. See Bernhard Spies, 'Georg Lukács und der sozialistische Realismus der DDR', in Heinz Ludwig Arnold (ed.), *Literatur der DDR. Rückblicke* (Munich: Text + Kritik, 1991), pp. 34–44 (at p. 42).
42. Stephan Ehrig, *Der dialektische Kleist. Zur Rezeption Heinrich von Kleists in Literatur und Theater der DDR* (Bielefeld: Transcript, 2018), pp. 14–31; Clé-

ment Fradin and Bénédicte Terrisse (eds), Special Issue: *Hans Mayer*. Revue Germanique Internationale 33 (2021).

Select Bibliography

Flierl, Thomas (ed.). *Bauhaus Shanghai Stalinallee Ha-Neu. Der Lebensweg des Architekten Richard Paulick 1903–1979*. Berlin: Lukas Verlag, 2020.
Jackes, Anja. *Halle-Neustadt und die Vision von Kunst und Leben. Eine Untersuchung zur Planung architekturbezogener Kunst*. Berlin: De Gruyter, 2021.
Jenkins, J.R. *Picturing Socialism: Public Art and Design in East Germany*. London: Bloomsbury, 2021.
Karrasch, Alexander. *Die 'nationale Bautradition' denken. Architekturideologie und Sozialistischer Realismus in der DDR der Fünfziger Jahre*. Berlin: Gebr. Mann, 2015.
Kuhl, Lena. 'Zwischen Planungseuphorie und Zukunftsverlust. Städtebau in Ost und West am Beispiel von Halle-Neustadt und Wulfen (1960–1983)', in Thomas Großbölting and Rüdiger Schmidt (eds), *Gedachte Stadt – Gebaute Stadt. Urbanität in der deutsch-deutschen Systemkonkurrenz 1945–1990*. Cologne: Böhlau, 2015, pp. 85–118.
Pugh, Emily. *Architecture, Identity, and Politics in Divided Berlin*. Pittsburgh: University of Pittsburgh Press, 2014.
Wakeman, Rosemary. 'Was There an Ideal Socialist City? Socialist New Towns as Modern Dreamscapes', in Jeffry M. Diefendorf and Janet Ward (eds), *Transnationalism and the German City*. New York: Palgrave Macmillan, 2014, pp. 105–24.
Zervosen, Tobias. *Architekten in der DDR. Realität und Selbstverständnis einer Profession*. Bielefeld: Transcript, 2016.

CHAPTER 16

The Rubble of History
Searching for the German Past in a European Present in Andreas Voigt's Ostpreußenland (Tales of East Prussia, 1995) and Volker Koepp's Kalte Heimat (Cold Homeland, 1995)

Jason Doerre

In the mid-1990s, after a period of brief uncertainty following the collapse of the Soviet Union, the picture of the emerging new global order came into sharper focus. The Cold War constellation of global power was shaken, leaving the capitalist West in a position of dominance. Tectonic geopolitical shifts ushered in a reconceptualization of the post-Soviet world that brought with it new attitudes, visions, desires and questions. At that moment in time, the widespread enthusiasm surrounding the *Wende* had dwindled noticeably. Expressions of mass euphoria soon came to be replaced by more practical concerns regarding the social, cultural and economic future of the new federal states within a recently unified Germany, and by questions about how the former German Democratic Republic (GDR) would – and should – be remembered in the public imagination. This chapter focuses on two documentary films from 1995 – Volker Koepp's *Kalte Heimat* (*Cold Homeland: Life in Northern East Prussia*) and Andreas Voigt's *Ostpreußenland* (*Tales of East Prussia*) – and considers not only why two filmmakers who had grown up in the GDR would travel east to explore a bygone region of

German history, but also the significance of these films for a renegotiation of German cultural identity in the post-*Wende* period.

Both Koepp's *Kalte Heimat* and Voigt's *Ostpreußenland* document journeys that lead the DEFA-trained filmmakers east to a territory that was once a part of Germany. Similarly, both document the former region of East Prussia by exploring the landscape, people, history and present state of this territory that now belongs to Poland, Lithuania and Russia. Nevertheless, as this chapter will demonstrate, the two films have several distinguishing features that set them apart. While both seek to document how historical processes have affected the lives of people in the region, Koepp's *Kalte Heimat* is primarily interested in probing the history of the region in the longer term and contextualizing the traumas of both the Second World War and the Stalinist period in the wider historical landscape of the region. Voigt's *Ostpreußenland*, by contrast, focuses to a greater extent on the historical processes that contributed to the collapse of the Soviet Union and prompted yet another reshifting of borders and political alignment in the region. While *Kalte Heimat* presents a collage of personal stories that present the region as a site of shared suffering among a group of nationalities including Russians, Lithuanians, Poles and Germans, *Ostpreußenland* documents the challenges that the current inhabitants of the region face and offers a critique of the economic and political upheaval under the new geopolitical order.

Volker Koepp, Andreas Voigt and DEFA Documentary Film

The filmmaking of both Koepp and Voigt is inextricably connected to DEFA documentary cinema. Even though both of the film projects discussed in this chapter are situated in the post-DEFA era, they bear markings that connect them to the East German background of their directors. The observational, poetic and reflective aspects of these films have their stylistic roots in a tradition of DEFA documentary filmmaking that can be traced back to the so-called middle generation of DEFA documentarists such as Jürgen Böttcher, Winfried Junge and Volker Koepp. For Marc Silberman, the tone of this type of approach demonstrates a 'kind of friendly collegiality toward interview subjects'.[1] This particular style, with its distinct restraint in respect of its subjects, is clearly evident in Koepp's 'Wittstock films' (1975–97), a series of documentaries that tracked factory workers over more than two decades, and established the director's reputation for documentary projects that investigate the subject matter in the *longue durée*. The extended scope of Koepp's films – both in terms of temporality and geography – is also evident in his post-*Wende* projects, which largely focus on the formerly German *Ostgebiete* (eastern territories) such as Pomerania, Lithuania, Russia, Bukovina, the Baltic Sea and more.[2] This is most evident in his highly successful film of 1999, *Herr Zwilling und Frau Zuckermann* (*Mr Zwilling and Mrs Zuckermann*), which provides a memorable portrait of the Bukovina territory and its inhabitants, which was then followed by *Dieses Jahr in Czernowitz* (*This Year in Czernowitz*) in 2004. Despite their disparate settings, his whole collection of so-called landscape films can be seen as separate parts of a single long-term project that connects the German national past of these regions with their European present. Through these films, Koepp has become the unofficial documentarian of these territories and his work has played a role in how they are remembered and indeed made a key contribution to the discourse of memory in post-reunification Germany.[3]

Koepp's orientation eastwards is already evident in his formative years and he credits the poems of Johannes Bobrowski – and in particular *Sarmatische Zeit* (*The Land of Sarmatia*, 1961) – as a catalyst for his sustained interest with the eastern regions. Bobrowski's influence on Koepp's filmmaking is evident in his fascination with East European landscapes, history and mythology. Koepp would later make the film *Grüße aus Sarmatien* (*Greetings from Sarmatia*, 1973), a portrait of the poet's work and life, and he further pays tribute to him in *Kalte Heimat* by narrating some of Bobrowski's verses. This initial 'eastward turn' generated further interest in the history, geography and people of these regions that has become even more pronounced after the collapse of communism, for as he explains:

> After a short awakening to this region after 1989, and a certain interest for the history there, it is once again too painstaking for most people to see what went on behind the Iron Curtain and they once again prefer to travel to France or Italy.[4]

Unlike the short wave of interest after the collapse of communism, Koepp's preoccupation with the history, landscape and people of the region reflects a commitment on his part that is both personal and political.

There is a remarkable consistency to Koepp's basic approach to filmmaking that informs both his early work for DEFA on the 'Wittstock films' and his later postcommunist documentaries about Central and

Eastern Europe. Unlike many documentarists who continually seek out new topics and new subjects to explore, Koepp's approach is based on building a personal relationship with people and landscapes over extended periods of time. As the filmmaker and critic Grit Lemke notes:

> There emerged – and continues to emerge – a solid edifice of relationships at the heart of which the filmmaker is located. Specific constellations that disintegrate but which can form anew. The director always returns to places and people already visited. Whoever was the protagonist today, can be the interpreter tomorrow. Friendship in any case. Thus, it is not only an exceptional relationship to geographic space that develops over the years, but rather more than anything else a distinct cosmos. People have a place in it just like the landscape.[5]

These themes of temporality, landscape, relationships and change have underpinned Koepp's filmmaking for over five decades.

As a young filmmaker, Voigt had worked with both Koepp on the film *Haus und Hof* (*Poor Soil*, 1980) and with Winfried Junge on his *Golzow* project (1961–2007), and was heavily influenced by the KAG Dokument of the DEFA-Studio für Dokumentarfilme (DEFA-Studio for Documentary). Voigt recalls this group as representing the 'cream of GDR documentary film', which included notable DEFA documentary filmmakers such as Böttcher, Junge and Koepp.[6] All three were already established names in the world of East German documentary cinema when Voigt began his work with them, and their intimate style of documentary filmmaking bears a noticeable influence on his own work.[7]

Voigt is perhaps best known for chronicling historical ruptures and the profound impact these historical processes have on individuals.[8] It is tempting to attribute this particular interest on Voigt's part to the much-cited belatedness of Voigt's generation of DEFA filmmakers, whose careers took off just as the Eastern Bloc was about to implode. One of his most notable works from this era is *Leipzig im Herbst* (*Leipzig in the Fall*, 1989), which documents the Monday demonstrations that took place in 1989.[9] He followed this with another film in 1990 titled *Letztes Jahr Titanic* (*Last Year Titanic*), in which he constructs a picture of the *Wende* through the varying perspectives of different individuals. In 1992, Voigt widened his scope to include Germany's eastern border in his *Grenzland – Eine Reise* (*Borderland – A Journey*) that focused on the shared border and shared history of Germany and Poland.[10] Voigt is drawn, in particular, to times of uncertainty, which he captures with raw and impromptu scenes that lend his work a sense of authenticity. Locating Voigt's style of filmmaking within the traditions of DEFA documentary film, Reinhild Steingröver notes that while he shares many affinities with the directors of the KAG Dokument, his films also bear the markings of the youngest generation of DEFA filmmakers, as can be seen with 'his interest in the very personal experiences and dreams of his individual subjects'.[11]

Documenting the Past, Present and Future of a Region

East Prussia occupies a complex position in German history. On the one hand, there is the colonization of the region through the Teutonic Knights, the extermination of the original inhabitants, the Pruss, and the many years of German rule and oppression of non-German subjects. The prevailing *Ostpolitik* made East Prussia into something of a shifting signifier throughout the duration of the Cold War. In the early years after 1945, refugees from the so-called eastern territories (Ostgebiete) were often seen as a burden on the Federal Republic. Yet, as Tim Bergfelder has pointed out, the memory of East Prussia came to symbolize German suffering in the early Federal Republic not only because of its loss, but also because of the crimes perpetrated against German civilians.[12] However, the public discourse about this German suffering often overshadowed other forms of suffering, such as the persecution and deportation of non-Germans and Jews by National Socialists. Nevertheless, this does not represent the complete range of activities in the Federal Republic dedicated to the memory of East Prussia and other eastern territories. Some of the discourse about the *Ostgebiete* in the Federal Republic was of a more apolitical nostalgic nature that had more to do with maintaining the memory of these territories through cultivating old traditions such as collecting objects, sharing recipes, anthologizing songs and literature, and preserving dialects.

During the Cold War, the memory of East Prussia was a contested topic, but the city of Kaliningrad posed particular problems for cultural historians. Up to the late 1980s, the past of Königsberg and the future of Kaliningrad were taboo themes in Soviet media, and travel to the exclave by foreigners was heavily restricted. The initial transformation of Königsberg to Kaliningrad was a result of the Potsdam Agreement drawn up by the victorious Allies in 1945.[13] Through this settlement, the map of Central and Eastern Europe was officially altered, but the ensuing Cold War would do even more to transform the region. However, some in the Federal Republic never accepted the fait accompli of Germany's territorial losses following the Second World War and sought to restore those lands they believed rightfully belonged to Germany. Special interest groups in the Federal Republic, such as the Bund der Heimatvertriebenen und Entrechteten (BHE – All-German Bloc/League of Expellees and Deprived of Rights) that represented refugees and persons expelled from their eastern homeland, disputed the dictates of the Potsdam Agreement that prescribed Germany's postwar borders on the basis of a right of residence (*Heimatrecht*). The position of the BHE seems exaggerated today considering the geopolitical reality after 1945, but in the immediate postwar period, the BHE wielded considerable political influence over both the Christian Democratic Union (CDU) and the Social Democratic Party (SPD).

Since 1945, East Prussia, and especially its former capital Königsberg, can be seen as what the historians Etienne François and Hagen Schulze call an *Erinnerungsort* or place of remembrance, modelled after French historian Pierre Nora's concept of *lieux de mémoire*. Only in an abstract space, such as that of memory, can people, places, things and concepts be crystallized as markers in the collective memories of nations. These *Erinnerungsorte*, François and Schulze expound, can wax or wane in importance, taking on new symbolic weight in different time periods. In the German context, East Prussia is simultaneously a place of German culture, a site of German aggression, an object of loss after 1945 and a symbol of hope for a more peaceful and unified Europe in the 1990s.[14]

As borders began to shift again after 1989, ideas emerged.[15] Not until after the break-up of the Soviet Union was the international community made aware of the severely decrepit state of the region. Voigt explains that it was precisely this mystique that initially attracted him to his subject matter:

> East Prussia, especially the Kaliningrad area, the former German Königsberg, became an area that was closed off and which one could not go to in GDR times. We were simply curious what was to be found there.[16]

In the early 1990s, Kaliningrad was opened up to the world in the hope that it could attract Western investment that would revitalize the area. Despite these efforts, very little foreign investment ever materialized. Despite a flow of German tourism by Germans with familial connections to the area (*Heimattourismus*), the Kaliningrad region failed to attract sufficient investment for any kind of major redevelopment.[17]

With this in mind, it is understandable why two East German filmmakers would turn their attention to this region in the mid-1990s. Randall Halle has commented that the eastward turn in the filmmaking of both Voigt and Koepp is a continuation of what was instilled in them in the GDR.[18] There is little doubt that the directors' backgrounds account for their predilection for the East, but both of these films are also an attempt to document and take stock of the momentous historical changes that just occurred. Describing the general mood surrounding the events of the *Wende* in an interview, Voigt comments:

> There was the great sense of hope, a vision, a brief moment of collective human happiness: Now we will change the world and shape it as we have always wished it to be . . . This optimism disappears again quickly, but at that moment it was there.[19]

And disappear it did. Already by the early to mid-1990s, the cloud of euphoria surrounding reunification and Helmut Kohl's promise of flourishing landscapes (*blühende Landschaften*) in the former GDR began to fade, and the new reality of an economic depression set in. While Koepp and Voigt were fortunate enough to continue making films after the dissolution of DEFA, they were the exceptions in this respect. Koepp, reminiscing about the dissolution of DEFA, notes: 'It's not easy when something like DEFA collapses, but it was clear to me that a production studio with 700 people in Babelsberg and Berlin could not be rescued in that form.'[20] Moreover, the legacy of DEFA came under scrutiny and was dismissed by some who believed it should be consigned to history and ignored. It is conceivable that many saw this as an attempted erasure of East German culture at the time, and the question of what would be spared from the rubble of a collapsed political system was certainly on the minds of many. As Helen Hughes has pointed out, the reflexive aspect of Voigt's *Wende* films that not only document the overhaul of the political system, but also chart the end of DEFA. Accordingly, in her essay of 1996, Hughes asks the following question: 'The name DEFA has, indeed, to all intents and purposes disappeared, but has the tradition also been extinguished?'[21] Addressing that question, this chapter argues that DEFA documentary traditions have indeed continued in the post-DEFA era, and that this continuity is evident in both Koepp's *Kalte Heimat* and Voigt's *Ostpreußenland*.

Kalte Heimat and *Ostpreußenland*

In *Kalte Heimat*, it is evident that Koepp's conception of East Prussia is one that connects the landscape to the history of the region. Through the many long takes of East Prussia's winter landscape and the personal testimonies of his subjects, the film connects people and places, as well as pasts and presents, although it is primarily the past that is Koepp's focal point. As Peter Jansen notes: 'The depth of focus is not only one of place but also one of time. The focus is directed into the past, the past before the film.'[22] Cinematographer Thomas Plenert's long takes of landscapes, the Baltic Sea, the River Memel and wildlife are breathtaking in terms of capturing the natural beauty of the region, but also impart a sense of melancholy and desolation. The title itself refers to a common name that East Prussians used to describe the harshness their homeland regarding the region's isolation and cold winters. However, for Koepp, this harshness is equally applicable to the history of the region and the personal stories of the subjects interviewed. Already in the opening voiceover, Koepp introduces his conception of East Prussia. His distinct voice, while speaking over long shots and diegetic sounds such as the splashing of waves on the sea, has become one of the hallmarks of his post-DEFA films. In this example we see Plenert's beautiful shots of the Curonian Spit off the coast of present-day Lithuania, while Koepp narrates the history of the region:

> 800 years ago, the Pruss people lived between Lithuania and Poland . . . The Pruss gave the region its name – Prussia. Yet, the Old Prussian language was soon not to be found . . . What followed was a long history of wars and destruction, division, and displacement, which affects everyone in the area: the Pruss, the Poles and Lithuanians, the Russians, and the Germans.

As contextualized in the *longue durée* of Koepp's film, the expulsion of Germans from East Prussia at the end of the Second World War is just one chapter in a long regional history of tragedy and trauma. Plenert's photography of the shifting sand dunes of the Curonian Spit provides the perfect natural metaphor for an ever-changing history of the region and its peoples. By the same token, images of isolated buildings and snow-covered train tracks reflect a harsh natural environment in a region whose future is always uncertain (Figure 16.1).

The subjects interviewed in *Kalte Heimat* come from a wide variety of backgrounds and nationalities. These interviews present the former East Prussia as a transnational space of memory, which in turn raises the question of whether East Prussia can actually be regarded as German at all. Among the subjects interviewed are Russians, Lithuanians, Germans as well as one Jewish woman, all of whom have created some form of sense of home (*Heimat*) in this region. Koepp weaves all their personal histories together into one pastiche of collective suffering. The suffering alluded to includes wartime trauma, displacement, loss of homeland, separation from families as well as the natural, political and economic hardships of this region. Here: 'Koepp does not seek to define the terms

Figure 16.1. Cinematographer Thomas Plenert capturing a cold winter landscape in Volker Koepp's *Kalte Heimat* (1995) © Edition Salzgeber.

of belonging and displacement; rather, he shows us the way that people negotiate them.'[23] Suffering is the common denominator. While there is no doubt that the anguish experienced across the nationalities was immense, one must question the ethics of collapsing all these forms of suffering into a single all-encompassing narrative of trauma. However, what is more problematic is the minimal attention paid to German atrocities in the Second World War. There are glaringly few references to German guilt for the pervasive suffering endured. This is exemplified in an interview with an elderly woman named Bluma Timofeyevna, the only Jewish subject in the film. As a former teacher, she recounts being on a class trip with students in Leningrad when the Germans invaded the Soviet Union. As the city came under attack, she and her students endured enormous hardships including hunger and forced labour. She recalls her pupils asking: '"Why is Stalin fighting? Why are Stalin and Hitler fighting? What is the reason for this war? We are dying, but we do not know why?" I said, "Children, I don't know why myself".' Here, the cause of the war and the totality of suffering endured is equally attributed to the agency of both Stalin and Hitler. What is also perplexing is that in the interviews with this sole Jewish subject in the film, the Holocaust is rarely referenced. Regarding her Jewishness, she only mentions that she feels connected to the former region of East Prussia, where she was relocated after the war, and not to Israel.

Koepp's non-interventionist style with his subjects on the one hand lends those interviewed agency in telling their stories, which affords a sense of authenticity. On the other hand, the absence of direction leaves blindspots in the collective narrative. One exception to this comes with an ethnic German man from Ukraine who was forced to resettle in the region after the war. Sitting in the man's kitchen, Koepp asks: 'Whose fault was it that life was so hard during this century?' The man replies: 'Stalin. Everything was under his sickle [sic!]. He oppressed the Germans, Tatars. He did not even think you were a human.' At this point Koepp intervenes, asking: 'And Hitler?' The man concedes: 'For Hitler, it was the Jew.' He goes on to recount a scene that he witnessed near his former home in Ukraine where *Einsatzgruppen* shot down Jewish civilians near a mass grave that was already dug for them. Despite the centrality of the Second World War in the film, this is the single reference to the Holocaust. Often Stalin's postwar policies of forced removal and resettlement of people are underscored as the primary source of this suffering. At the end of this scene, characteristic of a Koepp documentary, the shot of the man in his kitchen lingers for some time in silence. Considering the historical weight of this topic, this scene imparts a sense of frustration that Koepp does not search deeper, leaving one to question if form here takes precedence over content.

Although German guilt is not fully accounted for, there is no dearth of German perspectives in the film, from the few East Prussian Germans who stayed after the war, to ethnic Germans from Russia who were relocated there as well as tourists from Germany. The East Prussians who remained in the region mostly intermarried with Russians, Poles and Lithuanians, and integrated into the Soviet system. Their Germanness is only identifiable by language, memories and some East Prussian customs, such as one woman who is interviewed while cooking the East Prussian specialty *Königsberger Klopse*. In conversations with these subjects, the primary source of suffering among them is the sense of loss in terms of family. Most of them were separated from loved ones who fled to Germany after the war or were relocated by the Soviets to Siberia. One East Prussian woman, who remained after the war, articulates at the same time a sense of sadness and regret for what happened to the region, but also a determination to come to terms with the course of her life. She demonstrates the possibilities of maintaining nostalgia for an East Prussian past, while understanding and accepting what happened. Standing in front of her childhood home, Koepp asks her how she feels being there. She tells him: 'I have already come to terms with the thought that it no longer belongs to my parents.' She admits that the first time she returned, it was hard for her to see what her family had lost, but now she comes back to reconnect with her fond memories. By including subjects such as this, *Kalte Heimat* offers an alternative perspective on this *Erinnerungsort*, as exemplified by this woman having worked through the personal trauma of the war that had separated her from her family fifty years earlier.

More troubling, however, are the perspectives of German tourists visiting the region. Some have returned out of a general sense of curiosity, such as the two men who simply wanted to see their childhood home again. Standing outside the house, Koepp asks them if they want the property back, to which they vigorously reply in unison: 'Not at all!' Instead, they are thankful for being allowed to look around. When the current homeowner is asked what she thinks about the Germans, she remarks: 'Nothing bad. They are just people, like us.' While the twentieth-century trauma and suffering in the region was largely a product of nationalism, this scene displays a sense of transnational understanding coupled with hope for the future. However, in other interviews with tourists, a thinly veiled sense of resentment is discernible. One such case is an elderly woman who shows Koepp and his crew her former residence in what was the city of Tilsit (now Sovetsk). She shows the film crew the rooms in which her children were born during the Second World War before they fled in 1944. Koepp asks her if former residents are bitter about what happened, to which she replies:

> There are various attitudes. They are all sad how shabby it looks. We left a nice, tidy city behind, and we are sad that everything is now so run-down. At first, it was the soldiers' hatred of the Germans that drove them to destroy everything. It was the hatred they had been taught to have.

While the woman concedes that the Germans 'didn't think very well of the Russians either', there is little acknowledgement of the burden of responsibility that Germans bear for what befell the region.

Koepp's post-DEFA documentaries about former German territories in Eastern Europe have met with a mixed reception. A reviewer for the *TAZ* daily newspaper has nothing but praise for the slow-paced, reflective nature of *Kalte Heimat*. She writes: '*Kalte Heimat* is a journey through time from a bustling, chrome-gleaming present to another present that has been declared as past – precise, gloomy, zombie-like.'[24]

Likewise, another reviewer for the *TAZ* praises Koepp's aloof presence in the film as well as its apolitical agenda. She draws attention to the fact that his commentary becomes sparser as the film goes on: 'So the film develops on its own and without any revanchism into an important document about a *Völkerwanderung*, exiles and tourists in search of the past.'[25] While these reviewers of *Kalte Heimat* seem to endorse both Koepp's characteristic trait of connecting the histories of regions to their landscapes, and his non-interventionist style of interviewing, others have taken issue with these features. Koepp's film *Kurische Nehrung* (*Curonian Spit*, 2001), a follow-up to *Kalte Heimat*, was received with a degree of opprobrium, and his project of documenting these territories was called into question. The film scholar Alexandra Ludewig writes:

> Koepp has been accused of having a revanchist and tainted perspective that mythologizes the 'good old days' . . . Consequently, some critics saw the logical audience for Koepp's film as being extreme right wing.[26]

While such charges may seem harsh, it is understandable that Koepp's romanticization of the East Prussian past and landscape, without ever adequately underscoring German guilt for the suffering inflicted, would attract such criticism.

Both stylistically and thematically, Voigt's *Ostpreußenland* has much in common with Koepp's *Kalte Heimat*: the long takes of landscapes, the restrained style of interviewing subjects, as well as a general interest in the history and culture of the region. However, rather than primarily orienting the present with the past, Voigt's subjects are more preoccupied with the present and future of the region. This is especially evident in the interviews with the younger subjects who articulate their hopes for the region in the new postcommunist era. Like Koepp, Voigt includes the German memory of East Prussia, but places more emphasis on its problematic aspects. Yet, the primary focus is on the recent historical shifts and the lingering questions regarding the memory of the recent Soviet past and the challenges the region faces in the new era.

Voigt's documentary is structured as a journey that connects the recent communist pasts of Germany and the region now situated in Poland, Lithuania and Russia, as well as their postcommunist presents. In the opening sequence, a close-up shows snow melting off the outstretched hand of the soldier statue atop the Soviet monument in Berlin's Tiergarten Park. A quick cut to the face of the statue presents the viewer with the morose face of a Soviet soldier from a low-angle position, who stands guard over the nearby burial place of some 2,000 Soviet soldiers who fell during the Battle of Berlin in 1945. A subsequent full shot shows the statue confined by scaffolding that resembles a cage. Before the monument stands a man saluting the monument by raising a beer can. He pays homage to the monument with a noticeable Slavic accent: 'Kamerad, du hast uns das Leben gerettet' (Comrade, you saved our lives). Then the director's voice from outside the frame: 'Was ist, bauen sie das ab, das Denkmal?' (What is happening, are they dismantling the monument?). The man responds: 'Die Menschen, alles vergessen sollen' (The people are supposed to forget everything). The sequence ends with a cut to the man walking away. This opening scene establishes a depressing tone with images that call to mind the conflicts between Germany and the Soviet Union in twentieth-century history.

This first sequence in Berlin transitions to a dilapidated cemetery in Poland. The headstones are nothing more than crumbling ruins, giving the impression of an archaeological site rather than a cemetery. A half-buried gravestone with an engraving in German stands as a metaphor for a past that has been buried by time. Voigt asks his subject, a young Polish boy, about this cemetery, to which he replies: 'I don't know . . . Maybe there used to be Germans here.' This scene reflects on what becomes of forgotten cultures – in this case the culture of old East Prussia. But given that it was filmed in 1995, these reflections seem to have acquired a new significance in respect to events surrounding the *Wende* and the drastic changes that had recently taken place throughout the Eastern Bloc.

Ostpreußenland offers a perspective on the economics of the post-communist world. While the collapse of communism was met by many with a sense of optimism, Voigt's film depicts the more sober reality of the mid-1990s. The systems of production in the region have changed, but it remains uncertain as to whether this will bring economic progress. The fading sense of optimism frequently surfaces in the interviews with Voigt's subjects. One such scene takes place in a fish cannery in the city of Mamonowo in Oblast Kaliningrad where Voigt interviews the female workers about their lives and their outlook for the future. The scene begins with the women at work, performing a kind of factory labour that appears antiquated for the 1990s. The workers reveal that they became shareholders in the company after the collapse of communism. However, the women seem less than enthused by this. When Voigt asks how it works to be a shareholder, one woman responds that they have no idea. Their lack of enthusiasm stems from the fact that they have not been paid for six months. When Voigt asks them how they can live without money, one replies acerbically: 'You have to ask the manager and those at the top.' It is clear that these are lives and livelihoods that were negatively impacted by the collapse of communism. The enticing prospect of being a 'shareholder' in one's workplace does not match the harsh economic reality that these women must endure under the new capitalist order.

This scene contrasts sharply with another in a factory that produces electrical cables for automobiles and electronics in Poland. The high-technology manufacturing being done here seems worlds apart from packing sardines in tin cans. The camera floats around the work floor, showing the more modern, yet sterile space of the factory. Most striking in this scene is that Voigt does not speak with any workers. Instead, the only individual given voice is a representative of the German-owned company. The suit and tie of this manager distinguish him from the uniformed workers in the background. Voigt asks what occasioned a large company like Volkswagen to move production to Poland. In the nomenclature of neoliberalism, the manager first clarifies that the factory is part of a 'joint venture' with Siemens, but that it is the inexpensive cost of labour that brought them there. A more important reason, he explains, is to acquire a market foothold there to sell products. The scene ends here abruptly without further questions from Voigt, as if to say that is all that one needs to know about such enterprises. The names 'Volkswagen' and 'Siemens' are immediately recognizable as a metonymy for West German capitalism. Strikingly, when explaining why they opened a factory in Poland, the manager does not bother with free-market platitudes about bringing employment and opportunity to the region; instead, he is astonishingly candid that the company's primary motive is profit.

While *Kalte Heimat* presents German tourism to East Prussia ambivalently, *Ostpreußenland* accentuates its darker side. This is evident in an interview with an older man, whom Voigt asks to sing a *Heimatlied*, a folk song from the place of his birth. Without hesitation, he recites the lyrics of a song about Poland that he had learned as a member of the Hitler Youth. He promptly states that any attempts to label this as racist or antagonistic are mistaken. Voigt immediately counters that it was the Germans who attacked Poland, only for his interlocutor to contradict him: 'That too is a myth. The Poles absolutely wanted a war with us. And when you read reliable history books, you know that it was our side that wanted the war the least.' This jarring exchange demonstrates how nostalgia for the East Prussian past is sometimes bound up with unreconstructed nationalist sentiment and reminds the viewer that the process of coming to terms with the past is still a work in progress. With little provocation, Voigt exposes the persistence of national socialist attitudes. Mentalities such as this also go some way towards explaining the concerns some Europeans had about German unification in 1990. Nevertheless, not all critics at the time recognized the critical thrust of Voigt's film. One reviewer accuses him of giving a 'poorly researched' and 'superficial' documentation of the region. Among other things, he expounds that the film does not, or at least not adequately, address the environmental threats to the region, nor does it go into enough detail about the growing social tensions in the region due to the influx of Russian Germans. However, his most serious point of contention is that the film fails to critically confront the activities of German organizations that are depicted.[27] While Voigt remains characteristically reserved in his interview style, this reviewer misses the point that much of the critical confrontation is to be found in the editing; much of the material included speaks for itself (Figure 16.2).

Figure 16.2. Single mother, farmer, and cinéaste in Andreas Voigt's *Ostpreußenland* (1995). Reproduced with permission of Andreas Voigt.

Among the locals in *Ostpreußenland*, there is a pervasive desire to get away – certainly, a theme familiar to filmmakers from the former GDR. One young woman talks about her desire to leave the region, but she has no answer as to how or where she would go. Despite the longing for something else, this region, and especially the exclave of Kaliningrad, remained an isolated entity. The pervasive feeling of isolation among the population is articulated by Voigt in numerous scenes that have to do with mobility. In one scene, Voigt visits a lonely railway station that is the first and last stop in Kaliningrad. The dilapidated, outdated infrastructure highlights the isolation of the exclave both in time and space. While seismic shifts had drastically altered the geopolitical landscape in Europe in the early 1990s, this region is frozen in another temporal plane, disconnected from the world at large, yet its future is beholden to the processes of globalization. Another widowed Russian woman in the film runs a farm and a cinema alone. In juxtaposing shots, she is seen cleaning out a cow barn manually and preparing a film print in a projection booth. She explains that many of the films she shows are love films. In their discussion, it becomes apparent that for this woman, cinema offers a form of escapism. This is understandable considering the isolation of the region, coupled with her multiple obligations as a single working mother. However, it becomes even more poignant later on in the film when she tells of other tragedies in her life involving domestic violence and death. Moments such as this in *Ostpreußenland* align with what one favourable critic describes as Voigt's interpersonal style:

> Andreas Voigt listened to them, portrays the private in long and quiet takes and in doing so produced an account about personal stories that makes clear how individuals must endure and live through 'great' political shifts.[28]

Conclusion

The common theme running through both *Kalte Heimat* and *Ostpreußenland* is the notion of an individual's helplessness vis-à-vis historical and political processes. This is evident in the reactions to rumours of even more changes concerning Germany and the former East Prussia that were underway. Even before 1989, discussions about Germany's borders had heated up and in the mid-1980s, a scandal enveloped the CDU after the then Chancellor Helmut Kohl failed to adequately distance himself from hardliners refusing to recognize the post-1945 borders. By the 1990s, there were widespread rumours about a possible repatriation of East Prussia.[29] In *Kalte Heimat*, when one construction worker in Kaliningrad is asked about the future of his city, he responds: 'It will unite with Germany. What else?' This scene encapsulates an historical moment during which a deep sense of uncertainty about the future pervaded. The relative indifference of the individual interviewed underscores his lack of agency. Still, one could argue that it is precisely this sense of uncertainty that, more than anything, connects the past, present and future of the region. Likewise, a group of Russian soldiers in Kaliningrad collecting bricks from a rubble pile left over from the war tell Voigt that things will get better. He asks them when, to which they sardonically reply: 'Soon. That's what they've been telling us this our entire lives.'

As DEFA filmmakers of the middle and last generations, respectively, the careers of Koepp and Voigt were impacted significantly by the *Wende* and the subsequent collapse of DEFA. The bleak portraits that *Kalte Heimat* and *Ostpreußenland* paint of individual helplessness in the face of such large-scale geopolitical processes also speak volumes as to what East Germans felt by the mid-1990s as the new postcommunist reality set in. Exploring a region that was once a part of Germany, but that experienced possibly an even greater degree of turbulent change was for the two former DEFA filmmakers a personal, reflective exercise. Despite the enumerable similarities in content and form that *Kalte Heimat* and *Ostpreußenland* share, they diverge in their treatment of the historical-political processes at hand. Koepp's fixation on the desolate landscape and history of the region in *Kalte Heimat* has resulted in it becoming almost an ersatz post-DEFA *Heimat* for his filmmaking. However, instead of confronting the political, Koepp's film presents the landscape and distant past in the style of a romanticized documentary. Voigt's *Ostpreußenland*, by contrast, delves deeper into the current sociopolitical issues and offers a telling critique of the new economic and political order. Although this was a particularly turbulent period for postcommunist societies, the multifaceted approach of both films hold out the possibility of reconciling the memory of a difficult past with an uncertain present, while looking towards a European future.

Jason Doerre is Senior Lecturer of German Studies at Trinity College. His research and teaching focus on German cultural history from the nineteenth century to the present, as well as film studies. He has published articles and chapters on a number of different topics, including Berlin in the late nineteenth century, silent films of the Weimar era, and (anti)war films.

Notes

1. Marc Silberman, 'Post-Wall Documentaries: New Images from a New Germany', *Cinema Journal* 33(2) (1994), 22–41 (at 31).

2. A few such titles that further explore eastern regions after *Kalte Heimat* include *Kurische Nehrung* (*Curonian Spit*, 2001), *Schattenland – Reise nach Masuren* (*Shadowland – Journey to Masuria*, 2004), *Pommerland* (*Our Pomerania*, 2005), *Memelland* (*Memel Territory*, 2008) and *In Sarmatien* (*In Sarmatia*, 2013).
 3. For more on Koepp, see Tim Bergfelder, 'Shadowlands: The Memory of the *Ostgebiete* in Contemporary German Film and Television', in Paul Cooke and Marc Silberman (eds), *Screening War: Perspectives on German Suffering* (Rochester, NY: Camden House, 2010), pp. 123–42.
 4. Volker Koepp, 'Erkundungen in Landschaften', interviewed by Ingrid Poss, in Ingrid Poss, Christiane Mückenberger and Anne Richter (eds), *Das Prinzip Neugier. DEFA-Dokumentarfilmer erzählen* (Berlin: Neues Leben, 2012), pp. 445–65 (at pp. 455–56).
 5. Grit Lemke, 'Kollektiv im Krokodil oder: Dokumentarfilm als Lebensform', in Grit Lemke (ed.), *Unter hohen Himmeln. Das Universum Volker Koepp. Gespräche und Reflexionen* (Berlin: DEFA-Stiftung, 2019), pp. 9–13 (at p. 10). All translations are mine, unless otherwise noted.
 6. Andreas Voigt, 'Geschichten aus dem kleinen Menschenleben', interview by Christiane Mückenberger, in Poss, Mückenberger and Richter, *Das Prinzip Neugier*, pp. 557–91 (at p. 562).
 7. Ibid., p. 563.
 8. Reinhild Steingröver, *Last Features: East German Cinema's Lost Generation* (Rochester, NY: Camden House, 2014), p. 174.
 9. See Helen Hughes, 'Documenting the Wende: The Films of Andreas Voigt', in Seán Allan and John Sandford (eds), *DEFA. East German Cinema, 1946–1992* (New York: Berghahn Books, 1996), pp. 283–301.
10. For more about Voigt's film *Grenzland*, see Randall Halle, *The Europeanization of Cinema: Interzones and Imaginative Communities* (Champaign: University of Illinois Press, 2014), pp. 86–92.
11. Steingröver, *Last Features*, p. 176.
12. Bergfelder, 'Shadowlands', p. 124.
13. Potsdam Agreement, 2 August 1945, in Konrad Jarausch and Volker Gransow (eds), *Uniting Germany: Documents and Debates, 1944–1993*, trans. Allison Brown and Belinda Cooper (New York: Berghahn Books, 1994), p. 3.
14. Etienne François and Hagen Schulze (eds), 'Einleitung', in Etienne François and Hagen Schulze (eds), *Deutsche Erinnerungsorte*, vol. I (Munich: C.H. Beck, 2001), pp. 9–24 (at pp. 15–16).
15. See 'Moskau bot Verhandlungen über Ostpreußen an', *Der Spiegel*, 21 May 2010, https://www.spiegel.de/politik/deutschland/wiedervereinigung-moskau-bot-verhandlungen-ueber-ostpreussen-an-a-695928.html (retrieved 16 June 2023).
16. Voigt, 'Geschichten aus dem kleinen Menschenleben', p. 578.
17. Paul Rühl, 'Nicht einmal Grundbücher gibt es…: Was wird aus Kaliningrad?', *Osteuropa* 43(7) (1993), 358–59.

18. Halle, *The Europeanization of Cinema*, p. 86.
19. Voigt, 'Geschichten aus dem kleinen Menschenleben', p. 572.
20. Koepp, 'Erkundungen in Landschaften', p. 459.
21. Hughes, 'Documenting the Wende', p. 284.
22. Peter Jansen, 'Ostwärts', in Barbara Heinrich-Polte and Angelika Hölger (eds), *Volker Koepp. Menschen-Landschaften. Filme zwischen Wittstock und Czernowitz* (Berlin: Bundesarchiv-Filmarchiv, 2004), pp. 7–15 (at p. 11).
23. Halle, *The Europeanization of Cinema*, p. 96.
24. Anke Westphal, 'Es ist, wie es ist', *TAZ*, 11 February 1995, 13, https://taz.de/!1521062 (retrieved 16 June 2023).
25. Birgit Glombitza, 'Ohne Revanchismus', *TAZ*, 1 July 1996, 18, https://taz.de/Ohne-Revanchismus/!1449799 (retrieved 16 June 2023).
26. Alexandra Ludewig, 'Screening the East, Probing the Past: The Baltic Sea in Contemporary German Cinema', *German Politics and Society* 22(2) (2004), 27–48 (at 40).
27. Jürgen Burneleit, 'Historisch vergessene Region', *TAZ*, 22 December 1995, 24, https://taz.de/Historisch-vergessene-Region/!1479419 (retrieved 16 June 2023).
28. Thomas Plaichinger, 'Trachtengruppen im Regen', *TAZ*, 'Hamburger Kulturkalender', 1 August 1996, 1002, https://taz.de/Trachtengruppen-im-Regen/!1445086 (retrieved 18 June 2023).
29. For more on this, see the coverage in 'Königsberg für eine Hand voll Euro', *Der Spiegel*, 22 January 2001, https://www.spiegel.de/politik/deutschland/kaliningrad-koenigsberg-fuer-eine-hand-voll-euro-a-113527.html (retrieved 18 June 2023).

Select Bibliography

Bergfelder, Tim. 'Shadowlands: The Memory of the *Ostgebiete* in Contemporary German Film and Television', in Paul Cooke and Marc Silberman (eds), *Screening War: Perspectives on German Suffering*. Rochester, NY: Camden House, 2010, pp. 123–42.

Heinrich-Polte, Barbara, and Angelika Hölger (eds). *Volker Koepp. Menschen-Landschaften. Filme zwischen Wittstock und Czernowitz*. Berlin: Bundesarchiv-Filmarchiv, 2004.

Hughes, Helen. 'Andreas Voigt – Documenting the *Wende*', in Seán Allan and John Sandford (eds), *DEFA: East German Cinema, 1946–1992*. New York: Berghahn Books, 1999, pp. 283–301.

Lemke, Grit (ed.). *Unter hohen Himmeln. Das Universum Volker Koepp. Gespräche und Reflexionen*. Berlin: DEFA-Stiftung, 2019.

Ludewig, Alexandra. 'Screening the East, Probing the Past: The Baltic Sea in Contemporary German Cinema', *German Politics and Society* 22(2) (2004), 27–48.

Poss, Ingrid, Christiane Mückenberger and Anne Richter (eds). *Das Prinzip Neugier. DEFA-Dokumentarfilmer erzählen*. Berlin: Neues Leben, 2012.

Silberman, Marc. 'Post-Wall Documentaries: New Images from a New Germany', *Cinema Journal* 33(2) (1994), 22–41.

Filmography

35 Fotos – Blick ins Familienalbum (*35 Fotos – A Family Album*). Dir. Helke Misselwitz, DEFA Kinobox 39/1985.
Abschied von Afrika (*Farewell to Africa*). Dir. Ella Ensink, 1961.
Africa Addio. Dir. Gualtiero Jacopetti and Franco E. Prosperi, 1966.
Alltag eines Abenteuers (*The Daily Life of an Adventure*). Dir. Kurt Tetzlaff, 1977.
Aktfotographie, z.B. Gundula Schulze (*Nude Photography: The Case of Gundula Schulze*). Dir. Helke Misselwitz, 1983.
Apartheid – No! Dir. Günter Weschke, 1974.
Auf bald in Berlin (*See you in Berlin*). Dir. Kurt Tetzlaff, 1973.
Auf der Suche nach dem Glück (*In Search of Happiness*). Dir. Michael Unger, 1977.
Barfuß und ohne Hut (*Barefoot and without a Hat*). Dir. Jürgen Böttcher, 1964.
Beethoven. Dir. Max Jaap, 1954.
Begegnungen an der Trasse (*Encounters at the Line*). Dir. Kurt Tetzlaff, 1976.
Begegnungen der Freundschaft Libyen (*Meeting Friends – Libya*). Dir. Joachim Hadaschik, 1979.
Begegnungen der Freundschaft Mocambique (*Meeting Friends – People's Republic of Mozambique*). Dir. Joachim Hadaschik, 1979.
Begegnungen der Freundschaft Republik Sambia (*Meeting Friends – Republic of Zambia*). Dir. Joachim Hadaschik and Rolf Hempel, 1979.
Begegnungen der Freundschaft VR Angola (*Meeting Friends – People's Republic of Angola*). Dir. Rolf Hempel and Joachim Hadaschik, 1979.
Berlin heute (*Berlin Today*). Dir. Joachim Hadaschik, 1966.
Berlin im Aufbau (*Berlin Under Construction*). Dir. Kurt Maetzig, 1946.
Berlin – Die Sinfonie der Großstadt (*Berlin – Symphony of a City*). Dir. Walter Ruttmann, 1927.
Berliner Kneipen (*Berlin Bars*), Dir. Bodo Amelang, 1976.
Bertolt Brecht. Bild und Modell (*Bertolt Brecht. Image and Model*). Dir. Peter Voigt, 2006.
Bilder aus der Gießerei (*Images from the Foundry*). Dir. Andreas Voigt, DEFA Kinobox 37/1984.
Blutmai (*Bloody May Day*). Dir. Phil Jutzi, 1929.

Briefe – Gedenken an Dr. Maria Grollmuß; Listy (*Letters – In Memory of Dr. Maria Grollmuß; Listy*). Dir. Toni Bruk, 1985.
Bürgermeister Anna (*Mayor Anna*). Dir. Hans Müller, 1950.
Charlie und Co (*Charlie & Co*). Dir. Jürgen Böttcher, 1963.
Dämmerung – Ostberliner Bohème der 50er Jahre (*Dusk – East Berlin Bohemia in the 1950s*). Dir. Peter Voigt, 1993.
Das Gesetz heißt Glück (*The Law of Fortune*). Dir. Lotte Thiel, 1965.
Das Gesicht des neuen Afrika (*The Face of the New Africa*). Dir. Hans Dumke, 1960.
Das letzte Paradies (*The Last Paradise*). Dir. Hans Schomburgk, 1932.
Das russische Wunder (*The Russian Miracle*). Dir. Annelie Thorndike and Andrew Thorndike, 1959–63.
DDR-Magazin 13/1975 – Weltkongreß im Internationalen Jahr der Frau (*World Congress in the International Year of the Woman*). Dir. Barbara-Christa Enseleit, Joachim Hadaschik, Rolf Hempel, Alfons Machalz, Kurt Plickat and Heinz Sobiczewski.
Deep Throat. Dir. Gerard Damiano, 1972.
Der Auftrag (*The Mission*). Dir. Jochen Kraußer, 1983.
Der Dschungelkrieg (*The Jungle War*). Dir. Walter Heynowski and Gerhard Scheumann, 1983.
Der Fall Heusinger (*The Heusinger Case*). Dir. Joachim Hellwig, 1959.
Der Kinder wegen – Flucht ins Vaterland (*For the Sake of the Children – Escape to the Fatherland*). Dir. Winfried Junge, 1963.
Der goldene Strich. Bilder vom bürgerlichen Kunstbetrieb (*Gilded Whores. Pictures from the Bourgeois Art Business*). Dir. Peter Voigt, 1974.
Der lachende Mann (*The Laughing Man*). Dir. Walter Heynowski and Gerhard Scheumann, 1966.
Der schwarze Stern (*The Black Star*). Dir. Joachim Hellwig, 1965.
Der Sekretär (*The Secretary*). Dir. Jürgen Böttcher, 1967.
Der Weg nach oben: Chronik eines Aufstiegs (*The Way Up: Chronicle of an Ascent*). Dir. Andrew Thorndike and Karl Grass, 1950.
Der Zögling – Jawohl Brecht! (*The Apprentice – Yes Indeed, Brecht!*). Dir. Peter Voigt, 1998.
Deutschland – Endstation Ost (*Talking with Germans*). Dir. Frans Buyens, 1964.
Die Affäre Heyde-Sawade (*The Heyde-Sawade Affair*). Dir. Wolfgang Luderer, 1963.
Die Alliierten (*The Allies*). Dir. Joop Huisken, 1966.
Die andere Liebe (*The Other Love*). Dir. Axel Otten and Helmut Kißling, 1988.
Die Angkar (*The Angkar*). Dir. Walter Heynowski and Gerhard Scheumann, 1981.
Die Brücke von Caputh (*The Bridge of Caputh*). Dir. Eva Fritzsche, 1949.
Die Dreigroschenoper (*The Threepenny Opera*). Dir. Georg Wilhelm Pabst, 1930.
Die dritte Generation (*The Third Generation*). Dir. Heinz Müller, 1972.
Die erste Seite einer Chronik (*The First Page of a Chronicle*). Dir. Kurt Tetzlaff, 1961.

Die Karbidfabrik (The Carbide Factory). Dir. Heinz Brinkmann, 1988.
Die Mamais (The Mamais). Dir. Jürgen Böttcher, 1974.
Die Pflaumenbäume sind wohl abgehauen (The Plum Trees Have Surely Been Cut Down). Dir. Kurt Tetzlaff, 1978.
Dieses Jahr in Czernowitz (This Year in Czernowitz). Dir. Volker Koepp, 2003/2004.
Die Spur von meinen Erdentagen (The Trace of My Earthly Days). Dir. Lotte Thiel, 1968.
Die Teufelsinsel (The Devil's Island). Dir. Walter Heynowski and Gerhard Scheumann, 1976.
Die Wildnis stirbt (The Wilderness is Dying). Dir. Arnold Fanck and Hans Schomburgk, 1936.
Die Windrose (The Compass Rose). Dir. Joris Ivens, Alberto Cavalcanti, Sergey Gerasimov, Yannick Bellon, Gillo Pontecorvo and Alex Viany, 1957.
Die Wittkopfs – Eine Bauerfamilie in der DDR (Wittkopf – Farming Family). Dir. Rudi Hein, 1982.
Dorfkinder (Village Children). Dir. Heinz Müller, 1962.
Dort, wo die Sonne schnell versinkt (Where the Sun Sets Quickly). Dir. Konrad Herrmann, 1994.
Drei Briefe (Three Letters). Dir. Max Jaap, 1962.
Drei von vielen (Three of Many). Dir. Jürgen Böttcher, 1961/89.
Du bist min – Ein deutsches Tagebuch (You Are Mine – A German Diary). Dir. Annelie Thorndike and Andrew Thorndike, 1969.
Du und mancher Kamerad (The German Story). Dir. Annelie Thorndike and Andrew Thorndike, 1956.
Edeltraud D./Protokoll einer Erkundung (Edeltraud D./Protocol of an Exploration). Dir. Willi Urbanek, 1988.
Eine Lehrerin (A Teacher). Dir. Alfons Machalz, 1987.
Eine Delegierte (A Woman Delegate). Dir. Joachim Hadaschik, 1971.
Eine Hinterlassenschaft (A Legacy). Dir. Peter Voigt, 2004.
Eine Weiße unter Kannibalen (A White Person Among Cannibals). Dir. Hans Schomburgk, 1921.
Einheit SPD-KPD (Unity SPD-KPD). Dir. Kurt Maetzig, 1946.
Ein Tagebuch für Anne Frank (A Diary for Anne Frank). Dir. Joachim Hellwig, 1958.
Episches Theater (Epic Theatre). Dir. Peter Voigt, 2006.
Erinnerung an eine Landschaft – für Manuela (Memory of a Landscape – For Manuela). Dir. Kurt Tetzlaff, 1983.
Es genügt nicht 18 zu sein (Being 18 is not enough). Dir. Kurt Tetzlaff, 1964–1966.
Every Man for Himself (Jean-Luc Godard, 1980).
Etwas über die Lage der Genossenschaftsbauern (Something About Farmer Co-operators). Dir. Heinz Müller, 1973.
Exercises. Dir. Walter Heynowski and Gerhard Scheumann, 1981.
Familie Marx (The Marx Family). Dir. Helke Misselwitz, DEFA Kinobox 61/1988.
Feierabend (Leisure). Dir. Karl Gass, 1964.

Ferientage (*Holidays*). Dir. Winfried Junge, 1963.
Fliege, roter Schmetterling (*Fly, Red Butterfly*). Dir. Walter Heynowski and Gerhard Scheumann, 1980.
flüstern & SCHREIEN (*whisper & SHOUT*). Dir. Dieter Schumann, 1988.
Fotografien (*Photographs*). Dir. Peter Voigt, 1983.
Frauenschicksale (*Destinies of Women*). Dir. Slatan Dudow, 1952.
Freedom for Ghana. Dir. Sean Graham, 1957.
Freizeitkünstler (*Leisure Artists*). Dir. Regina Sommermeyer, 1982.
Für das Glück der Frauen und Familien (*For the Happiness of Women and Families*). Dir. Heinz Müller and Erwin Nippert, 1975.
Für das Selbstbestimmungsrecht der Völker (*For the Sake of National Self-Determination*). Dir. Frans Buyens, 1966.
Gabi – Vermittlung Platz 12 (*Gabi – Switchboard Position 12*). Dir. Uwe Belz, 1985.
Georg Friedrich Händel. Dir. Wernfried Hübel, 1960.
Gestern und die neue Stadt (*Yesterday and the New City*). Dir. Wolfgang Bartsch, 1968.
Globke heute (*Globke Today*). Dir. Walter Heynowski, 1963.
Grenzland – eine Reise (*Borderland – A Journey*). Dir. Andreas Voigt, 1992.
Grüße aus Maputo (*Greetings from Maputo*). Dir. Lisa Hadaschik and Joachim Hadaschik, 1979.
Grüße aus Sarmatien (*Greetings from Sarmatia*). Dir. Volker Koepp, 1973.
Guinea heute. Dir. Moussa Kémoko Diakité and Gerhard Jentsch, 1970.
Gulaschkanone (*Field Kitchen*). Dir. Inge Thieme, DEFA Kinobox 9/1982.
Halle-Neustadt – die Stadt der Chemiearbeiter (*Halle-Neustadt – City of Chemical Workers*). Dir. Kurt Barthel, 1975.
Halle – wie es war – und wie es ist (*Halle – How It Was – and How It Is*). Dir. Erwin Kreker, 1948.
Hangmen Also Die. Dir. Fritz Lang, 1943.
Häuser unterm Kreuz (*Houses Below the Cross*). Dir. Heinz Müller, 1966.
Haus und Hof (*Poor Soil*). Dir. Volker Koepp and Andreas Voigt, 1980.
Heim (*The Home*). Dir. Angelika Andrees, 1978/1989.
Herr Zwilling und Frau Zuckermann (*Mr. Zwilling and Mrs. Zuckermann*). Dir. Volker Koepp, 1998/1999.
Hier ist mein Platz (*This Is My Place*). Dir. M. J. Blochwitz, Armeefilmstudio, 1979.
Hinter den Fenstern (*Behind Closed Doors*). Dir. Petra Tschörtner, 1983.
Hirde Dyama. Dir. Moussa Kémoko Diakité and Gerhard Jentsch, 1971.
Hochwaldmärchen (*High Forest Fairy Tale*). Dir. Peter Rocha, 1987.
Ich bin meine eigene Frau (*I Am My Own Woman*). Dir. Rosa von Praunheim, 1992.
I'm a Negro. I'm an American – Paul Robeson. Dir. Kurt Tetzlaff, 1989.
Imbiß Spezial (*Snack Bar Special*). Dir. Thomas Heise, 1990.
Im Januar 1963 (*January 1963*). Dir. Kurt Tetzlaff, 1963.
Immer Bereit (*Always Prepared*). Dir. Kurt Maetzig and Feodor Pappe, 1950.
Im Pergamonmuseum (*In the Pergamon Museum*). Dir. Jürgen Böttcher, 1962.

In Sachen H. und acht anderer (*In the Matter of H. and Eight Others*). Dir. Richard Cohn-Vossen, 1972.
Institut der Freundschaft (*Academy of Friendship*). Dir. Heinz Fischer, 1964.
Jahrgang '45 (*Born in '45*). Dir. Jürgen Böttcher, 1966/90.
Jenseits von Klein Wanzleben (*Far from Klein Wanzleben*). Dir. Andreas Dresen, 1989.
Johann Sebastian Bach. Dir. Ernst Dahle, 1950.
Jubiläum einer Stadt – 750 Jahre Rostock (*A City's Anniversary – Rostock at 750 Years*). Dir. Winfried Junge, 1968.
Kalte Heimat – Leben im nördlichen Ostpreußen (*Cold Homeland – Life in Northern East Prussia*). Dir. Volker Koepp, 1994–1995.
Kampuchea – Sterben und Auferstehn (*Kampuchea – Death and Resurrection*). Dir. Walter Heynowski and Gerhard Scheumann, 1980.
Kommando 52 (*Commando 52*). Dir. Walter Heynowski, 1965.
Konzert im Freien (*A Place in Berlin*). Dir. Jürgen Böttcher, 2001.
Kreuzschnabellegende (*The Legend of the Crossbill*). Dir. Jochen Kraußer, DEFA Kinobox 8/1981.
Kuhle Wampe oder: Wem gehört die Welt? (*Kuhle Wampe Or Who Owns the World?*). Dir. Slatan Dudow, 1932.
Kurische Nehrung (*Curonian Spit*). Dir. Volker Koepp, 2001.
Le 17e parallèle (*The 17th Parallel*). Dir. Joris Ivens and Marceline Loridan-Ivens, 1968.
Le ciel, la terre (*The Threatening Sky*). Dir. Joris Ivens, 1966.
Leipzig im Herbst (*Leipzig in the Fall*). Dir. Andreas Voigt and Gerd Kroske, 1989.
Le joli mai (*The Lovely Month of May*). Dir. Chris Marker, 1963.
Le peuple et ses fusils (*The People and Their Guns*). Dir. Joris Ivens, Marceline Loridan-Ivens and Jean-Pierre Sergent, 1970.
Letztes aus der Da Da eR (*Last Things from the GDR*). Dir. Jörg Foth, 1990.
Letztes Jahr Titanic (*Last Year Titanic*). Dir. Andreas Voigt, 1990.
Loin du Vietnam (*Far from Vietnam*). Dir. Jean-Luc Godard, Joris Ivens, William Klein, Claude Lelouch, Chris Marker, Alain Resnais and Agnès Varda, 1967.
Liebe 2002 (*Love in the Year 2002*). Dir. Joachim Hellwig, 1972.
Lied der Ströme (*Song of the Rivers*). Dir. Joris Ivens, 1954.
Lok im Garten (*Locomotive in the Garden*). Dir. Jochen Kraußer, DEFA Kinobox 27/1983.
Looping. Dir. Kurt Tetzlaff, 1974.
Mädchen in Wittstock (*Girls in Wittstock*). Dir. Volker Koepp, 1975.
Made in GDR. Dir. Rudi Hein, 1981.
Mann mit Krokodil (*Man with Crocodile*). Dir. Andreas Voigt, DEFA Kinobox 34/1984.
Man with a Movie Camera. Dir. Dziga Vertov, 1929.
Meiers Nachlaß (*Meier's Estate*). Dir. by Walter Heynowski and Gerhard Scheumann, 1975.
Meiner ist bei den Soldaten (*My Boyfriend's a Soldier*). Dir. Heinz Killian, Armeefilmstudio, 1975.

Menschen am Sonntag (*People on Sunday*). Dir. Robert Siodmak and Edgar G. Ulmer, 1929.
Mondo Cane. Dir. Gualtiero Jacopetti, Paolo Cavara and Franco E. Prosperi, 1962.
Mord in Lwow (*Murder in Lwow*). Dir. Walter Heynowski, 1959.
Neugier und Bewährung (*Trying and Prevailing*). Dir. Dietmar Schürtz, Filmgruppe 82 (Armeefilmschau), 1988.
Nicht der Homosexuelle ist pervers, sondern die Situation, in der er lebt (*It Is Not the Homosexual That Is Perverse, But Rather the Society in Which He Lives*). Dir. Rosa von Praunheim, 1971/72.
Nuit et Brouillard (*Night and Fog*). Dir. Alain Resnais, 1955.
Ofenbauer (*Furnace Builders*). Dir. Jürgen Böttcher, 1962.
O.K. Dir. Walter Heynowski, 1965.
Optimistische Reportage (*Optimistic Reportage*). Dir. Harry Hornig, 1962.
Ostpreußenland (*Tales of East Prussia*). Dir. Andreas Voigt, 1995.
Piloten im Pyjama (*Pilots in Pyjamas*). Dir. Walter Heynowski and Gerhard Scheumann, 1967.
Plus und Minus (*Plus and Minus*). Dir. Werner Wüste, 1963.
Potsdam baut auf (*Rebuilding Potsdam*). Dir. Joop Huisken, 1946.
Quax in Afrika (*Quax in Africa*). Dir. Helmut Weiss, 1943–44.
Rencontre avec le président Hô Chi Minh (*Meeting with President Hô Chi Minh*). Dir. Joris Ivens, 1970.
Revanchismus in West-Berlin – Was wird aus West-Berlin? (*Revanchism in West-Berlin – What Will Become of West-Berlin?*). Dir. Dagobert Loewenberg, 1963.
Revolution einer Kultur (*Revolution of a Culture*). Dir. Heinz Müller, 1968.
Sans Soleil. Dir. Chris Marker, 1983.
Schiffshebewerk Niederfinow (*Shipyard Niederfinow*). Dir. Thomas Plenert, DEFA Kinobox. 32/1984.
Schlösser und Katen (*Castles and Cottages*). Dir. Kurt Maetzig, 1956.
Schmerzen der Lausitz (*The Pain of Lausatia*). Dir. Peter Rocha, 1990.
Shaft. Dir. Gordon Parks, 1971.
Sie, wie viele andere (*Portrait of a Woman*). Dir. Heinz Hafke, 1969.
Sokoł – P.S. ke kapitlej našich stawiznow / Sokol – P.S. zu einem Kapitel unserer Geschichte (*Sokoł – P.S. On a Chapter of Our History*). Dir. Toni Bruk, 1990.
Soldatenhochzeit (*A Soldier's Wedding*). Dir. Manfred Tzschaksch, Armeefilmstudio, 1964.
Sorge um Mutter und Kind (*Mother and Child*). Dir. Regina Thielmann, 1985.
Spur der Steine (*Trace of Stones*). Dir. Frank Beyer, 1966.
Staatsbesuch des Vorsitzenden des Staatsrates der Deutschen Demokratischen Republik, Erich Honecker in Mexico (*Honecker in Mexico*). Dir. Joachim Hadaschik, 1981.
Stahl (*Steel*). Dir. Joop Huisken, 1950.
Stars. Dir. Jürgen Böttcher, 1963.
TangoTraum (*Tango Dream*). Dir. Helke Misselwitz, 1985.
Theaterarbeit (*Theater Work*). Dir. Peter Voigt, 1975.

Tierparkfilm (*Tierpark Berlin*). Dir. Jürgen Böttcher, 1967–1968.
Todeslager Sachenshausen (*Sachsenhausen Death Camp*). Dir. Richard Brandt, 1946.
Todesmühlen (*Death Mills*). Dir. Hanuš Burger and Billy Wilder, 1945.
Tuba Wa Duo. Dir. Jörg Foth, 1989.
Turbine 1. Dir. Joop Huisken 1953.
Unsere alten Tage (*In Our Old Age*). Dir. Petra Tschörtner, 1989.
Unter der Sonne Ägyptens (*Under the Egyptian Sun*). Dir. Kurt Stanke 1956.
Unternehmen Teutonenschwert (*Operation Teutonic Sword*). Dir. Annelie Thorndike and Andrew Thorndike, 1958.
Urlaub auf Sylt (*Holiday on Sylt*). Dir. Annelie Thorndike and Andrew Thorndike, 1957.
Verriegelte Zeit (*Locked Up Time*). Dir. Sybille Schönemann, 1990.
Wäscherinnen (*Laundresses*). Dir. Jürgen Böttcher, 1972.
Wenn die Erde weiß vom Schnee (*Winter Sports in Oberhof*). Dir. Dieter Raue, 1986.
Wenn ich erst zur Schule geh'... (*When I go to School*). Dir. Winfried Junge, 1961.
Wenn wir schreiten Seit an Seit (*When We March Side by Side*). Dir. Götz Oelschlägel, 1958.
Wer fürchtet sich vorm schwarzen Mann (*Who's Afraid of the Bogeyman*). Dir. Helke Misselwitz, 1989.
Werke in Deutschland (*Factories in Germany*). Dir. Karl Gass, 1954.
Wieder in Wittstock (*Wittstock Once Again*). Dir. Volker Koepp, 1976.
Wer – wenn nicht wir (*Who – If Not Us*). Dir. Kurt Tetzlaff, 1971.
Wildbahn Afrika (*Hunting Ground Africa*). Dir. Hans Kubisch, 1956.
Winter Adé (*After Winter Comes Spring*). Dir. Helke Misselwitz, 1988.
Wir von ESDA (*Working for ESDA*). Dir. Gitta Nickel, 1976.
Wunschkinder (*Wanted Children*). Dir. Peter Petersen, 1981.
Zeitprobleme. Wie der Berliner Arbeiter wohnt (*Problems of our time. How the Berlin Worker Lives*). Dir. Slatan Dudow, 1929.
Zeltplatzgeschichten (*Camping Stories*). Dir. Konrad Weiss, DEFA Kinobox 15/1982.
Zu Hause in Schulzendorf (*Youth on the Land*). Dir. Regina Thielmann, 1984.

Index

1. Mai: Wir sind dabei! (1 May: We're taking part!), 320
  See also Auf der Suche nach dem Glück, 25, 236
35 Fotos – Blick ins Familienalbum (35 Fotos – A Family Album), 87
'61 Pontiac [artwork], 141

Abschied von Afrika (Farewell to Africa), 241–56
  colonial gaze, 246–48
  See also Black abjection; Black bodies, representation of
Adenauer, Konrad, 10, 266
Africa Addio, 254
African cinema, 25, 223–26, 236–37
Afrika 1979. See Begegnungen der Freundschaft
agra film studio, 182
Airstream [painting], 141
Akademie der Künste, 81, 283n15
Aktfotografie [print collection], 158
Aktfotografie, z.B. Gundula Schulze (Nude Photography: The Case of Gundula Schulze), 157–60
  nude photography, 157–59
alcoholism (in the GDR), 167–69, 174n17, 175n18
All Quiet in the Western Front [novel], 103
Alltag eines Abenteuers (The Daily Life of an Adventure), 126, 130–32
amateur filmmaking, 288, 308–9, 315–16, 324n21
Amelang, Bodo, 316–17, 319–20
Andrees, Angelika, 157, 160, 166–70, 172, 174n14
antisocial behaviour (in the GDR), 313–14

Apartheid, 244, 246–48, 255–59
  in East German film, 241–59
  Crime of Apartheid Convention, 255
  UN Special Committee on Apartheid, 255, 257–58
Apartheid – No!, 241–42, 247, 254–59
  and East Berlin, 257–58
  maps, 255
Apted, Michael, 19
Architecture, 329, 332, 334, 336–38, 341–45
Archive sagen aus, 9, 97–98, 103, 282n13
Arden Anderson and Nora Murphy [artwork], 141
Armeefilmschau, 288–89, 291–96
Armeefilmstudio (AFS), 2, 288–92, 294, 296, 298–99, 301–2
Auf bald in Berlin (See You in Berlin), 126
Auf der Suche nach dem Glück (In Search of Happiness), 317–22
  narration, 318
  use of documents, 319
Aufbau
  concept of, 329, 344
  in East German film, 8, 54, 330–32, 336–45, 348n28, 348n29
  symbolism, 329, 331–32, 343
  trope of, 5
Auslandsinformation, 53, 55–60, 63–69
  See also German Democratic Republic: soft power
Axen, Hermann, 258

Badel, Peter, 81–83
Barfuß und ohne Hut (Barefoot and without a Hat), 16
Barke, Lothar, 140

Barthel, Kurt, 338–39
Barthel, Erich, 179
Barthes, Roland, 205
Bartsch, Wolfgang, 330, 336–38
Baumert, Heinz, 36, 41, 47
Bechtle, Robert, 142
Beethoven [film], 7
Begegnungen an der Trasse (*Encounters at the Line*), 126, 128–30
  masculinity, 129–30
Begegnung der Freundschaft (*Meeting Friends*), 71n23
Behrend, Dieter, 294
Belz, Uwe, 296
Benjamin, Walter, 139
Berger-Fiedler, Róża, 11
Berghaus, Ruth, 147
Bergmann, Werner, 22
Berlau, Ruth, 140
Berlin, 5–6, 20, 55–58, 61, 64–67, 86, 88–89, 101, 140–41, 146, 148–49, 151, 163, 165, 182, 202, 204, 219n11, 243–45, 255, 257–58, 271, 273–74, 288–89, 307, 312, 317–18, 320, 330, 333, 356, 361–62
  See also Berlin Wall
Berlin – Die Sinfonie der Großstadt (*Berlin Symphony of a City*), 5
Berlin heute (*Berlin Today*), 57
Berlin im Aufbau (*Berlin Under Construction*), 5, 330
Berliner Ensemble, 17, 138, 140, 146–50, 152, 211
  See also Brecht, Bertolt
Berliner Kneipen (*Berlin Bars*), 320
Berlin Wall, 11, 13, 21, 28n13, 36, 55, 69, 98–99, 105, 194, 197, 331
Bertolt Brecht. Bild und Modell (*Bertolt Brecht. Image and Model*), 139, 148
Besson, Benno, 140
Biermann, Wolf, 18
Bilder aus der Gießerei (*Images from the Foundry*), 88
binary panic, 288, 291–99, 301–2
Bissert, Ingeborg, 11
Bitterfelder Weg, 12–13, 16, 316, 331
Black abjection, 17, 26, 241–59
Black bodies, representation of, 223, 241–59

Blutmai (*Bloody May Day*), 5–6
Bobrowski, Johannes, 352
Böhm, Volkmar, 292
Böttcher, Jürgen, 2–3, 12–16, 18, 22, 46, 56–58, 137, 144, 203, 348n28, 351, 353
Brandt, Richard, 5–6
Brandt, Willy, 10
Bräunig, Werner, 342
Brecht, Bertolt, 8, 17, 99, 101, 137–40, 142–43, 145–52, 211
  Coriolan (*Coriolanus*), 147
  Der Dreigroschenprozeß. Ein soziologisches Experiment, 142
  Der kaukasische Kreidekreis (*The Caucasian Chalk Circle*), 140
  Der Messingkauf (*The Messingkauf Dialogues*), 143
  Die Dreigroschenoper (*The Threepenny Opera*) [play], 147–49
  Die Gewehre der Frau Carrar (*Senora Carrar's Rifles*), 147
  Die Mutter (*The Mother*), 147
  Die unwürdige Greisin (*The Shameless Old Lady*), 145
  Die Verurteilung des Lukullus (*The Condemnation of Lukullus*), 149
  epic theatre, 138, 149
  'Fragen eines lesenden Arbeiters', 145, 147
  gestus, 17, 137, 139, 142–43, 145–46, 151–52
  Herr Puntila und sein Knecht Matti (*Mr Puntila and His Man Matti*), 140
  Im Dickicht der Städte (*In the Jungle of the Cities*), 147
  Kriegsfibel (*War Primer*), 139, 143, 211
  Leben des Galilei (*Life of Galileo*), 140, 149
  Mutter Courage [play], 148–49
  photography, 139, 143
  views on cinema, 138
  See also Berliner Ensemble; *Die Dreigroschenoper* [film]; *Mutter Courage* [film]
Brechts Wände (*Brecht's Walls*), 152
Brecht-Schall, Barbara, 150
Bredemeyer, Reiner, 204, 219n11
Breßler, Günter, 232

Brezhnev, Leonid, 98, 107
Briefe – In Gedenken an Dr. Maria Grollmuß (*Letters – In Memory of Dr. Maria Grollmuß; Listy*), 180, 183, 185–92
  concentration camps, 187–88
  evocations of Joan of Arc, 188
  resistance narratives, 186–88
  See also Grólmusec, Marja
Broomfield, Maurice, 131–32
Bruk, Franz, 15
Bruk, Toni, 180–81, 183–85, 188–90, 192, 197–98
  biography, 185
Budyšin (Bautzen), 182, 185, 194, 197
Burger, Hanuš, 5
Bürgermeister Anna (*Mayor Anna*), 54
Burkhardt, Bernd, 75, 80–81, 83–85, 90, 93n32
Burkhardt, Ulrich, 74
Busch, Ernst, 8
Buyens, Frans, 56, 58, 61, 67, 69

Calvino, Italo, 207
Cambodia (The People's Republic of Kampuchea), 201–4, 206, 208–10, 213–17
  in East German film, 201–17
  Phnom Penh, 204–5, 208, 210, 214
Camera DDR, 11, 18, 58–59, 60, 62–64, 66–68, 71n23, 232–33
  See also KAG Auslandsinformation
Carow, Heiner, 88, 119
Cayrol, Jean, 207, 217
CDU (Christlich Demokratische Union Deutschlands), 10, 277, 355, 365
Celan, Paul, 207
Cerna, Herbert, 193
Césaire, Aimé, 255
Charlie und Co (*Charlie & Co*), 56
children's homes (in the GDR), 173n9, 174n15, 174n16, 174n9, 175n18
  in East German film, 167–70, 172
Chile, 11, 17, 64
  in East German film, 64, 201–2
China (the People's Republic of), 44, 76, 203–5, 208–13, 216, 218n1
cinéma vérité, 12–14, 35–47, 48n13, 49n22, 77, 118–19, 256, 342

Cohn-Vossen, Richard, 307–8, 310, 312, 317
Cold War, 6, 18, 26, 60, 65, 98, 209, 350, 354
  See also Global Cold War
colonialism, 16, 208, 224–28, 234, 237, 242, 244–46, 248, 253, 255, 258–59
  in East German film, 224, 228, 236–37, 241–59
Coming Out, 88
compilation films, 8, 99–100, 105, 282n13, 317
  See also *Das russische Wunder*; *Du und mancher Kamerad*; *Ein Tagebuch für Anne Frank*;
concentration and death camps, 5, 43, 65, 116, 180, 186–90, 207–8, 212–13, 267, 277
  Auschwitz, 213
  Bergen-Belsen, 208, 272, 275
  Buchenwald, 65, 208
  Ravensbrück, 65, 180, 186–90
  Theresienstadt, 212
  Westerbork, 277
Congo, Republic of the, 16, 248–54, 259
  Congo Crisis, 248
  Congolese Liberation Movement, 251, 253
  in East German film, 241–42, 250–51, 255–56
construction sites, 5, 330–37, 343–44, 365
  See also urban planning
Cremer, Fritz, 188
cultural diplomacy. See soft power

Dahle, Ernst, 7
Dämmerung – Ostberliner Bohème der 50er Jahre (*Dusk – East Berlin Bohemia in the 1950*), 19, 148–52
Das Gesetz heißt Glück (*Care for Mothers and Infants in the GDR*), 59, 61–62, 68
Das Gesicht des neuen Afrika (*The Face of the New Africa*), 222
Das Kapital [animated film], 140
Das letzte Paradies (*The Last Paradise*), 245
Das russische Wunder (*The Russian Miracle*), 9–10, 98, 104–9, 112
  in the United States, 106–7
  use of archive material, 105, 107, 109
Das Stacheltier (*The Porcupine*), 7

Davis, Angela, 66
DDR-Magazin, 55, 60, 62, 64–66, 68, 72n34
de Andrea, John, 142
de Hondt, Joost, 225
de Kremer, Geert, 225
decolonization, 2, 11, 222
　in East German film, 2, 11, 222
　liberation movements in film, 17, 58, 120–23
DEFA
　Abteilung Kurzfilm, 6
　audiences, 79
　disco film, 79
　closure, 21, 356
　founding, 3–4
　post-Wende legacies, 1
　state film archive, 83, 112
　transnationalism, 1, 25
DEFA 70, 22
DEFA Außenhandel, 270–71
defa-futurum, 2, 18, 20, 78
DEFA-Gruppe 67, 18
DEFA-Gruppe Heynowski und Scheumann, 16–17, 20
　See also Studio H&S
DEFA-Studio für Dokumentarfilme, 18, 20–24, 75, 77, 81–83, 353
　See also DEFA-Studio für Wochenschau und Dokumentarfilme; DEFA-Studio für Kurzfilme
DEFA-Studio für Kurzfilme, 18, 337
DEFA-Studio für populärwissenschaftliche Filme, 7, 11, 18, 76–77, 179, 222
DEFA-Studio für Synchronisation, 270
DEFA-Studio für Trickfilme, 140, 181–82, 185, 191
DEFA-Studio für Wochenschau und Dokumentarfilme, 1–3, 7, 11, 18, 53, 55, 57–58, 97, 101, 140, 179, 225, 229, 251
　See also DEFA-Studio für Dokumentarfilme; DEFA-Studio für Kurzfilme
Demba Camara, Aboubacar, 231
Denecke, Gabriele, 19
Der Auftrag (*The Mission*), 85, 89
Der Augenzeuge, 4, 6, 20, 74–75, 105, 111, 222, 232, 238n3
　See also Kinobox, newsreels

Der Dschungelkrieg (*The Jungle War*), 201, 204, 214–15
Der ewige Jude, 4
Der goldene Strich. Bilder vom bürgerlichen Kunstbetrieb (*Gilded Whores. Pictures from the Bourgeois Art Business*), 141–43, 152, 153n9
　use of photography, 142
Der Hofmeister, 139
Der Kinder wegen – Flucht ins Vaterland (*For the Sake of the Children – Escape to the Fatherland*), 56
Der lachende Mann (*The Laughing Man*), 16, 140
Der Mensch muss auch wohnen: Bilder über das Leben in Halle-Neustadt (*People Must Have Homes, Too: Images of Life in Halle-Neustadt*), 330, 336, 338–45
　Alltag, 339
　cultural heritage, 338
Der schwarze Stern (*The Black Star*), 222, 225–29
　sound, 228
Der Weg nach oben. Der Film zum 1. Jahrestag der DDR (*The Way is Up*), 330
Der Weg nach oben: Chronik eines Aufstiegs (*The Way up: Chronicle of an Ascent*), 8, 99
Der Zögling. Jawohl Brecht! (*The Apprentice – Yes Indeed, Brecht!*), 137, 148
Dessau, Paul, 99, 103, 219n11
Deutscher Fernsehfunk. *See* East German television
Deutschland – Endstation Ost (*Talking with Germans*), 56–57, 61, 67–69
Diagne, Costa, 231
Diakité, Moussa Kémoko, 223, 229, 231
Die Alliierten (*The Allies*), 57
Die andere Liebe (*The Other Love*), 319
Die Angkar (*The Angkar*), 201–2, 204, 208–17
　parallels drawn with National Socialist Germany, 213
　use of documents, 210, 216–17
Die Brücke von Caputh (*The Bridge of Caputh*), 6
Die deutsche Wochenschau, 4

Index • **381**

Die Dreigroschenoper (*The Threepenny Opera*) [film], 138
 See also Brecht, Bertolt: *Die Dreigroschenoper* [play]
Die erste Seite einer Chronik (*The First Page of a Chronicle*), 121
Die Kinder von Golzow (*The Children of Golzow*), 19, 233, 353
Die neue deutsche Wochenschau, 74
Die Pflaumenbäume sind wohl abgehauen (*The Plum Trees Have Surely Been Cut Down*), 146
Die Spur von meinen Erdentagen (*The Trace of My Earthly Days*), 58
Die Teufelsinsel (*The Devil's Island*), 208
Die Todesmühlen (*Death Mills*), 5
Die Wildnis stirbt (*The Wilderness Is Dying*), 245
Die Windrose (*The Compass Rose*), 44
Dieses Jahr in Czernowitz (*This Year in Czernowitz*), 352
Dinter, Heinz, 228
direct cinema, 13, 35, 37–38, 44, 49n22, 119, 228, 342
Documenta, 141–42, 153n9
Dorfkinder (*Village Children*), 56
Dort, wo die Sonne schnell versinkt (*Where the Sun Sets Quickly*), 222
Drei Briefe (*Three Letters*), 56
Drei von vielen (*Three of Many*), 16
Dresen, Andreas, 237
Du bist min – Ein deutsches Tagebuch (*You Are Mine – A German Diary*), 22, 98, 109–12
 reception, 110
 use of documents, 111–12
Du und mancher Kamerad (*The German Story*), 8–9, 97, 99–103, 105, 107–8, 112, 269
 in the United States
 marketing, 99, 101
 use of archive material, 99–103
Dudow, Slatan, 5–6, 54, 138
Dumke, Hans, 222
Dymschitz, Alexander, 148

East German cultural and information centres, 10, 58
East German documentary film
 advertising films, 20, 77
 consolidation of socialism, 7, 54
 East German society, images of 18–19, 56–58, 66–67, 84–86, 202
 environmental themes, 19, 63–64, 75, 85
 gender, 18–21, 25, 54, 59–63, 63, 86
 generational shifts, 19–21, 81, 90n31
 humanist cultural traditions, 4, 7, 54, 58, 65, 75, 109, 338
 industry, films about, 12–13, 19, 82, 88, 101–23, 126, 128–31
 international cinema, influence of, 13–14, 35, 56, 58, 119
 international filmmakers, 8, 28n12
 mining themes, 63–64
 National Socialist past, 26, 41–43, 65, 202, 213
 sport, 59, 64–65
 technology, films about, 8, 11, 23
 transnationalism, 8, 18, 25
 women, depictions of, 54, 59–64, 65–68, 156–72, 187–91
East German radio, 83
East German television, 16, 20, 22–23, 37, 59, 68–69, 77, 97, 183, 204, 216, 273
 See also Studio Halle
East Prussia, 19, 20, 351, 354
 under National Socialism, 354
 during the Cold War, 354–55
 landscapes, 351–66
 in East German film, 350–52, 356–66
Ebeling, Rudi, 150
Eddy, Don, 142
Edeltraud D./Protokoll einer Erkundung (*Edeltraud D./Protocol of an Investigation*), 68
Ein Tagebuch für Anne Frank (*A Diary for Anne Frank*), 10, 266–81, 284n31, 285n39
 marketing, 276–77
 use of archival material, 267, 269, 275
 West German response, 272–73
Eine Delegierte (*A Female Delegate*), 63, 68
Eine Hinterlassenschaft (*A Legacy*), 143, 152
Eine Lehrerin (*A Teacher*), 59, 66–67
Eine Weiße unter Kannibalen (*A White Person Among Cannibals*), 245
Einheit SPD–KPD (*Unity SPD–KPD*), 4–6

Eisenstein, Sergei, 107, 248
Eisler, Hanns, 138, 270
elderly care homes (in the GDR), 164–66
Eleventh Plenum, 14–17, 41, 47, 49n22, 57–58, 126
Engels, Friedrich, 101, 105, 143–45
Engelhardt, Ludwig, 143–45
Enseleit, Barbara-Christa, 65
Ensink, Ella, 241, 243
Episches Theater (*Epic Theatre*), 139
Erfinder '82, 76, 82
Erinnerung an eine Landschaft – für Manuela (*Memory of a Landscape – For Manuela*), 116
Erpenbeck, Fritz, 149
Es genügt nicht 18 zu sein (*Being 18 is not enough*), 15, 123–26, 129
ethnographic film, 243–46
  in the Weimar Republic, 245
Exercises (1981), 201
exploitation cinema, 253–54

Familie Marx (*The Marx Family*), 85
Federal Republic of Germany
  East German criticisms of, 9, 17, 26, 41–43, 55–57, 60, 98, 101, 103–4, 140, 202, 241–54, 266–69, 272, 274–78, 280–81, 284n33
  Hallstein Doctrine, 10
  relations with the GDR, 10
Feierabend (*Leisure*), 12, 15, 46
  reception, 12
Ferientage (*Holidays*), 56
film clubs, 23, 81, 271
film exhibition, 23, 68–69, 77
film festivals, 35, 68
  Bergamo, 167
  Bilbao, 216
  Cannes, 236, 270
  Colombo, 62
  FESPACO, 231
  Leipzig, 13–14, 24, 36, 44, 48n3, 119, 130–31, 172n2, 231, 281, 283n24, 342
  Mannheim, 13
  Nationales Spielfilmfestival der DDR, 167
film stock, 6, 22–23, 233
  16 mm, 22, 38, 40, 46, 229, 231, 251, 253

35 mm, 22, 40, 46, 225, 229, 231, 233
  Kodak Eastman Color, 22, 212
  ORWO, 22, 225, 229, 233
film technology, 3, 6, 13, 21, 44–46, 49n22, 69, 101, 315–16
  in the GDR, 12, 18, 20–22, 38, 40, 46, 59, 110, 316
Filmgruppe 82, 288, 290, 296
  See also Armeefilmstudio and *Neugier & Bewährung*
Filmstudio der NVA. See Armeefilmstudio
Filmwissenschaftliche Mitteilungen, 14, 35–38, 40–41, 43–47, 48n1, 49n23
Fischer, Arno, 143–45
Fischer, Heinz, 56
Fischer, Klaus, 158–59
Five Car Stud [artwork], 142
Flaherty, Richard, 127
Flaschenballett (*Bottle Vallet*), 88
Fliege, roter Schmetterling (*Fly, Red Butterfly*), 201
flüstern & SCHREIEN (*whisper & SHOUT*), 79
Foreign Ministry Films. See Ministry of Foreign Affairs, films by
Foth, Jörg, 76, 79, 81, 84, 93n31
Frank, Anne, 10, 267–68, 271–72, 274–81
Frank, Otto, 273–75
Frauen für Frieden, 294
Frauenschicksale (*Destinies of Women*), 54
Freedom for Ghana, 229
Freie Deutsche Jugend (FDJ), 22, 62, 64–66, 81–82, 129, 329
Frenzel, Lenka, 196
Freudenberg, Nina, 86
Fritzche, Eva, 6
Für das Glück der Frauen und Familien (*For the Happiness of Women and Families*), 65
Für das Selbstbestimmungsrecht der Völker (*For the Sake of National Self-Determination*), 58

Gabi – Vermittlung Platz 12 (*Gabi – Switchboard Position 12*), 288, 296–99
Gagarin, Yuri, 104, 107–8
Gass, Karl, 2, 8, 12–15, 18, 26, 28n13, 46, 134n9, 172n2, 330
Gaus, Günter, 117

Gebser, Siegfried, 86
Gemmeker, Albert Konrad, 277
Georgi, Armin, 179
German Democratic Republic
    collapse, 19
    constitution, 8
    criticisms of the Federal Republic, 9, 17, 26, 41–43, 55–57, 60, 98, 101, 103–4, 140, 202, 241–54, 266–69, 272, 274–78, 280–81, 284n33
    cultural heritage, 7–8, 338
    diplomatic recognition, 10, 53–55, 59–60, 65, 222, 255. See also Hallstein Doctrine
    formalism debates, 6
    foreign policy, 10, 59–60, 65–66, 71n23, 204, 229, 241
    founding of, 6
    framings of the National Socialist past, 8, 265–66
    humanist cultural traditions, 54, 58, 109
    June 1953 Uprising, 150
    post-1989, 20, 350–51, 356
    racial politics, 242, 256–59
    Wende, 19, 21, 69, 350
Geschonneck, Erwin, 283n24
Gesellschaft für kulturelle Verbindungen mit dem Ausland, 55
Gestern und die neue Staat (*Yesterday and the New City*), 330, 336–37
    sculptures, 337
Ghana, 223, 225–29
    Ghana Film Industry Corporation, 229
    in East German film, 225–37,
Girnus, Wilhelm, 149
Global Cold War, 2, 17, 209–10, 222, 258–59
Global South, 2, 11, 16, 16, 144, 222–24
Globke, Hans, 266, 275, 282n6
Godard, Jean-Luc, 205, 207
Going, Ralph, 142
Gold Coast Film Unit, 229
Goodrich, Frances, 267
Gosse, Peter, 342, 347n26
Gräf, Roland, 167, 170
Graham, Sean, 229
Greif zur Kamera, Kumpel! (*Grab a Camera, Mate!*), 316

Grenzland. Eine Reise (*Borderland – A Journey*), 353
Grierson, Scot John, 13, 87
Greulich, Paul, 196
Grólmusec, Marja, 180, 185–91
Gronau, Manfred, 232
Große, Gerald, 336
Grotewohl, Otto, 7–8
Gruppe Kontakt, 126–27
Grüße aus Maputo (*Greetings from Maputo*), 223, 232–37
    education, depiction of, 235–36
    maps, 234
Grüße aus Sarmatien (*Greetings from Sarmatia*), 352
Guernica, 142
Guinea, 223, 229–32
    East German film week, 229
Guinea heute (*Guinea Today*), 229–30
Gulaschkanone (*Field Kitchen*), 85–86
Guten Morgen, du Schöne (*Good Morning, Beautiful!*), 163
Guzmán, Patricio, 24

Hackett, Albert, 267
Hadaschik, Joachim, 57–60, 63, 65, 71n23, 223, 232–33
Hadaschik, Lisa, 223, 232
Hafke, Heinz, 61–62
Hagenbeck, Carl, 243
Hager, Kurt, 105, 154n15
Halle – wie es war – und wie es ist (*Halle – How It Was – And How It Is*)
Halle-Neustadt, 5, 330, 333–45
    in East German film, 333–45, 348n28, 348n29
Halle-Neustadt – die Stadt der Chemiearbeiter (*Halle-Neustadt – City of Chemical Workers*), 330, 336–39
Händel [film], 7
Hangmen Also Die, 138
Hans Schomburgk – Mein Abschied von Afrika (*My Farewell to Africa*), 245
Hanson, Duane, 141
Harkenthal, Gisela, 79
Hartig, Kurt, 296, 300
Haufe, Gerhard, 11
Hauptverwaltung Film (HV Film), 7, 84–85, 182, 192, 194, 197, 270–76, 279

Haus und Hof (*Poor Soil*), 353
Häuser unterm Kreuz (*Churches in the GDR*), 58
Heartfield, John, 150
Heidemann, Gerd, 249, 251
Heim (*The Home*), 166–70, 172
Hein, Rudi, 69
Heinz, Wolfgang, 273
Heise, Thomas, 76, 81–83
Helbig, Walter, 288
Hellwig, Joachim, 10, 75, 78–81, 90, 222, 225, 229, 266–70, 272, 274–76, 279–82
Hempel, Johannes (Jan), 182
Hempel, Rolf, 65, 71n23
Hennecke, Adolf, 120, 134n10
Herder Institut, 56, 258
Herlinghaus, Hermann, 41, 44, 48n3, 49n23
Herr Zwilling und Frau Zuckermann (*Mr. Zwilling and Mrs. Zuckermann*), 352
Herrmann, Konrad, 192, 197, 222
Heynowski, Walter, 16–17, 24, 26, 35, 37, 41–43, 140, 201–17, 241, 248–54
Hier ist mein Platz (*This Is My Place*), 291
Hier, aujourd'hui, demain (*Yesterday, Today, Tomorrow*), 231
Hilscher, Robert, 337
Hinter den Fenstern (*Behind Closed Doors*), 160–63, 169
  housing shortages, 160, 162
  marriage, 161, 162
Hinterlassenschaft (*A Legacy*), 143, 152
Hippler, Fritz, 4
Hirde Dyama, 223, 229–32
  music, 230–32
Hochschule für Film und Fernsehen (HFF), 35, 76, 81–83, 118–19, 123, 185
Hochwaldmärchen (*High Forest Fairy Tale*), 19
Hofmann, Rolf, 179
Hoffmann, Jörg, 59
Hoffmann, Jutta, 147
Hohnstein, Maria, 179
Holocaust film, 265–66, 284n31, 285n39
  See also *Ein Tagebuch für Anne Frank*
Homosexuality
  attitudes to homosexuality in the GDR, 309–11, 321
  homophobic violence in the GDR, 307, 310–15
  See also queer
Homosexuelle Interessengemeinschaft Berlin, 2, 308–10, 316–17, 320–23, 325n30
Honecker, Erich, 16, 18, 59, 63–64, 66–67, 71n23, 83, 144, 154n15, 208, 232–33, 236, 316, 320, 330, 336, 339, 344
Honecker, Margot, 66
Hornja Łužica (*Oberlausitz*), 193
Howard, Ebenezer, 332
Hübel, Wernfried, 7
Huisken, Joop, 8, 24, 57, 134n9, 330
Hungarian Revolution 1956, 150

Ich bin meine eigene Frau (*I Am My Own Woman*), 88
Ickler, Paul, 57
If on a Winter's Night a Traveller, 207
Igel, Jayne-Ann, 302
I'm a Negro, 116
Imbiss Spezial, 82
Im Januar 1963 (*January 1963*), 13, 119–22
  brown coal (lignite) mining, 119–20
Immer bereit (*Always Prepared*), 22
Im Pergamonmuseum (*In the Pergamon Museum*), 56
In Sachen H. und acht anderer (*In the Matter of H. and Eight Others*), 25, 307–15, 317, 320
Institut der Freundschaft (*Academy of Friendship*), 56
Instituto Nacional de Cinema, 233–34, 236
Ivens, Joris, 8–10, 24, 28n12, 35, 43–47, 50n30, 50n31, 50n42, 99, 243

Jaap, Max, 7, 56
Jahrbuch der Millionäre (*Yearbook of Millionaires*), 101
Jahrgang '45 (*Born in '45*), 16
Jaldati, Lin, 275
Jenseits von klein Wanzleben (*Far from Klein Wanzleben*), 237
Jentsch, Gerhard, 179, 223, 229, 231
Jochmann, Rosa, 190
Johann Sebastian Bach [film], 7

Jubiläum einer Stadt – 750 Jahre Rostock (A City's Anniversary – Rostock at 750 Years), 58
Junge, Barbara and Winfried, 2–3, 19, 56, 58, 232–33, 351, 353
Jutzi, Phil, 5–6
juvenile delinquency (in the GDR), 307, 310–15

Kaden, Hans-Günter, 179
Kaiser, Wolf, 149
Kalte Heimat – Leben im nördlichen Ostpreußen (Cold Homeland – Life in Northern East Prussia), 350–52, 356–61, 364–66
    landscapes, 357, 361
    legacies of the Second World War, 357–60
Kampuchea – Sterben und Auferstehn (Kampuchea – Death and Resurrection), 201, 203–6, 216
    freeze-frame, 205–7
Kampuchea United Front for Salvation, 204
Khmer Rouge, 202–4, 206, 208–17
Kienholz, Edward, 142
Killing Fields, 202–4, 207, 209, 214
Kinobox, 2, 20, 74–91, 232, 238n3
    See also *Der Augenzeuge*, newsreels
Kinowagen, 23
Kipping, Herwig, 81, 83
Kißling, Helmut, 319
Kleiderbügel (Clothes Hangers), 88
Kleinert, Inge, 11
Koepp, Voelker, 2, 18, 20, 24, 350–53, 355–61, 365–66
Kommando 52 (Commando 52), 17, 241–42, 250–51, 255–56
    mercenaries, 252–54
    use of documents, 249–52
Konkret [gallery], 150
Konzert im Freien (A Place in Berlin), 144
Koplowitz, Jan, 342, 347n26
Kracauer, Siegfried, 139
Kraußer, Jochen, 76, 81, 83, 85, 89–90
Kreiseler, Werner, 179
Kreuzschnabellegende (The Legend of the Crossbill), 89

Kroske, Gerd, 82
Krug, Manfred, 119–25, 127–28
Krupp, 101–2, 142
Kubašec, Marja, 191
Kubisch, Hans, 222
Kuhle Wampe oder: Wem gehört die Welt (Kuhle Wampe Or Who Owns the World?), 138
Kunigk, Annelie
    See Thorndike, Annelie
Künstlerische Arbeitsgruppen, 11, 18, 20–21, 55–58
    KAG Auslandsinformation, 18, 57–58. See also Camera DDR
    KAG Dokument, 353–54
    KAG Gass, 18
    KAG Sach- und Zeichentrick, 11
    KAG Wochenschau, 11
Kurella, Alfred, 109
Kuxa Kanema, 233–34

Lammert, Willi, 188
Lang, Diana, 338
Lang, Fritz, 138
Le ciel, le terre (The Threatening Sky), 42n10, 50n42
Le joli Mai (The Lovely Month of May), 13, 15, 36, 50n39
Leacock, Richard, 13, 24, 36, 38, 49n22
Lechner, Ingrid, 150
Lehmann, Christian, 22
Leipzig im Herbst (Leipzig in the Fall), 353
Lepke, Irina (Gregor), 80–81
Lesben in der Kirche, 316
Letztes Jahr Titanic (Last Year Titanic), 353
Letztes aus der Da Da eR (Latest from the Da-Da-R), 81
Liebe 2002 (Love in the Year 2002), 79
Liebknecht, Karl, 101, 103
Liebknecht, Kurt, 329
Lied der Ströme (Song of the Rivers), 8, 10, 44, 50n32, 243
Liga für Völkerfreundschaft, 68
Lippold, Eva, 190–91
Loewenberg, Dagobert, 56
Lok im Garten (Locomotive in the Garden), 83, 89
Looping, 116

Lübbert, Barbara, 150
Luccas, Celso, 236
Lumumba, Patrice, 16, 249, 252, 258
Luthuli, Albert, 258

Machalz, Alfons, 59, 65, 67
Mädchen in Wittstock (*Girls in Wittstock*), 19, 351–52
Made in GDR (1981), 69
Maetzig, Kurt, 4–6, 22, 54, 99, 119, 123, 330
Man with a Movie Camera (*Chelovek s kinoapparatom*), 5, 205
Mann mit Krokodil (*Man with Crocodile*), 89
Marker, Chris, 13–15, 24, 36, 50n39, 203, 205, 207
Martha Lehmann – Eisenbahnerin (*Martha Lehmann – Railway Worker*), 145–46
Martin, Rudolf, 101
Martinez Correa, José Celso, 236
Marx-Engel Monument, 143, 152, 154n15
Marx, Karl, 85, 107, 140, 143, 145, 227
    Critique of the Golgotha Programme, 107
Maidorn, Georg, 22
May, Gisela, 147
Mayer, Hans, 345
Maysles, Albert, 13
Meiers Nachlaß (*Meier's Estate*), 36, 41–43, 46, 50n29
    Göring, Hermann, 41–43, 50n29
    use of montage, 42
Meiner ist bei den Soldaten (*My Boyfriend's a Soldier*), 290
Meinl, Trutz, 88
Meltke, Leaka, 196
Men of Aran, 127
Menschen am Sonntag (*People on Sunday*), 205
Middell, Margret, 144
Milestone, Lewis, 103
Ministry for Agriculture, Forestry and Food Industry, 182
    See also agra film studio
Ministry for Construction, 337
Ministry for Culture, 7, 16, 84, 182, 192. See also: HV Film

Ministry for Foreign Affairs, 10, 53, 55–56, 58, 66, 69
    films by, 10–11, 53–69
Ministry for National Defence, 288
Misselwitz, Helke, 2, 11, 19, 76, 80–81, 85, 87–88, 157–60, 163, 171
Mondo Cane, 254
Morris, Errol, 103
Mozambique, 223, 232–35, 255
    in East German film, 232–37
    Honecker visit, 232
Mückenberger, Jochen, 15
Müller, Friedrich, 16
Müller, Hans, 54
Müller, Heiner, 85, 148
Müller, Heinz, 56, 58, 65, 179
Müller, Siegfried "Congo", 140, 248, 250–51
Müller-Lankow, Helmut, 228
Mund, Karl-Heinz, 137
Mutter Courage [film], 138
    see also Brecht, Bertolt: *Mutter Courage*
My Child, 243

nation branding. *See* soft power
National Socialism
    film, 4, 6, 243, 246
    film bunker, 100
    Kulturfilm, 99
    See also concentration and death camps; German Democratic Republic; framings of the National Socialist past
Nationale Volksarmee (NVA), 25, 287–303
    conscription, 290, 294
    depiction of women in films, 287–303
    depiction of women's uniforms in films, 294–96, 299
    films about, 25, 288, 290, 296–99, 301–2
    trans soldiers, 302, 306n49
    women in the NVA, 287–90, 294
Natschinski, Thomas, 85
NATO, 9, 60, 204, 273
Négritude, 226–27, 255
neocolonialism, 242–44
Neugier und Bewährung (*Trying and Prevailing*), 288, 296–97, 299, 301–2
    depiction of uniforms, 299–300

newsreels, 2–4, 6–7, 20, 22–23, 53, 55, 60, 70n2, 74, 76–77, 83, 90, 98–99, 109, 112, 150–51, 222, 232–34, 287–93, 295–96, 300–302, 320
    See also Der Augenzeuge; Die deutsche Wochenschau, Kinobox
new towns, 331–33
    See also Halle-Neustadt
Ngakane, Lionel, 24
Nicht der Homosexuelle ist pervers, sondern die Situation, in der er lebt (It Is Not the Homosexual That Is Perverse, But Rather the Society in Which He Lives), 317–18, 322
Nippert, Erwin, 65
Nkrumah, Kwame, 228–29
Nickel, Gitta, 2, 11, 18
nouvelle vague, 14–16, 342
Nowak-Njechorński, Měrćin, 194, 196
Nuit et Brouillard (Night and Fog), 206–7, 217, 269–71, 278, 281, 283n24
    German commentary, 270

October: Ten Days That Shook the World, 107–8
O.K., 202
Ofenbauer (Furnace Builders), 12
Oley, Hans, 225, 229
Ostpreußenland (Tales of East Prussia), 350–51, 356, 361–66
    memorialisation, 361–62
    neoliberalism, 362–64

Pabst, G. W., 138
Palitzsch, Peter, 140
Pappe, Feodor, 22
Paulick, Richard, 334
Pehnert, Horst, 85, 192
Pennebaker, D. A., 38
Perry, Clarence, 332
Photorealists, 142, 153n9
Picasso, Pablo, 8, 142
Pieck, Wilhelm, 103, 130
Pietzsch, Jochen, 59
Piloten im Pyjama (Pilots in Pyjamas), 16–17, 208
Pinschewer, Julius, 77
Piontek, Helmut Karl, 228

Plenert, Thomas, 88, 357
Plickat, Kurt, 65
Plus und Minus (Plus and Minus), 121
Pol Pot (Saloth Sâr), 202, 206–16
polycentrism, 223–25, 231–33, 237
pornotroping, 252
postcolonialism, 26, 222–24, 226, 230, 234, 237, 253
Potsdam baut auf (Rebuilding Potsdam), 330
Prague Spring, 18
Prisma, 16, 36–37
Produktion Brandt, 6
Produktionsgruppen (Production Groups), 20–21
    See also Künstlerische Arbeitsgruppen
    PG 117, 21
    PG defa kinobox, 20, 74–76, 78–91
    PG Kinderfilm, 20
    PG Kronenstraße, 20. See also Studio H&S
    PG Video, 20
Progress Film, 77, 84, 183, 238n3, 277
Prometheus-Film GmbH, 5
P.S., 167, 170
public diplomacy. See soft power

Quax in Afrika, 246
queer
    as a cipher, 308–11, 314–15, 317, 321–22
    depicted in East German Super 8 films, 307–9, 315–23. See also Auf der Suche nach dem Glück
    queer rights in the FRG, 317–19, 325n31
    queer rights in the GDR, 307–8, 321–22
    See also homosexuality

Randel, Wolfgang, 225
Raue, Dieter, 59
Reinefarth, Heinz, 104
Reimann, Brigitte, 345, 348n37
Resnais, Alain, 203, 206–7, 269
Revanchismus in West-Berlin – Was wird aus West-Berlin? (Revanchism in West Berlin – What Will Become of West Berlin?), 56

Revolution einer Kultur (*Revolution of a Culture*), 58
Richter, Evelyn, 132–33
Ringsdorf, H. B., 208
Ritter, Claus, 78
Robeson, Paul, 8, 118, 243
Rocha, Peter, 19
Rock-Report in der DDR (*Rock Report in the GDR*), 79, 85
See also *flüstern & SCHREIEN*
Romm, Michail, 24
Rotha, Paul, 24
Rouch, Jean, 38–39, 46, 127, 203
Rücker, Günther, 103
Rundfunk der DDR. *See* East German radio
Ruttmann, Walter, 5–6

Sandmännchen, 20, 165
Sans soleil (*Sunless*), 205
Sarmatische Zeit (*The Land of Sarmatia*), 352
Sary, Ieng, 202
Sauve qui peut (la vie) (*Every Man for Himself*), 205
Schall, Ekkehard, 147, 150
Schaut auf diese Stadt, 28n13
Schernikau, Ingrid, 228
Scheumann, Gerhard, 16–17, 24, 26, 35–47, 49n18, 51n44, 140, 201–17
 biography, 37
 Prisma-Testament, 36
 television, 37, 49n18, 51n44
Schlecher, Raimund, 104
Schlemmer, Oskar, 150
Schlösser und Katen (*Castles and Cottages*), 54
Schmerzen der Lausitz (*The Pain of Lausatia*), 19
Schnabel, Rolf, 58, 121
Schöbel, Frank, 340
Scholz, Paul, 121
Schomburgk, Hans, 243–45
Schönemann, Sybille, 80
Schumann, Dieter, 85–86
Schürtz, Dietmar, 296–97
Schwartz, Dietrich, 122
Schwarz, Jaecki, 128
Schroeder, Ruth, 271

Seghers, Anna, 345
Seezmann, Harald, 141
self-reflexivity, 17, 26, 201–5, 207, 209
Senghor, Léopold Sédar, 255
Serbska filmowa skupina (Production Group Sorbian Film), 181–83, 185, 194, 197
Seven Up!, 19
Seydewitz, Fridolin, 190
Seydewitz, Max, 190
Shub, Esfir, 99, 107
Sie, wie viele andere (*Portrait of a Woman*), 61–62, 68
Sily-Cinéma, 230–31
Sindermann, Horst, 334–36, 339
Siodmak, Robert, 205, 207
Sitting Artist, 142
Sobiczewski, Heinz, 64–65
socialist personality 12–13, 62, 68, 163–64, 334
Socialist Realism, 13–14, 16, 41, 121, 138, 149–51, 257, 259, 330, 332, 344, 348n37
soft power, 2, 10, 53–60, 62, 68–69,
 See also Auslandsinformation; Ministry for Foreign Affairs: films by
Sokoł – P.S. ke kapitlej našich stawiznow (*Sokoł – P.S. On a Chapter of Our History*), 179, 183, 192–98
Soldatenhochzeit (*A Soldier's Wedding*), 290
Sontag, Susan, 205, 213
Sorabia Film Studio, 181, 185
Sorbs, 179–98
 Arbeitskreis Sorbischer Filmschaffender (Working Group of Sorbian Filmmakers), 181
 constitutional protection, 180–81, 198n2
 Domowina, 184–85, 199n7
 environmental loss, 181
 filmmaking, 25, 179, 182–98
 identity, 179–81, 186–191, 193
 in the GDR, 181, 186, 190–91
 Serbski Sokoł Association, 192–94, 196
 Sorbian film school, 185
 under National Socialism, 181–83, 186–87, 193–95
South Africa, 245–48, 254–59
 in East German film, 241–59

See also Apartheid
Soviet Zone of Occupation (SBZ), 3–4, 148
Sowjetische Militäradministration in Deutschland (SMAD), 3, 6, 265
Sozialistische Einheitspartei (Socialist Unity Party, SED), 1, 4, 6, 10, 12, 18, 41, 54–55, 57–59, 61, 64, 66, 71n23, 82, 99, 102, 109, 125, 138, 144, 148, 150, 156, 160, 222, 242, 258, 266, 268, 335
    Politburo, 55, 60, 105, 109, 203
Städte machen Leute (*Cities Make the Man*), 335–36, 342, 347n26
Stahl (*Steel*), 8
Stahnke, Kurt, 179
Stakhanov, Alexei, 120
Stanke, Kurt, 237
Stars, 14, 22, 46
Staudte, Wolfgang, 138
Steinmann, Hans-Jürgen, 342, 347n26
Sterne über dem Abgrund. Das Leben von Maria Grollmuß (*Stars above the Abyss. The Life of Maria Grollmuß*), 191
Stevens, George, 267, 272
Stötzer, Werner, 144, 149–50
Strempel, Horst, 150
Studio H&S, 2–3, 16–18, 20, 23–24, 26, 36–37, 39, 41, 46–47, 137, 140–41, 143, 146, 201–17,
    Cambodia Trilogy, 17, 201, 203–17.
    See also Kampuchea – Sterben und Auferstehn; Die Angkar; Der Dschungelking
    technology, 141, 210
    See also DEFA-Gruppe Heynowski und Scheumann; Heynowski, Walter; Scheumann, Gerhard
Studio Halle, 338–39
Svilova, Elizaveta, 205
Székely, Kati, 273, 277, 279

TangoTraum (*TangoDream*), 80
Tetzlaff, Kurt, 2, 13, 15, 116–33, 146
    biography, 116, 118–19
The Diary of a Young Girl
    book, 271
    East German reception, 271–73, 284n25
    film, 267, 272
    play, 267, 271–72

Theaterarbeit (*Theater Work*), 146–48, 152
The Fall of the Romanov Dynasty, 99
Thiel, Lotte, 58–59
Thin Blue Line, 103
Thoms, Franz, 122, 130
Thorndike, Andrew and Annelie, 2, 8–10, 14, 18, 22, 26, 97–112, 203, 207, 210, 269
    use of documents, 98–100, 103
    use of newsreels, 98, 112
Thorndike, Andrew, 18, 102–3, 112, 330
    biography, 99–100, 110
    See also Thorndike, Andrew and Annelie
Thorndike, Annelie, 103, 106–7, 109, 111–12
    biography, 99, 110–11
    Jeder Tag war schön, 111
    See also Thorndike, Andrew and Annelie
Tierparkfilm (*Tierpark Berlin*), 58
Todeslager Sachsenhausen (*Sachsenhausen Death Camp*), 5–6, 265–66
Touré, Ahmed Sékou, 230–31
Tschombe, Moïse Kapenda, 249, 251
Tschörtner, Petra, 2, 11, 19, 157, 160–72, 174n14
    depiction of ideological institutions, 160–61
    depiction of physical institutions, 160–61
    depiction of the elderly, 19
Tuba Wa Duo, 81
Turbine 1, 8
Turmakin, Igael, 150

Übersee-Filmgesellschaft, 243–44
Ulbricht, Walter, 15, 18, 104, 106, 121, 276, 330, 334, 336–37, 344
Ulmer, Edgar G., 205, 207
Unerlaubte Entfernung (*AWOL*), 302
Unger, Michael, 317
Unsere alten Tage (*In Our Old Age*), 19, 163–66, 168, 172
Unter der Sonne Ägyptens (*Under the Egyptian Sun*), 237
Unternehmen Teutonenschwert, 9, 103–4, 112, 210, 284n33
Urbanek, Willi, 68

urban planning, 329, 333–34, 336–43
Urlaub auf Sylt (*Holiday on Sylt*), 9, 97, 103–4, 112
    Use of archives, 104

Varda, Agnès, 203
Verband der Film- und Fernsehschaffenden der DDR, 21, 84, 215
Veriegelte Zeit, 80
Vertov, Dzhiga, 5–6, 13, 112, 119, 205, 248
Vietnam, 11, 16–17, 50n42, 201–4, 208–9, 211, 219n11
Vietnam War, 17, 45, 60
Voigt, Andreas, 20, 76, 79, 81, 86, 88–89, 350–51, 353, 355–56, 361–66
Voigt, Jutta, 150
Voigt, Peter, 17, 19, 26, 137, 139, 142–52
    biography, 139–40
    miniaturization, 145
    Marx-Engel Monument, 143–44
    photography, 137, 143–44
von Praunheim, Rosa, 88, 317–19, 322
von Schnitzler, Karl-Eduard, 99–101

Wandel, Paul, 4
Wander, Maxie, 163
Wäscherinnen (*Laundresses*), 18
Weigel, Helene, 137, 146, 148–49
Weimar Republic
    Weimar cinema, 5–6, 205, 245
Weiskopf, Grete, 71n13
Weiss, Konrad, 81, 83, 85, 89
Wekwerth, Renate, 11
Wendish culture, 180, 193
    See also Sorbs
Wenn die Erde weiß vom Schnee (*Winter Sports in Oberhof*, 1986), 59

Wenn ich erst zur Schule geh' (*When I go to School*), 19
Wenzel & Mensching, 81
Wer fürchtet sich vorm schwarzen Mann (*Who's Afraid of the Bogeyman*), 80
Wer – wenn nicht wir (*Who – If Not Us*), 126
Werkstatt H&S, 20
    See also Studio H&S
Werner, Hans, 294
Weschke, Günter, 241
Wićaz, Alfons, 196
Wieder in Wittstock (*Wittstock Once Again*), 19, 351–52
Wildbahn Afrika (*Hunting Ground Africa*), 222
Winter Adé, 19, 80–81, 163
Wir von ESDA (*Working for ESDA*), 18
Wladimir Iljitsch Ujanow Lenin [film], 22
Wolf, Christa, 345
Wormser, Olga, 269
Wrecking Yard 1 [artwork], 141
Würste, Werner, 121

Yutkevich, Sergei, 14

Zeitkinos, 23
Zeitprobleme. Wie der Berliner Arbeiter wohnt (*Problems of our time. How the Berlin Worker Lives*), 5
Zeltplatzgeschichten (*Camping Stories*), 83, 85
Zement (*Cement*), 148
Zentralinstitut für Jugendforschung, 79
Zeuchner, Gerd, 150
Zhdanov, Andrey, 149
Zimbabwe, 237, 243, 245–48, 255
Zmeškal, Vladimír, 193

www.ingramcontent.com/pod-product-compliance
Ingram Content Group UK Ltd.
Pitfield, Milton Keynes, MK11 3LW, UK
UKHW021851050225
454720UK00006B/15